INSTRUCTOR'S MANUAL TO ACC

FUNDAMENTALS OF MANAGEMENT
A Framework for Excellence

DONALD S. MILLER
EMPORIA STATE UNIVERSITY

STEPHEN E. CATT
EMPORIA STATE UNIVERSITY

JAMES R. CARLSON
MANATEE COMMUNITY COLLEGE

West Publishing Company
Minneapolis/St. Paul   New York   Los Angeles   San Francisco

WEST'S COMMITMENT TO THE ENVIRONMENT

In 1906, West Publishing Company began recycling materials left over from the production of books. This began a tradition of efficient and responsible use of resources. Today, 100% of our legal bound volumes are printed on acid-free, recycled paper consisting of 50% new paper pulp and 50% paper that has undergone a de-inking process. We also use vegetable-based inks to print all of our books. West recycles nearly 27,700,000 pounds of scrap paper annually—the equivalent of 229,300 trees. Since the 1960s, West has devised ways to capture and recycle waste inks, solvents, oils, and vapors created in the printing process. We also recycle plastics of all kinds, wood, glass, corrugated cardboard, and batteries, and have eliminated the use of polystyrene book packaging. We at West are proud of the longevity and the scope of our commitment to the environment.

West pocket parts and advance sheets are printed on recyclable paper and can be collected and recycled with newspapers. Staples do not have to be removed. Bound volumes can be recycled after removing the cover.

Production, Prepress, Printing and Binding by West Publishing Company.

 TEXT IS PRINTED ON 10% POST CONSUMER RECYCLED PAPER   Printed with Printwise
Environmentally Advanced Water Washable Ink   ∞

CONTENTS

CHAPTER 7: STAFFING AND TRAINING

CHAPTER 8: LEADING

CHAPTER 9: CONTROLLING

CHAPTER 10: MOTIVATING JOB PERFORMANCE

CHAPTER 11: SOCIAL RESPONSIBILITIES AND ETHICS

CHAPTER 12:   INTERNATIONAL MANAGEMENT

CHAPTER 13:   PRODUCTIONS/OPERATIONS MANAGEMENT

CHAPTER 14: WORKING WITH GROUPS

CHAPTER 15: MANAGING CHANGE AND CONFLICT

CHAPTER 20:   PREPARING FOR MANAGEMENT CAREERS

VIDEO CASES

PREFACE

This manual is developed to serve professors who use *Fundamentals of Management: A Framework for Excellence* by Miller, Catt, and Carlson. It is designed for new as well as experienced professors who desire a useful resource to use in preparing for class sessions and making classroom presentations.

A variety of supplements have been developed to accompany the text. An extensive test bank includes true/false, multiple-choice, fill-in-the-blank, and essay questions. WESTEST computerized software enables you to create, edit, store, and print exams. Transparency acetates contain full-color key figures and charts. In addition, a well-developed, comprehensive study guide is available in English or Spanish.

The format of this manual is designed to facilitate the instructional process. Each chapter includes these features:

1. A **Chapter Overview** gives a brief summary of topics that are covered.
2. **Teaching Objectives**, which are presented as learning objectives in the text, focus attention on key considerations.
3. A **Chapter Outline of the Text** shows major topic headings and subheadings of the content presentation.
4. A list of **Key Terms** provides handy reference to pertinent terminology.
5. The **Detailed Chapter Summary** uses an outline format to present a summary, which can serve as a guide for developing classroom presentations. Helpful teaching hints and highlights of selected readings, which may be assigned to students, are interspersed within each of the summaries.
6. Answers to **Consider This Questions**, which are included within each chapter of the text, represent plausible responses to questions that are useful for in-class discussion or out-of-class writing assignments.
7. Answers to the end-of-chapter **Review and Discussion Questions** and **Critical Thinking Incidents** provide a reference resource to use in guiding student discussions or grading homework.
8. The **Study Guide Assignments** refer to *individual* and *group* case-assignment materials included in the study guide that accompanies the text.
9. The **Video Case** section presents a summary of available videos and includes questions and answers to use in encouraging classroom discussion.

Sincere appreciation is given to West Educational Publishing for permission to include video-case material appearing in a video guide prepared by John Hall. We appreciate the guidance and thoughtful suggestions given to us by Susan Smart, our developmental editor. Also, Linda Miller deserves special thanks for her excellent work in typing this manual.

Management and the Workplace

Chapter Overview

This chapter examines the nature of management in today's workplace. The concept of management is defined, and a foundation is established for more detailed study in subsequent chapters. A major consideration is to establish the importance of communication as an important aspect of successful management.

Chapter 1 also discusses the basic managerial functions and differentiates among various levels of management. Roles performed by managers are identified, as are skills necessary for attaining desired results. The relevance of factors such as job satisfaction, productivity, and quality is explored.

The chapter concludes with an examination of forces that influence the business environment. In addition, characteristics of an increasingly diverse workplace are discussed.

Teaching Objectives

The teaching objectives of this chapter are to:

1. Explain the nature of management.

2. Identify functions included in the management process.

3. Differentiate among levels of management.

4.   Describe the importance of communication in the workplace.

5.   Discuss the various managerial roles.

6.   Specify four types of managerial skills.

7.   Identify key managerial concerns.

8.   Recognize the forces that fluence the business environment.

9.   Discuss the characteristics of an increasingly diverse workplace.

Chapter Outline of the Text

I.   AN OVERVIEW OF MANAGEMENT
II.   WHAT IS MANAGEMENT?
    A.   The Management Process
    B.   Managers: Who Are They?
    C.   Levels of Management
    D.   The Importance of Communication
III.   REALITIES OF MANAGEMENT
    A.   Managerial Roles
        1.   Interpersonal Roles
        2.   Informational Roles
        3.   Decisional Roles
    B.   Managerial Skills
    C.   Key Management Concerns
        1.   Efficiency and Effectiveness
        2.   Job Satisfaction
        3.   Productivity
        4.   Quality
IV.   UNDERSTANDING THE WORKPLACE
    A.   The Business Environment
    B.   Growing Globalization
    C.   Diversity and the Workplace
V.   LOOKING BACK
VI.   KEY TERMS
VII.   REVIEW AND DISCUSSION QUESTIONS
VIII.   CRITICAL THINKING INCIDENTS
IX.   SUGGESTED READINGS

Key Terms

These terms are introduced in the chapter. Definitions are included in the glossary of the text.

Communication
Communication skills
Communicator
Conceptual skills
Controlling
Decisional role
Disseminator
Disturbance handler
Economic forces
Effectiveness
Efficiency
Entrepreneur
Figurehead role
First-line manager
Informational role
Internal forces
Interpersonal role
Job satisfaction
Leadership role
Leading

Liaison management
Managers
Middle managers
Monitor
Multinational corporations
Organizing
People skills
Planning
Political forces
Productivity
Quality
Resource allocator
Societal forces
Staffing
Supervisors
Technical skills
Technological forces
Top management

Detailed Chapter Summary

I.   AN OVERVIEW OF MANAGEMENT

Teaching Objective 1: Explain the nature of management.

Everybody has opportunities to view the consequences of managerial actions. While some organizations are well managed, others do not attain high levels of success--frequently because of initiatives managers choose to take or else avoid. Management is both an art and a science.

II.   WHAT IS MANAGEMENT?

Management involves effective use of human, equipment, and information resources to achieve objectives.

A.   *The Management Process*

Teaching Objective 2: Identify functions included in the managerial process.

This process consists of performing five functions: planning, organizing, staffing, leading, and controlling. While top managers generally devote considerable time to planning and organizing, first-line management devotes much energy to performance of leading and controlling.

B.   *Managers Who Are They?*

Managers focus much effort on dealing with other people's problems and are responsible for product quality and customer satisfaction. Frequently, excellent job performance serves as the basis for promotion to supervisor; supervisors often become middle-level managers and so on up the managerial hierarchy.

Teaching Hint: Emphasize that managers wear many hats. Point out that all individuals must manage themselves each and everyday.

C.   *Levels of Management*

Teaching Objective 3: Differentiate among the levels of management.

Levels of management are classified in three ways: Top, middle, and first-line managers. Top managers are primarily concerned with setting goals, developing policies, and formulating strategies. Mid-level managers convert policies and strategies set forth by top management into specifics and act as intermediaries between the other managerial levels. Often called supervisors, first-line managers represent the lowest level of management and the only level having direct contact with nonmanagerial personnel.

D.   *The Importance of Communication*

Teaching Objective 4: Describe the importance of communication in the workplace.

Communication involves the sharing of meaning between senders and receivers of messages. This concept is extremely relevant because effective communication is a major consideration in avoiding waste, unnecessary expenditure of time, and interpersonal problems. The Ws of communication include who, what, when, where, and why.

Suggested Readings for this Section
Nohria, Nitin and James D. Berkley. "Whatever Happened to the Take-Charge Manager?" Harvard Business Review 72, January-February 1994, pp. 128-137.

Many managers fail to recognize the importance of pragmatic judgments. Trendy techniques and ready-made solutions may be useful; nevertheless, managers are obligated to take charge and reach objectives. Four aspects of pragmatism should be considered: sensitivity in adapting ideas to specific situations, willingness to "make do," emphasis upon attaining results without getting unnecessarily sidetracked, and openness to uncertainty. The present balance between innovativeness and management fundamentals needs to be reconsidered.

Hequet, Marc. "Giving Good Feedback." Training 31, September 1994, pp. 72-77.

Feedback is a very relevant aspect of communication. However, too many managers are inept at giving feedback. This article includes a feedback primer, which provides guidelines on how to provide better feedback to employees. Recommendations include a need for sharing feedback on a regular basis; setting clear expectations as baselines for subsequent feedback; and criticizing poor performance, not personalities. When administered effectively, feedback improves communication, boosts productivity, and reduces human relations problems.

III.   REALITIES OF MANAGEMENT

Successful managers understand their roles and recognize the importance of communication, people, technical, and conceptual skills. Also, the need to promote efficient and effective operations, encourage job satisfaction, emphasize productivity, and maintain quality cannot be underestimated.

A.   *Managerial Roles*

Teaching Objective 5: Describe the various managerial roles.

Henry Mintzberg classified the formal authority and status of managers in terms of interpersonal, informational, and decisional roles and believed that representative duties were associated with each of these roles.

Figure 1-5 summarizes the relationship between roles and representative duties.

1.   Interpersonal Roles

Managers participate in many interpersonal interactions with a variety of stakeholders. As figureheads, they are representatives at ceremonial functions. In the leadership role, they guide organizational operations. As liaisons, managers initiate and maintain contacts with personnel as well as individuals who are not employed by the firm.

2.   Informational Roles

Information is the key ingredient influencing managerial actions, and much time is consumed sending, receiving, and interpreting messages. As monitors, managers filter information to gain a grasp of factual information. In the disseminator role, information is distributed to those within the organization. Finally, the communicator role involves transmitting information to persons who are not direct subordinates.

3.   Decisional Roles

Decision making is a commonly recognized managerial activity. As entrepreneurs, managers seek innovative solutions to problems and look for new ways to accomplish tasks. While the disturbance-handler role involves resolution of disagreements, managers can also serve as negotiators to achieve beneficial outcomes that further a firms best interests. Finally, as resource allocators, managers decide how resources are divided among various units of a firm.

B.   *Managerial Skills*

Teaching Objective 6: Specify four types of managerial skills.

Managers are constantly challenged to meet an array of expectations set forth by stockholders, customers, employees, and others. Therefore, effective practice of communication, people, technical, and conceptual skills is quite relevant.

Communication skills stress the sharing of meaning to avoid complications related to the lack of or poor communication.

People skills involve abilities to lead, motivate, and understand the feelings and behaviors of others.

Technical skills relate to knowing how to perform job duties. These skills include understanding how equipment operates and being able to detect and correct employee mistakes.

Conceptual Skills involve abilities to consider abstract relationships.

C.   *Key Management Concerns*

Teaching Objective 7: Identify key management concerns.

Managers must deal with a variety of concerns, and a listing of all of them is limitless. Nevertheless, several prominent concerns merit attention and illustrate the types of challenges that must be confronted.

1.   Efficiency and Effectiveness

The meaning of these words is frequently confused. Efficiency refers to how well a task is performed. Effectiveness is to choose an appropriate task in the firstplace. Consequently, a person can select the proper task to perform and do an inadequate job of getting it done. Or, high levels of time and energy can be devoted to completion of a poorly selected task.

2.   Job Satisfaction

Actions and attitudes of managers impact employee job satisfaction, a feeling of enjoyment or contentment toward a job. In addition, job design is relevant, as personnel like to do meaningful and reasonably challenging work. Some companies encourage commitment through emphasis upon job security and provision of opportunities for career growth.

3.   Productivity

Productivity is a measure of output per worker. Firms must compete in an increasingly competitive marketplace; consequently, managers and employees need to recognize the close relationship between individual efforts and organizational productivity. Methods to increase productivity include selection of capable personnel, recognition of employee contributions, elimination of ineffective communication practices, and promotion of an efficient work environment.

4.   Quality

Quality refers to an anticipated level of excellence. To exceed customer expectations, organizations are challenged to emphasize teamwork, training, and product and service improvements. By delivering quality (as perceived by customers), firms build reputations for excellence and develop positive organizational images.

Teaching Hint: Point out that perceptions of quality change as circumstances change. On their television sets, people were once quite satisfied to receive somewhat fuzzy black-and-white pictures and availability of few channels. Today, quality assessment involves clearness of color-picture images, reception of many channels, and usage of a remote-control device to change channels.

IV.   UNDERSTANDING THE WORKPLACE

Contemporary organizations are influenced by technological, economic, societal, political, and internal forces. Today's workplace is characterized by increasing globalization and greater diversity.

Teaching Objective 8: Recognize the forces that influence the business environment.

A.   *The Business Environment*

Computers, dry copiers, and fax machines are examples of technological advances that have increased information processing and communication capabilities. Economic conditions influence a firm's ability to borrow funds, buy equipment, and sell products or services. Society expects behaviors to conform to established values, beliefs, and traditions. Businesses must comply with legislation enacted in the political arena. Finally, internal forces within an organization stipulate patterns of expectations for various departments or subunits.

B.   *Growing Globalization*

Greater numbers of firms are involved in international business. These companies seek to serve new markets and increase profitability, reduce expenses, or both. The global environment poses a new set of challenges for managers because of unfamiliar laws, cultures, political regimes, and languages.

Teaching Objective 9: Discuss characteristics of an increasingly diverse workplace.

     C.   *Diversity and the Workplace*

Demographics of America's workplace are changing. The labor force is growing older, and greater numbers of women are working. During the 1990s, more minorities will be represented in the workplace with the percentage of Hispanic workers expected to double. While American workers become more educated, greater levels of conceptual and applied skills will be needed to function successfully in an increasingly complex business environment.

Suggested Readings for this Section:
Stewart, Thomas A. "Welcome to the Revolution." <u>Fortune</u> 128, December 13, 1993, pp. 66-80.

The business world is confronted by an era of major changes involving trends toward greater globalization of markets, use of technology, and responsiveness to an information-age economy. Each trend is significant; however, (and most noteworthy) they are all happening simultaneously. The time has arrived where "management has to think like a fighter pilot."

Lee, Chris. "The Feminization of Management." <u>Training</u> 31, November 1994, pp. 25-31.

Similarities and differences in gender-related perspectives toward management are discussed. Several trends are noted. More women are working, and they are holding a greater number of management positions. Women-owned businesses are experiencing considerable growth; it is estimated that 10 percent of Americans work for such businesses. In an increasingly diverse workplace, it is possible that differences among genders will be recognized without being labeled as strengths or weaknesses.

V.   LOOKING BACK

This chapter provides an introduction to the concept of management and factors that influence the workplace environment.

Answers to CONSIDER THIS Questions   (Page 11)

1.   **Which function of the management process is most important?**

Students should justify the rationale for their response. Successful performance of all functions is necessary for organizations to grow and prosper. Some persons consider planning to be especially important because it provides a framework for guiding actions. Failure to organize resources or implement needed controls can lead to detrimental consequences. The value of staffing, the human-resource component, is often underestimated. Yet people are the key factor in organizational success. Persons who aspire to become managers should strive to acquire essential skills needed to master implementation of managerial functions.

2.   **How are people selected for managerial positions?**

Managerial selection is commonly based on prior job-performance accomplishments and demonstrated potential to be successful in a more responsible position. Relevant experience and an excellent work record as an employee provide a background for promotion from employee to supervisor. Likewise, middle-level managers are often chosen from supervisory ranks and so on up the management hierarchy. Many variables, such as personality and an ability to communicate effectively, can enter into the selection of managers. Individuals who possess especially well developed people skills often have an advantage in obtaining management positions.

3.   **What level of management is most responsibility for attaining organizational objectives?**:

Some students incorrectly believe that top management is solely responsible for efforts to attain objectives. In practice, every level of management, as well as all employees, has a responsibility to see that an organization succeeds. As the business environment becomes increasingly competitive, many managers strive to develop greater employee loyalty and increase their commitment to acceptance of organizational operating philosophy. We can speculate that managers will continually need to educate personnel and clearly communicate reasons for selecting particular strategies.

Answers to CONSIDER THIS Questions   (Page 16)

1. **How can managers learn to become better communicators?**

   Unfortunately, many problems can be traced to communication-related difficulties. Managers should learn from prior mistakes and can benefit by continually asking themselves, "Did I get my main points across?" Solicitation of feedback, which is frequently gained by asking questions, is a key to improved communication. Personal realization of the need to be a better communicator is a valuable factor, as this is a signal that a person is willing to exert the energy needed to improve. While informal efforts are worthwhile, many classes, seminars, and workshops are available to facilitate learning and development of communication skills.

2. **Which managerial role is the most challenging one for managers to perform?**

   Students can justify rationales for each of the managerial roles. The intent of this question is to encourage critical analysis of the nature of each of their roles: interpersonal (figurehead, leadership, and liaison); informational (monitor, disseminator, and communicator); and decisional (entrepreneur, disturbance handler, resource allocator, and negotiator). Some managers may be excellent decision makers but demonstrate less ability at serving as a figurehead or initiating communication with people. The extent to which a role may be challenging depends upon such things as a manager's personality, personal goals, comfort level with prevailing circumstances (giving an award vs. confronting those with opposing views), and prior job experiences.

3. **In the next decade, which managerial skill will be the most important for job success?**

   It is important for managers to excel at performance of all skills: communication, people, technical, and conceptual. Students can justify any skill as being most important. A key factor is to focus on the reason for selecting a particular skill. Effective communication will continue to be an essential concern, especially in an increasingly global economy and a workplace characterized by greater language-related diversity. Mastery of people skills certainly will be critical to successful performance of management functions. Technological advances will evidence a pattern of acceleration. Managers who can think critically and grasp relationships among complex concepts will possess a favorable advantage in a changing business environment.

Answers to REVIEW AND DISCUSSION Questions

1. *What are the five functions of the management process?*

    The managerial process consists of these functions: planning, organizing, staffing, leading, and controlling. Capable performance of each function is essential to survival and growth of a firm. Managers must examine their skills and consistently recognize how they are applied to implement these functions.

2. *How do the job responsibilities of workers differ from those of managers?*

    Workers are responsible for performance of job duties assigned to them. In contrast, managers guide the activities of others to reach organizational goals. It is important to note that successful employees who have mastered their job skills do not necessarily make excellent managers who are responsible for the work of others.

3. *Why should all personnel understand the concept of productivity?*

    Increased productivity (a measure of output per worker) is necessary for firms to be competitive in both national and international markets. Noncompetitive firms will encounter declining sales, loss of markets, and ultimately a need to layoff employees. Consequently, all personnel must continue to learn and keep abreast of changing business conditions.

4. *In what way will the labor force change during the remainder of the 1990s?*

    The American labor force will continue to grow older. Greater numbers of women and minorities will be employed. During this decade, the percentage of Hispanic workers will double. Workers will continue to be better educated, and business expenses for training will not decline. From a global perspective, greater mobility of labor will occur.

5. *Which type of skill is most important to managerial success: people, communication, technical, or conceptual skill?*

    Students will have different responses to this question. The key is to justify the rationale for their response. All of the skills are essential to successful management. Some students may give higher priority to communication and people skills because they think that technical skills are more easily learned. While relevant, the importance of conceptual skills is frequently underestimated.

6. *What is the difference between the job responsibilities of middle managers and those of first-line managers?*

Both levels perform all of the managerial functions. Much of a middle manager's time is spent on planning and organizing. A proportionately greater amount of supervisory time involves leading and controlling. However, one major factor distinguishes these managerial levels. Supervisors are the lowest level of management to interact directly with employees.

7. *Differentiate among interpersonal, informational, and decisional roles of managers.*

Figure 1-5 identifies the formal authority and status related to each of these roles. In addition, representative duties are illustrated. Interpersonal roles include figurehead, leadership, and liaison duties. While performing informational roles, managers serve as monitors, disseminators, or communicators. As decision makers, they seek innovative ideas, settle disputes, allocate resources, and strive to attain desired outcomes.

8. *How can managers increase employee job satisfaction?*

Employee-oriented managers strive to attain organizational objectives but also recognize the importance of human assets. These managers capably perform the managerial functions. However, they also demonstrate concern for their subordinates and encourage a collegial workplace environment. Job satisfaction is enhanced by managers who work "with" subordinates rather than expecting employees to work "for" them.

9 *What can managers do to emphasize the importance of product or service quality?*

Review the "boxed" material, which lists the ten commandments of quality. Managers who are concerned about quality can reward efforts to reduce defects, cut costs, and improve operations. Although it may not fully be recognized, managers are role models to subordinates who closely observe behaviors. Therefore, it is important for words to coincide with actions. Managers cannot simply talk about quality. Implementation of managerial functions needs to demonstrate that quality considerations have been recognized.

10. *How can a person determine if he or she is interested in becoming a manager?*

Knowledge can be acquired by observing practitioners and making inquiries about how they do their jobs. Any number of questions might be asked. What are the most favorable aspects of management? Why do you least like being a

manager? What preparation or training is necessary to become a manager.
How do you characterize an effective manager. Much can be learned by
reading about managers. Fortune magazine regularly features informative
articles about executives. Another strategy is to observe behaviors of managers
and listen to comments made by their subordinates.

Answers to CRITICAL THINKING INCIDENTS

Incident 1-1: WHY ME?

1. **Discuss John Hollander's perspective of management.**

   John can justify his reluctance to hire another person. Assuming Jane clearly
   communicated her feelings, John is not especially responsive to her concerns. As a
   manager, he should strive to maintain a positive work environment, which is a
   cornerstone to increased productivity and improved job satisfaction among personnel.
   Most likely, John desires to avoid a negative confrontation with Jane. However, an
   attitude of indifference toward Jane's concerns might ultimately lead to additional
   problems or possible termination of her employment.

2. **To what extent has Jane contributed to the difficulties she encounters with Herb
   and Joe?**

   To avoid unpleasantness, Jane has not strongly expressed her opinions or job-task
   preferences. Consequently, Herb and Joe do the most desired jobs. She has accepted
   criticism without voicing objections, and a pattern of expectations and predictable
   behaviors has emerged among the group members.

3. **Should Jane be more assertive and express her views to Herb and Joe? Explain
   your response.**

   Even though she risks being labeled as a complainer or stereotyped on the basis of
   gender, Jane could be more assertive in expressing her feelings. She does not need to
   deliberately antagonize Joe and Herb but should express her views and perhaps
   strongly emphasize her opinion about rotating job duties. Jane may not get results that
   she desires; however, she does focus attention on a major concern. Possibly, Joe and
   Herb have not really thought about the situation. Jane does face a difficult challenge,
   especially considering the view of John Hollander.

4   **Should Jane place greater emphasis to job satisfaction and less importance on family and financial considerations? Explain your response.**

Students will have numerous responses to this question, which does not have one correct answer. Individual preferences about the importance of job satisfaction versus family, financial, or other factors varies among people. Compared to personal job satisfaction, Jane will likely continue to place greater importance on family-related considerations. This is not a right or wrong choice but simply represents an individual priority.

5.   **Assuming John changes his mind, should a member of the group be designated as the manager? Explain your response.**

A member of the present group is not likely to be successful at managing all of the others. Past experiences and personal attitudes could be problematic and complicate acceptance of any one person by all members of the group. One possibility is for John to rotate the manager's position. While this approach does not alleviate personality complications, it does provide everyone with managerial experience. The ideal strategy is to appoint a new manager who is not presently a member of the group.

Incident 1-2: I'M THE CHIEF

1.   **How do the managerial responsibilities at Learning Consultants differ from those at Frontier International?**

At Learning Consultants, Carl is the top manager and has overall responsibility for managing the entire firm. He is encountering frustration in fulfilling interpersonal, informational, and decisional roles. Carl no longer has to contend with bureaucratic, structured formalities that commonly exist in the corporate world. In event the firm does not succeed, however, Carl will incur the loss of personal resources. This case illustrates a distinction between working as a middle-level executive and becoming an entrepreneur of a newly formed company.

2.   **Why is Carl experiencing difficulties with his managerial role at Learning Consultants?**

Various factors might contribute to Carl's difficulties. He is not accustomed to serving as a figurehead for an entire organization and has assumed a much larger informational role as a monitor, disseminator, and communicator. Finally, Carl has a broad range of obligations to negotiate and resolve differences of opinion. Students should recognize that Carl's position is not unique, and he encounters similar types of problems experienced by other managers who start their own firms.

3.   **Is Carl an effective manager? Explain your response.**

It is too soon to make a conclusive judgment on the success of Carl's ability to manage the company. He is facing challenges associated with the transition to chief executive of his own company. Carl has the expertise to manage effectively. Nevertheless, the new role is unfamiliar to Carl, and he needs to use all of his managerial skills to assure that operations run smoothly.

4.   **(Possible additional question)   How should Carl respond to Caroline's expressed interest in becoming a seminar leader?**

This request really puts Carl on the spot. He cannot risk offering seminars led by inexperienced personnel. However, Caroline is his wife, secretary, and colleague in the business; he cannot blatantly deny her request. She might be asked to develop an outline of the content for a possible training seminar and present a short program for critique by several experienced trainers and secretaries. At this point, Caroline must confront reality and take notice of her strengths and limitations. A key consideration is for Caroline to be given an opportunity to try her skills.

Incident 1-3: WHO GETS WHAT?

1.   **Is Marvin's dilemma unique to hospital administrators? Explain your response.**

Marvin's dilemma is not unique to hospital administrators or managers in other fields. Considering the external environment, hospitals must frequently compete for patients and initiate a range of strategies to attain objectives. Within organizations, departments or other subunits compete for resources, a situation that presents challenges to managers who usually cannot meet all funding requests.

2.   **What can Marvin do to gain the staff's support for his ultimate decision and to retain the cooperation of all hospital employees?**

Unanimous support is probably an unrealistic expectation. Marvin might call the subordinate members together as a group to help formulate the ultimate budget allocation. While this approach has its risks, a major benefit is for all managers to understand interrelationships among units, recognize priorities that cannot be ignored, and gain an overall perspective of the budget process. Assuming he does not seek their participation, Marvin should explain his decision-making rationale so that subordinate managers (and ultimately their employees) know the reasons for decisions. Managers who make secretive decisions generally experience difficulty in maintaining a cooperative work environment.

3.   **How should Marvin respond to the board's point of view?**

Marvin should explain and justify his perspective to the board. He could carefully review and illustrate anticipated consequences under several scenarios: no additional funding, partial funding, reduction of services, and elimination of programs. Communication is a key consideration. Marvin must use his persuasive talents and generate support for his views. Students should remember that the board is the ultimate source of authority, and Marvin is accountable to it.

4.   **Because she has threatened to resign, should Sally's request be given a top priority? Explain your response.**

Sally might be reacting without an informed understanding of budgetary priorities, or her comments may be quite accurate. Threatened resignations of key personnel should not be taken lightly. However, threats cannot represent a continual basis for establishment of program priorities and allocation of funds. Marvin should listen to Sally and consider how he might respond to her concerns.

Study Guide Assignments

The study guide includes excellent individual and group case-assessment exercises. You can use these exercises to give individuals an opportunity to develop their problem-solving skills. The group-case exercises enable students to work together and determine recommended solutions.

For this chapter, the individual case assessment asks students to differentiate between formal and informal groups, understand the functions of management, and recognize the importance of communication. Also, the case helps students gain insights into managerial roles and skills.

The group case assessment emphasizes an understanding of management functions. Students are encouraged to recognize differences between management of informal groups and formal organizations.

Video Case

Lanier Worldwide, Inc.

Focus: **Organizational Competencies, Management Skills, Quality, and Customer Orientation**

Summary:

Lanier Worldwide, Inc. is an organization whose entire market focus is reflected in a clear, unifying mission statement: *To be recognized as the preferred provider of office solutions dedicated to total customer satisfaction.* Lanier operated in more than 80 countries, and covers every county in the United States. The company has five main business areas: (1) copying, (2) facsimile systems, (3) information management systems, (4) dictation systems, and (5) presentation systems (overhead projectors and multimedia systems). Lanier's mission statement translates directly into its quest for customers to first think Lanier when they are in the market for these types of products and services.

Lanier's two core competencies are sourcing and distribution. Although it still manufactures dictation equipment and configures imaging equipment for its electronic filing systems for information management, it sources products for the other three product lines — copying, facsimile, and presentation systems. To ensure the utmost quality in these sourced products, Lanier's product and quality assurance engineers work closely with its manufacturing partners. Distribution is handled through 184 branches in 113 locations and 44 dealers in 110 locations, for a total of over 200 outlets. This dual-distribution system works well because it facilitates national coverage both within and outside metropolitan areas and, at the same time, enhances major account coverage.

Lanier has developed several programs to help achieve its mission. These include: (1) Customer Vision, (2) The Performance Promise, (3) 100 Percent Sold, and (4) The Lanier Team Management Process. The premise behind the Customer Vision program is that Lanier must see its business through the eyes of its customers and must respond to their needs as a team, at or above customer expectations. Lanier attempts to offer more than the competition through The Performance Promise, which offers guaranteed product satisfaction or replacement at no charge, guarantees on product up-time, free loaners, a 24-hour toll-free helpline, and a 10-year guarantee on availability of service, parts, and supplies. The 100 Percent Sold program has the ultimate goal of having every Lanier customer buy all of their office products from Lanier. Finally, The Lanier Team Management Process is a quality program that stresses a never-ending process of continuous improvement in quality, reliability, and performance in all things Lanier does at all levels of the company.

Industry analysts believe that Lanier is ready for the future. It has recognized what it does well: sourcing and distribution. Lanier reorganized to be more stream-lined, take advantage of synergy among product groups, and serve the customer better. The driving force behind the company is to look at the business through the eyes of the customers. Lanier appears to be well on its way to achieving its vision — to be recognized worldwide as the preferred provider of office solutions, dedicated to total customer satisfaction.

Discussion Questions:

1. Do you think external customers should have an impact when Lanier develops or refines products? If so, How? If not, why?

    In their book, *In search of Excellence*, Peters and Waterman argue that staying close to the customer is a tenet of an excellent manager. In *The Competitive Advantage of Nations*, Michael Porter advises companies to seek out the most sophisticated and demanding customers; if you can please them, you can please any customer.

2. To what degree are teamwork and employee involvement important to the quality of Lanier's Products?

    Experts in quality agree that a key ingredient to quality is the commitment of the organization's employees. Treating employees with respect, getting them involved in and committed to quality, and investing in their training and development are critical to the total quality organization.

Chapter 2

Philosophies of Management

Chapter Overview

This chapter examines how the field of management has evolved from the start of the Industrial Revolution to the present time. The main point to remember in studying this chapter is that present-day managers can learn a lot from the successes and errors of their predecessors.

Chapter 2 examines the early schools of management thought including: Classical, Administrative/Scientific, Behavioral, Management Science (Quantitative), Systems, Contingency, and two of the more recent approaches known as Japanese Management and Management Through Innovation.

Throughout the chapter, both positive and negative aspects of the earlier management approaches are discussed, as well as the role of communication or lack of communication at that time.

Teaching Objectives

The teaching objectives of this chapter are to:

1.   Understand some of the changes that have caused businesses to develop new management techniques.

2.   Appreciate and understand how many of the early management principles are still valid in today's business world.

3.   Comprehend the main points of emphases of the early classical approaches to management.

4.   Appreciate what the early developers of management thought were trying to accomplish.

5.   Identify the contributions the behavioral approach has made to the field of management.

6.   Comprehend some of the current ideas in management thought.

Chapter Outline of the Text

I.   A LOOK AT THE EVOLUTION OF MANAGEMENT: IS THERE ANYTHING TO LEARN FROM IT?
II.   EARLY HISTORICAL MANAGEMENT PRACTICES
III.   CLASSICAL MANAGEMENT
    A.   Scientific Management
       1.   Frederick Taylor
       2.   Henry Gantt
       3.   Frank and Lillian Gilbreth
    B.   Administrative Management
       1.   Henri Fayol
       2.   Max Weber
IV.   THE BEHAVIORAL SCHOOL OF MANAGEMENT
    A.   The Hawthorne Studies
    B.   Mary Parker Follett
    C.   Chester Barnard
V.   MANAGEMENT SCIENCE: THE QUANTITATIVE APPROACH
VI.   THE SYSTEMS APPROACH
VII.   THE CONTINGENCY APPROACH
VIII.   RECENT MANAGEMENT APPROACHES
    A.   Japanese Management
    B.   Management Through Innovation
IX.   LOOKING BACK
X.   KEY TERMS
XI.   REVIEW AND DISCUSSION QUESTIONS
XII.   CRITICAL THINKING INCIDENTS
XIII.   SUGGESTED READINGS

Key Terms

These terms are introduced in this chapter. Definitions are included in the glossary of the text.

Administrative management
Behavioral management
Bureaucracy
Classical management
Closed system
Contingency management
Cottage industry
Fayol's 14 principles of management
Gantt chart
The Hawthorne effect
The Hawthorne studies

Information based organizations (IBOs)
Innovative management
Japanese management
Management science (quantitative) approach
Synergy effect
Systems management
Taylor's principles of scientific management
Theory Z
Therbligs

Detailed Chapter Summary

I.   A LOOK AT THE EVOLUTION OF MANAGEMENT: IS THERE ANYTHING TO LEARN FROM IT?

Teaching Objective 1:   Understand the changes that have caused businesses to develop new management techniques.

The evolution of the field of management has definitely gone through a large number of changes. These changes, however, are primarily in the way various management techniques are accomplished, rather than an entirely new way to manage. As a manager, you can never get away from doing the five basic management functions of planning, organizing, staffing, leading, and controlling, but you can do each of them in a number of different ways. The historical and present approaches to management teach us some of the techniques that appear to work quite well, as well as some that do not work very well. One underlying theme that does seem to prevail throughout history, however, is the need to communicate with your employees, rather than to simply order them around. This can only be accomplished by establishing a very open communication system.

II.   EARLY HISTORICAL MANAGEMENT PRACTICES

Teaching Objective 2:   Appreciate and understand how many of the early management principles are still valid in today's business world.

While "some" form of management has been around since the time men and women formed groups on the face of the earth, it is only since the Industrial Revolution that the field of management has been formally studied. Prior to this time, there was not any great need as the "cottage industries" predominated in society. Many of these early management techniques are still valuable today.

III.   CLASSICAL MANAGEMENT

Teaching Objective 3:   Comprehend the main points of emphases of the early classical approaches to management.

Classical management was the first real attempt to study and try to figure out how to manage workers for better productivity and overall efficiency. Classical management contained two schools of management thought: scientific management and administrative management. Both of these schools of thought developed at approximately the same time, but scientific management was the first to be widely accepted.

Teaching Hint: Point out that the only two examples of formal management that the business world had to follow at this time were the military and the Catholic church, both of which were very autocratic and rigid.

A.   *Scientific Management*

This approach tried to "scientifically" analyze the job tasks that a worker was doing and then through experimentation see if a more efficient method of doing the job could be found. Many of the early scientific studies produced tremendous increases in efficiency and productivity. Unfortunately, even though some of the new techniques did benefit the worker, better treatment of workers was rarely, if ever considered.

1.   Frederick W. Taylor

Taylor is generally considered the first and biggest name in scientific management. Today, "scientific principles" are still utilized to try to increase efficiency. Taylor's four main principles of scientific management consisted of the following:

a. Develop a science or specific way to do each element of a job, instead of the "rule of thumb method."

b. Scientifically, or very carefully select, train, and develop each worker for a specific job.

      c. Work closely with the workers so that the task is being done as prescribed.

      d. Divide the work and responsibilities equally among management and the workers.

2.   Henry Gantt

Gantt was a close follower of Taylor and is the originator of the infamous Gantt chart. This bar graph chart is still used today by some small construction firms to schedule work and indicate progress. Gantt's biggest contribution, however, may have been his concern for the worker. Gantt was the first person to emphasize teaching workers as much as possible about their job, thereby utilizing an infant form of participative management. He also encouraged upward communication and advocated higher wages, believing the additional costs would be more than offset through increased productivity and quality.

3.   Frank and Lillian Gilbreth

This husband and wife team did extensive research utilizing time and motion studies. By studying workers with a movie camera, they were able to see how the workers picked up parts, handled them, and assembled them. They, in turn, would improve the workers' techniques and, therefore, their productivity. These pioneer researchers eventually found 17 basic hand motions which they termed "Therbligs" (Gilbreth spelled backwards transposing the t and the h) which applied to many manual labor jobs.

B.   *Administrative Management*

Teaching Objective 4: Appreciate what the early developers of management thought were trying to accomplish.

This school of management thought concentrated on how to "organize" the firm. The basic management functions were identified, as well as a number of basic principles that further define these basic management functions.

1.   Henri Fayol

Fayol was a large contributor to the school of administrative management. He developed five basic management functions which were: planning, organizing, command, coordination, and control. Fayol also developed 14 principles of management which further defined how to accomplish the five basic management functions. It is truly amazing how close Fayol's management functions are to the ones used today and how almost all of his principles of management continue to be valid.

2.   Max Weber

Weber was also heavily involved with organizational structure. Weber's "bureaucracy" advocated many rules and regulations to instruct workers how to handle different situations. Weber also utilized a very clear hierarchy which included specialization of labor and various types of authority. While Weber's "model" would rarely be effective today, almost every organization has some structure in the form of rules, regulations, policies, and procedures.

IV.   THE BEHAVIORAL SCHOOL OF MANAGEMENT

Teaching Objective 5:   Identify the contributions the behavioral approach has made to the field of management.

The behavioral school of management thought was the first to recognize that how you treat your employees can and will make a significant difference in how they perform. This school of thought came about almost accidently through the Hawthorne studies.

A.   *The Hawthorne Studies*

The Hawthorne studies were carried out originally from 1924 through 1932 as "scientific" studies in the Western Electric plant at Hawthorne, Illinois (just outside of Chicago). Some very significant finds resulted from these studies. Productivity can be increased through more humane treatment of workers; the social structure of work groups will set its own production norms informally; and new management skills are needed, which include good communication and interpersonal relationship skills, in order to manage workers in this "new" way.

B.   *Mary Parker Follett*

Follett's two main contributions to the behavioral school of management thought consisted of the following: (1) managers need to encourage group interacting to generate better problem solving ideas; (2) the best way to solve interpersonal conflicts is to use an "integrative process," which allows both parties in a conflict to find a mutual solution on their own. Interestingly, Follett seemed to be the forerunner for today's "quality circles" and "negotiated" methods of solving interpersonal conflicts.

Teaching Hint: Follett was a social worker, not a manager, yet her ideas and views are considered the right way to manage people even today.

C.   *Chester Barnard*

Barnard emphasized getting the employees involved and cooperating with management to achieve organizational goals. Barnard also stressed communication, both upward and downward, very strongly. He stated that it was through communication that a "feeling of harmony" can be created in an organization. Barnard also was the first person to realize that true authority only comes about if workers decide to accept the concept of authority. This bottom up view of authority was very radical for its time. It emphasized the fact that the "position power" of the manager was not all that was needed to control workers.

Suggested Readings for this Section

Linden, Dana Weschsler, "The Mother of Them All." <u>Forbes</u> *January 16, 1995, pp. 75-76.*

As early as 1920, Mary Parker Follett advocated flatter organizations, the benefits of teams and participative management, a kind of cooperative conflict resolution, and the idea that true leadership comes from ability, not from the position itself. Peter Drucker was so impressed with her thoughts and ideas that he personally wrote an introduction for a new publication entitled *Mary Parker Follett--Prophet of Management: A Celebration of the Writings from the 1920's* (Harvard Business School Press). Although she died in 1933, her insights and ideas are truly remarkable for her time. Follett was exposed to the business world while sitting on committees that set minimum wages for women and children.

Peterson, Peter B. "Training and Development: The Views of Henry L. Gantt (1861-1919) <u>SAM Advanced Management Journal</u> *51, Winter 1987, pp. 20-23.*

Henry Gantt is remembered primarily for his scheduling chart which bears his name. Upon further review, however, it can be seen that Gantt contributed much more to the field of management than his chart. Gantt, a former school teacher who studied directly under Frederick W. Taylor, favored a much more humanistic approach to workers than Taylor did. Gantt liked to use illustrations of data to teach workers the real impact of their actions. In fact Gantt was almost prophetic in his awareness of the need to train workers. Gantt's writings centered primarily on: training workers by teaching them their jobs; developing subordinates through leadership training so they could be advanced in the organization; utilizing effective and humane leadership; and giving workers fair compensation in the form of higher wages, which he believed would be more than offset by increased productivity.

V.   MANAGEMENT SCIENCE: THE QUANTITATIVE APPROACH

This approach to management attempted to make decision making more rational and logical. The quantitative approach, of course, utilizes mathematical analysis of all types. Some of the more common ones include: mathematical models, simulations, statistical trend analysis, and linear programming. There is also an entire series of computer programs which analyze costs, revenues, economic projections, forecasts of all types, production schedules, inventory control, and even "what-if" type of analysis. While this approach to management certainly has merit, it should never be used alone in making crucial decisions. Other "qualitative" factors or judgements based on experience and intuition must also be considered.

VI.   THE SYSTEMS APPROACH

This approach to management looked at an organization as a set of independent but interrelated sub-systems (departments, divisions, etc.) that must be coordinated and work in harmony for the firm to be successful. In order to accomplish this, the following techniques must be utilized: every person, department, and division must clearly understand how they fit into the organization and how they impact upon the other parts of the organization. A communication system must be established that encourages effective upward, downward, and horizontal communication. Finally, joint planning and problem solving techniques must be utilized to gain interdepartmental understanding and cooperation. If the systems approach is done properly and management encourages people to work together, then a "synergy" effect will occur. This means that the sum or output of all of the parts will be greater than if each sub-unit was working independently.

Teaching hint: Be sure to stress that the basic ideas utilized in the systems approach are applicable to any style of management and are found especially in the newest approaches to the field.

IV. THE CONTINGENCY APPROACH

This school of management thought states that there really is not any one best way to manage all organizations. The best way to manage any particular organization depends on a number of different variables. While there is debate as to which variables are the most important, most managers agree that the most effective style of management for a firm depends on the following variables: the stability of the external environment that the firm encounters, the complexity or simplicity of the tasks that workers are performing, the skill level of the workers, the amount of employee participation in decision making that is desired, the amount of risk and uncertainty in the decisions that must be made, the type of management/employee relations desired, and the size of the organization. Even after these factors have been analyzed and a style of management chosen, top management must remember that a re-evaluation of the factors is needed periodically, as these factors obviously change over time.

VIII. SOME RECENT MANAGEMENT APPROACHES

Teaching Objective 6: Comprehend some of the current ideas in management thought.

Many people feel that the field of management is entering into a new phase or school of management thought today. When you look at the main premises of some of the more popular management approaches, it is clear that many managers are managing by utilizing some interesting techniques. Two of the most popular new management approaches are Japanese Management and Management Through Innovation.

A.   *Japanese Management*

When Japan rebuilt its industries, after World War II, they began adopting many management techniques that American managers saw as unusual. At first, many U.S. managers dismissed the success that Japanese managers were having in Japan by simply believing that the style of management would only work in a Japanese culture. When the Japanese came to the U.S. and achieved the same results with American workers, U.S. managers started thinking differently.

While there are a variety of Japanese management styles, some of the factors that almost all of the successful Japanese firms have adopted include the following: a strong emphasis on long-term (life-time) employment, consensus decision making by all employees, non-specialized career paths, informal and implicit control procedures, group problem solving, shared responsibility, a strong emphasis on creating a family-type environment, and slow evaluation and promotion. Many of these Japanese techniques have now been adopted by both U.S. firms and Japanese firms operating in the U.S. and have been combined with some American management techniques such as job rotation and faster promotion schedules. This combination of Japanese and American management techniques is sometimes called "Theory Z," a term coined by Professor William Ouchi. This combination of Japanese and American management techniques has been very successful in many U.S. and Japanese firms located in the United States. Two other points of emphasis that the Japanese utilize significantly, which are now catching on very quickly with U.S. managers, are the emphasis on constant quality improvement and the use of significant profit sharing programs.

Suggested Readings for this Section:

Katzenstein, Gary, "Japanese Management Style, Beyond the Hype: What to Try and What to Toss," Working Woman February 1991, pp. 49-50, 98-101.

Gary Katzenstein spent a year working in Japan for Sony and for CSK, a large software firm. Katzenstein's experiences indicate both good and bad points of Japanese management. Some positive aspects of Japanese management include their use of observation and examination. Japanese automobile manufacturers purchase competitive models and tear them apart to see how they compare with theirs. Taking the long run perspective allows them to learn from their failures and to build better products in the future. The use of teamwork, which includes members from all departments, facilitates communication and understanding. On the negative side, Japanese workers are expected to work long hours, sometimes as much as six eleven-hour days. There is considerable pressure placed on workers and overseas assignments are common. Finally, even their "loyalty" is not what might be imagined, since employees who leave or are fired from a large firm are blacklisted and will not be hired by other large Japanese firms.

Kelly, Kevin, Neil Gross and James Treece, "Besting Japan," Business Week June 7, 1993, pp. 26-28.

U.S. automakers, computer manufacturers, and semiconductor producers are just some of the companies making significant strides against Japanese competitors. While the 1980s saw Japanese firms batter U.S. competitors, the tables are turning in the 1990s. The primary reasons for the switch include heavy investment in capital equipment, market research, government intervention, and economic changes in Japan. Because of fluctuating currency exchange rates and Japanese banks suffering from some major errors, money for capital spending is tight in Japan. U.S. firms, on the other hand, are increasing spending 10 percent to 11 percent on new equipment. Many U.S. companies have also brought the right products to the right markets at the right time by doing good market research. The U.S. government has also helped out by getting approval of the Japanese government to increase the purchase of computer chips and other U.S. parts, in some cases by as much as 20 percent. Finally, the economy in Japan is recovering slower than the U.S. economy. While all of the gains are nice for the U.S., the real question now is can we hold on to them and keep the momentum going?

B.   *Management Through Innovation*

This approach to management thought was originally developed by Thomas J. Peters and Robert Waterman, Jr. The essence of their philosphy is that successful organizations must learn to be very flexible and creative in finding new product market niches and innovative in developing new product/service offerings for the marketplace. The way to establish an organization to achieve these objectives is to use a comprehensive information gathering system, communicate continuously with customers, encourage new ideas from everyone (and do not be afraid to fail with some of them), establish a relationship of teamwork and trust with employees, and decentralize decision making and utilize self control as much as possible. It is important to communicate company values to everyone, exemplify these values to employees, and recognize the things the firm does well (core skills). Finally, all persons need to balance their personal and business lives. Although Peters and Waterman do have their critics, they point to firms that have had incredible success utilizing this style of management.

IX.   LOOKING BACK

This chapter provides an overview of how the field of management has "evolved" over time. The field of management is a dynamic field, which is constantly changing as new ideas and techniques are introduced.

▓▓ Answers to CONSIDER THIS Questions (Page 46)
■

1. **How different from Fayol's management principles are the five basic management functions that we utilize today?**

   Fayol's five main management elements are almost identical with the five management functions utilized today. There are some management authors who utilize only four main management functions: planning, organizing (which includes staffing), leading, and controlling. Fayol has all four of these plus coordination, which is certainly a management principle utilized by everyone in business today.

2. **What is wrong with taking a purely scientific approach toward managing a company such as a manufacturing firm?**

   The main problem with the purely scientific approach to management is that it tends to treat the worker as a tool or something to be manipulated in order to increase efficiency. We only need to look to the past to see numerous firms that had many labor problems because they utilized this approach. Management must realize that their employees are a most valuable asset; to be successful, management must treat employees with respect and trust.

3. **How do some of the principles advocated by Henry Gantt compare with modern management principles?**

   Gantt's principles compare very favorably with many of today's management principles. Gantt advocated a form of participative leadership. He stressed teaching workers as much as possible about their jobs, and he encouraged them to ask questions. This form of upward communication was rarely, if ever, used during his time. Finally, Gantt believed in giving workers a good wage, which he believed would be more than offset through increased productivity and higher quality. All of these principles are quite well accepted in today's management field.

Answers to CONSIDER THIS Questions   (Page 50)

1. **Why did the worker's productivity in the control group of the Hawthorne studies increase when nothing in the workplace environment was altered?**

   The increase in productivity in both the control group and the experimental group was caused by changes in how the workers were being treated. While the control group's work environment was not altered, they did "feel special" to be included as part of an important study. They were also treated much better by the researchers. Communication between the researchers and the workers was much better. They also enjoyed working in their own room; this was perceived to give them some elite status among the workforce.

2. **Why didn't the workers in the Bank Wiring Room experiment not increase production when economic incentives were provided?**

    The bank wiring room experiment was the first time that researchers realized that work groups do set their own production norms. These norms are based on what the group considers to be a fair reward for their work. Members who try to exceed this rate, even for economic incentives, were socially ostracized. For established work groups, the production norms may be so ingrained that the only way to change them may be to break up the group itself. Doing this, of course, may cause a whole new set of problems for the managers.

3. **Does raising morale through better treatment of workers always raise the level of production?**

    Unfortunately, the answer to the above question is no. There have been a number of recent studies that clearly show that raising morale does not always significantly increase production. Some workers are not motivated to perform at higher levels just because they are being treated better. For these workers, other forms of motivation are needed if an increase in production is the goal.

Answers to CONSIDER THIS Questions   (Page 55)

1. **What are the main forms of quantitative information being used in the business world today to assist managers in decision making?**

    While there are virtually an infinite number of computer programs and mathematical models in use today, the main forms of quantitative data appear to be the following: statistical trend analysis (for forecasting revenues and costs), breakeven analysis, ratio analysis, simulations, linear programming, scheduling programs (P.E.R.T. and C.P.M.), inventory control programs (J.I.T.), and computer spreadsheets which allow a manager to do "what-if" analysis.

2.   **Why can't managers rely on numerical data or statistics when they make decisions?**

The main problem with numerical data or quantitative data is that it only presents one view of the situation. For example, a cost breakdown on three different alternative advertising media mixes will only tell you which is the least expensive and which is the most expensive. A manager also needs to utilize qualitative data, or judgements from personal experience or from outside experts in order to zero in on the media mix that has the best appeals to the marketplace. Combining both quantitative and qualitative data is almost always the best way to arrive at a decision.

3.   **What are the main factors that can influence the style of management that should be used in a given situation?**

The contingency approach to management states that the proper style of management depends on the following main variables: (1) stability of the external environment that the firm operates in; (2) degree of complexity of tasks performed by the workers; (3) skill and proficiency level of the work force; (4) the degree or amount of participation desired; (5) amount of risk and level of uncertainty of the decisions that must be made; (6) the kind of management/employee relationship desired; and (7) the size of the organization.

Answers to REVIEW AND DISCUSSION Questions

1.   *What was the main problem with Max Weber's bureaucracy?*

Weber's bureaucracy was a very impersonal structure which allowed for very little if any interacting or creativity. Workers were not encouraged to communicate with each other or with management but were expected to simply do their job tasks as instructed. The main form of communication was downward and primarily in written format.

2.   *What were the main criticisms of Frederick Taylor's scientific management approach to management?*

The main criticism of Taylor's scientific management approach was the way the workers were viewed and treated. The worker was thought of as simply a tool or something to manipulate in order to achieve higher productivity. Virtually all of the changes in how the workers did their job, such as periodic rest breaks and incentive pay, were given only to increase productivity, not to make the worker's job easier or more enjoyable. If the added factor, (for example, periodic rest breaks) had not increased overall productivity, it would have been eliminated immediately.

3.   *What primary contribution to the field of management by Frank and Lillian Gilbreth make?*

The main contribution made by the Gilbreths to the field of management was their time and motion studies. By actually filming a worker doing a task, they could clearly identify wasted motion and then improve the worker's technique. The basic hand motions that they identified (called Therbligs) are applicable to virtually any manual labor job. Truly, this is an effective way to increase productivity.

4.   *What area did Mary Parker Follett feel should be of critical concern to managers?*

Follett was one of the first people to realize the crucial need to cultivate group interaction to solve problems. Follett saw the value in what we today call "participative management." Follett was also a strong advocate of utilizing a "negotiation" form of conflict resolution. She was certainly ahead of her time with these great ideas.

5.   *How can managers ensure that all systems and subsystems in an organization are working together?*

To get every subsystem and every person in an organization working together, management must clearly communicate the goals and objectives of the firm to every department and every person in the firm; everybody must understand how their departments interact and how their jobs impact those of others. Communication must be established through joint management/employee planning and problem solving sessions. In these sessions, participants need to be brought together to assure that all viewpoints are represented.

6.   *How does Japanese Management differ from Theory Z management?*

Theory Z is a combination of Japanese and American management principles. In Theory Z, primary Japanese principles are modified to some extent. Lifetime employment is changed to long-term employment with a real attempt to avoid layoffs. The evaluation and promotion process is not quite so lengthy. Finally, non-specialized career paths are modified to incorporate the use of job rotation.

7.   *What are the main management techniques that Thomas J. Peters and Robert H. Waterman feel a firm must utilize to stay out in front competitively in today's world markets?*

Peters and Waterman strongly advocate that a firm should organize to deal with the ever increasing amounts of change. To cope with this, firms need to be very flexible and innovative in the products and services that they market. Management must establish sophisticated information gathering systems which reach customers, suppliers, and employees on a continuous basis. Employees must be treated with respect. A real team approach must be established where everyone knows and accepts the values and core competencies of the firm. New product ideas must be tried with the knowledge that some of them are going to fail. The firm and everyone in it must accept these failures as the price they must pay to remain competitive. The organizational structure must be set up so that top management is kept to an absolute minimum, and decision making is pushed down to the lower levels. Finally, all persons need to maintain a balance between their personal and professional lives.

Answers to CRITICAL THINKING INCIDENTS

Incident 2-1: THE AMERICAN STEEL CORPORATION FACES BANKRUPTCY

1.   **What school of management thought most closely corresponds to the business philosophy practiced at American Steel prior to the company surveys?**

Prior to the surveys, American Steel's philosophy of management was based on the classical/scientific school of thought. Workers were treated as tools to be used, and communication with them was virtually nonexistent. Management's attempt to solve their problems through the hiring of more supervisors and quality control inspectors further illustrates how the firm ignores its employees in solving problems. Strikes, high turnover, and the number of grievances all indicate a very poor management/labor relationship which was very common during the classical era.

2.   **What specific areas does American Steel have to change it if is going to turn its problems around?**

First, and foremost, the management at American Steel needs to change the "adverse" type of relationship that it currently has with its employees. Employees must be treated with respect if this firm is ever going to gain their support. Next, management must reduce costs and/or increase revenues in order to turn the financial situation around. Strikes, high turnover, and absenteeism are all very costly factors. Also, revenues may be increased if the quality of the steel rises and delivery dates are met more often. Virtually all of the problems seen at this firm are traceable to the management/employee relationships.

3.   **What specific ideas do you recommend they implement to be more competitive?**

To have a new management/employee relationship, they must establish trust with their employees. To do this, they need to demonstrate more open communication with their employees. Management must work with employees to solve their grievances and to establish joint planning and problem solving sessions. Supervisors need human relations training on how to treat employees with respect and how to communicate with them more effectively. Incentives such as profit sharing and bonuses for cost saving ideas need to be established. Finally, a team orientation must be established through training and the constant communication of the firm's values and goals.

Incident 2-2: WHO IS RIGHT?

1.   **What type of management thought represents Bud Carraway's perspective?**

Bud Carraway is definitely a classical manager. His total disregard for the new-employee work schedule is causing the firm to experience high turnover of personnel, and yet he refuses to do anything about it. The hardships caused by working the late shift and the weekends/holidays schedule are not even considered. Utilizing this work schedule as a "test" to see who really wants to work in the hospitality field is very weak, especially since it does not seem to be giving him any positive results.

2.   **What kind of problems do you foresee the Ocala Inn having because of Bud's management style?**

Bud's style, as noted in the case, creates a lot of tension and stress on all employees and lower-level managers. No one works as well in a very stressful situation, and normally absenteeism and turnover both rise in this type of situation. Both of these factors raise costs and, therefore, reduce profits. Bud's style also reduces upward communication between the employees and management, which further reduces efficiency. Finally, Bud's style tends to permeate throughout the organization and eventually will even impact on the customers, which will reduce revenues in the long run.

3.   **If you were the new owner of the Ocala Inn, what changes would you make to increase its efficiency and profits? Why?**

The type of relationship that management has with its employees is crucial in any business but maybe even more crucial in a business that deals directly with the public. Since this is the case here, the new owner of the inn needs to replace Bud Carraway as the general manager. Since Bud has been in the field for 30 years already, it is doubtful that he would be receptive to changing his management style. Next, the new general manager needs to establish a team-oriented approach between the management and the staff. To establish this type of orientation, communication must be greatly expanded, company values firmly established in everyone's mind, and a more participative form of management must be used in planning and problem solving. Also some real incentives must be established to encourage employees to lower costs and increase profits.

Incident 2-3: TO WHOM DO I ANSWER?

1. **What management approach is the top management at Memorial Rehab primarily using?**

    Dr. Owens represents top management in this case. His style of management represents a classical management approach where lower-level managers are just given orders and expected to follow through without questions. This style of management almost always creates resistance by the lower-level managers and employees, especially when changes are introduced. It is only natural to somewhat fear and, therefore, want to fight changes that you had no knowledge of beforehand and no input into developing.

2. **What systems approach would you recommend be implemented to get the two units to work together?**

    In order to get the two units to work together effectively, a joint committee, which has representation from all departments in each unit, must be established to determine the best way to achieve this goal. Committee members must be briefed on why these changes need to be made and on the mutual benefits to them and to patient care. They, in turn, need to go back to their departments and communicate these points to everyone. All persons in each department should be asked for ideas on how to accomplish this goal, and all of their questions and concerns need to be addressed. If this procedure is followed, in time the committee should be able to come up with an effective way to accomplish this goal, and it should be well received by the great majority of the employees and lower-level managers.

3. **What kind of a management approach do you think is needed here to increase efficiency and improve employee morale?**

Certainly a more participative and creative approach is needed in this case. Right now there is a total lack of respect between top- and lower-level managers, and there is also an adverse relationship. To turn this around, communication must be opened up considerably, and the goals and values of the organization need to be discussed and established in everyone's mind. Next, both lower-level managers and employees need to be encouraged to openly discuss problems, ideas, and concerns. Management must address these points and establish a more positive, caring, and respectful atmosphere with everyone in the organization. Patient follow-ups should continue to be completed and used as a guide to inform the staff on how well they are doing. Patient care must become the main goal in this situation. Finally, top management needs to give lower-level managers the training and assistance needed to run their departments more efficiently. Once they are able to do this, then decision making authority needs to be pushed down to the lower levels.

Study Guide Assignments

The individual case assignment in the study guide is a good way to help your students see how the various principles of management are integrated into a real situation. If each of the members work independently, they will fail to utilize the specialized talents that each possesses. By working as a team, they will get a "synergy" effect; therefore, they will become more productive and efficient.

The group case assignment continues the individual case scenario somewhat but points out the value of analyzing how the management of a firm can influence its potential market value. This case asks students to actually research and compare the management style of a firm currently on the Fortune 500 list with one that was not on it 10 years ago. The contrast should indicate the importance of having an effective management team.

Video Case

Lincoln Electric

Focus: **Scientific Management Principles**

Summary:

Lincoln Electric Company is the world's leading manufacturer of welding machines, with sales in excess of $800 million. Despite being located in the heart of America's rust belt, this non-union Fortune 500 company has prospered as have its employees. Lincoln can boast of the highest paid factory workers in the world, with an average wage of over $45,000. Some workers have seen their annual wage exceed $85,000. Added to these wages are annual bonuses. In a recent year, $48 million in profit was divided among 2,650 employees. Workers were graded on such factors as attendance and cooperation; the highest-rated worker received a bonus of $37,000, while low-grade workers received only a few thousand dollars. In addition to the high wages, Lincoln is also proud of the fact that it does not lay off workers. Even when sales declined 40 percent between 1982 and 1983, no workers were laid off.

How is Lincoln able to achieve these results? It uses a system that ties workers' pay directly to their output. Lincoln uses this piecework pay system exclusively. Workers only get paid for good products manufactured. Workers receive no paid sick days or holidays. They are paid only when they produce. Many employees choose to work straight through their shifts, minimizing or eliminating lunch and rest breaks. They also often report to work when they are sick. In fact, to curb employees' enthusiasm for work, Lincoln has posted a sign at the employees' entrance telling workers not to come to work more than 30 minutes early.

Although unions have fought against piecework for years, Lincoln Electric does not apologize for its system. Don Hastings, CEO of Lincoln, asserts that "to get paid for what you negotiate and not for what you produce does not make sense." He contends that the recent emphasis on job satisfaction with happy workers exercising and singing company songs is baloney. Workers come to Lincoln to earn a good living, he says. Although many Lincoln workers may not be particularly fond of their jobs, they do like the money and want no part of unions or strikes.

Discussion Questions:

1.   Critics of Lincoln's system contend that if it were used throughout American industry, it would throw us back into the nineteenth century, rivaling the worst days of the Industrial Revolution. Discuss the rationale that would lead to such a prediction.

Arguments against a wide-scale implementation of Lincoln's system include: problems with no sick leave, questions about the ability of some employees to continue to perform at high levels as they age, and problems with employees if they become disabled.

2. Some people say that Lincoln is behind the times, while others see it as ahead of the times. Provide support for each side of the argument.

In many respects, Lincoln operates like an American company at the turn of the century: pay based on piece work, no paid holidays or vacations, and strict adherence to pay for performance. However, the system works at Lincoln, and some argue that many American companies have strayed too far from linking pay to performance.

3. How do you think the compensation system at Lincoln affects salaried, mid-level managers?

There is some evidence that mid-level managers are squeezed in the middle. They are under pressure to perform from their bosses and from the piecework employees who work for them.

Chapter 3

The Role of Communication

Chapter Overview

This chapter emphasizes that for communication to occur between a sender and receiver, there must be a sharing of meaning between them concerning a message. For managers, the number of situations in which they must communicate well are endless.

The communication process is discussed in this chapter. In doing so, key aspects of this process are examined. Miscommunication that occurs due to the making of inferences is also examined. Due to the fact that managers send and receive many nonverbal messages, the topic of nonverbal communication is covered. The important topic of listening is also discussed. A distinction between formal communication and the grapevine is made. In terms of formal communication, the topics of downward, upward, and horizontal communication are examined. Important issues associated with the grapevine are also discussed.

Teaching Objectives

The teaching objectives of this chapter are to:

1. Explain the communication process.

2. Identify strategies for avoiding miscommunication that results from inferences.

3. Identify the functions of nonverbal messages.

4. Explain the difference between hearing and listening.

5.   Distinguish between downward, upward, and horizontal communication.

6.   Identify ways to deal with the grapevine.

Chapter Outline of the Text

I.   TO MANAGE, YOU MUST COMMUNICATE
II.   WHAT IS COMMUNICATION
III.   THE COMMUNICATION PROCESS
    A.   Participants
    B.   Messages
    C.   Channels
    D.   Noise
      1.   Environmental Noise
      2.   Psychological Noise
      3.   Semantic Noise
    E.   Feedback
IV.   INFERENCES CAUSE MISCOMMUNICATION
    A.   How Inferences Can Cause Miscommunication.
    B.   Strategies for Avoiding Miscommunication Due To Inferences
      1.   Be aware of your important inferences
      2.   Label your important inferences
V.   NONVERBAL COMMUNICATION
    A.   Nonverbal Communication Defined
    B.   Functions of Nonverbal Messages
      1.   To Accent and Complement
      2.   To Repeat
      3.   To Contradict
      4.   To Regulate
      5.   To Substitute
    C.   Nonverbal Communication Can Motivate
VI.   LISTENING
    A.   Hearing Versus Listening
    B.   Listening is Good Business
    C.   Strategies for Comprehensive Listening
      1.   Ask Questions to Enhance Understanding
      2.   Confirm Your Understanding
      3.   Maximize Your Excess Thought Time
      4.   Listen for the Speaker's Main Idea
      5.   Listen for Supporting Details
      6.   Listen for Key Words
      7.   Take Notes

Key Terms

These terms are introduced in the chapter. Definitions are included in the glossary of the text.

Communication channel
Communication
Communication process
Comprehensive listening
Decoding
Diagonal communication
Downward communication
Encoding
Environmental noise
Excess thought time
Feedback
Formal communication
Grapevine

Horizontal communication
Inference
Key word
Listening
Noise
Nonverbal communication
Psychological noise
Rumor
Semantic noise
Semantics
Supporting detail
Upward communication

Detailed Chapter Summary

I.   TO MANAGE, YOU MUST COMMUNICATE

The functions of management cannot be fulfilled if managers lack the ability to communicate. The situations in which managers must communicate well are endless. For example, as a manager you will need to provide employees with directions and guidance on how they should perform certain job duties. You also will need to collaborate with other managers. In addition, you will be expected to interact with customers. Throughout these activities, your boss will observe how well you communicate with others.

II.   WHAT IS COMMUNICATION?

Communication is the sharing of meaning between the sender and the receiver of a message.

III.   THE COMMUNICATION PROCESS

Teaching Objective 1:   Explain the communication process.

The communication process involves sending and receiving messages for the purpose of sharing meaning. The sender encodes a thought into message form. The receiver decodes the message. This encoding and decoding process is influenced by the sender's and the receiver's fields of experience. The sending, receiving, and interpreting of messages may be hindered by various forms of noise.

A.   *Participants*

People differ in their backgrounds. Furthermore, different backgrounds provide individuals with different experiences, and we interpret statements and events based on our experiences. Therefore, the sender of a message should not assume that the receiver will automatically interpret a message as intended.

B.   *Messages*

You are *always* sending messages. For example, your physical appearance sends messages to others about your age, height, weight, and so on. When you are angry or happy, your facial expressions probably signal the emotion you are experiencing. Furthermore, the words you speak and the letters you send to others are also examples of messages that you may send as a manager.

However, although you can send a message, you cannot send meaning. That is, others can receive your messages, but they cannot receive the meaning you intend. Instead, others must give meaning to your messages. *The extent to which the receiver of your message gives the same meaning to it as you intended, is the degree to which communication has occurred.*

C.   *Channels*

In the communication process, a communication channel represents both the path of a message and the means by which the message is transmitted. A message conveyed by a sender to a receiver travels in the direction of the receiver. A feedback message conveyed by a receiver to a sender travels in the opposite direction.

Managers communicate through many channels. Common channels include light and sound. However, people can use any of their five senses to communicate. Communication channels for managers often include face-to-face discussions, memorandums, and telephone calls.

D.   *Noise*

When two people are attempting to communicate with each other, noise
represents any interference with the message that hinders the sharing of
meaning.

   1.   Environmental Noise

          All of the surrounding sights and sounds that distract people who are
          attempting to communicate with each other are known as environmental
          noise. Clothing styles, a loud car horn, the conversation of others, and
          the color of a room represent distractions that hinder communication.

   2.   Psychological Noise

          The thoughts and feelings that hinder communication while we interact
          with others are referred to as psychological noise. Day-dreaming is a
          classic example of this type of noise. Psychological noise can act as a
          distraction, causing your mind to wander while you attempt to listen to
          others. Biases or prejudices that lead to closed-mindedness are also
          examples of psychological noise.

   3.   Semantic Noise

          Alternative meanings for a message that hinder communication because
          they are different from the meaning intended by the sender represent
          semantic noise. For example, "dorms" at colleges are now often
          referred to as "residence halls" by school administrators. Actually,
          some administrators are offended when a person naively refers to
          student housing as a "dorm." This offense is due to semantic noise; no
          disrespect was intended, but the administrator interpreted the reference
          negatively. As another example, innocent use of the term "stewardess"
          instead of "flight attendant" in the airline industry may anger female
          employees due to semantic noise. Jargon and ambiguous terms that
          cause confusion are also forms of semantic noise.

E.   *Feedback*

Any type of response to a message represents a form of feedback. The
feedback you receive as a manager will give you an idea of how well you have
communicated with others. For example, an employee's response to a
suggestion you make may clearly indicate to you that miscommunication has
occurred. On the other hand, even without saying a word, an employee's

actions can provide feedback that your instructions have been interpreted correctly. Furthermore, feedback helps managers to become aware of and deal with communication problems as they are developing.

Teaching Hint: Emphasize that communication is more than just sending and receiving messages; there must be a sharing of meaning. That is, the receiver's interpretation of your message may be different than you intended.

IV. INFERENCES CAUSE MISCOMMUNICATION

Making inferences is a common cause of miscommunication by managers. An inference can be defined as the act or process of drawing a conclusion about something unknown based on facts or indications. Unlike a fact, which can be proved to be true, an inference is a guess that seems correct. The act of inferring works as follows. A manager gains information, perhaps by observing something, hearing comments from others, or reading certain material. The manager then analyzes the information and draws a conclusion from it. The conclusion or inference that results may be correct or incorrect.

A. *How Inferences Can Cause Miscommunication*

The inferences you make while interacting with others on the job can lead you to incorrectly interpret their statements. Miscommunication then results. For example, Carol, a manager for a large company, was asked to speak for 30 minutes regarding her company's expansion plans during a luncheon meeting for the local Chamber of Commerce. Carol agreed to speak and asked what time she should arrive for the meeting. She was instructed to be there at noon.

Carol *inferred* that she would begin speaking at noon. Based on that inference, Carol scheduled a 1:00 p.m. meeting in her office with an important client. Unfortunately, when Carol arrived at the luncheon meeting to give her presentation, she learned that she was not scheduled to speak until the lunch was over at 12:30 p.m. Carol quickly realized that she could not speak at 12:30 and make her 1:00 meeting. Carol's inference caused miscommunication and put her in a difficult situation.

B. *Strategies for Avoiding Miscommunication Due To Inferences*

Teaching Objective 2: Identify strategies for avoiding miscommunication that results from inferences.

First, be aware of the important inferences you make. You cannot deal with your inferences if you are not aware of them. Second, label the important inferences you make.

Teaching Hint: Emphasize that it is acceptable to make inferences. However, it is important to clarify any inference that could cause a major problem if it is incorrect.

V.   NONVERBAL COMMUNICATION

Managers send and receive many nonverbal messages on the job each day. Interestingly, according to one estimate, 93 percent of a message's impact is influenced by nonverbal behavior, which leaves only 7 percent accounted for by word selection. As a result, managers should be aware of important aspects of nonverbal communication and how it works.

A.   *Nonverbal Communication Defined*

Nonverbal communication is communication other than through actual words that are spoken.

B.   *Functions of Nonverbal Messages*

Teaching Objective 3:   Identify the functions of nonverbal messages.

Research into nonverbal communication has revealed that nonverbal messages serve several functions. Specifically, nonverbal messages can accent and complement, repeat, contradict, regulate, and substitute for verbal messages.

C.   *Nonverbal Communication Can Motivate*

Many managers overlook the fact that their nonverbal behavior can act as an important motivational tool. Subtle aspects in the way in which a manager interacts with employees can influence their level of motivation. For example, if a manager shows an interest in employees and what they are doing, this behavior probably will have a positive effect on their level of motivation. On the job, when you interact with employees, it is appreciated when you express warmth, respect, concern, equality, and a willingness to listen.

Too often, managers are unaware of the negative nonverbal messages they send to employees. Although they are unintentional in some cases, these messages may be interpreted as demonstrations of coolness, aloofness, disinterest, and/or disrespect. Needless to say, when employees are left with such impressions, their levels of motivation are likely to decrease. On the other hand, if a manager's nonverbal messages indicate support for employees and satisfaction with their performances, their levels of motivation are likely to increase. Your efforts, for example, to maintain good eye contact, use a pleasant tone of voice, show enthusiasm, and acknowledge others with a smile will be noticed and appreciated by employees.

VI.   LISTENING

To manage effectively, you need to receive information that will assist you in accomplishing goals. Much of that information comes to you in verbal form, and for that reason, you must be skilled at listening. Listening is paying attention to what the speaker says and giving meaning to what you have heard.

A.   *Hearing Versus Listening*

Teaching Objective 4:   Explain the difference between hearing and listening.

Hearing is automatic; you have little control over your ability to hear. However, listening only occurs when you make an effort to pay attention to what a speaker says and give meaning to what you have heard. Therefore, listening requires mental effort beyond just hearing.

B.   *Listening is Good Business*

Listening errors by employees can be very expensive for companies. Large numbers of organizations are incorporating listening training as part of their employee-development programs to enhance employee performance on the job.

C.   *Strategies for Comprehensive Listening*

When you listen for the purpose of understanding and remembering the information contained in a verbal message, you are engaging in comprehensive listening.

1.   Ask Questions to Enhance Understanding

It is a good idea to ask questions if you are confused by a speaker's statements or if you are uncertain about whether your interpretation is accurate.

2.   Confirm Your Understanding

Especially when the consequences of a misunderstanding are high, you want to confirm your understanding of the speaker's statements.

3.   Maximize Your Excess Thought Time

You should use your excess thought time to review what the speaker has said. During this review, think of relevant questions to ask or comments to make. As a result, you will stay in tune with the speaker.

4.   Listen for the Speaker's Main Idea

While listening, it is important to identify and remember the speaker's main idea. Listeners seldom remember all of a lengthy verbal message. However, remembering the main idea is most important.

5.   Listen for Supporting Details

In addition to listening for the main idea, it is also important to listen for details that support the speaker's main idea. Supporting details confirm the speaker's main idea, although they are secondary in importance to the main idea.

6.   Listen for Key Words

Specific words that aid you in remembering parts of what a speaker says are called key words.

7.   Take Notes

If you take notes while listening, there is less need to rely on your memory to recall what a speaker says.

Suggested Readings for this Section:

Deeprose, Donna. "Listen Your Way to Better Management." <u>Supervisory Management</u> *38, May 1993, pp. 7-8.*

This article begins with a listening quiz that contains nine items. The items in the quiz relate to realistic situations a listener could reasonably expect to experience on the job. Following the quiz is an examination of the available responses to various items on the quiz. In doing so, a guide to effective listening is offered.

Watson, Arden K. and James R. Bossley. "Taking the Sweat Out of Communication Anxiety." <u>Personnel Journal</u> *74, April 1995, pp. 111-119.*

Facilitating a team meeting can provoke communication anxiety among many managers. The Whirlpool Corporation, Clyde Division in Ohio, experienced this problem as it introduced self-directed work teams. This article discusses how Whirlpool is dealing with the problem of communication anxiety.

VII   FORMAL COMMUNICATION PATHS

Organizations have both formal and informal communication networks. Formal communication can be defined as communication between individuals in the organization about formal, work-related matters. Formal communication paths are dictated by the organizational hierarchy or by job function. Furthermore, formal communication generally occurs along downward, upward, and horizontal paths.

Teaching Objective 5:   Distinguish between downward, upward, and horizontal communication.

Downward communication refers to the flow of messages from managers to employees. Upward communication represents the flow of messages from employees to managers. Horizontal communication is the lateral exchange of messages among people at the same level of authority.

VIII.   A FOCUS ON QUALITY IN COMMUNICATION

Effective use of the different forms of formal communication is necessary for the successful implementation of quality management programs in organizations. There needs to be a fostering of communication across departments and between the planners of total quality management programs and the employees responsible for making the plans work.

Suggested Readings for this Section
Harari, Oren. "Open the Doors, Tell the Truth." Management Review 84, January 1995, pp. 33-35.

The author recalls a flight on an airplane that developed engine difficulty. Open and honest communication from the pilot helped develop cohesiveness among the passengers. The positive impact of open communication on empowerment and teamwork in organizations is discussed.

Rao, Spikumar S. "Welcome to Open Space." Training 31, April 1994, pp. 52-56.

One morning in 1993, Rockport Company closed for two days. All production, shipping, and regular meetings were cancelled. With the exception of a few employees who remained to answer telephone calls, the company's entire work force of 350 people met in a warehouse to attend an "open space" meeting. In an open space meeting, any employee can identify a work-related issue that the employee believes should be discussed. A time and place for those who wish to discuss the issue is then posted. Suggestions that evolved from these discussions are expected to save the company more than four million dollars. This article discusses how an open space meeting works.

IX.   THE GRAPEVINE

In organizations, the grapevine represents the informal communication system or the unofficial flow of information about people and events. Information that is not official or required by job conditions, company rules, or procedures is considered grapevine information.

A.   *Dealing with the Grapevine*

Teaching Objective 6:   Identify ways to deal with the grapevine.

Managers can minimize grapevine activity by developing a climate of open communication with their employees. In doing so, they should keep their employees informed. Also, managers should engage in behaviors that lead employees to view them as approachable people.

B.   *Handling Rumors*

A rumor is an unofficial piece of information that travels through the grapevine without evidence to confirm it. Rumors can be true, but they frequently are either partially or completely false. In general, the best way for a manager to handle a false rumor is to release the correct facts quickly, without restating the rumor itself.

X.   SUGGESTIONS FOR EFFECTIVE COMMUNICATION

Managers, by the very nature of their job, usually find it necessary to interact with many individuals. In doing so, managers should be honest and direct in communicating with others; summarize important decisions; and limit messages to those that are necessary. They should also time messages properly and give and seek feedback.

XI.   LOOKING BACK

This chapter examines communication concepts that managers must understand to succeed on the job.

Answers to CONSIDER THIS Questions (Page 78)

1.   **The term "communication" is misunderstood and misused by many managers. As discussed earlier, communication can be defined as the sharing of meaning. How is the term "communication" misused in the following statement? "The communication was communicated, but no communication occurred."**

The term "communication," or a variation of it, is used three times in the above statement. These three instances are numbered as follows: (1) "the communication was (2) communicated, but no (3) communication occurred." In the first instance, the term "communication" refers to "message." In the second instance, "communicated" refers to "sent." In the third instance, "communication" refers to the "sharing of meaning." The third instance represents the most appropriate use of the term "communication." When the term "communication" is used to mean many things, it becomes vague and imprecise. The statement under consideration here should be rephrased as follows: "The message was sent, but no communication occurred."

2.   **We interpret statements and actions based on our field of experience. Why, then, is there a natural tendency for communication problems to occur between employees and executives in organizations?**

Employees and executives, by the nature of their jobs, often have different experiences. They may see things from a different perspective, and they may interpret events differently due to their different experiences. One executive, for example, thought a particular meeting he conducted went well until he was informed that the material covered didn't affect a few of the employees present at the meeting. Suddenly, the executive realized that those few employees wasted their time in the meeting. The executive's experience did not allow him to see that the time of some employees was wasted in the meeting until he was informed of the problem.

3.   **Think of an inference you made that caused a communication problem. In looking back at the situation, what should you have done to avoid the communication problem?**

One student who was a manager at a fast food restaurant indicated that when more French fries needed to be fried, he would yell out "drop the fries." Then, the employee closest to the machine that fried the French fries would lower a basket of frozen fries into the hot grease. A new employee, after hearing the manager say "drop the fries," dumped the fries from the basket into the hot grease, creating a mess. The new employee should have been informed how to interpret the jargon "drop the fries" during a training program.

Answers to CONSIDER THIS Questions   (Page 87)

1.   **People have an invisible bubble around them that represents their personal space. How does it make you feel when people invade your personal space by standing too close to you?**

One student explained that some customers stand too close to him at work and it makes him feel uncomfortable when this happens. The student said he does his best not to make others feel uncomfortable by standing too close to them. Another student indicated that we need to be aware of the fact that the size of the invisible bubble may vary among different cultures.

2.   **It has been said, "To be a good listener, you must accept the speaker as he or she is." What does this statement mean to you?**

The intent of this statement is that when listening, we must guard against being unduly influenced by the age, race, sex, religion, dress, etc., of the speaker. Instead, we should concentrate on what the speaker says. For example, discounting what a person says because the speaker is in some way different from us, is an unfortunate trait of many poor listeners.

3. **It is often claimed that information is power. How does this assertion explain why some managers withhold important information from employees?**

Some managers believe that by withholding important information from employees, they will be perceived as having something employees want. The managers then conclude that this behavior will give them control over the employees. Too often, however, this behavior creates problems for companies, and it reduces job satisfaction for employees. Any attempt by a company to empower employees will be hindered if managers withhold important information from them.

Answers to REVIEW AND DISCUSSION Questions

1. *In addition to sending and receiving a message, what else is needed for communication to occur?*

There must be a sharing of meaning between the sender and receiver. If the receiver of a message interprets the message the same way the sender of the message intended, very good communication has occurred.

2. *How does the communication process work?*

The communication process involves the sending and receiving of messages for the purpose of sharing meaning. When you wish to express a thought, you must create (encode) a message. Next, you send your message to a receiver, who interprets (decodes) the message. For communication to occur, the outcome or result of this process must be a sharing of meaning between the sender and the receiver of the message.

3. *We give meaning to messages based on what?*

We give meaning based on our experiences. For a farmer, for example, the word "dinner" may refer to the meal served at noon. To a person raised in a large city, "dinner" may refer to the meal served around 6 p.m. Different backgrounds and experiences can produce different interpretations or meanings for the same message.

4.   *How can inferences cause miscommunication?*

Inferences can cause people to incorrectly interpret others' statements. This problem often occurs when we mistakenly treat an inference as a fact. To illustrate, a manager asked an employee how work on a particular report was progressing. The employee replied, "I will be finished with my part of the report this afternoon." The manager inferred that all other necessary sections of the report were finished. As a result, the manager told her superior that the report would be finished that afternoon. Actually, other sections of the report being prepared by additional individuals had not been completed and would not be finished for several days. The manager would have realized that it was inappropriate to promise completion of the report that day had she responded to the employee by saying, "I'm inferring that when you finish your part of the report, the report will be finished." Then, the employee would have explained that other sections were not near completion.

5.   *Why are managers often unaware of important inferences they make when interacting with others?*

Our expectations, based on our experiences and what makes sense to us, can make it difficult for us to realize the difference between what we are guessing at and what we know. In a multicultural workforce, for example, managers may infer that perceptions held by employees of one culture are shared by employees from different cultures. If this inference is acted on as if it was a fact, problems may occur for the manager.

6.   *Why are so many communication problems associated with nonverbal messages?*

Part of the explanation is that such a large number of the messages we send are nonverbal in nature. With so many of our messages being nonverbal, communication problems are more likely to show up in that area. In addition, we are always sending nonverbal messages. However, people are often unaware of many of the nonverbal messages they send. This lack of attention increases the chances that we will behave in ways that leave the wrong impression with others.

7. *How can you use your excess thought time to enhance your listening effectiveness?*

Use your excess thought time while listening to review what the speaker is saying. This review can help you gain more from what the speaker said. While reviewing the speaker's comments, think of questions to ask that will clarify uncertain aspects of what was said or that will help you better understand how to benefit from the speakers comments. Excess thought time, therefore, can be used to help you get more out of a speaker's comments.

8. *As a manager, how can you facilitate good upward communication?*

Show a positive attitude toward receiving upward communication so employees will know that you are interested in knowing ideas they have to share. Let them know the type of information they can share with you that is especially helpful to you and listen carefully when they share that information with you. As you listen to upward communication, be open-minded and respond to suggestions and ideas that are presented to you. To further encourage the flow of valuable upward communication, establish a mechanism that helps employees to communicate upward.

9. *How should management respond to a false rumor that is harming the organization.*

In most cases, the best way for a manager to deal with a false rumor is to release the correct facts quickly, without restating the rumor itself.

Answers to CRITICAL THINKING INCIDENTS

Incident 3-1: A TROUBLED BANK

1. Was it a good idea for top management to introduce the award system to promote competition among departments? Explain.

It was not a good idea to introduce the award system. Organizational goals must take precedence over departmental goals. Top management is responsible for making sure that various groups in a company work together, not against each other. The award system at Metropolitan Bank has departments working against each other. Competition that promotes the accomplishment of company goals by all departments is needed. This type of competition, perhaps against another bank, will encourage departments to work together.

2.   **What mistake did Sharon make in acting on the information she received from the employee concerning the free-checking account? Explain.**

Sharon instructed her employees to spend valuable time preparing a marking strategy based on second-hand information. Sharon proceeded on the send-hand information because she wanted it to be true, not because she knew it was correct. Before acting on the information, Sharon should have checked with a person who could have made the information official. Failure to do so was a mistake.

3.   **What mistake did Jeff make in dealing with the information he received from Carol? Explain.**

Jeff made an inference that Carol got the information directly from the company president. Jeff then treated the inference as a fact and canceled plans to attend the president's meeting. Jeff should have labeled his inference by saying "I assume you received a message directly from the president indicating that the meeting had been canceled." After learning that the information did not come directly from the company president, Jeff could have tactfully rechecked on the status of the changed meeting. In doing so, Jeff may have learned that the meeting was still scheduled for Tuesday.

4.   **What suggestions do you believe Mark Fletcher should make to the bank?**

A communication training program for managers at the bank would be appropriate. In this training program, it should be emphasized that communication is more than just sending and receiving messages. Instead, communication is the sharing of meaning. Also, when making important decisions, the training program should encourage managers to confirm the accuracy of the information on which they are relying. In addition, the training program should examine methods of improving upward communication as one important source of ideas for improving company efficiency.

Incident 3-2: QUALITY IS JOB 4

1.   **What communication mistakes is Harvey making?**

It is unwise for Harvey to assume it is unnecessary for him to discuss with employees the expectations of their jobs or what should be done to make needed improvements in quality. Two-way communication between Harvey and employees on these issues can benefit him, the employees, and the company. As a matter of fact, the employees want to engage in upward communication, but it is unlikely to happen unless Harvey shows an interest in employees' ideas. Once Harvey receives upward communication, he needs to respond and indicate how the ideas are being used. Harvey is making a mistake when he assumes employees know he is interested in receiving upward communication. He must demonstrate that interest. No feedback from Harvey can be interpreted by some employees as an indication of dissatisfaction with their work.

2. **What should Harvey do differently to improve his performance as manager?**

Harvey should not dismiss the K & A survey. Instead, he should take the survey seriously. He needs to help the company develop a way to educate consumers about the hidden quality that exists in Sleek Craft boats. Solving quality problems after the boats reach customers is not an effective quality program. He should not assume that work performed by his employees is of high quality. It is important to monitor quality as the work of employees occurs. Harvey should be promoting continuous quality improvement. If Harvey is unwilling to change, his company will probably be unable to compete effectively as customers demand higher-quality boats.

3. **What is your assessment of Harvey's view that quality is an outcome, rather than a process?**

Harvey's view is wrong and risky. A process generally produces an outcome. A flawed process can be expected to produce something with deficiencies. If there is quality in the process, quality will likely be present in the outcome. A quality process usually reduces or eliminates the need to solve quality problems in the outcome of the process.

Incident 3-3: A SLOW PERK

1. **What communication problems is the company experiencing?**

There is a problem with downward communication. The engineering department thinks it has been instructed to design a coffee maker for commercial use. However, the marketing department is under the impression that the coffee maker produced will be for home use. Also, employees are not being kept informed about this new product, so grapevine activity is increasing. In addition, upward communication is not encouraged in the company. As a result, employees believe management is not interested in their ideas. There-fore, employees are reluctant to provide upward communication that could benefit the company.

2.   **What problems can you predict will occur with the process the company is using to develop the new product?**

As the different departments work independently on the new product, much time may pass and much money may be spent before the company realizes that a communication problem has created some wasted effort. The fact that the various departments are not engaging in horizontal communication means that when problems surface, they will probably be harder to correct than if they had been identified earlier.

3.   **What should the company do differently in developing the new product?**

In addition to using downward communication, the company should request feedback to make sure that miscommunication does not occur. Employees should be kept informed of new developments in the company so they will not be forced to use the grapevine in an effort to learn what is occurring. Also, programs to encourage upward communication from employees should be established. In addition, there should be more horizontal communication and greater coordination among the departments working on the new product.

Study Guide Assignments

A matching exercise is provided to help students review key terms. In addition, a concept application exercise offers six scenarios that challenge students to apply the information they have learned in this chapter. These scenarios cover key concepts presented.

An individual case assessment and a group case assessment are also available to students in the study guide. These assessments enable students to utilize the chapter's learning objectives in a practical way.

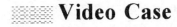 # Video Case

Price/Costco

Focus: **Communication**

Summary:

Price/Costco was formed on October 21, 1993 as a result of a merger of The Price Company and Costco Wholesale Corporation — two of the top three membership discount retailers in the United States. Price/Costco operates a chain of cash and carry membership warehouses that sell high quality, nationally branded and selected private label merchandise at low prices. Their target markets include both businesses that purchase merchandise for commercial use or resale and individuals who are employees of select organizations. The company's business is based upon achieving high sales volumes and rapid inventory turnover by offering a limited assortment of merchandise in a wide variety of product categories at very competitive prices.

In order to coordinate the merger and manage the transition as smoothly as possible, effective communication was critical. Communication at Price/Costco occurs in many forms and at many levels. For example, formal communication, which follows the normal chain of command, was the primary channel of information about merger activities. Top management had the responsibility for communicating accurate, up-to-date, and necessary information about the merger to the company's stakeholders. In turn, this information was carried through the informal channels of communication, namely the grapevine. Surprisingly, perhaps, information passed through the grapevine was quite accurate.

The management of Price/Costco had worked diligently to ensure the effectiveness and the accuracy of the information being circulated within Price/Costco. As they found out, communication was key to the success of the merger.

Discussion Questions:

1. Although communication is important in all organizations at all times, discuss why communication is even more important during a merger.

    During a major organizational change like a merger, the question going through virtually all stakeholders' minds is: What does this change mean to me? Employees are concerned about job security, stockholders about the value of their investment, and customers about the continued availability of their store. During such a change, stakeholders need to be kept up-to-date with clear, accurate information.

2.   Describe some negative consequences that could have resulted if the management of Price/Costco did not pay careful attention to the communication.

If the managers at Price/Costco were not careful in their communications about the merger, good employees might leave, stockholders might sell their stock, and customer could decide to find another store.

Chapter 4

Decision Making

Chapter Overview

This chapter explains the concept of decision making and discusses the role of human behaviors in decisions. The presentation emphasizes how managers can avoid making faulty decisions and identifies guidelines that are useful in reaching decisions.

Key characteristics of the decision process are identified and discussed. The presentation describes the decision environment, notes advantages and disadvantages of group decision making, and explains group decision techniques.

Finally, the concept of creativity and the stages of the creative process are presented. The chapter concludes with coverage of information technology, including management information systems, decision support systems, and expert systems.

Teaching Objectives

The teaching objectives of this chapter are to:

1.   Understand the behavioral aspects of decision making.

2.   Identify steps in the decision-making process.

3.   Describe the conditions of certainty, risk, and uncertainty.

4.   Explain the approaches to group decision making.

5.   Discuss the role of creativity in the workplace.

6.   Provide an overview of business information systems.

Chapter Outline of the Text

I.   THE ROLE OF DECISION MAKING
      A.   Teamwork in Decision Making
      B.   What Is a Good Decision?
      C.   The Search for Quality
II.   BEHAVIORAL ASPECTS OF DECISION MAKING
      A.   Prior Decisions
      B.   Attitudes and Opinions
      C.   Knowledge
      D.   Emotions
      E.   Intuition
      F.   Current Circumstances
      G.   Communication Practices
III. MANAGERS AS DECISION MAKERS
      A.   How to Avoid Faulty Decisions
      B.   Programmed and Nonprogrammed Decisions
      C.   Decision Guidelines
IV.   THE DECISION-MAKING PROCESS
      A.   Identify the Problem
      B.   Develop and Evaluate Alternatives
      C.   Select the Best Alternative
      D.   Implement the Alternative
      E.   Follow Up
V.   THE DECISION ENVIRONMENT
      A.   Conditions for Decision Making
            1.   Certainty
            2.   Risk
            3.   Uncertainty
VI.   THE ROLE OF GROUP DECISIONS
      A.   Advantages and Disadvantages of Group Decisions
VII. GROUP DECISION TECHNIQUES
      A.   The Ordinary Group Technique
      B.   The Nominal Group Technique (NGT)
      C.   The Delphi Technique
VIII. CREATIVITY AND THE WORKPLACE

      A.   Understanding Creativity
      B.   The Four Stages of the Creative Process
      C.   Encouraging Creativity
IX.   USING INFORMATION TECHNOLOGY
      A.   Functions of Business Information Systems
      B.   Management Information Systems (MIS)
      C.   Decision Support Systems (DSS)
      D.   Expert Systems
X.   LOOKING BACK
XI.   KEY TERMS
XII.   REVIEW AND DISCUSSION QUESTIONS
XIII.   CRITICAL THINKING INCIDENTS
XIV.   SUGGESTED READINGS

Key Terms

These terms are discussed in the chapter. Definitions are included in the glossary of the text.

Brainstorming	Groupthink
Certainty	Management Information System (MIS)
Creative process	Nonprogrammed decision
Creativity	Nominal Group Technique (NGT)
Data	Ordinary group technique
Decision making	Programmed decision
Decision Support System (DSS)	Quality circles
Delegation	Risk
Delphi Technique	Uncertainty
Expert system	

Detailed Chapter Summary

I.   THE ROLE OF DECISION MAKING

Decision making involves choosing among various courses of action. Managers can choose to do nothing; this choice is still a decision. In practice, some managers often spend much time fretting about decisions over which they have no control.

A.   *Teamwork in Decision Making*

Increasingly, teams are involved in the decision process. Team members strive to identify problems, discuss alternative courses of action, and implement solutions.

B.   *What Is a Good Decision?*

Good decisions do not just happen. Such decisions recognize the best interests of an organization and its employees.

C.   *The Search for Quality*

To remain competitive, managers must recognize the importance of quality. A valuable strategy is to maintain lines of communication with suppliers and seek input from employees.

II.   BEHAVIORAL ASPECTS OF DECISION MAKING

Teaching Objective 1:   Understand the behavioral aspects of decision making.

Decisions are made and implemented by people who possess different attitudes, experiences, and viewpoints. Behavioral factors can have much impact on decisions that need to be reached.

A.   *Prior Decisions*

Managers learn from past decisions. These experiences provide knowledge and insights that can be considered in developing responses to future decisions.

B.   *Attitudes and Opinions*

Attention is focused on aspects of problem situations perceived to be important. Opinions are the basis for favoring or not favoring a course of action in circumstances necessitating decisions. Together, attitudes and opinions are subtle influences on the decision-making process.

C.   *Knowledge*

Knowledge provides a foundation for making informed choices. Decision makers seek to gain as much information as possible in order to make the most opportune selection among alternatives.

D.   *Emotions*

Emotions can impact decisions and often prevail over logic. It is important for managers to retain objective perspectives toward issues.

E.   *Intuition*

Intuitive decisions frequently cannot be justified on the basis of accumulated information. Nevertheless, intuition does play a role in many decisions and influences some decision makers to a greater extent than others.

F.   *Current Circumstances*

The major events and issues of today will not necessarily be those of tomorrow. Prevailing circumstances cannot be overlooked but need to be scrutinized by managers who use them as a basis for making decisions.

G.   *Communication Practices*

Growing globalization of markets necessitates maintaining a balance between differences in behavioral and communication practices. Differences among cultures include the importance of "saving face" to avoid embarrassment, the role of informal talk before business discussions, and the need for having written contracts.

III.   MANAGERS AS DECISION MAKERS

Decision making is not necessarily a calm, rational process and can involve trying to reach agreement among people having different perspectives. It is important for managers to avoid making inappropriate decisions and be committed to chosen courses of action. Wise managers continually review merits of their decisions.

A.   *How to Avoid Faulty Decisions*

Decisions will not always be correct. Faulty decisions can be minimized by focusing on priorities, hiring capable personnel, and providing clear explanations. Effective delegation helps to avoid poor decisions and likely results in fewer mistakes.

B.   *Programmed and Nonprogrammed Decisions*

Programmed decisions are routine and repetitive in nature. Examples include ordering replacement inventory and completing information for credit applications. Nonprogrammed decisions are not repetitive in nature. A reduction in employees and consideration of a proposed merger are illustrations of nonprogrammed decisions.

C.   *Decision Guidelines*

Various guidelines assist decision makers. These include the need to base decisions on reliable, accurate information; review decisions; focus on relevant problems and issues; and defend decisions. Other guidelines emphasize the importance of communication, development of assessment tools, and consideration of unanticipated precedents.

Suggested Reading for this Section
Bridges, William. "The End of the Job." <u>Fortune</u> 130, September 19, 1994, pp. 62-74.

This article emphasizes the changing nature of jobs and is useful as a reference to discuss how decisions influence the workplace of the future. Many organizations have reengineered toward flatter hierarchies and greater usage of computers to do routine work. Such decisions have been a part of the change from jobs to the concept of a field of work that needs to be accomplished. Decisions to select key people are a major consideration. Increasingly, personnel take cues from demands of the situation rather than job descriptions or order giving by managers. The article includes a list of rules for breaking into a "de-jobbed" world.

IV.   THE DECISION-MAKING PROCESS

Learning Objective 2:   Identify steps in the decision-making process.

The decision-making process provides a framework to assist in making decision choices. The process involves five steps: identify the problem, develop and evaluate alternatives, select the best alternative, implement the alternative, and follow up.

A.   *Identify the Problem*

A key is to distinguish between a problem and symptoms of a problem. Asking questions involving who, what, where, and when can provide guidance. Individual perspectives do influence perceptions regarding what constitutes a problem.

B.   *Develop and Evaluate Alternatives*

A sufficient number of alternative should be generated, but limiting factors (such as laws, company policies, budget restrictions, or time) do need to be considered. Evaluation of alternatives requires foresight and consistency of purpose.

C.   *Implement the Alternative*

Decision makers need to recognize the importance of actually implementing decisions. Communication is a necessary consideration. When implementing negative decisions, good interpersonal skills are especially important.

D.   *Follow Up*

Follow up activities cannot be overlooked, as outcomes do not always occur as anticipated. These activities serve as checks to determine whether changes are necessary.

V.   THE DECISION ENVIRONMENT

From the decision makers perspective, prevailing business conditions involve a number of variables. While accurate information is desired, available information may be incomplete or incorrect. In the international arena, political considerations often complicate decision making.

Learning Objective 3:   Describe the conditions of certainty, risk, and uncertainty.

A.   *Conditions for Decision Making: Certainty, Risk, and Uncertainty*

Under conditions of certainty, a decision maker knows which events will occur and simply selects the one having the largest payoff value. With the risk criterion, a decision maker does not know which event will occur but can determine probabilities of occurrence for various events. Uncertainty acknowledges that events, which influence decisions, and their probabilities of happening are not known.

VI.   THE ROLE OF GROUP DECISIONS

The group format is widely used as an approach to decision making. Groups tend to function best in situations where a range of potential solutions is available and when personal needs of members do not predominate.

   A.   *The Advantages and Disadvantages of Group Decisions*

   Review Figure 4-4 for a listing of advantages and disadvantages. The group structure facilitates discussion of ideas and encourages acceptance of the ultimate decision. Nevertheless, group decision making consumes considerable time, and dominant personalities may unduly influence decisions.

Teaching Hint: Ask several students to indicate their favorite flavor of cake. Continue asking the question until four different flavors are named. Then, ask students who named these four flavors to decide on one "best" flavor. Emphasize the similarity between this exercise and the challenge of reaching decisions among people possessing individual perspectives in the real world of business.

VII.   GROUP DECISION TECHNIQUES

Teaching Objective 4:   Explain the approaches to group decision making.

Groups vary in different ways, including size, frequency of meetings, and extent of personal contact among members.

   A.   *The Ordinary Group Technique*

   This is a frequently-used approach, which emphasizes interpersonal dialogue among members in an unstructured setting. Brainstorming can be used to encourage communication and generate ideas. In cohesive groups, participants need to avoid groupthink by carefully scrutinizing views of colleagues before accepting them.

B.   *The Nominal Group Technique (NGT)*

With the NGT, each member independently writes ideas, which are recorded, subsequently discussed, and ultimately voted upon. While the technique can generate many alternatives, personal interaction among members is minimal.

C.   *The Delphi Technique*

This approach uses mail questionnaires to collect responses and develop a consensus of opinions among participants who do not interact on a personal basis. While the Delphi Technique preserves anonymity, it consumes time and does not include the benefits resulting from direct verbal communication.

VIII.   CREATIVITY AND THE WORKPLACE

Teaching Objective 5:   Discuss the role of creativity in the workplace.

A.   *Understanding Creativity*

Sources for creative ideas are unlimited. Previous experiences and current needs may serve as the basis for a potentially creative solution to a problem.

Teaching Hint: Point out that people often tend to limit their own creativeness. New employees may be an excellent source of creative ideas because they may not be aware of reasons why ideas cannot be implemented.

B.   *The Four Stages of the Creative Process*

The creative process involves preparation, incubation, insight, and verification. Review Figure 4-5, which summarizes these stages.

C.   *Encouraging Creativity*

Managerial philosophies and actions influence creativity. To stimulate creativity, managers should give subordinates credit for their innovative ideas and provide a workplace environment that encourages creative thinking.

Suggested Readings for this Section
Michalko, Michael. "Bright Ideas." Training and Development 48, June 1994, pp. 44-47.

This article discusses 15 steps to stimulate employee creativity. These steps include a need to stress positive thinking, brainstorm, exchange ideas about successful accomplishments, and establish creativity committees. The author recommends asking people to display personal items that illustrate creative accomplishments.

Farnham, Alan. "How to Nurture Creative Sparks," Fortune 129, January 10, 1994, pp. 62-66.

Highly creative people are very dedicated to their work and tend to have several characteristics in common. These include self-motivation, a high tolerance for risk, and a healthy attitude toward ambiguity. The author stresses that creativity can be taught and notes the importance of accommodating the needs of creative persons and granting them greater autonomy.

IX. USING INFORMATION TECHNOLOGY

Teaching Objective 6:   Provide an overview of business information systems.

Successful decision making involves an interdependence among information, communication, and productivity. While data consist of numbers and facts, information involves meaningful interpretation of data. Future applications of computer technology are limitless.

A. *Functions of Business Information Systems*

Figure 4-6 summarizes the functions of business information systems. These functions include satisfying the needs of users, sharing common data, integrating information flow, providing flexible output presentation, and providing interactive inquiry/analysis.

B. *Management Information Systems (MIS)*

Management information systems are generalized in nature to serve nonspecialized information needs of entire departments or units. These systems help to monitor and control managerial activities, generate periodic and special reports, and aid in development of tactical plans.

C. *Decision Support Systems (DSS)*

Decision support systems provide managers with specialized types of information and are useful in resolving semistructured problems. The focus is to provide support to decision makers who are dealing with specific problem situations.

D. *Expert Systems*

Through computer programs, expert systems use information to reason like knowledgeable human experts. Opportunities exist for application of expert systems at all levels of management. While these systems do assist understanding of the decision process and often reduce the need for human resources, they are costly to maintain and do not have the flexibility of a human mind.

X. LOOKING BACK

This chapter introduces the concept of decision making and explains the decision-making process. In addition, the role of creativity in the workplace and an overview of information technology are presented.

Answers to CONSIDER THIS Questions (Page 116)

1. **What is the most important step in the decision-making process?**

This thought question is designed to encourage reflective thinking about decision making. While every step is essential, proper identification of the problem is extremely critical and generally considered to be the most important step. Failure to identify the problem means that subsequent steps will not be focused on actions that will result in needed solutions. The text discussion emphasizes the importance of the Ws—who, what, where, and when, and also cautions against confusing symptoms of a problem with the problem itself.

2. **When should managers change their decisions?**

If new information becomes available to evidence an incorrect decision, a decision needs to be changed. Environmental conditions generally do not remain static, and as events occur, decisions need to be reviewed for possible revision. It is important for students to realize the benefits gained by following the steps of the decision-making process. This process encourages systematic consideration of factors entering into decisions and serves to minimize the number of changes that may be necessary.

3. **How can managers improve their decision-making skills?**

Students will have many different responses to this question. The steps outlined in the decision-making process encourage managers to carefully contemplate courses of action prior to taking them. Managers learn from personal experiences and from observing the decision practices of successful colleagues. Formal training, such as seminars or courses, often provides useful insights into improvement of managerial skills.

Answers to CONSIDER THIS Questions   (Page 129)

1. **Why is group decision making becoming more widespread?**

The business environment is becoming more competitive and complex with greater utilization of advanced technology. In addition, employees desire more involvement in decision making. To meet these challenges, many organizations are moving toward flatter organizational hierarchies and introducing participatory personnel strategies to a greater extent. As members of groups, employees are increasingly involved in quality initiatives, reengineering efforts, and teamwork structures.

2. **What is the key to successful brainstorming sessions?**

Students will make numerous comments about the key factor, and various answers are feasible. The reason for having a brainstorming session needs to be clearly explained to participants. It is worthwhile to generate as many ideas or suggestions as possible. It is also important to avoid criticism of ideas as they are given. Brainstorming sessions can be too lengthy. When this occurs, fewer pertinent ideas are expressed, and a session tends to lose its focus.

3. **How can creative people encourage greater acceptance of their ideas?**

Creative people are challenged to educate others and help them understand their ideas. Effective communication is a key consideration. Too often, acceptance of creative ideas suffers because they are not explained in an understandable manner. Explanations are too abrupt, or too much jargon is used. A focus on benefits is an important strategy, as people tend to be more interested and receptive toward ideas that will benefit them.

Answers to REVIEW AND DISCUSSION Questions

1. *Why is a manager's choice of doing nothing about a problem or issue considered to be a decision?*

   By definition, decisions involve choices. Selection of "yes" or "no" alternatives are easily categorized as decisions. However, some persons hesitate to classify the "no choice" option as a decision. In practice, it represents a choice and therefore constitutes a decision.

2. *How do attitudes and opinions influence decisions?*

   Persons who make decisions have dissimilar experiences in their personal and professional lives. Consequently, they may hold different views. The likelihood of having a negative (or positive) attitude depends on the extent to which previous experiences have (or have not) led to undesired difficulties. Decision makers form their own opinions, which may be influenced by others. The importance of a problem, issue, or event varies among people. As alternatives are contemplated, decision makers do not always fully recognize the relationship among attitudes, opinions, and final choices.

3. *Why do managers make faulty decisions?*

   Faulty decisions occur for any number of reasons: personality factors, biases or prejudices, incorrect assumptions, and failure to get input from appropriate persons. Also, factors such as inaccurate opinions, insufficient knowledge, emotions, or personal intuition can impede decision making. Thorough understanding of steps included in the decision process helps decision makers to attain preferred outcomes.

4. *What is the difference between a programmed and a nonprogrammed decision?*

   Programmed decisions are routine and repetitive in nature. Generally, these decisions do not generate much discussion over whether or not they should be implemented. Nonprogrammed decisions are nonrepetitive and do not involve routine choices. By comparison, nonprogrammed decisions are more subjective and commonly representative of decision making at upper levels of management.

5.   *Why is follow up a necessary step in the decision making process?*

Events do not always unfold as anticipated. Equipment breakdowns occur; miscommunication causes unexpected complications; and people make mistakes. Follow-up activities serve as a check to determine if events are progressing as originally planned. In practice, it is not uncommon to revise a decision before attaining objectives.

6.   *Why should a decision maker be knowledgeable about the conditions of certainty, risk, and uncertainty?*

These conditions describe characteristics of the business environment and provide guidance to managers who make choices among alternative courses of action. Risk and uncertainty, the most commonly utilized criterions, help mangers assess consequences associated with possible decision choices. With risk, knowledge of probability is useful; however, uncertainty helps managers structure decisions in circumstances where the concept of probability is meaningless. Even though certainty does not commonly describe business decisions, understanding this criterion enables managers to focus attention on the relationship between events and potential outcomes.

7.   *What are the advantages of group decision making?*

These are presented in Figure 4-4. The group approach promotes discussion of ideas and suggestions. Alternatives can be considered from the perspective of persons who have different backgrounds and experiences. Participants can collect, review, and discuss a considerable amount of information. Involvement encourages acceptance of the ultimate decision. Group members gain greater insights into complexities of problems being considered.

8.   *What are the useful aspects of the ordinary group technique?*

This technique promotes interpersonal dialogue in an unstructured setting. Participants have opportunities to express views and listen to those of others. Generation of more options than a single individual might formulate and discussion of various views enable the group to identify a choice having the greatest potential for goal attainment.

9.   *How can managers encourage creativity?*

Creativity is encouraged by managers who do not take credit for worthy ideas of subordinates and do not react negatively to their suggestions. Creative managers listen to the merits of ideas, even if different from their own views.

These managers recognize that mistakes will occur but allow sufficient flexibility so that workers will not be afraid to take some reasonable risks. Creativity is encouraged by managers who are coaches and facilitators rather than arbitrary rule enforcers. Finally, creativeness is enhanced by helping employees to develop confidence in themselves and their abilities.

10. *What stages are involved in the creative process?*

The creative process consists of four stages. *Preparation* involves defining the problem, collecting and reviewing of information, and finding a reason to do something in a different way. *Incubation* refers to subconscious mental reflection about the problem, and *insight* is where a spark of awareness occurs as a solution is recognized. *Verification*, which is the final stage, involves observing how the solution works and testing to determine if the insight is useful.

Answers to CRITICAL THINKING INCIDENTS

Incident 4-1: MORE WORK: IS THIS A JOKE?

1. **How effectively does Sally make decisions?**

Sally appears to have a successful career. She seems to receive support from her managers, as evidenced by approval for the new assistant director's job. However, Sally might be criticized for not thinking about how this position increases Jill's workload. In practice, this is not an infrequent occurrence. Too many managers do not consider how personnel changes impact jobs of subordinates who are not included in decision processes.

2. **Since she did not get the entry-level management job, did Jill make a wise decision to continue her high level of productivity? Why or why not?**

Jill's decision was correct. In the workplace, there is no substitute for excellent job performance. Managers influence career opportunities of subordinates. In the future, an attractive position may become available at Coleman. If Jill applies, management support will be essential. Should she seek employment with other firms, Jill will still need excellent references from her boss.

3.   **What can Sally do to improve her decision making abilities?**

Most managers can improve their abilities to make decisions. Continued focus on steps of the decision-making process is an important consideration. A good recommendation is to review the decision guidelines, which are explained in the chapter. If Sally recognizes the importance of effective communication, she will likely encounter fewer problems related to decisions.

4.   **Should Jill schedule an appointment with James to state her concerns?**

This choice should be carefully considered. While the desire to express her views is understandable, Jill risks not getting a sympathetic understanding from Jim and at the same time irritating Sally. Unless circumstances change, prior decisions are not likely altered. Most likely, a formal appointment is not necessarily in Jill's best interests. Since she is known for her capable job performance, Jill's future career interests are probably best served by continuing to do good work and informally expressing her interests in other job opportunities.

Incident 4-2: WE'VE GOT TO DO SOMETHING

1.   **After hearing Janet's recommended plan, why should the board not vote immediately to make the final decision?**

The board needs to discuss further implications of the plan, consider additional information, and revise the plan for gaining greater consensus among board members. Sufficient time should be set aside for alternatives to be expressed and discussed. Too much haste may cause the board to make an inappropriate decision without paying adequate attention to a range of possible concerns that may ultimately prove to be of importance.

2.   **How should Janet react to the difference of viewpoints between Manual and Jane?**

Differences of opinion are commonplace in business decision making. As discussion transpires, Janet serves as a facilitator. It is important for her to encourage participation and assure that all members have opportunities to state their views. A key concern is to keep the discussion focused on issues and not let personality differences needlessly hinder the exchange of perspectives. As a strategy, Janet might avoid expressing her personal opinion until the others have stated their viewpoints.

3.   **What can the group do to avoid making an unfortunate decision?**

Hindsight is always more accurate than foresight. The group has no guarantees that the final decision will be the best in terms of getting preferred outcomes. Following steps outlined in the decision process (identify the problem, develop/evaluate alternatives, select the best alternative, implement the alternative, and follow up) helps to assure that relevant considerations are not overlooked. Available information and desired expectations are guidelines to help reach a decision that best serves group interests. Should circumstances change, the decision will need to be modified.

4.   **What course of action should Joan ultimately favor to arrive at a decision?**

Students will have a variety of responses to this question. Several possibilities are identified: appointing a subcommittee, designating an outside consultant, meeting with employees, or supporting her own plan. Since the decision involves personnel changes, employee views are important. They may suggest possible alternatives that have not previously been considered. The subcommittee approach is worthwhile; composition of the group should reflect various opinions held by members. The subcommittee could conduct a comprehensive examination of the problem and possibly suggest additional options. Hiring outside consultants is the most expensive course of action; however, it is a way to attain nonbiased professional perspectives. Joan's plan might prevail as the ultimate choice. She should not become needlessly defensive about her recommendations. The plan represents an initial starting point for examination of the problem.

Incident 4-3: CREATIVITY AND THE MARKETPLACE

1.   **Why is creativity an important publication consideration?**

A new text competes with many well-established competitors, which have been successfully marketed and extensively adopted. Professors use texts as the basis for developing classroom presentations and are not easily motivated to choose other texts. Therefore, innovative features are important considerations. In essence, the proposed text should be well written and technically accurate, but it also must be sufficiently differentiated from competitors. Sales representatives who call upon college instructors play major roles in the marketing process. It is important for them to be excited about a text and believe that the product can generate sales revenue.

2.   **How can Bill and Gloria generate additional creative ideas?**

Students will suggest a number of possibilities. Lists of ideas can be developed and discussed. Bill and Gloria might solicit suggestions from students, colleagues, or salespersons who represent publishing companies. A key factor is to let people know that ideas are desired. Even though much time may be consumed discussing ideas that are not feasible, just one worthwhile idea can have a major positive impact.

3.   **Can a well written text be successful in the marketplace without any special creative efforts? Explain your response.**

Many students will say "yes;" however, it is difficult for a new textbook to gain adoptions without being differentiated from competitors. Students should be reminded that textbook changes necessitate revision of teaching notes used for classroom presentations. Readableness, writing style, and comprehensive discussion of content are not the only factors influencing adoption choices. Ancillary items (such as availability of overhead transparencies, computerized test banks, study guides, and videos) often have much influence on decision making.

4.   **Should Stan extend an offer to Bill and Gloria to publish the text? Why or why not?**

Students can justify positive or negative responses. Stan has received mixed comments from reviewers; this does not make the decision any easier. The manuscript appears to be well written and include coverage of timely topics. These are essential factors to consider in development of a competitive publication. On the other hand, Stan is not personally excited about creative ideas suggested by the authors and notes the lack of enthusiasm from several reviewers. Potential users might be surveyed and asked about features that should be incorporated into a new text. Bill and Gloria could be given additional time to refine the manuscript with emphasis upon creativity. At this time, Stan can justify a rationale for not extending an offer to the authors.

Study Guide Assignments

In the individual case assessment, one manager gives an immediate answer to a problem situation. Another manager prefers a more reasoned, methodological approach. As consultants, students are asked to give advice.

The group case assessment provides an opportunity for students to understand the brainstorming technique and its merits. It enables students to recognize how problems are created when managers do not choose a proper format for discussing a problem situation.

 **Video Case**

Team Xerox

Focus: **Decision Making**

Summary:

The 1960s were golden years for Xerox: the company's 914 model copier was the first on the market to produce high quality, low cost copies. But Xerox became a victim of its own success because it lost its focus on its customers. In the 1970s, the Japanese introduced low cost copiers, a market Xerox ignored. By the late 1970s, Japanese companies could sell a copier for what it cost Xerox to make one.

Xerox took several steps to regain market share. First, it thoroughly checks out the competition. Xerox engineers and designers literally take apart competitors' copiers in order to develop a set of standards by which they can judge their own work. This benchmarking also provides Xerox with new ideas.

Xerox also developed a new relationship with its suppliers, working with them to increase quality and decrease price. Xerox went from over 5,000 suppliers to just 300.

As a result, defects are down 50 percent, and Xerox has won back market share from the Japanese.

Discussion Questions:

1.   How did decision making change at Xerox?

Xerox went from a hierarchical, individual model of decision making to a team approach in making decisions and solving problems. This approach brings greater expertise, more information, more satisfaction, and greater commitment to the decisions.

2.   What are the advantages of Xerox's new relationship with its suppliers? Are there any disadvantages?

The major advantages of Xerox's new relationship with its suppliers are the quality and price improvements. The potential disadvantages are that Xerox could become dependent on a key supplier and pay higher than market rates for key materials.

Chapter 5

Planning

Chapter Overview

Planning is an essential management function. This chapter discusses the role of planning and identifies steps in the planning process. The presentation differentiates among various types of plans and explains each of them.

Important characteristics of strategic management are included with emphasis upon how to develop strategies, implement strategies, and monitor results. SWOT analysis is explained as an approach to identify strengths and weaknesses and recognize opportunities and threats. Finally, details of corporate, business, and functional strategies are examined.

Coverage of corporate strategy includes explanation of the grand strategies and the Boston Consulting Group matrix. Discussion of business strategies emphasizes the adaptation model and Porter's framework. The chapter concludes with a definition and overview of functional strategies.

Teaching Objectives

The teaching objectives for this chapter are to:

1. Differentiate among policies, procedures, and rules.

2. Describe each step in the planning process.

3. Explain the importance of strategic management.

4.   Identify the grand-strategy alternatives.

5.   Recognize strategies in the adaptation model.

Chapter Outline of the Text

I.   THE ROLE OF PLANNING
    A.   Developing Effective Plans
    B.   Key Concerns: Communication and Quality
II.   THE PLANNING PROCESS
    A.   Determine the Goal
    B.   Review the Present Situation
    C.   Recognize Limiting Factors
    D.   Develop the Plan
    E.   Implement the Plan
III.   TYPES OF PLANS
    A.   Strategic Plans
    B.   Intermediate Plans
    C.   Operational Plans
    D.   Contingency Plans
IV.   UNDERSTANDING STRATEGIC MANAGEMENT
    A.   Define the Mission and Identify Strategic Objectives
    B.   Develop and Implement Strategies
    C.   Monitor Results
V.   THE SWOT ANALYSIS
    A.   Identifying Strengths and Weaknesses
    B.   Recognizing Opportunities and Threats
VI.   CORPORATE STRATEGY
    A.   The Grand Strategies
    B.   A Portfolio Strategy: The BCG Matrix
VII.   BUSINESS STRATEGY
    A.   The Adaptation Model
    B.   Porter's Framework
VIII. FUNCTIONAL STRATEGY
IX.   LOOKING BACK
X.   KEY TERMS
XI.   REVIEW AND DISCUSSION QUESTIONS
XII.   CRITICAL THINKING INCIDENTS
XIII. SUGGESTED READINGS

▧ Key Terms

These terms are introduced in the chapter. Definitions are included in the glossary of the text.

Adaptation model
Analyzer strategy
BCG matrix
Business strategy
Combination strategy
Contingency plan
Corporate strategy
Defender strategy
Functional strategy
Goal
Grand strategies
Growth strategies
Intermediate plan
Mission statement
Operational plan
Planning
Policy

Portfolio strategy
Procedure
Prospector strategy
Reactor strategy
Retrenchment strategy
Rule
Stability strategy
Strategic business unit (SBU)
Strategic management
Strategic objective
Strategic plan
SWOT analysis
  Strengths
  Weaknesses
  Opportunities
  Threats

▧ Detailed Chapter Summary

I.   THE ROLE OF PLANNING

Planning involves looking to the future and developing courses of action to attain business objectives. Through planning, managers set expectations and priorities; they establish patterns of reaction to uncertain environmental conditions. The purpose of the planning function is the same for both domestic and international markets, but plans to do business internationally are often complicated by economics, political, cultural, and technological factors.

Teaching Objective 1:   Differentiate among policies, procedures, and rules.

Policies are guidelines that are quite general in nature. A procedure refers to the step-by-step sequence of events needed to implement a policy. Rules are more restrictive than policies or procedures and represent detailed guidelines for job performance.

A.   *Developing Effective Plans*

Formalized planning enables planners to share their perspectives, respond to other viewpoints, and gain insights into pros and cons of alternatives. Effective planning forces managers to be future oriented and is a continual process that should not restrain managerial flexibility.

B.   *Key Concerns: Communication and Quality*

To avoid misunderstandings, clarity of communication is a foremost consideration. When plans are updated or revised, information needs to be communicated to all personnel who are affected by the changes.

Capable planners recognize the need for continuous quality improvement. Consequently, plans should include standards and measurement criteria. A concern for quality needs to be considered by all persons from top managers to recently-hired employees.

II.   THE PLANNING PROCESS

Teaching Objective 2: Describe each step in the planning process.

The planning process provides a framework to guide planners. It encourages decision makers to look ahead and consider potential responses to various circumstances that can occur.

Teaching Hint: Ask students what career they desire to pursue. Then, ask what steps (training, academic degrees, certifications or examinations) are necessary to prepare for this chosen career. Use the steps of the planning process to illustrate similarities between career and business planning.

A.   *Determine the Goal*

Managers need to specify what the firm seeks to achieve. Without goals, planners do not know how to allocate resources and simply cannot function.

B.   *Review the Present Situation*

Planning activities need to reduce any discrepancies between desired goals and the current status of affairs.

C.   *Recognize Limiting Factors*

A failure to attain plans can occur because of inadequate human, equipment, or financial resources. Potential limiting factors need to be considered; unexpected circumstances can necessitate revision of plans.

D.   *Develop the Plan*

This step involves "putting it all together." It is worthwhile to consider "if/then" choices. Planners should ask probing questions and strive to avoid obstacles that might arise and cause difficulties later.

E.   *Implement the Plan*

At this point, the plan is actually put into action. All participants should understand their obligations and responsibilities.

III.   TYPES OF PLANS

A.   *Strategic Plans*

Strategic plans provide a long-term sense of direction. They indicate major goals and represent a framework for the allocation of resources. Top management should clearly communicate the firm's position on strategic courses of action.

B.   *Intermediate Plans*

Intermediate plans are largely a responsibility of middle management and cover a time period between a few months and two years. Managers must be knowledgeable about corporate goals so that specific plans can be formulated to achieve them.

C.   *Operational Plans*

Operational plans are narrowly defined, cover relatively short periods of time, and relate to the lowest organizational level. Examples of these plans include weekly work schedules, monthly budgets, and lists of tasks for employees to perform.

D.   *Contingency Plans*

Contingency plans specify alternative courses of action and enable managers to react to situations within a relatively short period of time. These plans help managers to weigh potential outcomes, which can help alleviate pressures arising from crisis management.

IV.   UNDERSTANDING STRATEGIC MANAGEMENT

Teaching Objective 3:   Explain the importance of strategic management.

Strategic management is the process of defining an organization's mission, identifying long-term objectives, developing and implementing strategies, and monitoring results.

A.   *Define the Mission and Identify Strategic Objectives*

The mission statement includes a description of an organization's purpose, philosophy, customers, products or services, and philosophy. It is the basis for answering these questions: What is our business? Who do we serve? What do we sell? Strategic objectives emphasize outcomes sought from selection of a particular strategy.

B.   *Develop and Implement Strategies*

Strategies are developed at three levels of a firm. Corporate strategy specifies the major thrust of an organization. Business strategies indicate how various business units or clusters of subunits should operate. Functional strategies involve courses of actions for specific areas such as marketing or human resources. Figure 5-5 highlights the principal tasks involved in strategy implementation.

C.   *Monitor Results*

The monitoring process enables managers to know if the plan is achieving desired results. Feedback is important as a basis for knowing whether changes are necessary, as internal and external environmental factors do not remain static.

Suggested Readings for this Section
*Mintzberg, Henry. "The Fall and Rise of Strategic Planning." <u>Harvard Business Review</u>
72, January-February 1994, pp. 107-114.*

Strategic planning is not the same as strategic thinking. While planning is focused on
analysis, strategic thinking involves *synthesis*. Formal planning uses existing categories
(levels of strategy, established products, and current organizational structures). However,
strategic change necessitates innovativeness with invention of new categories. Those
persons who encourage conventional strategic planning serve to lessen management's power
over development of strategy. Fallacious assumptions of conventional strategic planning
include the fallacies of predictions, detachment, and formalization. Two different types of
planners are identified: analytic thinkers and creative thinkers.

DeMott, John S. "New Mission." <u>Nation's Business</u> 82, November 1994, pp. 20-27.

Loss of defense-related government contracts has caused considerable economic and job
losses to individuals and communities that experienced closing of military bases. These
communities, like firms experiencing misfortunes, have to focus on development of new
missions to attract business. In a process called "defense conversion," some communities
have enticed firms to open or expand local operations. Successful efforts have involved
strategies to rapidly organize key business people and local officials, recruit many smaller
(rather than one large business) employers, and accept a reality of future business
expectations that differ from those of the past.

V.   THE SWOT ANALYSIS

SWOT analysis enables managers to access a firm's competitive position. Strategy
selection is a key consideration in maximizing a firm's internal strengths and
minimizing weaknesses. Figure 5-6 illustrates factors to consider in preparation of a
SWOT analysis.

*Teaching Hint: Emphasize the practical importance of understanding the SWOT concept.
Note how this analysis enables managers to initiate the most appropriate actions.*

A.   *Identifying Strengths and Weaknesses*

Strengths are capabilities in which strong advantages are perceived to exist;
weaknesses negatively impact the likelihood of getting desired results. The
focus of identifying strengths and weaknesses is on functional areas:
marketing, production/operations, finance and accounting, research and
development, and human resources.

B. *Recognizing Opportunities and Threats*

Opportunities identify areas in which market shares can be gained. Threats represent potential obstacles that may adversely influence competitiveness. Managers must consider implications of opportunities and threats for various sectors of the business environment: socioeconomic, technological, government, customer, supplier, competitor, and international.

VI. CORPORATE STRATEGY

Corporate strategy, which covers a time period between three to six years, provides an overall sense of direction and specifies the primary plan of action to reach goals. When selecting a corporate strategy, managers focus on the grand strategies or a portfolio strategy, such as the BCG matrix.

Teaching Objective 4: Identify the grand-strategy alternatives.

A. *The Grand Strategies*

Grand strategies identify the goals sought by a firm and can also be used in formulation of business-level strategies. With a growth strategy, management strives to acquire additional market shares, open more outlets, and introduce new products. A stability strategy attempts to preserve the status quo. Firms do not always reach goals and may need to follow a retrenchment strategy, which involved activities such as withdrawal from the marketplace or personnel layoffs. In addition, grand strategies can be used in combination.

B. *A Portfolio Strategy: The BCG Matrix*

The BCG matrix compares high and low growth rate with high and low market share. Business units are classified into one of four quadrants: stars, cash cows, question marks, and dogs.

Stars are business units that demonstrate high growth and high market share and include products such as diet colas and VCRs. *Cash cows* represent low-growth business units with large shares of the market; examples are Hershey chocolate bars and Cheerios breakfast cereal. *Question marks* reflect high growth and low market share; the introduction of some prescription drugs illustrates this type of product. *Dogs* are business units in mature markets that show little profitability. For example, many drive-in movies might be classified in this category.

VII. BUSINESS STRATEGY

Less broadly oriented than a corporate strategy, a business strategy is focused on attaining goals for each business unit or cluster of business units. Strategic business units (SBU)s are separate operating units designed to sell distinctive products or services to identifiable customer groups.

Teaching Objective 5: Recognize strategies in the adaptation model.

A. *The Adaptation Model*

This model attempts to match business strategies with environmental conditions. A defender strategy, which emphasizes competition in a relatively narrow market, is feasible in stable environments. The prospector strategy emphasizes introducing new products and seeking new customers. Positioned between prospectors and defenders, the analyzer strategy balances stability with conditions involving risk and uncertainty. The reactor strategy evidences failure. Ultimately, reactors must adopt one of the other strategies or else cease to function.

B. *Porter's Framework*

Michael E. Porter, a Harvard professor and leading business strategist, cites several factors that influence competitiveness.

1. Threat of New Entrants

2. Rivalry among Competitors

3. Availability of Substitute Products

4. Economic Strength of Buyers

5. Economic Strength of Suppliers

Porter recommends three generic strategies to utilize in a competitive marketplace to gain a performance advantage.

1. Overall Cost Leadership

Low overall costs provide a firm with advantages over its competitors. High cash margins give firms an advantage by providing available funds for necessary purchases.

2.   Differentiation

This approach emphasizes provision of products with unique characteristics. Firms can capitalize these distinctions in development of marketing and promotional efforts.

3.   Focus

Firms using the focus strategy stress low costs, product differentiation, or both approaches to a narrow target market.

Suggested Readings for this Section
Porter, Michael E. "The Competitive Advantage of the Inner City." Harvard Business Review 73, May-June 1995, pp. 55-71.

Michael E. Porter, a well-known business strategy expert, proposes implementation of an economic model to remedy inner-city problems. Rather than focus on wealth redistribution, Porter stresses wealth creation including emphasis on strategic location, local market demand, and human resources. A major recommendation is to build profitable (not subsidized) businesses with government's role directed toward improving the business environment (rather than providing direct funding or services). To maximize its competitive advantage, inner-city development necessitates changing roles and responsibilities for business, nonprofit entities, and government.

Hamel, Gary and C. K. Parahalad. "Seeing the Future First." Fortune 130, September 5, 1994, pp. 64-70.

Managers do not spend sufficient time taking long-term views of their industries. The authors estimate that senior management spends less than 3 percent of its time to develop a useful futuristic perspective. They recommend that top managers discover or exploit opportunities before the competition takes such initiatives. Development of a curiosity characterized by depth and breadth is important.

Managers must do more than simply meet articulated needs of customers. It's a challenge for customers to submit ideas related to concepts that are unknown to them. For example, customer suggestions were not a factor in development of Chrysler's minivan, a concept that was initially rejected by Ford. Successful plans and strategies involve responding to changes in lifestyles, geopolitics, demographics, and government regulations.

VIII. FUNCTIONAL STRATEGY

Functional Strategies relate to activities of a firm's functional units. These units include marketing, production/operations, finance, research and development, and human resources.

IX. LOOKING BACK

This chapter explains the importance of planning, provides an overview of the planning process, and presents an introduction to the concept of strategic planning.

Answers to CONSIDER THIS Questions   (Page 161)

1. **How can managers improve their effectiveness as planners?**

Managers need to realize the importance of planning and recognize that time spent on planning activities is not wasted. A key factor is to use the steps of the planning process as a guideline for development of improved plans. In addition, it is important for managers not to overlook the importance of communication. They must strive to assure that plans are understood; when revisions become necessary, persons who are affected need to be informed about the changes. It is important for managers to look ahead, anticipate likely outcomes, and *think* before initiating actions.

2. **Why should first-line managers be concerned with strategic planning?**

Strategic plans provide a firm with long-term direction and communicate its purpose to employees as well as external stakeholders. These plans influence how resources are allocated, a most important concern to first-line managers. Supervisors need to recognize how plans for their units will mesh with strategic plans of their organizations. Knowledge of strategic planning assists supervisors to gain personal insights into how their actions contribute to attainment of goals.

3. **What is the most important task for a manager to consider when implementing a strategy?**

The most important task involves whether a strategy can, in fact, be successfully put into action to reach a desired goal. By focusing their attention on the importance of strategy implementation, managers are more likely to avoid undesired, and often unexpected, consequences. Figure 5-5 gives an overview of primary tasks involved in strategy implementation.

Answers to CONSIDER THIS Questions   (Page 166)

1.   **How can the BCG matrix be of the most value to managers?**

The BCG matrix enables managers to examine the relationship between a product's growth rate and its market share. As a result, it helps managers realize the importance of marketplace realities and gives them a better understanding of how various products are actually doing in the marketplace. Even though it is sometimes criticized as being overly simplified, the matrix does provide a framework to guide formulation of plans.

2.   **What is the relationship between a firm's mission and its corporate strategy?**

The mission indicates an organization's purpose, identifies major goals, and recognizes obligations to stakeholders. (Who is to be served? What is to be sold?) Corporate strategy, which generally covers a three- to six-year period, specifies plans of action to attain goals. While the mission is somewhat generalized in nature, corporate strategy tends to be more specific in identification of particular strategies.

3.   **Referring to the adaptation model, why is the defender strategy feasible in stable environments?**

A stable environment provides opportunities for organizations to focus on retention of customers and preservation of market share. The defender strategy enables firms to concentrate on serving relatively narrow markets with quality goods and services. Consequently, firms can become quite efficient at providing specialized goods and services.

Answers to REVIEW AND DISCUSSION Questions

1.   *How does effective planning benefit managers?*

Through planning, managers are encouraged to think—anticipate future events, recognize potential obstacles, and consider strategies for attaining desired outcomes. Planning assists managers in setting priorities and developing courses of action in response to uncertain environmental conditions. Formalized planning provides a structured approach to gain insights and weigh the pros and cons of alternative choices.

2.   *What are the differences among policies, procedures, and rules?*

While policies are generalized operational guidelines, procedures involve step-by-step sequences of events needed to implement policies. Rules are more restrictive than policies and procedures. They prescribe how actions are to be accomplished and customarily do not give managers discretionary flexibility. Managers must comply with an organization's rules.

3.   *What steps are involved in the planning process?*

The planning process consists of five steps: determine the goal, review the present situation, recognize limiting factors, develop the plan, and implement the plan. The chapter includes a detailed discussion of each step. It is important for students to note that successful planning is not a haphazard activity. It requires time, effort, and thought.

4.   *What is the relationship between the concepts of corporate and functional strategy?*

Corporate strategy, which is broadly oriented, provides an overall sense of direction for an organization and identifies a primary approach to accomplishment of goals. Functional strategy, however, involves activities of a firm's functional units, including marketing, production/operations, finance, and human resources. These activities are rather specific and focused upon gaining results within the various component functional areas.

5.   *Why should planners understand the concept of grand strategies?*

These strategies identify the "big picture" toward which organizations have options to direct resources. They provide guidance for firms desiring to alter fundamental purposes, revise product lines, or change direction in serving market segments. Students should remember that successful implementation of grand strategies requires development and implementation of numerous more detailed, specific plans.

6.   *What is the purpose of a business strategy?*

This strategy is designed to attain goals for each business unit or grouping of business units. A business strategy is more narrowly focused than a corporate strategy and may involve concerns ranging from growth to retrenchment. In firms with many subunits, separate business strategies help to avoid complications involving attempts to adapt the same or similar strategies to diverse types of business operations.

7.   *What are functional strategies?*

Functional strategies relate to activities categorized according to actual functions performed. The functions include marketing, finance, production/operations, and human resources. At the functional level, these strategies, which may be referred to as policies, provide guidance in organizing work activities and helping to assure completion of tasks. Students should realize that desired outcomes necessitate successful performance in all functional areas. A strategy implemented in production can influence what occurs in the area of marketing.

8.   *How does the adaptation model assist managers?*

This model enables managers to understand the relationship between alternative strategies and economic conditions. Figure 5-8 compares defender, prospector, and analyzer strategies with corresponding environmental variables. In addition, the figure shows that managers cannot maintain a position of ignoring environmental factors.

9.   *Identify each quadrant of the BCG Matrix and explain differences among the quadrants.*

The matrix, which compares market growth rate and market share, consists of these quadrants: stars, cash cows, question marks, and dogs. Stars (high growth and high market share) are products with strong potential for long-term growth. Cash cows (low growth and high market share) generate large revenues but demonstrate little promise of gaining additional market growth. Question marks (high growth and low market share) have promise of obtaining growth in the marketplace but require a commitment of additional financial resources. Dogs (low growth and low market share) are businesses in mature markets and hold little promise of becoming profitable. They are likely candidates for liquidation.

10.   *What factors should be considered in development of a SWOT analysis?*

Refer to Figure 5-6, which lists possible sources of strengths, weaknesses, opportunities, and threats. Common opportunities and threats involve economic, political-legal, social, technological, and industry forces. Advertising, decision making, labor relations, and financial resources are examples of factors that represent an organization's strengths or weaknesses.

Answers to CRITICAL THINKING INCIDENTS

Incident 5-1: A CHANGE OF PLANS

1. **What is the relationship between the planning function and Sam's concern about dependable customer service?**

   The essence of planning is to prepare courses of future action to reach objectives. Increasingly, firms are challenged to be productive, meet competitive pressures, and adapt to change. Meeting (and exceeding) customer expectations is an essential priority and a key to business success. Planning is a tool to link a company with its customers. Satisfied customers are instrumental in building favorable perceptions toward a company. Progressive firms that emphasize the planning function may be more likely to develop customer-service strategies.

2. **How could Jean have minimized Sam's criticism of her implementation of her new plan for revamping the recordkeeping system?**

   Prior to implementing her proposal, Jean should have met with Sam to explain the new system and discuss its pros and cons. Better communication is a key to keeping Sam informed and making him aware of possible future problems. Nevertheless, it is possible for Sam to criticize Jean anyway. Students need to recognize that effective communication can improve interpersonal relations and serve as a basis to justify plans. If Sam is aware of Jean's plan, she is in a better position to explain the rationale for her actions and defend them.

3. **During her performance evaluation, should Jean plan to tell Sam how she really feels? Explain your response.**

   Performance-review discussions do provide opportunities to communicate views with superiors. If Jean does not express her views, no changes are likely to occur. Should Sam ask if she has any questions, Jean has an ideal "opening" for stating her concerns. If such a request is not made, she should plan for an appropriate moment, preferably toward the end of the meeting, and state her views. Jean might begin by saying, "Sam, I have a couple of concerns. . ."

   Jean needs to consider how she can elicit a desired response from Sam without unduly risking a negative reaction. Her "game plan" should include making comments in a cordial, yet straightforward, manner and sticking to issues without any personal attack upon Sam. It is important for Jean to communicate the concern about time pressures and changing expectations from a perspective of how they negatively impact her job performance.

4.   **How can Sam be encouraged to become a more capable planner?**

It is not easy for a subordinate to encourage the boss to change established behaviors. When being critical of a boss, caution and diplomacy are most relevant considerations. Sam may not respond positively to any suggestions, and there is a strong likelihood that he is not aware of any needed changes in his planning capabilities.

Subordinates might take the initiative and periodically remind Sam of their desire to know about time-consuming events related to performance of their job duties. Generally, best results are attained if this approach is practiced informally over an extended duration of time. Another recommendation is for subordinates to compliment Sam whenever his actions demonstrate recognition of successful planning strategies.

Incident 5-2: LOOKING AHEAD

1.   **How much thought has been given to the plan for using the former campus facility?**

Although not known for certain, it appears that Mr. Winters has not developed a formalized, comprehensive plan to outline and target most promising options. Awareness of limiting factors and adherence to the planning process will yield worthwhile results. Specifics should not be overlooked. How many office units are possible? What types of housing units should be built for senior citizens? How large a shopping mall is necessary? Then, relevant questions focus on whether facilities can be leased or rented to generate a reasonable return on investment. Even though Winters and Associates apparently has a successful track record, the basic essentials of planning cannot be ignored.

A key purpose of this question is to help students realize that planning involves consideration of relationships among goals, limitations, resources, and feasibility of implementation. Too often, alternatives are not adequately considered, and insufficient attention is given to examination of details. There is frequently a tendency to move quickly from conception of a plan to its implementation.

2.   **What factors might necessitate revising a plan to purchase the facility?**

Students will have a variety of responses to this question. They may cite changing interest rates, population trends, governmental regulations, tax rates, cost/availability of labor and so on. Another possibility includes unanticipated negotiation complications with the seller. The question is intended to help students realize that plans must be flexible and may need to be altered because of changing circumstances.

3.   **What should Charles include in any contingency plan that might be developed?**

A contingency plan should specify courses of action for situations that unexpectedly arise and hinder success probabilities of an original plan. Numerous responses are possible. A contingency plan might include strategies for alternative uses of space that cannot be leased or rented. If a suitable commercial lender cannot be located, other sources of funds, such as entrepreneurial lenders, need to be identified. It is important for students to understand that events do not necessarily occur because of prior expectations. Even though a contingency plan is not used, time set aside to develop it is not wasted.

4.   **Why is it important for Charles to review content of the plan before it is finalized?**

Review helps to assure that all relevant factors are considered. Frequently, relevant factors are incorrectly taken for granted, and if not examined, assumptions may be unrealistic. Charles needs to consider the likelihood of present and future competitors, highway route changes, and attractiveness of location. As far as senior citizens are concerned, proximity of living facilities to grocery stores and medical facilities is important. A key point is for students to grasp the importance of reviewing plans before implementing them.

Incident 5-3: WHERE FROM HERE?

1.   **In planning for his business, what factors should Wilbur consider?**

Several factors are especially relevant. Obtaining a down payment is a crucial strategic concern. Assuming a loan is obtained, sufficient cash is necessary to pay overhead expenses, interest, and ultimately the principal loan amount. Wilbur's plan should consider specification of target markets, personnel needs, location options, inventory requirements, and promotional approaches. In practice, important factors are too often not given sufficient thought and, as a consequence, emerge as major problems.

2.   **Since he is already skilled and experienced at his profession, why is it still important for Wilbur to plan?**

Skill and experience at performing jobs are not necessarily equated with the ability to be a successful planner. Many businesses fail because of poor management practices, and a failure to plan is a major part of the problem. Sometimes, students need to be reminded that "failing to plan is planning to fail." Planning provides a path to help assure attainment of objectives. It is a method of forcing managers to think ahead, anticipate occurrences, and consider alternatives. Given the number of start-up business failures, Wilbur cannot overlook the importance of realistic business planning.

3. **As it relates to planning his business, identify the most relevant long-term question for Wilbur to consider?**

Several answers are possible. Students need to emphasize that a major priority is to develop a business mission. Relevant concerns are to target potential customers and provide quality goods and services that exceed customer expectations. Key questions are: What is our business? Who are our customers? How can we satisfy and exceed customer expectations? Sometimes, the movie industry is cited as an industry that emphasized the movie business rather than its more comprehensive aspect of providing entertainment. "Know thy customer" is a key to corporate growth and long-term customer satisfaction in the financial brokerage industry.

4. **Why do short-term plans need to be developed for the new business to be successful?**

The business cannot neglect the short term because of the critical need for resources and development of a blueprint to guide actions. A most critical immediate need is for a plan to obtain necessary funds. Other short-term priorities involve plans for determining whether to serve retail or commercial customers, advertising, building an inventory, and hiring personnel. These are major considerations that demand Wilbur's immediate attention. Well-formulated short-term plans will enable Wilbur to consider key priorities and be prepared to act expediently. It is important that short-term plans not be considered less important than long-term plans; both are necessary and essential to successful operations.

5. **Assuming Martin, Gerald, and Sally are hired, why should Wilbur involve them in the planning process?**

By soliciting participation, Wilbur has opportunities to gain ideas that may be worthwhile and also develop employee loyalty. Martin possesses relevant job capabilities and experience. Gerald may not initially be in a position to make significant contributions. Through dedicated effort and a willingness to learn, however, he will gain greater professional competence. Sally's prior retailing experience might be a source of valuable insights, especially if the firm expands into retailing. Assuming they are hired, these employees might choose to remain with the firm because of a participatory work environment in which their input is valued.

Study Guide Assignments

The individual case assignment involves a discussion of a readily understood application of SWOT analysis. Since students are familiar with the college environment, they can grasp implications of key factors that are considered in determining strengths, weaknesses, opportunities, and threats.

In the group case assignments, students have an opportunity to actually perform a SWOT analysis for their school. They are also asked to consider their group's analysis from the perspective of faculty, administration, trustees, and the community. This exercise enables students to learn how viewpoints can differ and gain practical knowledge about the SWOT approach.

Video Case

Minnesota Twins

Focus: **Planning, Strategy, Mission, and Culture**

Summary:

The Minnesota Twins are an American League baseball team based in Minneapolis, Minnesota. Although some might think that a major league baseball team would be very different from a typical business organization, that's just not so, especially when it comes to organizational planning. The Twins, like any other organization, consider strategic planning critical to their long-term success.

With regard to strategic analysis, the Twins face many internal and external issues. Internally, the organization must cope with fan relations, marketing issues (such as promotions and ticket sales) and limitations on their stadium, the Metrodome (such as seating, vendors, and other tenants). One of the most important aspects of the internal organization is human resources. In baseball, this takes on tremendous significance, since the quality of the product is so highly dependent on having strong human resources out on the field.

Externally, competition for the consumer's entertainment dollars presents challenges for a major league baseball team. Legal issues are also relevant because, like any other business organization, baseball teams have to deal with antitrust issues, tax regulations, and potential lawsuits. Technology has affected the game in many ways as well. For example, computer networking now makes it easier to purchase tickets at kiosks throughout the city. All of these external environment issues have a significant impact on the Twins' strategic plan.

The Twins have a formal mission statement that sets out the organization's reasons for existence, as well as its fundamental goals. While the most visible goal of the organization is to win on the field, it has other important goals related to total sales, profit, and other financial measures of success. Based on these goals, the Twins have pursued a growth strategy directed at attracting more fans to the games, as well as better media coverage.

Functional strategies are necessary at many levels of the organization. For example, the Promotions Department has developed a number of strategies designed to increase attendance at the games. These strategies range from simply advertising games with strong competitors heavily to elaborate in-stadium giveaway plans to attract fans to less competitive games. Marketing efforts to attract more media coverage of the games are essential to implementing the strategy of growth as well. Strategies for recruiting players, assessing talent, building a strong roster, and enhancing player relations are also important at the functional level of the organization.

The management and players of the Minnesota Twins feel that, in the end, it is their organizational culture that sets them apart from other major league teams. The Twins take a great deal of pride in maintaining a culture that values hard work, having fun, playing the best game possible, and not carrying a briefcase to work. The Twins culture is a function of their commitment to give 100 percent of their energy, effort, and enthusiasm to building a team that their fans can be proud of.

Through strategic planning, the Twins have charted a path for their future success.

Discussion Questions:

1.   Develop a list of the external and internal issues that would likely affect the strategic plan of the Twins. Describe how these issues would affect their strategic plan.

        Internal issues include: attracting and keeping outstanding players; ticket sales; stadium capacity; and fan relations. External issues include: competition; legal issues; and the potential for a baseball strike.

2.   What performance goals do you feel would be most important to the Twins?

        A dual approach to measuring performance is probably appropriate here: one set of goals on team performance (such as standing in the league) and another set on financial performance.

3. Develop a comprehensive list of functional strategies that would be necessary to implement a strategy of growth and thereby meet the goals identified in Question 2.

   A long-range functional strategy for attracting outstanding players could involve emphasis on the Twins' minor league team; functional strategies to support financial performance would include marketing plans.

Chapter 6

Organizing

Chapter Overview

This chapter emphasizes that the way firms are organized can influence their ability to succeed. Many traditional and new ways of organizing are available to large and small organizations. Managers should be familiar with different ways of organizing in order to select an approach that will help them accomplish organizational goals.

A distinction is made between the formal and informal organizational structures that exist in companies. Each of these structures is served by its own communication system. Some companies are highly centralized, whereas other companies are more decentralized. Reporting functions in a company are identified by the company's chain of command. The need for managers to delegate is examined. Traditional forms of departmentalization used in companies are discussed. In addition, new trends in organizing are described.

Teaching Objectives

The teaching objectives of this chapter are to:

1. Explain the difference between line departments and staff departments in organizations.

2. Identify common ways in which organizations practice departmentalization.

2.   Identify common ways in which organizations practice departmentalization.

3.   Identify the key factors that should be considered when designing jobs, according to the job characteristics model.

4.   Indicate how process management is distinguished from management by function.

5.   Explain how the modular approach to organizing works.

6.   Describe the virtual corporation approach to organizing.

Chapter Outline of the Text

I.   TRADITIONAL PRINCIPLES OF ORGANIZING
        A.   Formal and Informal Organizational Structures
        B.   Centralization and Decentralization
        C.   The Scalar Principle
II.   LINE AND STAFF STRUCTURES
III.   DELEGATION
        A.   Accountability
        B.   Personal Power
        C.   Obstacles to Delegation
        D.   Determining what to Delegate
IV.   SPAN OF MANAGEMENT
V.   DEPARTMENTALIZATION
        A.   Departmentalization by Function
        B.   Departmentalization by Product
        C.   Departmentalization by Customer
        D.   Departmentalization by Geographic Location
        E.   Departmentalization by Matrix Design
VI.   MECHANISTIC STRUCTURE VERSUS ORGANIC STRUCTURE
VII.   JOB DESIGN
        A.   Job Specialization and Standardization
        B.   Beyond Specialization
               1.   Job Rotation
               2.   Job Enlargement
               3.   Job Enrichment
               4.   The Job Characteristic's Model
VIII.   THE NEW FLEXIBLE ORGANIZATION
        A.   Breakthrough in Organizing
        B.   The Modular Approach
IX.   THE VIRTUAL CORPORATION

Key Terms

These terms are introduced in the chapter. Definitions are included in the glossary of the text.

Authority	Job rotation
Centralization	Line department
Chain of command	Line organization
Decentralization	Matrix design
Delegation	Mechanistic structure
Departmentalization	Modular approach
by customer	Organic structure
by function	Organizing
by geographic design	Process management
by product	Reengineering
Flat organizational structure	Responsibility
Formal organizational structure	Scalar principle
Informal organizational structure	Smoke screen communication (SSC)
Internal motivation	Span of management (span of control)
Job characteristics model	Staff department
Job design	Tall organizational structure
Job enlargement	Virtual corporation
Job enrichment	

Detailed Chapter Summary

1.   TRADITIONAL PRINCIPLES OF ORGANIZING

Organizing is the process of determining what tasks should be assigned to employees, how the tasks should be grouped into departments, and how resources can be appropriately allocated to accomplish organizational goals. Traditional forms of organizing in companies include departmentalization by function, product, customer, geographic location, and matrix design.

A.   *Formal and Informal Organizational Structure*

The formal organizational structure is based on the positions and functions in a company and is represented by the firm's organizational chart. The informal organizational structure refers to the relationship patterns that develop as a result of the interests and informal activities of members of an organization.

B.   *Centralization and Decentralization*

Centralization exists when most important decisions are made by top managers. Decentralization occurs when lower-level employees engage in decision making.

Teaching Hint: Emphasize that for decentralization to work in companies, the employees who are given increased responsibility for decision making must be trained to assume the new responsibilities.

C.   *The Scalar Principle*

According to the scalar principle, a clear line of authority should connect every person from the top to the bottom of a company. Through this clear line of authority, everybody in an organization knows who reports to whom.

II.   LINE AND STAFF STRUCTURES

Learning Objective 1:   Explain the difference between line departments and staff departments in organizations.

Line departments in a company contribute directly to the accomplishment of company goals. On the other hand, staff departments provide specialized advice and assistance to members of line departments. Staff departments do not contribute directly to the accomplishment of company goals; they assist line departments.

III.   DELEGATION

When managers delegate, they empower employees with the authority and responsibility to use company resources to accomplish assigned tasks.

A.   *Accountability*

Managers must be careful not to delegate a task to an employee who is untrained to fully perform the task. Managers are always responsible for the performance of tasks they delegate to others.

B.   *Personal Power*

Managers can use their personal power to accomplish job-related responsibilities, especially when they are faced with a situation where they have limited authority.

C.   *Obstacles to Delegation*

Managers who fail to provide employees with adequate training make delegation difficult. Inadequate planning by managers eliminates many opportunities for orderly delegation. Managers who trust only themselves to do a job right preclude much appropriate delegation from occurring. Expecting perfection and being unwilling to accept reasonable risks associated with giving responsibilities to others can also make delegation unlikely.

D.   *Determining What to Delegate*

Many routine duties can be delegated by managers, as well as specialized tasks. Through appropriate delegation, managers can help employees with valuable experiences and opportunities to develop professionally.

IV.   SPAN OF MANAGEMENT

In organizations, span of management refers to the number of employees a manager is responsible for supervising. Span of management can influence whether organizations have relatively flat or tall organizational structures.

V.   DEPARTMENTALIZATION

Learning Objective 2:   Identify common ways in which organizations practice departmentalization.

The common ways in which organizations practice departmentalization are by function, product, customer, geographic location, and matrix design.

VI. MECHANISTIC STRUCTURE VERSUS ORGANIC STRUCTURE

In a mechanistic structure, employees specialize, job descriptions are precise, authority and power are centralized at the top, many formal rules and policies exist, and downward communication dominates. In an organic structure, employees assume responsibility for a wide array of tasks, job descriptions are informal and general, authority is decentralized, minimal formal rules exist, and communication is encouraged both vertically and horizontally.

VII. JOB DESIGN

Job design determines what tasks are to be performed, how they are to be completed, and the expectations, responsibilities, and authority associated with the job.

A. *Job Specialization and Standardization*

The way jobs are designed at the new United Motor Manufacturing plant in California demonstrates that a hierarchical organization can use great discipline to implement detailed standards as part of specialized jobs and, at the same time, encourage employee innovation and commitment.

B. *Beyond Specialization*

Managers face the challenges of making tasks meaningful to employees so they will be motivated to perform their jobs well. Four traditional alternatives are available to meet this challenge: Job rotation, job enlargement, job enrichment, and use of the job characteristics model.

1. Job Rotation

Job rotation is the systematic movement of employees among various jobs in an organization in order to broaden their experiences.

2. Job Enlargement

Job enlargement increases the number of tasks to be performed in a job.

3. Job Enrichment

Job enrichment involves increasing the responsibility, scope, and challenge of the work performed in a way that gives workers more control over how they do their jobs.

4.   The Job characteristic Model

Teaching Objective 3:   Identify the key factors that should be considered when designing jobs, according to the job characteristics model.

According to the job characteristics model, the design of jobs should take into consideration the workers' competency, their need for personal growth, and their level of satisfaction with the work context. Employees who are well matched to their jobs will experience an internal motivation that is influenced by how meaningful their work is to them, by their level of accountability, and by how much feedback they receive. Five core job characteristics that affect the three conditions of internal motivation are skill variety, task identity, task significance, autonomy, and feedback. Furthermore, for employees to respond positively to complex and challenging jobs, their growth needs must be strong.

Suggested Readings for this Section:
Harari, Oren. "The Brain-Based Organization." Management Review 83, June 1994, pp. 57-60.

The author claims that a company's success is now determined more by knowledge in the company than by the traditional attributes of land, labor, capital, and sheer size. According to Oren Harari, "Knowledge is the full utilization and exploitation of information, coupled with the optimal application of people's competencies, skills, talents, thoughts, ideas, intuitions, commitments, motivations and imaginations. In line with this view, companies must reduce their large pyramid organizational structures and expand their knowledge. That is, the trend in organizational design is away from the bureaucratic big body/little brain structure to the big brain/little body design.

LaBarre, Polly. "The Dis-Organization of Oticon." Industry Week, July 18, 1994, pp. 23-28.

Lars Kolind, president of Oticon, the Danish hearing-aid manufacturer, realized that a shift was occurring in that industry from products being technology-based to knowledge-based. That is, instead of building every smaller hearing aids, Oticon needed to build better hearing aids to dominate that market. As a result, Kolind reorganized the structure and design of Oticon. For example, projects no longer were worked on in traditional departments within the company. Instead, the projects were initiated and pursued by

informal groups of interested employees. The development of the first fully automatic
hearing aid followed quickly from this reorganization.

VIII.   THE NEW FLEXIBLE ORGANIZATION

A trend in organizational design, especially in high-technology companies, is the
creation of generally interdependent business units within a company. The
organizational designs that provide the best forms of direct communication channels
between managers, employees, and customers are being given the greatest attention.

A.   *Breakthrough in Organizing*

It has been shown that productivity can be improved by focusing on business
processes rather than on functional departments.

**Teaching Objective 4:   Indicate how process management is distinguished from
management by function.**

Three characteristics distinguish process management from management by
function. First, instead of focusing on intradepartmental objectives, process
management looks at how well the various integrated functions in a company
are working together. Second, employees who possess different skills work
together as a team to accomplish tasks, instead of performing functions in a
series. Third, in process management, information is provided directly to
where it is needed, without going through a hierarchy that can distort messages
and cause miscommunication.

B.   *The Modular Approach*

Teaching Objective 5:   Explain how the modular approach to organizing works.

The modular approach to organizing concentrates a company's efforts and
resources on core activities in which it has special expertise and contracts
required services to others.

*Teaching Hint: Emphasize that it is difficult for one company to perform well in every aspect
of delivering a product to customers. To be competitive, it may be best for a company to
focus on performing certain core competencies well and having other necessary tasks
performed by companies that specialize in those areas.*

IX. THE VIRTUAL CORPORATION

Teaching Objective 6:   Describe the virtual corporation approach to organizing.

The virtual corporation is a temporary combination of independent companies that are linked by information technology to allow them to share skills, reduce costs, and enter new markets

---

Suggested Readings for this Section:
Spee, James C. "Addition by Subtraction: Outsourcing Strengthens Business Focus." HR Magazine 40, March 1995, pp. 38-43.

Companies are finding that they can maintain core competencies while becoming more cost-effective by outsourcing some human relations (HR) tasks. For example, outsourcing may be appropriate for HR tasks such as creating a safety program or recruiting for a specific position. This article offers six questions managers should answer when considering whether to oursource HR tasks.

Denton, D. Keith. "Process Mapping Trims Cycle Time." HR Magazine 40, February 1995, pp. 56-61.

Many companies are attempting to reduce their cycle time, which represents how much time transpires from the moment a customer places an order to the moment payment for the order is received. To develop a strategy for reducing cycle time, a company should first map out its process to see what barriers exist. This article examines how Owens-Corning and Asea Brown Boveri have used process mapping to reduce cycle time.

X.   REENGINEERING

Reengineer is the design and implementation of wide-ranging changes in business processes to produce breakthrough results. In reorganizing a company, reengineering starts from scratch, as if the company was being created for the first time. As a matter of fact, managers who are responsible for reengineering ask themselves, "If we could start all over again, how would we run this company?" Then, with intense dedication, they make the company fit their vision.

XI.   LOOKING BACK

This chapter provides an introduction to the traditional approaches to organizing and examines innovations to organizing that are being introduced in organizations.

Answers to CONSIDER THIS Questions   (Page 186)

1.   **Some managers are detail-oriented and focus on specifics. Other managers look at the broad picture and focus on abstract ideas. Which type of manager is likely to do better at organizing and why?**

There is, perhaps a natural tendency to conclude that managers who are detail-oriented and focus on specifics are better at organizing. However, as students often indicate, without a broad picture of what is going on in a company and an ability to focus on future needs, a manager may need to frequently reorganize the way company operations function in reaction to changes in the internal and external environment. Therefore, the ability to be proactive rather than reactive as a manager can enhance efforts to be effective at organizing. Efforts by a manager to empower employees and to decentralize can reduce the need for the manager to be detail-oriented and to focus on specifics in order to be effective at organizing.

2.   **Staff departments, such as the training (personnel) department, are often the first to experience budget cuts when companies are looking for ways to reduce costs. How wise is this strategy?**

It is important to examine what tasks are being performed by a staff department that may experience budget cuts. Critical tasks performed by the staff department should not be eliminated simply due to the need to cut budgets. Eliminating necessary training as part of budget cuts, for example, would be unwise. Reassigning the critical tasks to another department or outsourcing the tasks may be appropriate as a way to deal with budget cuts in staff departments.

3.   **What traits, if any, do you have that make you reluctant to delegate responsibilities to others?**

Many students often indicate that there is a specific way they want certain tasks performed, and they do not want others performing the tasks a different way. Therefore, they do little delegating. Some students indicate that you need to be organized to delegate. That is, you cannot reasonably delegate tasks to people who have not been properly trained or who do not know where to find the necessary resources to complete the tasks. In these cases, students say they find it easier to do the tasks themselves than to organize things well enough for others to perform the tasks.

Answers to CONSIDER THIS Questions (Page 199)

1. **Would you feel most comfortable as a manger with a large span of management in a flat organization or with a narrow span of management in a tall organization?**

   Students often indicate that they think a large span of management would require more effort from a manager than is necessary for a narrow span of management. However, as they analyze the situation, they frequently realize that the employees' level of job-related motivation and ability should be considered. That is, a large span of management consisting of employees who are very motivated and capable is less difficult for a manager compared to a narrow span of management in which employees must be closely monitored.

2. **Why is it difficult for managers who like to provide a lot of direction and control to succeed when they have a wide span of management?**

   Providing a lot of direction and control as a manager takes much time per employee in most cases. To spend this amount of time per employee in a large span of management can be overwhelming for a manager. Under these conditions, it is difficult for a manager to be effective.

3. **What do you think is the biggest obstacle to getting companies to make an appropriate switch from a vertical structure to a process-oriented, horizontal design?**

   Certainly a major obstacle to the switch is the resistance from people in a company who will complain that "We have always done things the other way!" These individuals must realize that great leaps in quality, for example, can occur only when a focus on quality exists throughout a process, not just at the end of the process. Problems associated with quality and efficiency are more easily identified and corrected in a process-oriented rather than a horizontal design. Students also often indicate that getting employees to change their focus from departmental goals and objectives to focusing on the needs of internal and external customers is another significant obstacle.

▓ **Answers to REVIEW AND DISCUSSION Questions**
■

1. *What is the difference between a centralized and a decentralized organizational structure?*

    In organizations, centralization exists when most important decisions are made by top managers. Conversely, decentralization occurs when lower-level employees engage in decision making. In highly centralized companies, top management maintains much control. As a result, it is common for these companies to have standardized operating procedures that apply to all departments. On the other hand, more empowerment exists in companies that are very decentralized. Lower-level employees in these companies can act quickly to solve problems on the job because they have been given the authority to make decisions.

2. *Why is the distinction between line and staff functions becoming blurred in many companies today?*

    In the past, bloated bureaucracies in many companies isolated staff functions from market realities. However, downsizing in companies, through a reduction in the number of individuals employed, has forced more staff departments to assume increased responsibilities for company performance. Furthermore, with increased frequency, staff departments are being expected to be self supporting by selling their services competitively to line units.

3. *What communication problems seem to be inherent to flat versus tall organizational structures?*

    A common communication problem plaguing flat organizational structures is *communication overload.* That is, with so many employees reporting to one person in a flat organizational structure, the manager can be overwhelmed with the demands for information. Although the manager has a lot of control in this situation, it is difficult for a flat organization to expand because too many demands are placed on the manager. Tall organizational structures, however, encounter the inherent communication problem of *communication distortion.*

4. *Why is departmentalization by function common in many companies?*

    Departmentalization by function is common in many companies because it has two key advantages. First, it permits employees to specialize and become experts in a certain area. Second, supervisors' tasks are simplified due to the fact that they are only responsible for understanding and coordinating the duties of one functional task or skill.

5.   *What is the logic behind job enlargement, and why does this logic often fail?*

Job enlargement increases the number of tasks to be performed in a job. The additional tasks are usually taken from other jobs that have been eliminated. Part of the logic behind job enlargement is that the additional tasks keep workers busy, and busy workers do not have time to be bored. Boredom, however, is more a function of how workers feel about the work they perform than how much work they have to perform. That is, adding a lot of simple tasks to an already simple job does not change the nature of the job much.

6.   *Why don't all employees respond positively to jobs that are complex and challenging?*

The essence of internal motivation, according to Hackman and Oldham, is that positive feelings result from good performance and negative feelings result from poor performance. Unfortunately, if a job has low motivating potential, internal motivation can be expected to be low, and an employee's feelings will probably be unaffected by personal performance. Therefore, the design of such a job offers little incentive to employees to perform well to feel good. Interestingly, however, for individuals to respond positively to complex and challenging jobs, their "growth needs" must be strong. Growth needs refer to an individual's need for personal accomplishment, for learning, and for improvement. Without strong growth needs, and especially if employees lack the necessary knowledge and skills to perform a job, they will probably not respond positively to jobs that are complex and challenging?

7.   *Why are many companies abandoning their traditional vertical organization in favor of a process-oriented, horizontal organization?*

Fundamental changes are occurring in the organizational designs of many companies. The impetus for this change is the need to accommodate the rapid pace of technological developments, global competition, and the dawning of a knowledge-based economy. As a result of these developments, increasing numbers of companies are abandoning the traditional monolithic and rigid organizational designs. The emerging organizational designs are ones that can accommodate innovation and change in an effective manner. Evidence indicates that productivity can be improved by focusing on business processes rather than on functional departments. The process-oriented horizontal organization does not have traditional department heads such as "manager of sales." Instead, there is a manager of "getting-things-to-customers," which integrates sales, shipping, and billing. It has been estimated that organizations can cut their cost base by one-third or more by adopting a process-oriented organizational design.

8.   *How does the modular approach enable companies to become more efficient and competitive?*

The modular approach to organizing concentrates a company's efforts and resources on core activities in which it has special expertise, while contracting required services to others. Use of the modular approach is enabling more companies to avoid the burdens of operating unprofitable plants and maintaining inefficient bureaucracies. Outsourcing noncore activities offers two advantages to modular companies. First, it minimizes the financial investment needed to produce new products quickly. Second, it enables companies to funnel their scarce capital into areas where they have a competitive advantage, such as hiring the best people to design new products or enhancing customer service.

9.   *How does the concept of a virtual corporation enable companies to act quickly to take advantage of new market opportunities?*

The virtual corporation is a temporary combination of independent companies which are linked by information technology allowing them to share skills, reduce costs, and enter new markets. The collaborative web of companies eliminates the need for a single organization with a new product idea to be responsible for every aspect of bringing the product to market. With each company in the collaboration doing something especially well, new products can be developed and marketed much faster and with a higher level of quality than if one company tried to do everything by itself.

Answers to CRITICAL THINKING INCIDENTS

Incident 6-1: THE NEW MANAGER

1.   **What key mistake is Warren making as a new manager?**

Warren is trying to do too much himself. He doesn't realize that a leader accomplishes goals with and through *others*. For example, Warren performs some tasks himself that employees could perform, if only he would take the time to train them. This problem is perpetuated by the fact that Warren is a perfectionist and believes that many tasks can only be performed correctly by himself. Warren is not good at delegating.

2.   **Why is Warren failing to delegate departmental responsibilities properly?**

One reason is that his employees lack complete training. This situation gives Warren an excuse not to delegate. Also, inadequate planning by Warren eliminates many opportunities for orderly delegation. The fact that Warren often believes that only he can do the job right precludes much appropriate delegation from occurring. This limitation is made worse by the fact that Warren is a perfectionist

3.   **What changes do you recommend that Warren make to increase the likelihood that he will succeed as a manager?**

When Warren became a manager, he had high hopes that employees in his department would perform well and that he would succeed. These expectations can still come true for Warren, but he must first become better at delegating. Warren is less productive than other managers in the company because he tries to do too much himself. To be more productive, Warren needs to delegate more. For employees in Warren's department to be able to accept more responsibility, Warren must make the effort to provide them with appropriate training. Warren must also be willing to take some risks that employees might make some mistakes or fail to do a job as well as he can. In doing so, employees will develop on the job and become more capable of accepting even more responsibility. Last, Warren should expect excellence, not perfection in the work performed by employees in his department.

Incident 6-2: FINE TUNING A MERGER

1.   **Should Susan recommend a wide or narrow span of management for the East Plant? Why?**

A wide span of management will work at the East Plant for several reasons. To begin with, the employees in the East Plant perform similar job functions and their jobs are simple and routine. In addition, the planning required to keep the East Plant operating at peak performance is not that great. Last, little coordination of the work performed by employees at the East Plant is required.

2.   **Should Susan recommend a wide or narrow span of management for the West Plant? Why?**

A narrow span of management is appropriate at the West Plant due to the following circumstances that exist there. The jobs performed by the employees at the West Plant are very dissimilar, and they are complex and varied. A great deal of planning is needed at the West Plant and much coordination of the work performed by employees there is required.

3.   **What strategies should Susan recommend to reduce the problem of information overload that managers in the two plants are experiencing?**

The managers in the merged organization enjoy maintaining large amounts of control. As long as they attempt to assume much responsibility and control over what happens in the company, they will experience information overload as employees must seek information and approval from them. The problem of information overload will get worse as the company work force expands. To reduce information overload for managers, more needs to be done to empower employees who have the willingness and ability to accept increased responsibility. Increasing the number of managers as the work force expands will also help to reduce information overload for existing managers.

Incident 6-3: A GROWING COMPANY

1.   **Why is Omega Craft successful with its boats but not with the kit-car parts?**

As mentioned in the chapter, part of organizing involves the appropriate allocation of resources to accomplish organizational goals. Keith Selby, president of Omega Craft, is afraid the company is losing its "golden touch." When companies do well, it is usually due to using all forms of company resources well; not a golden touch. Managers who believe success in some areas will automatically lead to success in any new area due to the "golden touch," can get companies into trouble. Building fiberglass body panels and other parts for kit cars is different than building boats. Omega Craft is very good at building fiberglass molds. However, it is not so good at maintaining color consistency in large production runs or filling orders for parts on time. Also, its costs are high in the kit-car division. The company's expertise with boats is not necessarily transferable to kit cars. As a result, the company is not automatically experiencing success with kit cars.

2.   **Would the concept of a virtual corporation be appropriate for the kit-car division? Why or why not?**

Several leading business experts believe the virtual corporation is an appropriate way for many companies to organize. The virtual corporation is a temporary combination of independent companies which are linked by information technology allowing them to share skills, reduce costs, and enter new markets. The Omega Craft company is limited in its ability to do everything associated with designing, producing, and marketing kit car products. The company is good at building fiberglass molds, and the company should focus on its strengths. As a result, the Omega Craft company could create a virtual corporation by sharing key tasks in the kit car project with other companies. Omega Craft could, for example, make the fiberglass molds and allow them to be used by a company that is good at maintaining color consistency in large production runs at a lower cost. Another company that is expert at processing orders and delivery might also be included in the new virtual corporation created.

3.   **Although Omega Craft is successful at building fishing boats, what problems will this company probably experience as it expands?**

As a maker of small fishing boats, Omega Craft has a relatively flat organizational structure. However, as the company expands, it will be much harder for Keith Selby to run the company effectively. For one thing, Keith will experience increased information overload. There will then be a need to hire more managers as the company begins to acquire a taller organizational structure. The way Omega Craft is expanding, there is a real danger that the kit car division will drain valuable resources from the company without being profitable. The production problems with this division will likely continue and will probably monopolize much of Keith's valuable time. Keith should determine the type of organizational structure with which he feels comfortable. If the size of the company is not appropriate for that structure, Keith should rethink his expansion plans for the company.

Study Guide Assignments

For this chapter, the study guide contains an excellent concept application section that provides six scenarios for students to analyze in relation to key organizing concepts. An individual case assessment is also provided that helps students to better understand the implications of organizing trends in companies.

The group case assessment provided offers students an opportunity to discuss in groups how they will deal with some of the unique situations that will emerge through the creation of virtual corporations.

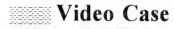 **Video Case**

Cormier Equipment Corporation

Focus: **Job Design**

Summary:

Cormier Equipment Corporation rents, services, and sells heavy industrial equipment. When the president of the company began to suspect that the economy was going into a recession, he began to prepare for a potential loss of revenues. Through a reengineering project that affected job design as well as other aspects of the organization, Cormier continued to prosper even through the recession.

When describing the reengineering project, Cormier says, "We reviewed the way we did business." All aspects of the organization's operation were reviewed with an eye on improving quality and efficiency. The following were among the actions eventually implemented:

- Managers were told to be more attentive to worker suggestions.
- Jobs were enlarged, and workers were given more responsibilities.
- Monetary incentives were provided for doing better jobs.
- Cost-reduction goals were set, and strategies for achieving them were developed.
- Annual reviews of paperwork eliminated duplication and unneeded reports.
- A new billing system produced quicker, more error-free invoicing.
- A system of processing equipment before it was rented out again improved service quality.
- In need of improved marketing, Cormier created a marketing director's position. The new marketing director's primary emphasis was on creating long-term client loyalty.

Through reengineering with a focus on changing the way jobs were designed and tasks were completed, Cormier weathered the recession successfully. As evidence of that success, profitability rose 2 ½ times from October 1990 to October 1992.

Discussion Questions:

1.   Discuss how Cormier adapted job design to prepare for an economic downturn.

Cormier made jobs more flexible through job enlargement and increasing the responsibilities of employees. Cost reductions and monetary incentives produced additional savings at cormier.

2.   How can reengineering improve productivity, quality, and job satisfaction?

Reengineering, also known as process innovation and core process redesign, requires radical change in the way a business operates in order to achieve major results. In effect, companies undergoing this process ask the question, "If we were starting from scratch, how would we do things?" As a result, radical improvement in productivity, quality, and job satisfaction are possible. However, given the magnitude of the change, employee morale can plummet, and employees at all levels in the organization need to be involved in and aware of what is going on during the change process.

Chapter 7

Staffing and Training

Chapter Overview

Human resources are key assets, and the performance of personnel influences is a critical factor in the success or failure of organizations. This chapter provides an introduction to the staffing function and explains the role of human-resource needs. Sources for locating employees are discussed, and emphasis is focused on the important concepts of recruitment and selection.

The presentation discusses the role of training, recognition of training needs, and types of training methods. In addition, the chapter examines methods used to evaluate the effectiveness of training activities.

Teaching Objectives

The teaching objectives of this chapter are to:

1.   Understand the staffing process.

2.   Explain the purpose of equal employment opportunity legislation.

3.   Differentiate between internal and external recruitment practices.

4.   Identify the techniques used in the selection process.

5.   Discuss various types of job-training methods.

6.   Specify methods to evaluate training activities.

Chapter Outline of the Text

I.   STAFFING: PEOPLE AND JOBS
        A.   The Staffing Model
        B.   Equal Employment Opportunity (EEO) Legislation
            1.   Adverse Impact
            2.   Affirmative Action Programs (AAPs)
II.   HUMAN-RESOURCE NEEDS
        A.   Job Analysis
        B.   Job Descriptions
        C.   Job Specifications
III.   RECRUITMENT
IV.   SOURCES OF EMPLOYEES
        A.   Internal Recruitment
        B.   External Recruitment
V.   SELECTION
        A.   Selection Techniques
            1.   Application Forms
            2.   Job References
            3.   Employment Testing
            4.   Interviews
            5.   Assessment Centers
VI.   THE ROLE OF TRAINING
VII.   RECOGNIZING TRAINING NEEDS
VIII.   TRAINING METHODS
        A.   On-the Job Training
            1.   Job Instruction Training (JIT)
            2.   Job Rotation
            3.   Special Assignments
        B.   Off-the-Job Training
            1.   The Lecture Method
            2.   Case Study Method
            3.   Role Playing
            4.   Audiovisual (AV) Training
IX.   EVALUATION OF TRAINING
        A.   Formal Evaluation
        B.   Observation and Informal Evaluation

X.	LOOKING BACK
XI.	KEY TERMS
XII.	REVIEW AND DISCUSSION QUESTIONS
XIII.	CRITICAL THINKING INCIDENTS
XIV.	SUGGESTED READINGS

Key Terms

These terms are introduced in the chapter. Definitions are included in the glossary of the text.

Adverse impact	Job instruction training (JIT)
Affirmative action program (AAP)	Job rotation
Assessment center	Job specification
Audio visual (AV) training	Lecture method
Bona Fide occupational qualifications (BFOQ)	Off-the-job training
	On-the-job training
Case-study method	Prejudice
Disparate impact	Recruitment
Disparate treatment	Reliability
Discrimination	Role playing
Equal employment opportunity (EEO) legislation	Selection
	Special-assignment method
Glass ceiling	Staffing
Job analysis	Training
Job description	Validity

Detailed Chapter Summary

I. STAFFING: PEOPLE AND JOBS

Teaching Objective 1: Understand the staffing process.

Staffing, which involves attracting, hiring, and retaining of personnel, serves to match employee skills needed to perform jobs with human-resource capabilities. Staffing is an essential concern because businesses depend on human resources to meet and exceed customer expectations. While employees need jobs, employers seek to hire people who are capable of making the contributions needed to attain corporate objectives.

A.   *The Staffing Model*

Figure 7-1 illustrates components of the staffing model: determination of human resource needs, recruitment, selection, training, and performance appraisal. All companies perform the staffing function. In practice, a key purpose is to hire knowledgeable personnel who are dedicated to the concept of continuous quality improvement.

B.   *Equal Employment Opportunity (EEO) Legislation*

Teaching Objective 2:   Explain the purpose of equal employment opportunity legislation.

The intent of EEO legislation is to prevent discrimination in job selection or in the performance of job duties after employees are hired. It is important to differentiate between prejudice and discrimination. Prejudice is an *attitude* toward a person or group that is based on incomplete information. Discrimination refers to either favorable or unfavorable *actions*. The chapter includes a listing of various laws designed to promote fair employment practices and assure equal employment opportunity.

1.   Adverse Impact

Adverse impact refers to the application of an employment practice that unjustly affects members of one or more protected groups. It involves disparate impact, which implies discrimination against a group, or disparate treatment, which is discrimination against an individual. Criteria developed to evidence adverse impact include comparative statistics, labor market statistics, and concentration statistics.

2.   Affirmative Action Programs (AAPs)

These programs attempt to correct previous workplace discrimination against females and minorities. Typically, AAPs include utilization and availability analyses, specified goals, and time guidelines.

II.   HUMAN-RESOURCE NEEDS

The job analysis, job descriptions, and job specifications are tools that help managers meet human-resource needs. By focusing on these needs, firms are more likely to attract capable personnel and successfully match employee qualifications with needed job skills.

A.   *Job Analysis*

Job analysis seeks to identify and record job tasks and the human qualifications needed to perform these tasks. It justifies the rationale for a position and specifies reporting relationships between managers and employees. In addition, job analysis is an important resource for development of job descriptions and job specifications.

B.   *Job Descriptions*

Job descriptions are unwritten statements that outline duties and responsibilities involved in performing jobs. They include descriptions of job duties and illustrate types of activities completed by job holders.

C.   *Job Specifications*

Job specifications list the human qualifications needed to perform job duties. These involve knowledge, skills, experience, and education requirements.

III.   RECRUITMENT

Recruitment is the process of building a pool of available job candidates from which persons are ultimately selected for employment. Companies hope to attract people who are qualified and willing to accept invitations for employment. Formal recruitment activities can be expensive and time-consuming.

Suggested Readings for this Section:
Downs, Alan. "Planned People Obsolescence." Training 32, February 1995, pp. 54-58.

Often, companies recruit on the basis of trying to match applicant qualifications and *yesterday's* job needs. Recommended recruitment strategies involve personnel who readily adapt to change, a feature that characterizes the workplace of the 1990s. Successful candidates for tomorrow's jobs need talents in these key areas: broad technical knowledge, organizational competencies, management skills, and learning skills.

Henkoff, Ronald. "Finding, Training, and Keeping the Best Service Workers." Fortune 130, October 3, 1994, pp. 110-122.

In an era dominated by demands for excellent customer service, more firms are paying attention to recruitment of personnel who can help them meet customer-service expectations. Many service firms do not necessarily place a priority on hiring persons with high levels of formal education or extensive technical skills. These companies seek employees who are empathetic, enterprising, and creative. A tendency is to recruit people who have pleasant personalities, evidence enthusiastic attitudes, and require minimum supervision. The article includes examples of front-line recruitment strategies used by Marriott Hotels, Credit Uniform Corporation, and Walt Disney World Resort.

IV.   SOURCES OF EMPLOYEES

Sources of job candidates include current employees and persons who are employed elsewhere. Figure 7-3 summarizes advantages and disadvantages of internal and external sources of job applicants.

Teaching Objective 3:   Differentiate between internal and external recruitment practices.

A.   *Internal Recruitment*

Promotions, transfers, job rotation, and rehires are internal sources of job applicants. Internal recruitment efforts are less expensive than development of formal recruitment programs to attract persons from external sources. Promotions are especially noteworthy, as they formally recognize past performance and evidence a commitment on behalf of the firm.

B.   *External Recruitment*

External recruitment sources include referrals, employment agencies, schools, and trade associations. Companies with reputations for providing quality products and services have an advantage in recruiting talented personnel. Many job applicants equate the marketplace success of employers with career employment possibilities for themselves.

V.   SELECTION

Selection involves the choice of a successful job candidate from available job applicants. A good match between applicants and jobs serves the interests of employees and employers.

Teaching Hint: Emphasize the importance of selection by pointing out types of complications that accompany an inability to match employee interests and skills with job requirements.

Teaching Objective 4:   Identify the techniques used in the selection process.

A.   *Selection Techniques*

The selection decision is a critical choice. Components of the selection process may include application forms, job references, employment testing, interviews, and assessment centers

1.   Application Forms

These forms include various types of information about the applicant and serve as a way to screen candidates. Some application forms even contain introductory information to help applicants understand job expectations.

2.   Job References

The practice of asking applicants to list references is quite common. However, candidates themselves select references, and it is unlikely that a name will be listed unless a positive reference is expected.

3.   Employment Testing

Testing programs seek to predict job-related performance capabilities. Tests must exhibit validity (actually measure what they say they measure) and reliability (evidence consistency over a span of time).

4.   Interviews

Job interviews are highly utilized, as almost all employers desire to meet applicants on a personal basis and discuss job openings. The text includes guidelines to help managers conduct job interviews and also lists suggestions for job applicants to consider in preparing for interviews.

5.   Assessment Centers

Assessment centers provide comprehensive evaluation of prospective employees and of current employees being considered for promotion or career-development programs. Trained assessors and managerial personnel observe performances and prepare evaluations.

VI.   THE ROLE OF TRAINING

Training involves acquiring the knowledge, skills, and abilities needed to do job tasks. The business community has expressed concerns about the educational capabilities of workers. Training is essential to assure that firms are productive and competitive. Given the inevitable technological advancements and greater pressures to achieve objectives, employees will be retrained more frequently. As business becomes more globalized, greater interactions will occur among personnel trained in various parts of the world. The text lists several strategies that are useful to train personnel who originate from other countries.

Figure 7-5 lists several benefits of training, which are key factors to reducing time and costs and increasing job satisfaction of workers. Trainers have varied backgrounds and experiences. Figure 7-6 summarizes advantages and disadvantages of using various types of trainers.

Teaching Hint: Stress that the costs of training can be viewed as an investment in human resources with the potential to pay considerable dividends in the future.

Suggested Readings for this Section:
Carr, Clay. "The Three R's of Training." Training 29, June 1992, pp. 60-67.

When viewed as a system, training can be improved by devoting attention to several critical components: requirements, resources, and results. Also, it is important to recognize the importance of process orientation. "An effective training process combines clear *strategy*, careful *analysis and design*, appropriate *media and methodology*, and continuous *evaluation*." Since providing customer satisfaction is the key result of effective training, it is essential for businesses to clearly understand customer expectations.

Meister, Jeanne C. "Training Workers in the Three C's." Nation's Business 82, September 1994, pp. 51-53.

To attain company goals, training programs need to provide workers with insights into the C's: culture, context, and core competencies. This knowledge helps them to make productive contributions and better understand organizational goals. Unitech Corporation and Empire Air Line have cooperated to offer training, including a special program designed to give top managers skills needed for teaching line personnel about corporate culture and values. Knowledge of company goals and values enables personnel to better serve customers.

VII.   RECOGNIZING TRAINING NEEDS

Training activities consume time and involve expenses. Therefore, identification of training needs and meeting them in a timely fashion are relevant concerns. Workers can be asked to suggest topics for training sessions. By reviewing production records, examining finished products, and listening to customer comments, managers can become more aware of the need for training. Also, summary statistics compiled from job-related examinations frequently reveal areas where additional training is necessary. Evaluation of employee job performance identifies strengths and weaknesses.

VIII.   TRAINING METHODS

Teaching Objective 5:   Discuss various types of job-training methods.

Selection of a training method or combination of methods should be carefully considered. Training methods can be classified in two ways: on-the-job training or off-the-job training.

   A.   *On-the-Job Training*

         On-the-Job Training includes job instruction training, job rotation, and special assignments. Job instruction training features a four-step approach (preparation of the learner, presentation, performance, and follow up). Job rotation involves moving learners among a series of jobs. With the special-assignment method, learners are assigned nonroutine work responsibilities to gain experience and develop career skills.

   B.   *Off-the-Job Training*

         Off-the-job training includes lectures, case studies, role playing, and audiovisual techniques. The lecture method emphasizes spoken presentations. With the case-study method, trainees are given information that describes certain decision-making situations and asked to recommend solutions. Acting out roles is a feature of role playing. Audiovisual training involves the use of videotapes, slides, and audio cassettes.

IX.   EVALUATION OF TRAINING

Teaching Objective 6:   Specify methods to evaluate training activities.

The purpose of training is to enhance productivity and quality. Evaluation is a critical consideration and serves as a basis for determining the extent to which training activities are successful.

A.   *Formal Evaluation*

Questionnaires are commonly used evaluative tools. Examinations represent
another type of evaluation technique. Rather than rely upon the opinions of
trainers and trainees, evaluation is based on actual measurements and can serve
as a way to document whether training is effective.

B.   *Observation and Informal Evaluation*

Managers have opportunities to observe the job performance of employees.
These observations help to evaluate previous training and provide insights into
the need for additional training. Persons who participate in training are usually
willing to comment informally about their experiences.

X.   LOOKING BACK

This chapter provides an overview of the importance of staffing and examines
fundamental concepts related to training.

Answers to CONSIDER THIS Questions   (Page 227)

1.   **What is the most common mistake that job applicants make during
preemployment interviews?**

Students will have many different responses to this question, which is designed
to encourage them to think about job interviews. Many types of mistakes are
possible; these include the failure to dress properly, arrive promptly, or
evidence an enthusiastic attitude toward the prospective job. A very common
mistake is a lack of planning, not learning enough about the company (its
products, services, or past history) and the nature of the job itself. Another
mistake is to communicate ineffectively. Here, complications range from a
lack of eye contact with an interviewer to answering questions without
sufficient forethought.

2.   **How can managers prepare themselves to interview prospective employees?**

The text cites several guidelines to assist managers. Planning is the key to
successful interviewing. It is important to review applicant files with an
emphasis on relevant skills, pertinent experiences, education requirements, or
special talents necessary to perform a job. It is useful to develop a list of
interview questions based on job-related factors. Managers must remember to

avoid questions that illegally discriminate among job candidates. Figure 7-4 presents examples of inappropriate preemployment inquiries.

3. **Why should managers be knowledgeable about recruitment practices?**

Managers should be knowledgeable because successful recruitment is a key to having a sufficiently large "pool" of qualified applicants from which to make selection decisions. From a formal perspective, managers need to know the appropriate procedures for making referrals to the human resource department. Managers serve as informal recruiters on a daily basis. Their comments about subordinates and the company itself may influence whether prospective employees elect to seek employment.

Answers to CONSIDER THIS Questions (Page 237)

1. **In the next decade, what changes in training methodology are likely to occur?**

Usage of computers will become more widespread in the years ahead. Future software applications will likely be more user friendly and include more innovative capabilities. The concept of interactive communication between trainers and learners will continue to evolve, enabling trainers to target their presentations, respond to questions, and provide instant feedback. Regardless of anticipated changes, classroom instruction will continue to be widely practiced as a methodology, largely because of its traditional acceptance as a flexible method of instruction and the personalized interaction between trainers and trainees.

2. **How can managers improve their capabilities as trainers?**

A key factor is to recognize the important role of training in the workplace and develop a commitment to becoming more proficient as a trainer. With a desire to improve, managers are more likely to be actively involved in various types of on- and off-the-job training activities. Sources of additional knowledge include formal classes, seminars, workshops, conferences, and home study. Membership in professional associations provides many opportunities to acquire new skills, learn from others, and gain insights into training strategies. In addition, managers can observe the practices of colleagues who are skilled trainers.

3.   **Who is responsible for company efforts to train personnel?**

It is easy to conclude that people who have specific assignments in the area of training are responsible for the success of training activities. In reality, all managers and employees share responsibility for effectiveness of the training function. While human resource departments and training specialists generally have formal responsibility to design and implement training programs, employees can make informal recommendations. These may involve providing input related to training needs, recommending types of training activities, or even suggesting capable trainers.

Answers to REVIEW AND DISCUSSION Questions

1.   *Why is staffing considered to be a key to corporate success?*

Capabilities of human resources are essential to achievement of corporate objectives. Some people express this importance by saying, "Firms are only as good as the people working for them." It is through the efforts of managers and employees that quality is attained and productive results occur.

2.   *How are a firm's human-resource needs influenced by its strategic plans?*

Strategic plans set forth courses of action to reach identified goals. A close relationship exists between these plans and usage of human resources. A growth-oriented firm seeks to hire additional personnel as revenues increase, and it expands into new markets. In a stable business environment, companies attempt to maintain the status quo. Consequently, the number of employees does not fluctuate to any great extent. Retrenchment and consolidations imply that fewer human resources will be needed; frequently, layoffs can be anticipated.

3.   *Why should job descriptions and job specifications be developed?*

Job descriptions describe the type of work activities that jobholders are expected to perform. When personnel know job-performance expectations, there is less likelihood for mistakes and miscommunication to happen. Job specifications state human qualifications needed to perform job duties. They set standards for comparing capabilities of applicants to those deemed essential by employers. Preparation of formal job descriptions and specifications forces employers to review the content of jobs and specify skills necessary to perform them.

4.   *How do recruitment practices affect selection decisions?*

Effective recruitment is a key to selection. Ideally, a large pool of qualified applicants provides an opportunity to review a wide range of abilities. Students should remember that the size of applicant pools can dwindle rather quickly. For example, applicants accept other job offers, cannot work during certain hours, or consider the salary to be unacceptable. If unqualified candidates are recruited, available positions cannot be staffed. If advertisements of vacancies are not widely disseminated, potential applicants may not learn of vacancies. Opportunities to select top candidates are increased by targeting announcements of job openings to reach persons who possess desired attributes. For instance, recruiting through college placement services is an excellent strategy to reach students seeking employment upon graduation.

5.   *What are the advantages and disadvantages of recruiting from internal sources?*

The practice of promotion from within gives personnel opportunities for career advancement and also helps strengthen employee loyalty. An accurate assessment of job capabilities and prior work records can quickly be determined for currently-employed persons. Internal recruitment is not necessarily a strategy to advocate innovative change. In addition to gaining the value of their prior experience, new hires from other firms are often considered as valuable sources of ideas. People who remain at a position for an extended duration of time can become "job stereotyped," which is not professionally advantageous in terms of career advancement. For example, it may be difficult for a secretary to make a smooth transition and become an office manager (at the same firm) because he or she may continue to be perceived as a secretary.

6.   *During pre-employment interviews, what type of questions should interviewers avoid asking?*

Refer to Figure 7-4, which gives examples of inappropriate inquiries. As a general guideline, interview questions should be directed toward job-related considerations. Questions related to race, gender, age, or national origin should be avoided. Before conducting interviews, some managers find it useful to make a list of potential questions. This approach helps the interviewer avoid asking "off-the-cuff" questions, which may not be proper or legal.

7.   *For the purpose of employment testing, what is the difference between validity and reliability? Why are these concepts important?*

Validity implies that a measurement instrument actually measures what it is supposed to measure. A reliable test is consistent and evidences similar results over an extended number of administrations. Validity and reliability represent the essence of testing and are crucial for test data to be useful. Sometimes, these concepts are not given sufficient attention. When this occurs, test results are likely to be inaccurate.

8.   *Why are assessment centers a recommended method for training managers?*

Assessment centers provide an opportunity to appraise a person's potential for success as a manager. The assessment process involves being interviewed, completing exercises, and taking tests. A considerable amount of data are compiled and available for analysis. Information can be utilized to help determine if a person is qualified for a specific position or has the necessary interpersonal communication skills to function successfully as a team member.

9.   *What major benefits are derived from training?*

Through training, employees and managers acquire knowledge and skills to do their jobs. In an era of growing globalism and rapid technological change, training prepares personnel to better meet customer expectations, improve competitiveness, and increase productivity. The need to seek continuing professional education has become a necessity, not an option. If job knowledge is kept up to date, individuals are more likely to experience a pattern of increasingly successful career growth.

10.   *Why is Job Instruction Training (JIT) recommended as a method for training employees to perform jobs that involve repetitive tasks.*

JIT consists of a basic four-step process to learn new job skills. It involves a logical progression. Learners are prepared; content is presented; and newly-acquired skills can be practiced under the watchful eyes of trainers. The technique provides structure and guidance to learners and can be adapted to most learning situations. Since repetition is emphasized, tasks can be mastered rather quickly. Observation of learner performance by skilled trainers provides immediate feedback and enables mistakes to be corrected before much time has elapsed.

Answers to CRITICAL THINKING INCIDENTS

Incident 7-1: WHO'S NEXT?

1. **How should Stan have responded to Omar's inquiry?**

In response to telephone inquiries, many managers and human resource department personnel will either give no information or only verify job titles and periods of employment. Stan may be acquainted with Omar or at least know of him. Nevertheless, the call caught him by surprise, a circumstance which frequently occurs in the real world of business. Assuming a willingness to share information, the response was a positive and accurate assessment of Wilma's job performance.

Students will have a variety of answers to the question. A key point is to recognize the importance of protecting oneself from legal problems related to references. Stan might have said, "With Wilma's permission, I'll be glad to discuss her work record. Please have her contact me." In practice, persons who provide references are often willing to share positive comments but are more hesitant about expressing negative views.

2. **What, if anything, should Stan say to Wilma about receiving the call from Omar?**

This is a difficult question, and the answer frequently depends upon the nature of interpersonal relationships. If respectful, trusting, and cordial relations prevail, it is more likely that Stan will comment informally about the call. Some students will suggest that Stan be candid and simply tell Wilma about the inquiry. Others will recommend that nothing be said. A personable approach might be for Stan to relate specifics (his comment about her fine performance and hope that she is not hired away from Haywards) of the reply to Omar. This response expresses how Stan feels about Wilma's job performance and might evoke an explanation of her reason for seeking other employment. Hearing how the boss feels is important to most subordinates and might encourage Wilma to remain at Haywards.

3. **In addition to the career-advancement opportunity, what factors should Wilma consider if Omar makes a job offer?**

Wilma must consider the extent of her interest in becoming a regional manager. Acceptance of a new position involves making adjustments—new superiors, subordinates, and job responsibilities. Learning these new responsibilities will be time consuming, and added travel could be a necessary consideration. Accepting the job may necessitate moving to another geographical location. Omar may not have the same managerial philosophy, and the new employer will likely have different operating policies and procedures. Also, Wilma should consider her ultimate career goal and determine whether Omar's position is a step toward attaining it.

4.   **Assuming that Wilma does leave Haywards, how should Stan go about recruiting her replacement?**

Replacement of capable personnel is generally a challenge. To fill vacancies, many firms follow the practice of promoting from within. This approach conveys a message that job-performance excellence is recognized and rewarded. On the other hand, a person recruited from outside the company may possess needed expertise and be a source of new ideas. In addition, such a person is not disadvantaged because of prior managerial decisions that may have alienated people. The recommended procedure is for Stan to promote from within if possible.

Incident 7-2: GREATER EXPECTATIONS

1.   **What type of training is recommended for Judy?**

Judy's initial concern is to become computer literate, as computer skills are essential in today's office environment. The company will likely provide training for employees to learn the new system. However, Judy will likely find it worthwhile to take evening management courses as a way of learning about management. She has demonstrated an ability to handle a heavy workload, but this is not the same as managing others who are expected to get tasks accomplished. On-the-job development of management skills will generate pressure on Judy's time and energy. Nevertheless, there might be opportunities to oversee persons doing various job tasks.

2.   **How could the special-assignment method be used to train Judy?**

Special assignments (perhaps completing a needed project, developing a proposal, or preparing a plan for change) serve as a technique for professional development. Assignments might involve an array of activities, including those that are community related. Many insights into management can be gained by participation in fund raising drives for the United Way.

If special assignments are used, Don should not overlook Judy's already heavy workload. He needs to remember that this technique is best utilized in circumstances where trainees have control over the flow of work. Quite likely, Judy does not have the flexibility to control the sequence and timing of many required job tasks. Practically speaking, some assignments may have to be completed on her own time. If she is interested, however, the learning might be quite valuable to her future career.

3. **Should Judy be considered as a potential candidate for the office-manager position? Explain your response.**

Judy has compiled an excellent performance record. The case is somewhat vague about the extent of Judy's managerial experience. Some experience might have been gained by supervising the department's former receptionist and part-time secretary. Her abilities to organize tasks, assume a heavy workload, meet deadlines, and cooperate with colleagues demonstrate potential for success as a manager. Seemingly, Judy possesses considerable talent. Her biggest drawback is the lack of significant managerial experience.

4. **If approval is granted to hire a part-time employee, what duties should be stated in the job description for the position?**

This question is designed to help students understand the content of a job description. Various answers are possible. Refer to the figure illustration in the text. Students will likely list some duties currently performed by Judy that might be delegated to a new assistant. Representative responses are: (1) type letters, memos, and reports; (2) file correspondence; (3) serve as a receptionist to greet customers and answer the telephone; (4) provide information about job vacancies to potential applicants; and (5) assist in processing employment applications.

Incident 7-3:   WE'VE GOT A PROBLEM

1. **How effective is the existing approach to training at Beauty Cosmetics?**

The present approach to training seems to be fragmented and dependent upon skills possessed by each individual who sponsors new recruits into the organization. If sponsored by skilled trainers, training is likely to be quite adequate. However, it appears that training is not receiving sufficient attention, and consequently, consumer complaints have emerged as a problematic concern.

2. **What training options could Helen be overlooking?**

Helen might consider development of a series of seminars to be held periodically at various locations. These seminars can be designed to include lectures, role playing exercises, and discussions. Videotaped instruction is easily integrated into the seminar format. Also, these tapes can be made available to persons who are unable to attend training sessions. And, it's feasible to prepare self-study materials for new recruits to review at their own leisure.

3.   **Will a simplified consultant's training manual and the proposed "training skills checklist" remedy difficulties with customers? Explain your answer.**

These items are not likely to remedy all consumer-related difficulties; however, they represent an important first step. Simplification of the manual could make it more practical and increase its use. Perhaps, the current manual is incomplete, confusing, or difficult to read. If so, it probably is not being used effectively. The checklist will serve as a reminder of important factors that should be explained and discussed with new recruits. Sometimes, more experienced consultants may take too much for granted and wrongly assume the extent of knowledge and understanding possessed by newcomers.

4.   **How can recruiters of new consultants become better trainers?**

Trainers must be concerned about both content and training methodology; each is critical to instruction. They need to understand how people learn and be familiar with various training methods. And, knowledge of the subject matter is absolutely essential. It's important for trainers to set aside sufficient time for training activities and demonstrate empathy toward learners who are embarking upon a new experience.

5.   **What is the most important training priority at Beauty Cosmetics?**

Students will have a variety of responses to this question. Seemingly, the training function should receive greater attention in order to assure that new recruits receive sufficient preparation. Product knowledge, sales techniques, and communication skills are primary areas in which additional training is needed.

Study Guide Assignments

The individual case assessment presents the experience of two students who apply for the same job and explains key criteria used by an employer to select one of the applicants. In this exercise, students are encouraged to think about pros and cons of an employer's approach to interviewing, especially the heavy reliance on nonverbal signals.

Even though qualifications are similar, do interviewers favor different job applicants? This question serves as a basis for the group case assessment, which involves a role playing and then invites students to discuss their observations.

Video Cases

3 cases from the Blue Chip Enterprise Initiative*

Rhino Foods

Focus: **Staffing and Training**

Summary:

You might think Ted Castle would have been all smiles over a corporate customer's appetite for his chocolate-chip cookie dough. However, he knew that the customer's sudden demand for a mountainous increase in supply could give his small business a critical case of indigestion.

Castle's Rhino Foods, Inc., of Burlington, Vt., had comfortably been making various dessert products for years when, in 1991, Ben & Jerry's Homemade, a large producer of ice cream and ice cream novelties, put Rhino dough in a new product it was introducing, chocolate-chip cookie dough ice cream.

Ben & Jerry's released the flavor to retailers in April and by June was selling it in unimagined quantities. Castle, who had been supplying 32,000 pounds of cookie-dough pellets a week, was asked to quadruple that amount in three weeks. If he didn't answer yes within 48 hours, he was told, Ben & Jerry's would get a secondary supplier. As he drove to Burlington from Ben & Jerry's headquarters in Waterbury, Vt., 40 minutes away, Castle stewed over the need to expand production in a rush that could lead to accidents, errors, even loss of the Ben & Jerry's account altogether. Also, he had limited funds.

But the opportunity was too good to miss. He bought new equipment and had a wall moved for more space, getting a loan from Ben & Jerry's and negotiating extended-payment terms from suppliers. Procedures for making the dough pellets had to be redesigned, and Castle, a believer in employee empowerment, relied for ideas on the employees who were doing the work.

Within the year Rhino moved to larger premises and bought more equipment, thanks to loans from the U.S. Small Business Administration, Vermont's Industrial Development Association, and Burlington's Community Economic Development Office.

Ben & Jerry's was providing 80 percent of Rhino's business. But occasionally it cut orders, leaving some skilled production workers with little to do. Castle hated layoffs for their effect on remaining employees' morale, on unemployment compensation insurance rates, and on the quality of job-seekers when Rhino was ready to rehire. Also, it was costly to train new workers.

Brainstorming among employees produced a creative solution: exchanges with other companies that also had up-and-down staffing needs. Two firms have taken six Rhino employees temporarily, and Rhino, which has a staff of 60–up from 16 in 1991–is planning to repay the favor.

(Castle is also repaying Burlington for its support. He has set up a job whose function is to give time, money, product, and personnel to community needs.)

To avoid over dependence on Ben & Jerry's, new products were created and marketers hired. Sales accounts were maintained by building relationships: Customers receive regular phone calls to be sure things are going well.

A New Jersey grocery chain requested an Irish cream cheesecake. Rhino created one, along with appropriate packaging, and the product was in the stores inside a month.

Today Ben & Jerry's represents only 50 percent of Rhino sales, which totaled $5.5 million in 1993–a fivefold increase over 1990–and are projected to rise strongly this year. Castle is very glad he didn't miss that big opportunity.

Discussion Questions:

1. How was Rhino Foods able to meet higher production expectations necessitated by the large order received from Ben & Jerry's?

    In addition to the purchase of equipment, redesign of procedures, and modifications to gain additional space, Ted Castle initiated goal setting, solicited employee involvement, and listened to views of workers. Effective staffing and hiring practices are keys to productivity accomplishments. Likely, Rhino Foods did an excellent job of preparing personnel to handle the increased volume of production.

2. Why was it important to address the problem of occasional underutilization of facilities, which could ultimately necessitate layoffs of personnel?

    Reducing employee turnover and retaining the services of trained people can certainly have positive impacts on a firm's "bottom line." A stable labor force helps assure availability of persons who possess needed job skills. Layoffs have a negative impact on morale and may make it more difficult to hire employees who will not accept jobs involving high probabilities of consistent layoffs.

Carolina Fine Snacks

Focus: **Staffing and Disabled Workers**

Summary:

"The day David Bruton showed up for work was the day things began to take a dramatic change for the better," says Philip Kosak, a vice president of Carolina Fine Snacks.

Kosak and two fellow Ph.D. food scientists, Craig Bair and Ray Leander, left good jobs at a big company to try entrepreneurship, founding Carolina Fine Snacks in 1982. The Greensboro, N.C., firm, a manufacturer of popcorn, fried cheese curls, fried pork skins, and similar munch food, faced one tough challenge after another. The toughest, Kosak says, was finding reliable workers.

On average, one employee in five would be absent on a given day. Turnover? "With 15 full-time employees, we had over 200 people on the payroll in a little more than a year." Theft was high, productivity low.

Bruton's last job had been with a hotel chain, third shift, cleaning floors. At Carolina Fine Snacks' plant he "immediately began asking what he could do to help, a question we had never heard out of an employee," ways Kosak. "He loved the work and was always on time and anxious to start."

His enthusiasm was infectious, and soon there was a new climate in the plant. Other employees worked harder. Some quit.

Invariably, those who quit were replaced by job candidates sent by a local vocational rehabilitation office. Carolina Fine Snacks had hired Bruton there when it took part of an exercise to teach people with disabilities how to handle job interviews. Bruton had a learning disability and was legally blind.

"Within a year over half our staff were persons with disabilities," Kosak says. "The revolving door closed. Turnover and absenteeism dropped to next to nothing. productivity skyrocketed."

The company raised wages and offered full health benefits and paid vacations to all its employees, who number 20 today.

For three years following its founding, Carolina Fine Snacks had no employees—just Kosak, Bair, and Leander. "We would make a sale and then come back and manufacture the order ourselves." Kosak says.

After volume rose enough to permit hiring, the company ran into a problem comparable in gravity to that of employee quality. Food retailers had begun to charge manufacturers for space on their shelves. In North Carolina the fee was as high as $1,500 per food. "Even if we had the money, we were unwilling to participate," Kosak says.

Carolina Fine Snacks looked for niche markets. Technology it had developed gave its pork skins a shelf life much longer than competing products'. that provided an edge that landed the firm a government contract. The firm began pursuing international sales, eventually winning approval to sell four products in Japan. It also has two Pacific Rim joint ventures.

When a market developed for nutritionally superior snack foods, the company produced some with lower fat content, higher fiber, less salt, etc. It won contracts with enterprises like Weight Watchers and Amway.

A good reputation won it the opportunity to supply pork skins for George Bush et al at the 1988 G.O.P. Convention. Subsequent publicity brought the firm to the attention of the vocational rehabilitation office where it found David Bruton.

Today, with annual sales at the $1.2 million level, Carolina Fine Snacks is thriving in an industry where many small firms are collapsing. Says Kosak: "The cream will rise to the top."

Discussion Questions:

1.   Why did Carolina Fine Snacks originally experience such high employee turnover?

Turnover occurs for any number of reasons: improper job design, low wage rates, lack of promotional opportunities, management styles, difficult-to-operate equipment, or a poor match between job demands and worker expectations. Possibly, some combination of these factors contributed to the high turnover experienced by the firm.

2.   Why did Carolina Fine Snacks begin to hire persons with disabilities?

David Bruton was an enthusiastic, capable worker who possessed a positive attitude. In essence, his actions encouraged management to focus on positive qualities that disabled persons might bring to the workplace. David likely served as a role model for many persons who subsequently became employees of the company.

Lewis Services

Focus: **Staffing and Training**

Summary:

Lewis Services, a custodial-janitorial company, would not be in existence today if its owner-general manager had not taken the right steps after three disasters.

- In 1984 the company lost half of its clientele in a 60-day period.
- In 1992, through no fault of its own, the business got in big-time trouble with the Internal Revenue Service, was fined heavily, and as a result was unable to borrow funds.
- Also in 1992, because of what owner Lenden Lewis describes as staff incompetence, a client responsible for almost half of the company's revenues left it.

A severe downturn in the oil industry, home of about 80 percent of Lewis Services clients then, caused the 1984 trauma. Owner Lewis, who had started the company three years earlier, reacted with a new marketing strategy. He added services that would appeal to companies outside the oil industry–landscaping, lawn service–and gained new clients. With an increased cash flow, he was able to buy equipment and add food service.

Lewis Services didn't live happily ever after, though. As already indicated, it had a very bad year in 1992.

An outside accountant was hired to do payroll, bookkeeping, account payables, and account receivables. At year's end a shocked Lenden Lewis was notified that payroll taxes had not been filed for some of the year.

The accountant was replaced with a new, in-house accountant, and arrangements were made with the IRS to set up a plan for payment of the fines and tax delinquencies. The company obtained new clients, built up receivables, and got by without additional credit. Last year, its tax problem solved, the company became computerized.

Lenden Lewis suffered an injury in 1992 that disabled him for eight months. Without his supervision, he says, employees were unable to perform competently, resulting in loss of the major client.

To remedy the situation, Lewis hired an operations manager who oversees the 40-odd employees, makes sure jobs are completed on time, and acts as general manager in Lewis' absence. A human relations manager was hired to interview job applicants, check references, and help in employee training and evaluations. Employees who were not performing were terminated. All employees go through a 30-day evaluation period now and must pass any drug tests administered.

The improvement in hiring practices improved the quality of Lewis Services' work and helped it add to its client list, bringing annual sales to an impressive figure. One addition, after 13 months of negotiations, was the major client lost in 1992.

Discussion Questions:

1.   In what ways does the case of Lewis Services illustrate the importance of staffing and training?

      An outside accountant did not keep accurate records and contributed to problems involving the Internal Revenue Service. On the other hand, the screening process, which involves accountability for previous employment and character references, appears to aid in the selection of capable workers and also helped reduce employee turnover. Improved hiring practices enable the firm to be more competitive and attract additional customers.

2.   Why is the quality of personnel an especially relevant concern to Lewis Services?

      Capable, well-trained staff members are essential to a firm's ability to be profitable and meet competitive challenges. When workers successfully perform their jobs, managers can devote efforts to meeting managerial responsibilities with less likelihood of encountering unexpected problems, such as those related to expenses that are out of control or unmet governmental obligations.

Source: excerpted from Real-World Lessons for America's Small Businesses 1994, pp. 24-25, 27-28, and 134-135, Connecticut Mutual Life Insurance Company

Chapter 8

Leading

▤ Chapter Overview

As indicated in this chapter, leadership is a complex skill that requires careful study to understand and practice effectively. If effective leadership was always simple and easy to practice, organizations would have a surplus of capable leaders. Instead, there is a shortage of such talent in many companies.

To help students analyze different leadership situations and select an appropriate style of leadership, this chapter reviews a wide range of expert views on leadership. In doing so, important aspects of the trait approach to leadership and key leadership strategies associated with the behavioral approach and the situational approach to leadership are discussed. The concept of transformational leadership is also examined. Last, the importance of self-managing work teams is explained.

▤ Teaching Objectives

The teaching objectives of this chapter are to:

1. Define leadership.

2. Explain the trait approach to leadership.

3.   Identify and describe key theories of the behavioral approach to leadership.

4.   Identify and describe important theories associated with the situational approach to leadership.

5.   Describe a self-managing work team.

▨ Chapter Outline of the Text

▨ Key Terms

These terms are introduced in the chapter. Definitions are included in the glossary of the text.

Behavioral approach
Consideration
Contingency model of leadership
    effectiveness
Employee orientation
Initiating structure
Leader-member relations
Leader position power
Leadership
Leadership continuum
Leadership Grid
Management

Path-goal theory of leadership
Production orientation
Relationship behavior
Self-managing work team
Situational (contingency) approach
Situational control
Situational Leadership Model
Task behavior
Task structure
Trait approach
Transformational leadership

▨ Detailed Chapter Summary

I.   LEADERSHIP DEFINED

Learning Objective 1:   Define leadership.

Leadership is the process of directing and influencing the activities and behaviors of others through communication to attain goals.

II.   MANAGEMENT VERSUS LEADERSHIP

Management involves using human, equipment, and information resources to achieve various objectives. On the other hand, leadership focuses on getting things done through others. Thus, you manage things (budgets, procedures, etc.), but you lead people.

III.   THE TRAIT APPROACH TO LEADERSHIP

Learning Objective 2:   Explain the trait approach to leadership.

The trait approach to leadership seeks to identify key characteristics found in all successful leaders. No single personality trait or set of traits consistently differentiates leaders from nonleaders. However, certain core traits significantly contribute to a leader's success. These core traits include drive, the desire to lead, honesty and integrity, self-confidence, cognitive ability, and knowledge of the business.

Suggested Readings for this Section
Dreyer, R.S. "What It Takes to be a Leader--Today!," *Supervision 55 (May 1994), pp. 22-26.*

The author of this article cites Elton J. Masterson as indicating that leaders must be good at coaching and guidance. In this regard, leaders must be able to earn the loyalty and gain the cooperation of employees. The best employees are attracted to companies led by managers who create a work environment that promotes employee development. According to the author, managers who can help employees develop on the job are also effective communicators.

Kinni, Theodore B. "Leadership Up Close: Effective Leaders Share Four Major Characteristics," *Industry Week (June 20, 1994), pp.21-25.*

Companies depend heavily upon capable leadership to succeed. Research by James Kouzes indicates that four characteristics are especially important to business leaders. First, a manager must be honest. In this regard, managers are cautioned not to make a promise they cannot keep. Being forward-looking is the second characteristic. Capable managers look beyond the present to anticipate future needs of the company. Forward-looking managers have a vision they can communicate well to employees. A third characteristic present in many outstanding managers is the ability to be inspiring. In addition to having a vision, capable managers have the ability to inspire others to adopt and pursue the vision. The fourth characteristic is competence. That is, outstanding managers must have the competence to implement an effective business strategy.

IV.   THE BEHAVIORAL APPROACH TO LEADERSHIP

Learning Objective 3:   Identify and describe key theories of the behavioral approach to leadership.

The behavioral approach to leadership focuses on behaviors that differentiate effective leaders from ineffective leaders. The Ohio State Leadership studies and leadership research at the University of Michigan have identified two broad classifications of behavior associated with successful leaders: an emphasis on production and quality relationships with subordinates. In turn, the Leadership Grid states that the most effective managers have a high concern for both production and people.

Teaching Hint: Encourage students to consider the short-run <u>and</u> the long-run implications of different leadership behaviors. A manager's behavior that produces quick results may hurt the long-run performance of employees.

V.   THE SITUATIONAL (CONTINGENCY) APPROACH

Learning Objective 4:   Identify and describe important theories associated with the situational approach to leadership.

According to the situational approach to leadership, there is no single best leadership style. Instead, the situation determines the appropriate leadership style. Established situational or contingency leadership theories include:

- Tannenbaum and Schmidt's leadership continuum, which illustrates leadership behaviors that reflect the varying levels of authority exercised by managers. Forces in the manager, subordinates, and situation determine which leadership behaviors are selected.

- House's path-goal theory of leadership proposes that a manager's leadership style will be motivating to the extent that subordinates believe it will help them to achieve things that they value.

- Fiedler's contingency model of leadership effectiveness theorizes that the appropriate leadership style depends on the leader's personality and on how favorable the leadership situation is to the leader.

- Hersey and Blanchard's situational leadership model considers the readiness level of an employee to be the critical factor in determining an appropriate leadership style.

Teaching Hint: Emphasize that managers need to take some risks and empower employees if they want to see those employees develop on the job. For example, continuous use of high task behavior by managers practically guarantees that employees will become dependent individuals on the job with limited ability to accept much responsibility.

VI.   TRANSFORMATIONAL LEADERSHIP

Transformational leadership occurs when leaders inspire and motivate followers to put aside their individual self-interests and work diligently to accomplish organizational goals.

VII.   GENDER AND LEADERSHIP STYLES

Large numbers of women are continuing to acquire the experience and professional training needed for positions as managers. As women move into more managerial jobs, one expectation is that they are drawing on the skills they have acquired from their own experiences instead of automatically adopting the traditional leadership styles used in male-dominated jobs. Another expectation is that female managers in general do not actually lead much differently than male managers. In either case, successful leaders in organizations include both men and women.

VIII.   RECOMMENDATIONS FOR EFFECTIVE LEADERSHIP

It is suggested that managers should carry through with decisions, train employees, show respect for employees, provide necessary resources for employees, and demonstrate confidence in employees. Managers should also set a good example, set realistic but challenging goals, be fair and consistent, and monitor the progress of important tasks.

Suggested Reading for this Section
Bartlett, Christopher A. and Sumantra Ghoshal. "Changing the Role of Top Management: Beyond Systems to People." <u>Harvard Business Review</u> 73, May-June 1995, pp. 132-142.

The Norton Company, an industrial abrasives manufacturer, was a competitor of the 3M Company until its poor performance led it to be absorbed by a French company in 1990. 3M succeeded because, unlike Norton, its leaders utilized a people-centered entre-preneurial model. This article discusses how personal interaction and communication between managers and employees is much more effective than statistical reports at helping employees utilize their abilities.

Harari, Oren and Chip R. Bell. "Is Wile E. Coyote In Your Office?" <u>Management Review</u> 84, May 1995, pp. 57-61.

In the roadrunner cartoon, the roadrunner prevails, and Wile E. Coyote fails. Roadrunners have many positive characteristics that enable them to succeed. This article offers leaders a list of six suggestions on how to create a "spirit of the roadrunner" culture. Each of the suggestions is discussed and companies that apply these techniques are identified.

IX.   SELF-MANAGING WORK TEAMS

Learning Objective 5:   Describe a self-managing work team.

A self-managing work team is a group of well-trained and cross-trained employees who have the specified responsibility and authority to complete a well-defined task.

A.   *The Benefits of Self-managing Work Teams.*

Even within a large organization, self-managing work teams can recreate the entrepreneurial spirit that exists in the start-up stage for most small companies. As a result, team members typically generate a high level of energy, commitment, and performance. Self-managing work teams also allow company operations to be streamlined in a way that often provides added flexibility, quality, and cost savings.

B.   *Creating Self-managing Teams*

When creating a self-managing work team, make sure that the duty to be performed by the team is clear. Also, determine what skills and resources are necessary for the team to complete its assigned function successfully. Select team members who possess the skills needed by the group, and make sure the team has a leader to get things going.

X.   LOOKING BACK

This chapter provides an introduction to the concept of leadership and an examination of approaches for selecting an appropriate leadership style.

▦ Answers to CONSIDER THIS Questions   (Page 260
■

1.   **Think of a person you consider to be a good leader. What leadership traits do you observe in this person?**

The traits many students have identified in the past are closely associated with the core traits of drive, the desire to lead, honesty and integrity, self-confidence, cognitive ability, and knowledge of the business. These traits are discussed in the section dealing with the trait approach to leadership in this chapter.

2.   **Why, in your opinion, are many people who could be leaders reluctant to accept leadership roles?**

Several students have indicated that it is due to low self-confidence. That is, people who have low self-confidence do not realize that they may have leadership potential. As a result, they are reluctant to accept leadership challenges that could help them develop their leadership potential.

3.   **What should a leader do to earn the trust and loyalty of subordinates?**

To cement a trusting relationship between themselves and their followers, successful leaders know that it is important to be truthful and reliable. They are open with employees, and they do what they say they will do.

Answers to CONSIDER THIS Questions   (Page 268)

1.   **Think about the leadership style you prefer to use when you are in a leadership position. How would you characterize what appears to be your natural style of leadership?**

Many students indicate that they prefer to use a democratic leadership style. That is, they want to focus more on having good rapport with their followers than on exerting a lot of task behavior. They probably lean toward this approach to leadership because they generally want to be treated this way by their bosses.

2.   **What leadership approach do you think has the best chance of working well in the majority of situations leaders face.**

Many students agree with Blake and Mouton that a team management style of leadership often works well. However, students may disagree with the view of Blake and Mouton that this style of leadership is best for all leadership situations.

3.   **Is it easier to lead a large number of independent or dependent employees?**

It is easier to lead a large number of independent employees. The reason is that independent employees who are motivated and capable do not need close supervision. They can run their own show. As a result, a manager can realistically be in charge of a large number of independent employees and expect for tasks to be performed well.

Answers to REVIEW AND DISCUSSION Questions

1. *How is management distinguished from leadership?*

   Management involves using human, equipment, and information resources to achieve various objectives. On the other hand, leadership focuses on getting things done through others. That is, you manage things (budgets, procedures, etc.), but you lead people. Management, therefore, is a broader concept, compared to leadership.

2. *What are some of the problems that plague the trait approach to leadership?*

   Four problems plague the trait approach. First, just being in a leadership position necessarily requires a manager to behave differently than employees. However, changes in behavior brought about by the requirements of a job do not mean that the manager has leadership skills. Second, the possession of any group of leadership traits by a manager does not automatically assure success. Some managers, for example, who look good on paper, fail on the job. Third, the trait approach does not consider the nature of the leadership situation itself. As a result, all leadership situations are viewed as being the same, which is not the case in reality. The traits of a successful religious leader, for example, may not be the same as the traits of a successful military leader. Last, not all successful leaders are exactly alike.

3. *What contribution has the trait approach made to the understanding of leadership?*

   No single personality trait or set of traits has been found that consistently differentiates leaders from nonleaders. However, evidence from trait research indicates that the possession of certain core traits significantly contributes to a leader's success. These core traits include drive, the desire to lead, honesty and integrity, self-confidence, cognitive ability, and knowledge of the business. Possession of these core leadership traits appears to contribute greatly to leadership success. Furthermore, these traits aid leaders in developing a vision for the organization and turning that vision into reality.

4. *According to Blake and Mouton, what is the best leadership style for managers to use?*

   Blake and Mouton have long claimed that team management is the one best style or approach for managers to take in leading employees. They state that through the use of a team management approach, communication between the manager and employees is enhanced. In addition, they believe conflict is more easily resolved, employees are more committed, and creativity blossoms when a team management style is employed. Blake and Mouton also claim that managers generally identify the team management approach as the best overall leadership style for achieving excellence.

5.   *How were the results of the Ohio State University and the University of Michigan leadership studies similar?*

Research conducted independently by Ohio State University and the University of Michigan led to the same conclusion. That is, some very successful leaders tend to focus primarily on the task to be completed, whereas equally successful leaders focus mainly on the needs of employees. Therefore, both approaches to leadership can be very successful. It is not that one approach is automatically better than the other.

6.   *According to Tannenbaum and Schmidt, what forces in a leadership situation should a manager consider when determining the appropriate way to lead?*

Tannenbaum and Schmidt identified four forces affecting the manager that stem from the leadership situation. First, a manager should consider the values and traditions of the organization. The second force relevant to the situation is group effectiveness. That is, how well employees work together as a group. The third force to be considered is the problem itself. Specifically, the manager needs to determine whether the problem is too difficult for the group to handle on its own. Time pressure is the fourth force relevant to many leadership situations.

7.   *According to the contingency model of leadership effectiveness, a manager's success in leading a work group is contingent upon what factors?*

Fred Fiedler's Contingency Model of Leadership Effectiveness states that a manager's success in leading a work group is contingent upon the task or relationship motivation (leader personality) of the leader and the extent to which the leader has situational control and influence.

8.   *According to Fiedler's research, why do task-motivated leaders generally perform best when their situational control is either high or relatively low?*

Task-oriented managers are determined to get the job done one way or another. Their self-esteem derives more from measurable performance than from how they are perceived by their subordinates. If the work group supports the task-oriented manager's strategy, he or she will step back and let the group implement the strategy. These managers can be very pleasant when things are going their way. However, they are going to make sure the job gets completed, even if subordinates do not like the job or how it is being done. Therefore, under conditions of low support, high task orientation may be the only way to get the task completed.

9.   *According to the path-goal theory of leadership, what determines whether a manager's leadership style will be motivating to his or her employees?*

Path-goal theory proposes that a manager's leadership style will be motivating to the extent that employees believe it will help them achieve things they value. The theory emphasizes the need for managers to clarify for employees the paths for obtaining goals and rewards valued by employees.

Answers to CRITICAL THINKING INCIDENTS

Incident 8-1: DESIGNING A LEADERSHIP APPROACH

1.   **According to Hersey and Blanchard's situational leadership model, how do the job-relevant levels of readiness differ for the designers and the sewing machine operators?**

The designers are highly trained and experienced in designing men's and women's fashions. They are proud of their designs, they take their work very seriously, and they are well paid. The designers are given the time and artistic freedom to produce outstanding designs. In addition, they like their jobs. As a result, the level of readiness for the designers is probably high. On the other hand, the work performed by the sewing machine operators is fairly routine and uninteresting. Their work requires little skill and does not pay well. The jobs of the sewing machine operators is very structured, and the operators do not desire much responsibility. As a result, the level of readiness for the sewing machine operators is generally low.

2.   **Why is Tony having problems in the manufacturing plant? State the most likely reason.**

Tony's natural leadership style is to give employees responsibilities and leave them alone to make decisions. This approach is fine if the readiness level of employees is high. However, it usually does not work well for employees who have a low level of readiness. As a result, Tony's leadership style is inappropriate for the sewing machine operators. Specifically, the operators do not want a lot of responsibility. Their jobs must be performed according to specific procedures, and allowing them a lot of flexibility in how they perform their work is likely to create manufacturing problems. Instead, a leadership style that utilizes high task behavior is appropriate for the sewing machine operators.

3.   **How should Tony attempt to lead the employees in his company?**

Tony should use a high task and low relationship behavior style of leadership in leading employees whose level of readiness is low. He should use a low task and low relationship behavior leadership style in leading employees whose level of readiness is high.

Incident 8-2:   THREE'S A CHARM

1.   **How appropriate is Dan's leadership style for the employees he must lead?**

Actually, for leading employees who are inexperienced, Dan's leadership behavior of closely supervising their work is appropriate. That is, they need a lot of guidance. Inexperienced workers need to be shown what needs to be done and how the work should be performed. However, assuming they are lazy and chastising an employee in front of others is usually unwise.

2.   **What is your reaction to Dan's statement that he doesn't think his employees are ever going to be ready to accept greater responsibility?**

With Dan's negative assumptions about the employees, it is unlikely that they will soon be ready to accept greater responsibility. The employees observed the harsh treatment given to the worker who did attempt to improve the way a job was performed. As a result, they do not see anything to be gained by showing initiative.

3.   **What recommendations can you make that will enable Dan to become a more effective leader?**

Although Dan hires workers who are inexperienced, they will basically stay inexperienced if Dan continues to operate under the philosophy of "If you want something done right, you have to do it yourself." To develop the workers into employees who can perform increasingly challenging work without such close supervision, Dan needs to gradually give the workers increased responsibility and encourage them. Dan should realize that he will be more productive with workers who are being developed and can work with less supervision, than always engaging in close supervision and making important decisions himself. Dan should avoid chastising an employee in front of others.

Incident 8-3: CHANGING WEATHER PATTERNS

1.   **According to path-goal theory of leadership, what key aspects of the weather analysts' job at Weathertronics should be considered in determining an appropriate leadership style for the new manager?**

In selecting an appropriate leadership style, the new manager should take into consideration the following key aspects of the weather analysts' job. The job of the weather analysis is ambiguous. The weather analysts must evaluate reams of technical data collected by various means. There is no single formula available that will always convert the data into a completely accurate weather forecast. Instead, the weather analysts must continuously refine their forecasting techniques and build on their collective wisdom to create superior weather predictions. They must continue to monitor new data relevant to their forecasts. As a result, their job is very stressful.

2.   **What is known about the analysts that will be important in determining an appropriate leadership style?**

The weather analysts employed by Weathertronics are competent, but many are young and realize they will benefit from all the help they can get. They understand the importance of getting reactions from other company analysts to their forecasts before releasing them. They perform an ambiguous and stressful job.

3.   **What leadership approach does path-goal theory suggest for the new manager?**

The fact that the weather analysts' job is ambiguous indicates that some directive leadership behavior is needed by the new manager to let the young analysts know what is expected of them, how they are to do their job, and how they will be evaluated. Efforts by the new manager to be supportive will be valued by the analysts, because their jobs are naturally stressful and frustrating. The weather analysts realize they are competent. As a result, they will require a participative leadership style by the new manager to be most productive. The fact that the analysts have much ability also indicates that they will benefit from the new manager showing much confidence in them.

Study Guide Assignments

For this chapter, the study guide contains a valuable concept application section that contains six leadership scenarios for students to consider. An individual case assessment has also been prepared that challenges students to determine whether sufficient evidence of leadership ability exists for an employee named Jim.

The group case assessment provided gives students an opportunity to share their views on encouraging upward communication and employee involvement in decision making. After the group discussion occurs, the students are given additional information about the situation to consider in relation to their discussion earlier. A helpful self assessment leadership checklist is also available to help students evaluate their potential leadership ability.

Video Case

Northern Telecom

Focus: **Self-managed Work Teams**

Summary:

Northern Telecom, incorporated under the laws of Canada in 1914, is a large designer and manufacturer of fully digital telecommunications equipment. The company operates 42 manufacturing plants in eight countries, including the United States and Canada. Wireless Systems Plant, a subsidiary of Northern Telecom, is located in Calgary, Alberta, Canada. This facility has discarded the traditional corporate management structure and adopted the concept of self-directed teams.

Central to the operations at Wireless are the auto insertion teams. These self-directed teams come up with ideas to correct problems and address cost issues at the operator level. The philosophy is to focus on opportunities for improvement that may have been overlooked. The team approach provides the framework to act on these ideas without having to rely on management to solve problems.

Managers had to change their views on management and learn how to function as part of the team. Even the compensation system had to be adapted to support the team concept. With the old management method, people were unaware of the actual progress or quality of the products they were manufacturing. There was no direct day-to-day feedback. Now, an operator can go directly to a controller to ask a question and the controller will respond openly and willingly. Information sharing is a key part of feedback and at Wireless Systems charts are an essential part of the distribution of information.

Team members rotate functions and self-delegate responsibilities, but agreement as a team takes learning. Interpersonal skills training is often necessary to assist team members in communicating. Open communication is essential, and peer appraisals let team members know where they stand with the rest of the team before they hear it from their managers.

The reasoning at Wireless Systems is that rules should serve people. This plant is one big team with one big purpose. Even modest savings and detail improvements contributed by teams (towards zero defects) add up. As Mike Garrett, manufacturing manager, states, "The only way to remain viable is to be the most cost effective, quality product, delivered on time to the customer." With self-directed teams, Wireless is achieving this goal.

Discussion Questions:

1. Why did Wireless Systems plant break away from the old management methods to self-managed teams? What was involved in changing from the traditional system to self-managed teams?

    Wireless changed to self-directed teams primarily to become more cost efficient; teams on the factory floor are more capable of identifying cost-saving opportunities than managers in an office. Among the changes needed were learning to function as a team, access to information, and the compensation system.

2. What steps did the company take to assure that the self-managed teams would be successful?

    The company provided interpersonal skills training to assist employees in communicating and set up a system of peer appraisals for feedback.

3. What was the attitude of management at Wireless towards self-managed teams?

    There was most likely some skepticism at first. As teams made progress toward improving operations, any objections faded.

Chapter 9

Controlling

Chapter Overview

Control is a basic management function. The importance of the control function cannot be over emphasized, since it is through this function that management is made aware of how the firm is progressing in terms of their goals and objectives.

The basic control process as well as several different types of controls are analyzed in this chapter. Financial controls in the form of budgets and ratio analysis are particularly stressed. Finally, the characteristics of a good control system and some of the more common reasons why employees and managers may resist controls are discussed.

Teaching Objectives

The teaching objectives of this chapter are to:

1. Understand the main role of the control function in management.

2. Explain the control process.

3. Identify various types of control systems.

4. Discuss how controls vary, depending on the managerial level.

5.   List the characteristics of an effective control system.

6.   Examine why people tend to resist control systems.

▓▓ **Chapter Outline of the Text**

I.   THE IMPORTANCE OF CONTROL
   A.   The Role and Definition of the Control Process
   B.   The Control Process
      1.   Setting Performance Standards
      2.   Measuring Performance
      3.   Comparing Performance to the Standard
      4.   Taking Corrective Action
   C.   The Importance of Communication in the Control Process
II.   TYPES OF CONTROL SYSTEMS
   A.   Control of the Functional Areas
      1.   Human Resource Controls
      2.   Production Controls
      3.   Marketing Controls
      4.   Information Controls
      5.   Financial Controls
   B.   Budgets
      1.   The Advantages and Disadvantages of Budgets
      2.   Zero-based Budgeting
   C.   Ratio Analysis
      1.   Liquidity Ratios
      2.   Leverage Ratios
      3.   Operating or Activity Ratios
      4.   Profitability Ratios
      5.   Breakeven Analysis
   D.   Control Systems Based on Timing
      1.   Feed-Forward Controls
      2.   Concurrent Controls
      3.   Post-Action Controls

   E.   Controls Based on the Level of Management
      1.   Strategic Controls
      2.   Tactical Controls
      3.   Operational Controls
III.   CHARACTERISTICS OF A GOOD CONTROL SYSTEM
IV.   RESISTANCE TO CONTROL SYSTEMS
V.   LOOKING BACK
VI.   KEY TERMS

Key Terms

These terms are introduced in the chapter. Definitions are included in the glossary of the text.

Acid test ratio	Leverage (debt) ratio
Balance sheet	Liquidity ratio
Breakeven analysis	Marketing controls
Breakeven point	Nonmonetary budget
Budget	Operating (activity) ratio
Capital expenditure budget	Operating budget
Cash-flow budget	Operational controls
Concurrent controls	Overcontrol
Control function	Post-action controls
Control standard	Preventive corrective action
Current ratio	Production controls
Deviation from the standard	Profitability ratio
Feed-forward controls	Ratio analysis
Financial controls	Strategic controls
Human-resource controls	Tactical controls
Income statement	Total asset turnover ratio
Information controls	Zero-based budgeting
Inventory turnover ratio	

Detailed Chapter Summary

I. THE IMPORTANCE OF CONTROL

Every firm wants to know how they are doing in terms of reaching goals and objectives. The control function answers this question. Without an effective control system, a business can quickly encounter major financial troubles and take wrong courses of action. The control function gathers information from a variety of sources and tells managers if their plans are working properly. By monitoring different critical areas in a timely and accurate manner, management is made aware of changes and deviations in the direction that the firm is going. Control then tells managers where they have been as well as the direction they are heading.

A.   *The Role and Definition of the Control Process*

Teaching Objective 1:   Understand the main role of the control function in management.

Control is defined as "the process that helps to ensure that the firm's plans and objectives are being achieved or to determine what adjustments must be made in order to reach them." The control and planning functions are very closely related to each other. By gathering data from both external and internal sources, management is able to see if plans are working properly and, if not, what changes need to be made. A good control system should help management identify why plans are not working. Control activities should always be geared directly to tactical and operational plans, which are directly related to top management's long-term strategic plan. Finally, it is from management's plans that the standards, which will be monitored, are established.

B.   *The Control Process*

Teaching Objective 2:   Explain the Control Process

An excellent communication system is at the very heart of every effective control system. Everyone in the firm must be briefed on how the control system works and why it is necessary. Management must also be sure that all of the data are gathered very accurately and analyzed properly with the results communicated to appropriate personnel in the firm.

Teaching Hint: Be sure to stress the fact that a firm's control system will only be effective if everyone in the firm accepts the control process. In order to gain this acceptance, managers must be sure everyone understands the control process and why it is necessary.

The control process itself consists of the following four points:

1.   Setting Performance Standards.

The control standards usually come from the firm's planning process. Typically a firm will specify its goals and objectives in numerical terms. These numbers then become the standard against which measurements are based. The standards must be very clear, specific, and measurable. While not every objective is numerical in nature, some type of measurable number must be determined, even if it must be stated as a range of acceptable tolerances, or the firm's management will not be able to measure it. Everyone in the firm must know the standards that apply to them and to the firm as a whole.

2.   Measuring Performance.

Several questions must be answered in this step of the control process. Exactly what information or data will be gathered? How should it be gathered? How frequently should it be gathered? This step may be the most crucial to the control process. Many times, a firm must experiment to determine the answers to these questions. For example, how often should a milk bottling company stop the assembly line to check the bottles for proper full levels, etc.? Also, how many bottles should be randomly pulled off of the line? A very large number of bottles pass through the line every minute. If management only checks once an hour, then a lot of errors can be made if a problem should occur. If the line is stopped every five minutes, however, a lot of time and money may be wasted. By trying different time frames and learning the normal frequency of problems occurring, the answers to these questions can be found.

Teaching Hints: To illustrate the difficulty of this control step, ask your students to determine how they would measure learning in a management class, how often they would measure it, and what type of measuring devices should be used.

3.   Comparing Performance Against the Standard.

First, management must be sure that the right information has been gathered and that it is accurate. If the information does not directly relate to the standard being measured or has been gathered in a careless or very subjective manner, then the information may be useless. In any case, comparing questionable information against a standard is worse than not having any information at all, since you are now going to draw conclusions based on inaccurate information. Normally there is a range of acceptable deviation from the standard, since it is highly unlikely that specific goals, such as those for sales or profits, are hit exactly. In many cases, this range may be derived from experi-mentation or from industry averages.

4.   Taking Corrective Action.

If results are outside of the acceptable range of variation, then corrective action may be necessary. The main problem is to determine the real cause of the variation. Until this is known, management cannot formulate a new course of action. Many times, but not always, the cause will be quite obvious. When the cause is not obvious management must research internal and external sources to determine the cause. Once the true cause has been determined new plans can be derived. Occasionally, the cause may be beyond management's control, such as a downturn in the economy, and then new standards themselves will have to be set.

C.   *The Importance of Communication in the Control Process*

One possible problem that can subvert almost any control system is lack of employee acceptance. If employees and lower-level management do not completely understand why the control system is necessary, exactly how it works, how deviations from the standard may occur, and what to do about them if they do occur, a firm's control system will not be very effective. Only by communicating the answers to the above questions in a clear and specific manner, which also allows for employee questions and input, will a firm ever win them over.

Teaching Objective: Identify various types of control systems.

II.   TYPES OF CONTROL SYSTEMS

Control systems can take many forms. Some of the more common types of control systems involve: control of functional areas within the firm, controls based on timing during the production process, and controls based on the level of management.

A.   *Control of the Functional Areas*

Typically a firm has the following functional areas, each of which needs to have some type of control system in place.

1.   Human Resource Controls.

Controlling the quality of newly hired personnel, the progress and development of a firm's personnel and monitoring and controlling daily performance all fall under this area. Common types of controls include performance appraisals, disciplinary programs, observations, and training and development assessments. Since the quality of a firm's personnel, to a large degree, determines the firm's overall effectiveness, controlling this area is very crucial.

2.   Production Controls

All of the control systems in this area are designed to increase efficiency, cost/effectiveness, and quality in the production of products or services. Key areas that are typically controlled here include: quality, inventories, purchasing, scheduling, and waste management. With global competition increasing, all of these areas must be controlled very carefully, or a competitor may gain a company's customers and/or potential customers.

3.   Marketing Controls

Market controls are concerned with every aspect of the firm's market plan. This includes matching products to markets, promotion, distribution, and pricing. Every product or service offered by a firm is monitored to determine how successful it is and when the product should be discontinued or new approaches developed. New product development is another major aspect in this area. Finally, controlling the day-to-day activities of sales and customer service personnel is very important to every firm.

4.   Information Control

Firms have some confidential and sensitive information that they would not want to become general knowledge. Controlling access to computer data bases is the key to this area. Every firm must determine a balance between information employees need to do their jobs effectively and information that is considered to be nonessential. Firms also need to have a very good management information system that gathers accurate information on a continuous basis.

5.   Financial Controls

The importance of financial controls cannot be overstated. Understanding financial statements, budgets, and ratio analysis are some of the most common forms of control utilized in this area. The number of firms that has experienced bankruptcy due to losing financial control is endless. Every manager, therefore, must have a good understanding of these very basic financial controls.

B.   *Budgets*

Budgets are the most common form of financial controls used in business today. Normally, budgets are for a one year period of time, but they may be shorter or considerably longer. Some of the most common types of budgets are: operating budgets which estimate revenues and expenses for the firm for one year; cash flow budgets which illustrate whether the firm will generate enough revenues each month to cover its expenses; capital expenditure budgets which are developed to ascertain the expense and revenues associated with making major purchases of equipment (this type of budget typically covers several years in time.); and finally, nonmonetary or miscellaneous budgets which are used to allocate resources other than cash, such as floor space or materials.

1.   Advantages and Disadvantages of Budgets

The primary advantages of budgets are that they help the firm control expenditures, allocate resources fairly, and communicate to everyone the main areas of commitment within the firm. They can also be used to measure the firm's monetary performance.

The main disadvantages of budgets appear to be the following: (1) They take a lot of time to produce and are, therefore, costly. (2) They may be wasteful by encouraging managers to "pad" figures in case their budgets are cut or encouraging managers to always spend all of their budgets every year out of fear that next year's budget will be reduced if they do not spend it all. Budgets can also give an erroneous picture of managers who exceed their budgets because of circumstances beyond their control. Finally, budgets only show the monetary side without considering the long-term effect of an action.

In summary, budgets need some "flexibility" and should be developed and used in a manner that does not reward padding or excessive spending.

2.   Zero-based Budgets

This form of budgeting process asks managers to start each budget from zero and rejustify all items. It is intended to get managers to rethink the whole budgeting process and not simply add more to last year's budget.

Suggested Readings for this Section

Steward, Thomas A., "Why Budgets are Bad for Business," Fortune *(June 4, 1990), pp. 179-90.*

Budgets work fine for tracing where the money goes. However, when they become the main tool that top management uses to gauge performance, then they have gone too far. In firms where this is the case, lower-level managers will many times do all kinds of gaming tactics to make their budgets look good. When this occurs, the performance of the entire company suffers. Budgets can even discourage managers from doing appropriate actions out of fear of running over budget. The author of the article concludes by giving the following five points on how to build an effective budget:
1. Measure output, not input.   Look at earnings as well as costs.
2. Plan first, budget later.   Do not work off of last year's budget for next year's plan.
3. Budget for managers, not accountants.   Management budget reports should stress
    the areas of prime importance to their functional area.
4. Design against turf wars.   Try to look for ways to link budgets together
    horizontally, not vertically.
5. Build budget busting into the system. Include some contingency plans in your budget.

Gruner, Stephanie, "The Employee Run Budget Work Sheet," INC, *(February, 1995), pp. 81-83.*

Mid-States Technical Staffing Services, an engineering services firm in Davenport, Iowa, was experiencing declining revenues and profits in 1991 due to departmental power struggles between each other. To solve the problem, Mid-States instituted "open book" management where a company's financials are presented to all employees. Employees and managers were trained to manage fixed-cost line items in the budget with a bonus program tied to it. Employees actually picked budget line items for which they would be responsible, and these choices were matched with other employees who were involved in the daily operation of that area. Once the budget was all approved, employees would track expenses and note discrepancies. This bottom-up budget took a lot of training and coaching by managers, but the results for 1994 show costs down 15 percent over 1991 levels and profits at 11.3 percent as compared to 3.5 percent in 1991.

C.   *Ratio Analysis*

Ratio analysis is a way to show how the firm is doing in specific financial areas over a period of time or make comparisons to similar firms in the industry. Ratio analysis is utilized extensively by bankers and possible investors as well as the firm's management. Ratios are derived by taking figures from the firm's balance sheet or income statement and calculating the relationship that one figure has to the other figure. The following are the five most common ratios used in business today.

1.   Liquidity Ratios

     This ratio indicates a firm's ability to pay its current debts. The most common type of liquidity ratio is the current ratio, which takes a firm's current assets and divides them by the firm's current liabilities. An even more strict form of liquidity ratio is the acid test ratio, which removes the value of the firm's inventories from its current assets before calculating the ratio. This ratio states how well a firm could pay its current debts without selling any of its products.

2.   Leverage Ratios

     This ratio is also sometimes referred to as the debt ratio. It indicates the percentage of debt financing that a firm currently has against the value of its assets. To find this ratio, take the firm's total liabilities and divide that number by the firm's total assets. A high leverage ratio compared to the industry average may indicate that the firm would be at a competitive disadvantage if an economic downturn occurred, since it has a higher debt service to pay each month.

3.   Operating or Activity Ratios

     The two main forms of operating ratios are the inventory turnover ratio and the total asset turnover ratio. The inventory turnover ratio indicates how many times during a given year a firm turned over or sold its average inventory. This ratio is found by dividing a firm's net sales by its average inventory (beginning and ending inventories divided by two). This ratio is a good indication of how efficient a firm is in utilizing its inventory investment. The total asset turnover ratio indicates how efficiently a firm is utilizing its assets to generate sales. It is found by dividing the firm's net sales by its total assets.

4.   Profitability Ratios

     This ratio indicates how efficiently a firm is utilizing its assets to generate a profit. The most common profitability ratio is return on investment (ROI). This is found by dividing a firm's net profit (after taxes) by its total assets. This ratio indicates a percentage of return that a firm is getting for every dollar it has invested in assets. This ROI percentage is extremely crucial to investors and management of all profit seeking firms.

5.   Breakeven Analysis

This analysis indicates the level of sales that is required to cover all of a firm's costs. Breakeven analysis is normally done before starting a new business or launching a new product or service. It is also done when making a major purchase of equipment, etc. To find a firm's breakeven point in units or products, take the total fixed costs and divide by the product's selling price minus its variable costs. To find the breakeven point in sales, multiply the breakeven number of units times the selling price.

D.   *Control Systems Based on Timing*

Control systems can also be classified in terms of when they are used in the production process. The three most common types of control based on timing are feed-forward controls, concurrent controls, and post-action controls.

1.   Feed-Forward Controls

These are also known as preliminary controls as they are designed to be preventive in nature. Controls here try to eliminate problems before they occur. For example, a control system that checks all raw materials and component parts for quality before production starts would be a feed-forward control.

2.   Concurrent Controls

As the name implies, these controls take place as production is occurring. The various inspection points in producing a product are examples of this type of control. These types of controls are also referred to as "yes-no" concurrent controls, since production will stop if the control indicates a problem.

3.   Post-Action Controls

This type of control examines the results after the product or service has been produced. Comparing actual costs versus budgeted costs is one example of this type of control system. Based on the results, a firm may have to make adjustments in its production process or financial estimates.

Teaching Objective 4:   Discuss how controls vary, depending on the managerial level.

E.   *Controls Based on the Level of Management*

The type of controls used at different levels of management are different. Since top managers are concerned with long-range strategic planning, they are going to need different types of controls than supervisory managers who are concerned with the day-to-day operations.

1.   Strategic Controls

Since the long range strategic plans are the main concern of top managers, they are going to need controls which allow them to see "emerging patterns" in the business environment. In particular, these are controls such as trends in sales, costs, profits, and market share of entire product lines or of subsidiaries. Ratio analysis is another common form of control utilized at this level to identify trends. At this level, controls, must help top management to see the future as well as the past.

2.   Tactical Controls

Middle management is primarily concerned with tactical controls. Here, controls relate to store, division, or product sales, costs, profits, market share, growth trends, and budget data. By comparing figures to objectives and strategies, management will know whether changes need to be made in the firm's plans.

3.   Operational Controls

Lower-level managers or supervisors are concerned primarily with operational controls. At this level, controls are designed to assess the performances of individuals or work groups against performance standards. Operational controls are very precise and measure factors such as quantity produced or sold, quality levels, costs, and profitability. However, these controls are changing somewhat as more companies switch to more participative management styles. When this style of management is utilized, there is less emphasis on individual performance and more on group performance.

Suggested Readings for this Section

Kellinghausen, Georg and Klaus Wubbenhorst, "Strategic Control for Improved Performance," Long Range Planning (June 1990), pp. 30-40.

The difficulties of tying together strategic objectives with operational control is well documented. In this article, the authors illustrate how a $1 billion paper manufacturer/printing corporation, which operates in eight countries, solved this problem by translating strategic objectives into operating targets that are understood and accepted by line managers. To achieve this, each individual profit center must be analyzed both operationally (Are we doing business efficiently?) and strategically (Are we in the right business?). By getting local managers involved with a task force group, data were collected, analyzed, and sent to headquarters for further review. Inclusion of local managers in the process also helped in overcoming problems related to acceptance of the final strategic and operational targets.

Francis, Robert, "A New Vision of Quality Control," Datamation (April, 1990), pp. 70-72.

The use of new technology to increase quality is hardly new at General Motors Corporation (GM). What is new, however, is how they are using this new technology. In the past, GM used vision machines at the end of the line to check the quality of the parts it was manufacturing. What they, and many other manufacturing firms, are doing now is using vision systems to monitor the entire manufacturing process. To do this, many U.S. companies are following the lead of many Japanese firms. These firms utilize several less costly vision machines that monitor even small changes and stop the line so that defective products can be caught early. Even more important, the cause of the defects can be ascertained and corrected before any more defective products are made. Using technology to improve the manufacturing process rather than to just identify defective products is a major step forward in quality control.

III.   CHARACTERISTICS OF A GOOD CONTROL SYSTEM

Teaching Objective 5:   List the characteristics of an effective control system.

An effective control system must give management timely, accurate, and useful data, but it must do so in a manner which is acceptable to the employees affected by it.

Teaching Hint: Point out the fact that if the employees or lower-level managers feel that the controls on them are excessive or possibly even unfair, then there is a high probability that they will resist them and possibly even subvert them.

A.   *Involvement in the Control System*

Some form of employee involvement in the control system is absolutely essential. A good way to do this is to get them involved in helping to design the system right from the start as well as in making periodic revisions..

B.   *Control Strategies*

While various business situations require different control strategies, there are some common characteristics which seem to be present in virtually all effective control systems.

1.   The control must fit the organization and task characteristics.

The firm's business environment and preciseness of data that can be measured will influence the type of controls used. For example, quite informal controls will normally be used to monitor a research and development department or a new product development department. More explicit controls will be used where specific performance data are available such as in sales or production.

2.   The control system must provide timely and accurate information.

Accuracy and timeliness are critical. Management must consider three main factors: potential losses, potential dangerous outcomes, and the cost and complexity of the control system itself. Control systems do normally slow down productivity and, therefore, they are costly in terms of time as well as efficiency.

3.   The control system must be acceptable, clearly communicated, and understood by the people directly involved with it.

It is only natural for people to resist anything they do not understand. If everyone involved knows why these controls are essential and exactly how the system works, then resistance is normally reduced. Management must also be sure that the control system is not measuring factors that are beyond the employees control, or resentment is sure to build up.

4.   The control system should be cost-effective.

The control system cost must be measured against the total potential losses. In looking at costs of a control system, management must not only consider the initial cost of the system but also the costs of lost productivity due to work stoppages (in order to gather data and record it).

5.   The control system needs to monitor strategic elements of the business.

Management needs to be sure that the control system is monitoring the areas of the firm where the greatest potential losses may occur. For example, if potential losses from sales people padding their expense accounts is $5,000 per year while inventory shrinkage is $50,000 per year, it obviously makes sense to have a much larger control system on inventory control.

6.   Control systems should be difficult to manipulate.

Every organization has people in it who will go to great lengths to avoid "looking bad." The control system needs checks and balances for this reason, as well as to deter outright theft. There are numerous examples of companies who literally were thrown into bankruptcy because employees in key positions subverted the system and stole millions of dollars from them.

IV.   RESISTANCE TO CONTROL SYSTEMS

Teaching Objective 6:   Examine why people tend to resist control systems.

Almost everyone dislikes being very tightly controlled, and over-controlling people can be very expensive.

A.   *Problem Areas Related to Control Systems*

1.   Strict output control systems definitely increase job tension and stress levels.

Employees must understand why the controls are necessary and how the results will be used. Also, by controlling only strategic areas, stress can be lessened to some degree.

2.   Employees may engage in "gaming" tactics or behaviors that appear beneficial to management but really are not.

When only one control point, such as sales or costs, is used then employees may use some very questionable tactics to get these figures to look right. For example, low production cost figures are nice but not at the expense of quality.

3.   Information may be manipulated in several different ways.

"Smoothing" occurs when employees try to even out costs or sales figures from one month to another or one project to another. "Focusing" occurs when employees greatly enhance positive data while barely mentioning negative data. An example is submission of "inaccurate" figures, such as inflated budget requests, because they anticipate their budgets being reduced by management.

B.   *Possible Reasons for Resistance to Control*

1.   Overcontrolling employees

When even minor areas are being controlled tightly or control procedures are extremely detailed and time consuming, then a firm may be overcontrolling. Also, when an employee's every word and activity is monitored electronically, a lot of resistance will normally be the result.

2.   If management only uses one control point, or stresses the importance of one point over all others, that point will become an employee's total focus.

Multiple control points which have appropriate values are the best way to set up control points. The control points should also not conflict with each other, or resistance is sure to occur.

3.   Objectives that are being monitored must be fair and realistic in terms of the current environment.

When employees feel that the objectives being monitored are unfair or unrealistic, resistance is sure to follow. Management must work with employees in setting these objectives and be willing to change them when changes in the business environment warrant it.

V.   LOOKING BACK

This chapter has examined some of the varieties of control methods and techniques
utilized in the business world today. Every firm must achieve a balance between too
little and too much control. Two critical aspects that are clear, however, are that
management must make certain that key critical areas are properly controlled and that
a firm's employees understand and accept the control system in place.

Answers to CONSIDER THIS Questions (Page 290)

1.   **Where do performance standards come from, and why is it so important
       that they must be clearly understood by everyone?**

       Performance standards in areas such as sales, costs, profits, quantity, and
       quality are taken from the firm's organizational objectives. The control
       function completes the loop back to planning and sets the stage for new plans
       based on the results achieved. Everyone must clearly understand exactly what
       these standards are, or they will not know what specific data to collect, how
       often to collect it, or what comparison to make between the data collected and
       the standards.

2.   **How do you determine what information to gather, how often to gather it,
       and where to get it?**

       As stated in question one, everything starts with the standards themselves.
       Once a person understands them, he or she can start determining what exact
       information is needed in order to make a comparison between the data gathered
       and the standard. In areas that are easily quantified (like revenues, costs, or
       profits), the answer is obvious. In areas where numerical data are not always
       available, however, it becomes much more difficult, but even here, some
       measurements must be made. For example, if a standard was to increase the
       efficiency of the clerical pool by 10 percent next year, some forms of cost data
       and output data would have to be gathered over the year to see if efficiency
       had increased by 10 percent. The standard itself influences how frequently
       data are collected.   If the standard is long term, such as a 20 percent increase
       in market share by 1998, then six month or quarterly figures will probably
       suffice. For monthly standards, weekly or even daily figures may be needed.
       Finally, data should be gathered in a timely and accurate manner. For
       example, sales or cost data can easily be retrieved from the financial
       statements. Reliable data on customer satisfaction requires some form of
       customer contact in sufficient numbers to be statistically reliable.

3.   **Why is preventive corrective action so important?**

Preventive corrective action anticipates potential problems before they occur. Checking the quality of component parts and raw materials before production begins is the most common form of control in this area. Another form of control is to track repetitive breakdowns so that management can learn the normal life expectancy of various pieces of equipment and replace them before they malfunction and cause problems. Preventive corrective action also includes routine maintenance on equipment to keep it working as long as possible. All of these types of preventive corrective action have been found to be very cost effective.

Answers to CONSIDER THIS Questions   (Page 301)

1.   **Why do some firms not believe in doing extensive budgeting?**

While budgets do play a role in the financial control of almost all firms, some firms have determined that doing extensive budgeting in all areas may not be totally beneficial to them. For instance, budgets can be restrictive in areas such as research and development where costs versus returns are very difficult to determine. Budgets may also unfairly evaluate the effectiveness of managers who exceed their budget if top management does not look at the returns and/or circumstances surrounding the situation. Strict budgeting may also lead to "game playing," such as inflating budgets in anticipation of reductions. Finally, doing extensive budgeting costs a lot of money and takes a lot of time. In some very dynamic industries, things change so fast that the value of a budget may be limited.

2.   **How does a manager determine whether a firm's ratios are good or bad?**

A firm's ratios indicate a relationship between two different numbers taken from the firm's financial statements. A ratio, by itself, has little meaning. To give the ratios meaning, they must be compared against industry averages. Ideally, these industry averages will also be available and classified according to firm and marketsize. By comparing ratios against its ratios from pervious months or years, the firm can also see if it is moving in the right direction.

3.   **How can the results of a firm's break even analysis be deceiving?**

Breakeven figures for both units and sales volume simply tell a firm the point at which it stops losing money. While that in itself is valuable, most firms have a desired profit level in mind, and to be more useful, the breakeven analysis should also be done with this figure factored into the equation. The breakeven analysis also assumes constant fixed and variable costs, as well as a constant price per unit. Therefore, it does not take into consideration any cost savings from economies of scale or any price reductions which are usually necessary to reach higher sales levels. Finally, competitors, suppliers, and even consumer tastes are constantly changing, making the effective life of a breakeven analysis rather short in most business situations.

Answers to REVIEW AND DISCUSSION Questions

1.   *What is the main function of the control process?*

The control process helps a firm ensure that plans and objectives are being reached. The control process monitors various activities of the firm and allows management to know when deviations occur so that corrective action can be taken. Based upon the control process, new plans and strategies are developed which will hopefully put the firm back on track to reach desired goals and objectives.

2.   *How are the planning and control functions connected to each other?*

First, control takes the standards, which are part of the firm's goals and objectives, and uses them as a basis of comparison against the data collected. Control indicates any variation from these standards; if sufficiently large, management will institute new plans or new goals and objectives to rectify this situation.

3.   *How are the four basic steps in the control process related to each other?*

The standards are first identified in the control process from the firm's organizational plans. Next, performance in each standard area is measured accurately and as frequently as necessary. Third, a comparison is made between the data gathered and the performance standard. Finally, if deviations are sufficiently large enough to warrant action, corrective action is taken. If the results are positive, an analysis and continuation of the plan is implemented.

4.   *Why does communication play such a critical role in the control process?*

For the control process to work properly, everyone involved must understand (1) what the control process is trying to do, (2) accept the process as meaningful, (3) know how to accurately collect the data and how often to collect it, (4) understand what the data findings really mean, and (5) have some ideas on how to correct for negative deviations. If employees or lower-level managers do not understand any of these points completely, then there is probably going to be a breakdown in the firm's control process. Only by communicating the **what, why, how**, and **when** of the process can management ever expect employees to accept and properly carry out the control process.

5. *What is the breakeven point both in units and in dollars if a firm's fixed costs are $10,000.00, its variable costs are $15.00 per unit, and the selling price is $25.00 per unit?*

$$\text{Breakeven in units} = \frac{\text{Total Fixed Cost} \quad \$10,000}{\text{Selling Price} \ (\$25) - \text{Variable Costs} \ (\$15)} = 1000 \text{ units}$$

Breakeven = 1000 units x 25.00 (selling price) = $25,000 in dollars

6. *How can top management keep middle- and first-level management from continually increasing every new budget?*

The use of zero-based budgeting forces managers to start every new budget from zero, and then they must rejustify every expense item. This forces managers to look at the real necessity of every expense item, rather than simply adding a given amount to each item on last year's budget. Top management can also offer bonuses or some other incentive for managers who can reduce their budgets without reducing quality or efficiency.

7. *What information does a liquidity ratio provide to management? In addition to the managers of a firm, who else may be interested in this ratio?*

The liquidity ratio indicates a firm's ability to pay its current debt. It is found by dividing a firm's total current assets by its total current liabilities. While this ratio varies between different industries, a commonly accepted current ratio in the manufacturing industry is 2.0. This ratio indicates that the "typical" manufacturer has $2.00 in current assets for every $1.00 in current liabilities. There is also an even stricter liquidity ratio called the "acid test ratio." This ratio removes inventory from current assets and indicates how well a firm could pay off its current liabilities without selling any of its products. Besides management, bankers and suppliers would be very interested in the liquidity ratio. Also, current stockholders and potential investors or buyers would also be interested in this ratio.

8. *If a firm has a leverage ratio of 0.85 and the industry average is 0.70, is this good or bad for the firm? Why?*

The leverage ratio indicates the percentage of debt financing a firm currently has against their assets. It is found by dividing a firm's total liabilities by its total assets. If a firm had a leverage ratio of .85, 85 percent of the value of its assets are financed by debt, or for every $1.00 of assets, 85 cents is still owed. If the industry average is .70 or 70 percent debt on assets, this indicates that the firm is more heavily indebted than the average firm in its industry. A firm with a heavier than average debt service will have higher fixed costs than its competitors and be less able to handle a downturn in sales due to a recession.

9. *List at least four characteristics which exist in all good control systems.*

1. The system "fits" the organization and the tasks it is doing. The control system has the proper amount of flexibility to fit the firm's competitive environment, and it fits the work tasks being done in each area of the firm.
2. The control system provides timely and accurate information.
3. The control system is understood and acceptable to all people directly involved with it.
4. The control system is cost effective.
5. The control system monitors only strategically important elements in the business.
6. The control system is difficult to manipulate.

10. *Why might some employees attempt to subvert a control system?*

1. They are thieves and are stealing from the company.
2. If the controls are very strict, they may feel too much stress. Therefore, they may try to subvert the system.
3. If employees or managers "learn" that controls, like budgets, will normally be reduced by say 20 percent, then they may engage in a gaming tactic and artificially inflate the budget by 20 percent or more.
4. If the control system only focuses on one or two points, then these areas will always "look good" even if they have to smooth or even out figures, focus very strongly on them, or even report inaccurate figures.

▓▓ **Answers to CRITICAL THINKING INCIDENTS**
■

Incident 9-1: THE BREAD BOX RESTAURANT

1. **What do you think Ralph should do about this matter? What are the main issues that he has to deal with?**

Many students reading this incident will want to just deal with Jackie Ode, the dishonest employee. While this issue certainly must be dealt with, there is another equally important issue that also must be dealt with here, namely Mr. Leonard's poor financial control system. Mr. Leonard must revise his cash control system so this never happens again. He could possibly use pre-numbered checks with one copy going to the kitchen and the original to the cashier. Any "lost" checks would carry a substantial fine for the waitress. He also needs to personally total out the register against the checks every night.

Mr. Leonard also needs to decide what he wants to do with Jackie Ode. He can simply fire her, which is probably the most common solution utilized in the business world today. Another alternative, however, would be to continue her employment since it is a small town and he obviously knows her very well after six years. If he really believes that Jackie Ode is basically an honest person who simply became "too tempted" during tough financial times, then keeping her on is a logical alternative. This alternative also has the advantage of the possibility of getting his two or three thousand dollars back.

2. **What are the pro's and con's of keeping Jackie on as an employee? Of firing her? Which action do you recommend and why?**

First, let us look at the case for firing Jackie. The pro's for this choice are:
(1)   By firing her, you get rid of this whole situation once and for all.
(2)   By firing her, you are setting an example for your other employees as to what they can expect if they should decide to dip into the register.
(3)   Firing her is the logical thing to do because employees who steal from you once may do it again.

The con's of firing Jackie are:
(1)   You lose virtually any real chance of getting the money back.
(2)   You lose a well trained, well liked, waitress who may not be easy to replace.
(3)   If you fire her, it will be very difficult for her to get another job.
(4)   If you fire her, co-workers may react angrily.

The pro's of keeping Jackie Ode as an employee are:

(1)   You retain an otherwise good employee who may now become your most honest employee.

(2)   You may be able to work out a repayment schedule out of her salary or get her to agree to take out a bank loan and repay you immediately.

(3)   By giving her a second chance, you are showing both Jackie and your other employees that you are a compassionate and understanding person.

(4)   If there is another position available that she is qualified to handle that does not require handling money, this may be a possibility.

The con's of keeping Jackie are:

(1)   Some people strongly believe "once a thief, always a thief." Does a person want to have a non-trustworthy employee around that must be constantly watched?

(2)   An incorrect message may be sent to her co-workers. "It's OK to borrow from Mr. Leonard. If you get caught, just agree to pay him back."

(3)   If she now has the additional payment for the money she has stolen Jackie may not be able to make ends meet financially.

Recommendations for firing her or keeping her on are both acceptable and easily justified with the limited information provided in this case. One of the main points to stress is that there is another alternative besides simply firing her.

3.   **Do you feel it was ethical for Ralph to put $20.00 in the cash register to try to catch Jackie?**

This question is not a question of legality. Many businesses periodically do so to check on their cashiers. Some even tell their employees that this will occur occasionally, while others do not inform them. On the question of ethical behavior, both sides of this question usually will be raised. Students who are going to be managers someday need to learn to think like a manager and realize that what Mr. Leonard did was not done in a mean or malicious way. He was simply testing the honesty or accuracy of an employee. For students who still feel that putting twenty dollars in the register is unethical, you may want to see whether their view changes if the employees are told about this checking routine when they are hired.

Incident 9-2: SAIL RIGHT INC.

1.   **Find the BEP, both in terms of the number of sales that must be sold (units) and in terms of total sales.**

In solving both the breakeven problems and the ratios, it is very important to stress that this is not just a mathematical exercise. The real importance of these figures is determined when a manager asks this question, "What do these figures really mean to my business?" For example, once top management finds the breakeven point in units and dollars for their new sails, they then must ask themselves the following questions:
"How realistic is it to think that Sail Right will be able to sell 36 sails a month at a price of $750.00?" "How difficult would it be to sell 48 sails at $750.00?"
Both of these questions will, of course, force them to look at the market in terms of the total number of sails sold per month right now, competitive products, etc. Breakeven points force a firm to do some initial cost and marketing research and are used in a "preliminary" feasibility study. If these figures look good and the market data are favorable, then normally a firm will do more in-depth cost and market studies before actually making a decision on adding a new product line.

The ratio analysis is also a situation where you need to point out that the ratios, by themselves, are almost meaningless. They become meaningful when a manager understands what each ratio really means in terms of the firm's financial condition and when they are compared with industry averages or against a firm's previous monthly or yearly ratios. The comparison is really the most important part of the ratio exercise.

SAIL RIGHT

<u>BEP Problem</u>
Total Fixed Costs =	$14,100
Variable costs =	$350/unit
Selling Price =	$750

BEP

$$\text{in units} = \frac{TFC}{SP - VC} \qquad \frac{14,100}{750 - 350} = \frac{14,100}{400}$$

BEP/units   35.25 or 36 units (all decimal points indicate a partial sail and must be rounded up to the next whole number.)

BEP in sales   BEP X Selling Price

BEP/sales   36 X 750 = $27,000

2.   **Find the BEP in question 1 if the company wants to make a per-month profit of $5,000.00.**

BEP   =   TFC   +   P.G.   (profit goal)
                S.P.   -   V.C.

BEP   =   14,100   +   5000   19,100   =   47.75 or 48 units
                750   —   350   400

BEP in sales   =   BEP   X   S.P.   =   48 X   750   = $36,000

1.   Liquidity Ratio   =   Current assets   =   899,000   =   3.26
                          Current liabilities   276,100
                          Comparative rating   =   Good
    (The firm has over 3 1/4 dollars of assets for each $1 current debt.)

2.   Leverage Ratio   =   Total liabilities   =   852,100   =   .55
                          Total Assets   1,553,000
                          Comparative rating   =   Fair
                          (same as industry average)
    (Approximately 45 percent of the firm's assets are debt free.)

3.   Inventory   =   Net Sales   =   1,718,000   =   5.95
    Turnover   Average Inventory   288,500
                          (328,000 + 249,000)
                                  2
                          Comparative rating   =   Good
    (The firm sold the equivalent of their entire inventory almost 6 times.)

4.   Total Assets   =   Total Sales   =   1,824,000   =   1.17
    Turnover Ratio   Total Assets   1,553,000
                          Comparative rating   =   Poor
    (The firm could only generate $1.17 in sales for every $1 of assets.)

5.   Return of Investment   =   Net Profit   =   374,400   =   .241 or 24.1 percent
    R.O.I.   Total Assets   1,553,000
                          Comparative rating   =   Good
    (The firm received a 24 percent return on their investment.)

Incident 9-3: HOME FEDERAL SAVINGS AND LOAN

1. **What is the heart of the real problem here?**

    In trying to identify the heart of the problem in this incident, you are really asking, "What caused this problem to occur?" The main cause of the problem is clearly Mr. Taylor's erroneous assumption that the larger banks and savings and loans were about to enter the Toledo market, now that deregulation allowed them to do so. It should be noted that this trend of thought was very common among both bankers and the airline industry, which was also deregulated at the same time. Nowhere in the incident is any information given that actually points to this event happening. Other causes that lead to Home Federal's problems include purchasing savings and loans that were losing money without determining why there were in such bad financial shape and the onset of an economic recession with high inflation. There was not anything Home Federal could do about the recession, but as a lending institution, it certainly should have seen it coming and held off on any expansionary plans.

2. **Who is responsible for causing this problem to occur?**

    While the president, Mr. Harry Taylor, is the main person at fault, the board of directors is also to blame. Anytime a firm makes a decision that puts its future existence at serious risk, the top management staff and/or board of directors must demand the most thorough and complete analysis possible. They cannot approve any decision unless the odds of failure appear very small, since they are literally staking the future life of the firm on this decision. Neither the board or Mr. Taylor did this type of analysis.

3. **How can Home Federal stop this problem from getting any worse right now?**

    This question is something phrased in the business world as, "How do we stop the bleeding?" Home Federal has to stop their financial losses immediately. To do this, both the cost and revenue sides of the business need to be examined. First, costs must be cut severely and immediately. Each new savings and loan that is losing money must have its costs cut as much as possible. Personnel at all branches and at Home Federal will have to be let go, and all operating costs severely analyzed for possible reductions. On the revenue side, Home Federal needs to take a good look at possible sources of new revenues. A new marketing plan, which has minimal costs, needs to be developed and launched as soon as possible.

4. **What is your long-term solution to this problem?**

    The long-term solution appears to be a retrenchment strategy. Home Federal needs to get back to what it was doing well before this disastrous expansion plan was implemented. The first need is to analyze each new branch in terms of real turnaround potential. Those that look very poor should be closed and put on the market immediately for resale. If Home Federal is not able to sell the branches at a profit (which is probably going to be the case), they should let them go for the best price available and take the losses.

Home Federal also needs to take a good hard look at the makeup of its top management team. Mr. Taylor was dishonest with the board and instituted an extremely high risk venture on very little background or research data. He probably needs to be replaced. Although the incident never mentions them, one can only wonder about the rest of the top management team. Was there even one vice president who seriously questioned this venture? Finally, the makeup of the board itself obviously needs to be changed. Currently, it appears to be a "rubber stamp" board rather than a board seriously concerned with the interests of the stockholders.

If Home Federal can stop its losses and regain some loanable funds through the sale of some or all of the branches or some other assets, it might start making home loans again and slowly emerge from this disaster.

5.   **What is your contingency plan in case your first solution fails?**

If Home Federal is not able to stop its losses, then the only two real options are to either file for bankruptcy or try to merge with another bank or savings and loan. A merger is the preferred solution but very difficult to implement.

Study Guide Assignments

The individual case assignment for this chapter asks the student to play the role of a management consultant who is being brought in to help solve a quality control problem. In this case, a department manager is taking samples of inputs and outputs at the same time each day. He makes no changes if quality is acceptable when sampled. Since the department is not producing quality products, his system obviously is not working.

This case asks students how they would approach this problem and solve it. It is a good case to use to see if a student could develop a logical plan which starts with identification of defective parts in the products, determination of the causes, implementation of preventive controls, and development of a better concurrent and post-action control system.

The group project is a very good case to discuss the real meaning of ratios. The case asks members of a group to discuss what the numbers that are included in the ratio calculations really mean. While actual ratios are not calculated or given, the case is valuable from the perspective of helping students to gain some insight into what ratios are really telling them about the firm's financial situation.

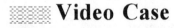

Video Case

Fullwood Foods

Focus: **Control and Performance Standards**

Summary:

Harlan Fullwood, Jr., left the police force after 24 years to go into business for himself. Through a unique program sponsored by Kentucky Fried Chicken (KFC), Fullwood now owns four of the country's most successful KFC outlets.

Fullwood lacked both the capital and experience to qualify for a fast food franchise. However, as part of the Reverend Jesse Jackson's program, Operation Push, KFC gave Fullwood an opportunity to purchase a KFC franchise. Fullwood worked hard and set an example to his employees; he took no pay for the first 18 months of operation.

Fullwood focuses on finding and encouraging the best employees and developing managers internally. He provides his employees with a generous benefits package. Today, Fullwood owns four KFC franchises in the Baltimore area, and two of them are among the busiest KFCs in the country.

Discussion Questions:

1.   What approach to control does Harlan Fullwood use?

        Fullwood appears to favor an organic approach. He talks about focusing on encouragement and working with people rather than emphasizing rules or regulations.

2.   What kind of feedforward and concurrent controls are found in a fast-food restaurant?

        In this environment, a number of control methods are likely. Feedforward controls include a budget; concurrent controls include having a manager on duty at all times.

Chapter **10**

Motivating Job Performance

▓▓▓ Chapter Overview

In this chapter, the fundamentals of motivation are presented with an emphasis on the importance of understanding the nature of this complex topic. Various theories of motivation are explained, including McGregor's Theory X and Theory Y, Maslow's hierarchy of human needs, Alderfer's ERG theory, and Herzberg's two-factor theory. In addition, expectancy, equity, and reinforcement theories are discussed.

The chapter concludes with coverage of motivation as it relates to self-motivation, empowerment of employees, goal setting, and development of organizational morale. These are relevant topics for persons aspiring to become successful managers.

▓▓▓ Teaching Objectives

The teaching objectives of this chapter are to:

1.   Define motivation and understand the motivation process.

2.   Discuss several commonly recognized motivation theories.

3.   Examine how communication influences motivation.

4.   Explain the concepts of self-motivation, empowerment, and goal setting.

5.   Understand how morale affects job performance.

Chapter Outline of the Text

    I.   UNDERSTANDING MOTIVATION
        A.   The importance of Motivation
        B.   The Motivation Process
   II.   PERSPECTIVES ON MOTIVATION
        A.   Management Perspectives
        B.   Communication Considerations
  III.   THEORIES OF MOTIVATION
        A.   McGregor's Theory X and Theory Y
        B.   Maslow's Hierarchy of Human Needs
        C.   ERG Theory
        D.   Herzberg's Two-Factor Theory
        E.   Expectancy Theory
        F.   Equity Theory
        G.   Reinforcement Theory
        H.   Motivation Theories: Implications for Managers
  IV.   MOTIVATION TECHNIQUES
        A.   Self-Motivation
        B.   Empowering Employees
        C.   Goal Setting
        D.   Building Organizational Morale
    V.   LOOKING BACK
   VI.   KEY TERMS
  VII.   REVIEW AND DISCUSSION QUESTIONS
 VIII.   CRITICAL THINKING INCIDENTS
   IX.   SUGGESTED READINGS

Key Terms

These terms are introduced in the chapter. Definitions are included in the glossary of the text.

Content theories of motivation
Continuous reinforcement
Cs of motivation
    Confidence
    Challenge
    Commitment
    Competence
Empowerment
Equity theory
ERG theory
Esteem needs
Existence needs
Expectancy theory
Extinction
Fixed-interval schedule
Fixed-ratio schedule
Goal setting
Growth needs
Hygiene factors
Intermittent reinforcement
Management by walking around (MBWA)

Maslow's hierarchy of needs
Motivation
Motivator factors
Needs
Negative reinforcement
Open-door policy
Organizational morale
Positive reinforcement
Probability assessment
Process theories of motivation
Punishment
Reinforcement theory
Relatedness needs
Safety and security needs
Self-actualization needs
Self contract
Social needs
Survival needs
Theory X
Theory Y
Variable-interval schedule
Variable-ratio schedule

Detailed Chapter Summary

I.   UNDERSTANDING MOTIVATION

Teaching Objective 1: Define motivation and understand the motivation process.

Motivation is an internal process for satisfying human wants, needs, and desires. Each person is unique and possesses different experiences, attitudes, and opinions. An understanding of motivation is needed by managers who face the challenge of motivating themselves and others.

A.   *The Importance of Motivation*

Human resources are essential to an organization's success. Managers should
recognize what factors are important to personnel. Employees who are treated
with respect, encouraged to excel, and rewarded for their efforts are more likely
to demonstrate motivated job performance.

B.   *The Motivation Process*

This process involves identification of needs and initiation of behaviors to
satisfy them. Fulfillment of needs leads to satisfaction. If needs are not
fulfilled, frustration will occur.

II.   PERSPECTIVES ON MOTIVATION

Managers play key roles in influencing employee behaviors. Employees do observe
behaviors of managers. It is important for managers to understand the Cs of
Motivation, which include confidence, competence, commitment, and challenge.

*Teaching Hint: Have students suggest words that describe motivated behavior and explain
reasons for choosing these words. Conclude the discussion by relating the suggested words
to the Cs of motivation.*

A.   *Management Perspectives*

Managers and workers do not necessarily have the same perspectives toward
job-reward factors. Management expectations can influence motivation. With
growing globalization, managers are increasingly challenged to motivate
employees in multicultural and multinational environments.

Teaching Objective 2:   Examine how communication influences motivation.

B.   *Communication Considerations*

Communication influences motivation to a greater extent than is often realized.
Lack of communication creates anxiety; unclear messages create confusion; and
miscommunication needlessly consumes time. Effective communication helps
managers to understand the needs and wants of their employees.

Suggested Readings for this Section:
Farnham, Alan. "Mary Kay's Lessons in Leadership." Fortune 128, September 20, 1993, pp. 68-77.

The philosophy of Mary Kay Ash, founder of Mary Kay Cosmetics, has motivated many beauty consultants to achieve outstanding sales accomplishments. At Mary Kay, recognition is earned through sales production. Organizational politics does not play a role in the firm's motivation and reward structure. May Kay is quite adept at convincing people that they can accomplish almost anything. Mary Kay Cosmetics has an impressive record of growth. Sales grew from $198,000 in 1963 to over $613 million by 1993.

Filipezak, Bob. "Why No One Likes Your Incentive Program." Training 30, August 1993, pp. 19-25.

Reward systems often fail because they are not designed to cure long-term business problems. Also, many firms do not pay enough attention to obstacles that can negatively impact performance. Different views prevail concerning merits of cash and noncash rewards. As related to noncash rewards, managers should not overlook the concepts of trophy value (having a reward to show peers) and perceived value (the perception of cost for an award versus its actual cost). Communication is a relevant concern, as employees talk about some types of rewards more than others. Managers need to communicate status reports so employees know how their efforts are progressing in relation to goal accomplishment.

III.   THEORIES OF MOTIVATION

Teaching Objective 3:   Discuss several commonly recognized motivational theories.

Various theories have evolved to explain motivation. Content theories of motivation are concerned with identifying the specific internal needs that motivate individuals. Process theories of motivation describe and analyze how internal personal factors impact certain behaviors.

A.   *McGregor's Theory X and Y*

Theory X emphasizes control to assure compliance. Theory X managers often practice an autocratic management style and may use the threat of punishment to induce employee productivity. Theory Y stresses management through employee input and delegation of authority. Managers advocate the Theory Y approach solicit ideas from employees and delegate responsibilities to them.

B.   *Maslow's Hierarchy of Human Needs*

According to Maslow, needs are arranged in a hierarchical order. Lower-order needs are satisfied before efforts are directed toward satisfaction of higher-order needs. Once satisfied, a need is no longer motivational.

1.   Survival Needs

Survival needs include food, shelter, air, water, and clothing. These are the most basic needs, which must be met before people are motivated to satisfy other needs.

2.   Safety and Security Needs

Safety and security needs refer to avoidance of physical and economic dangers. Safety legislation has promoted a safer and healthier workplace.

3.   Social Needs

Social needs are fulfilled through development of affiliations with others. Working with others and being accepted as a member of the group illustrates how this type of need is satisfied.

4.   Esteem Needs

Esteem needs involve improving self esteem and gaining recognition from others. Satisfaction of these needs enables people to feel good about themselves.

5.   Self-Actualization Needs

Self-actualization needs are at the top of Maslow's hierarchy and involve reaching the maximum potential for growth and fulfillment. Few people ever are truly self-actualized.

C.   *ERG Theory*

Clayton Alderfer condensed Maslow's five categories of needs to three: existence needs, relatedness needs, and growth needs. *Existence needs* include basic life necessities; *relatedness needs* focus on interpersonal relationships; and *growth needs* incorporate Maslow's self-actualization and esteem needs.

Compared to Maslow's hierarchy, Alderfer's model is probably more representative of actual human behavior.

D. *Herzberg's Two-Factor Theory*

In Herzberg's view, motivator factors contribute to job satisfaction and serve to motivate. These factors include opportunities for advancement, achievement, and recognition. Hygiene factors represent potential sources of job dissatisfaction. Good salaries and positive relations with the boss are examples of hygiene factors.

E. *Expectancy Theory*

According to expectancy theory, motivation is influenced by the relationship between the desire for preferred outcomes (value) and the likelihood of attaining them (expectancy). Major components of this theory are effort, performance, and outcomes. Expectancy theory recognizes the importance of individual differences in skills and abilities and considers how role perceptions influence performance.

F. *Equity Theory*

Equity theory examines perceptions of fairness. The premise is that employers strive for equality and make subjective comparisons of their inputs and outcomes to others in similar circumstances. The comparison aspect of equity theory is a key consideration.

G. *Reinforcement Theory*

The essence of reinforcement theory is to examine the consequences of past experiences on subsequent behaviors. Four types of reinforcement are utilized. Positive reinforcement recognizes desired behaviors. While positive reinforcement recognizes desired behaviors, negative reinforcement focuses on behavior to avoid undesirable consequences. Punishment, which involves penalties, minimizes undesirable behaviors. When formerly rewarded behaviors cease to be recognized, extinction occurs, and unwanted behaviors diminish.

With continuous reinforcement, every correct response is reinforced. Since this is impractical in business settings, intermittent reinforcement is applied. Four intermittent schedules of reinforcement are used: fixed-ratio (administers a reward after a preselected number of correct responses), variable-ratio (randomly reinforces behavior according to an average number of responses), fixed-interval (reinforces behavior after a specified amount of time has elapsed), and variable-interval (varies the time between reinforcement of behaviors).

H.   *Motivation Theories: Implications for Managers*

Maslow, Alderfer, and Herzberg stress *what* motivates behavior. Expectancy, equity, and reinforcement theories emphasize *how* motivated behavior occurs. Maslow's hierarchy and ERG theory stress the importance of satisfying needs. Herzberg encourages managers to look beyond factors that contribute to job dissatisfaction. Equity theory stresses managerial awareness of employee views toward fairness. Expectancy theory gives managers insights into the relationships among effort, performance outcomes, rewards, and goal attainment.

IV.   MOTIVATION TECHNIQUES

Teaching Objective 4:   Explain the concepts of self-motivation, empowerment, and goal setting.

Greater numbers of organizations are involving employees in problem solving, seeking their recommendations and loyalty, and giving them greater authority to make decisions.

A.   *Self-Motivation*

As a prelude to managing others, managers must be capable of motivating themselves. A positive attitude is a major factor in self-motivation. Many managers who excel have excellent insights into their own behaviors. A self contract, which is a written agreement you make with yourself to do certain tasks, can be useful as a motivational technique.

Teaching Hint: Emphasize that managers serve as role models to subordinates. If a manager is perceived to be unmotivated, he or she will experience difficulty in attempting to motivate others.

B.   *Empowering Employees*

Empowerment involves giving workers knowledge, confidence, and authority to make decisions. Trained employees are essential to successful usage of empowerment, and the managerial role often changes from order giver to coach and adviser. To retain capable managers, some firms make a priority of noting management concerns and recognizing the value of empowerment.

C.   *Goal Setting*

Goal setting involves making a conscious effort to achieve specified goals. Along with provision of feedback, specific and challenging goals, which are accepted by employees, are most motivational. Employee participation in goal setting increases the likelihood of goal acceptance.

Teaching Objective 5:   Understand how morale affects job performance.

D.   *Building Organizational Morale*

The generalized attitude of an employee group toward the company, management, or job-related factors is termed organizational morale. Actions of managers and factors in the business environment influence organizational morale. Strategies to improve organizational morale include giving recognition, gaining perspectives, and emphasizing the positive.

1.   Giving Recognition

Employees like to receive compliments. Handwritten notes of praise, personal compliments, and public acknowledgement are pertinent non-monetary morale builders. Cultural differences should not be overlooked in terms of giving recognition.

2.   Gaining Perspectives

Employees want opportunities to express their views. Some managers practice an open-door policy, which involves inviting subordinates to come in and discuss topics of interest. Managers can employ the concept of managing by walking around to become better acquainted with employee job responsibilities and problems.

3.   Emphasizing the Positive

Managers and their subordinates encounter many types of obstacles. When managers have a positive attitude, subordinates are encouraged to have higher morale.

Suggested Readings for this Section:
Filipczak, Bob. "Are We Having Fun Yet?" Training 32, April 1995, pp. 48-56.

This article emphasizes the benefits of taking work seriously but still having fun on the job. A strategy for having fun at work can help firms reduce costs and also stimulate productivity. By setting examples, executives can encourage creation of a productive and fun work environment. Employees who are excited about their jobs are more likely to give excellent customer service, which is a way to gain an advantage over competitors. Management support for a fun-oriented environment is essential to its success. Most experts agree that personnel cannot be *forced* to have fun.

Tully, Shawn. "Why to Go for Stretch Targets." Fortune 130, November 14, 1994, pp. 145-158.

In an era of growing competitiveness, firms cannot afford to be satisfied with mediocrity. Stretch targets are intended to motivate performance so that challenging milestones can be reached. Key factors are to set clear long-term goals, identify one or two primary stretch targets, implement benchmarking to help assure personnel that the goal is attainable, and then give sufficient freedom for operating personnel to get tasks accomplished. Examples of successful application of stretch targets include a major cost savings for the coal division of CSX railroad and Boeing's significant reduction of time and manufacturing expense in the production of new airplanes.

V.   LOOKING BACK

This chapter examines the concept of motivation, an important and complex topic. Motivation is essential to attainment of an organization's goals and professional goals of personnel.

Answers to CONSIDER THIS Questions   (Page 326)

1.   **Why is employee motivation so frequently regarded as a major concern in the workplace?**

To be competitive in today's business environment, firms must attain and exceed goals. We can speculate that many companies will encounter similar or even greater competitive pressures in the future. High levels of job performance are needed to increase productivity, provide quality goods and services, meet deadlines, and assure prompt response to customer expectations. Consequently, much attention will continue to be focused on ways for encouraging all personnel to be motivated and excel at doing their jobs.

2. **What is the most important factor to recognize about motivating employees?**

Students will have a variety of responses to this question, which is designed to encourage them to think about the concept of motivation. A key factor is to recognize that people are motivated differently. An enthusiastic, positive managerial attitude contributes to development of a motivated workplace environment. Review Figure 10-2, which shows disagreement between factors valued by employees and those considered to be important by supervisors. This figure can serve as the basis for a discussion concerning the priority of motivational factors.

3. **How can managers better understand the motivational needs of their employees?**

Managers must take the initiative and be willing to *make an effort* to understand motivational needs. A manager's attitude is relevant. When employees are viewed as valued human assets, their motivational needs are more likely to be considered. Insights can be gleaned by listening to employees, soliciting input from them, and practicing an open style of communication. When workers observe that managers are concerned and responsive, desired levels of motivation are more likely to occur.

Answers to CONSIDER THIS Questions   (Page 338)

1. **Which theory best explains the motivation of today's workers?**

Because real-world circumstances and individual motivations vary to a large extent, students can have different responses to this question. However, they should include a rationale to justify their conclusions. Content theories of motivation, such as Maslow and Herzberg, focus on specific internal needs. While basic needs of most workers are met, many social and esteem needs are unmet. Few employees have satisfied Maslow's self-actualization needs. Herzberg's motivator factors are especially appropriate to motivate today's workers.

Process (equity, expectancy, and reinforcement) theories are relevant in today's business environment. Workers do consider the equity of how they are treated compared to others, and the relationship between valuation placed on rewards and likelihood of attaining them has motivational implications. Various approaches to motivation are currently used by businesses. Positive reinforcement and variable reinforcement schedules are frequently used to elicit desired levels of motivated job performance.

2.   **What can managers do to maintain perceptions of equity or fairness among employees?**

Quite likely, few managers are considered to be fair and equitable by all subordinates. Nevertheless, several strategies can enhance perceptions of fairness or equity. One strategy is to solicit input for important issues and then explain the rationale for subsequent decisions and actions. Often, managers who practice openness of communication are apt to be perceived as being fair because subordinates feel more comfortable to ask questions or express views. Another strategy is to avoid perceptions of playing favorites among employees, which can destroy reputations for fairness in treatment of personnel.

3.   **Why do so few people attain Maslow's level of self-actualization?**

According to Maslow, lower-order needs must be fulfilled before people are motivated to satisfy higher-order needs. Therefore, self-actualization is experienced by few people. Numerous workers are challenged to satisfy social and esteem needs. Many obstacles, personal and nonpersonal as well as real or perceived, hinder people from attaining their maximum potential for growth and fulfillment.

Answers to REVIEW AND DISCUSSION Questions

1.   *Why is motivation a complex topic?*

Motivation is an internal process. While all behavior is motivated, people are unique; have a variety of experiences, attitudes, and backgrounds; and are motivated differently. Understanding human behavior is a challenge. While one person may put forth much effort to attain a goal, it may have little or no meaning to another individual.

2. *How do the assumptions of Theory X differ from those of Theory Y.*

Theory X, a traditional management approach, emphasizes control to assure compliance. It represents an autocratic management style and makes negative assumptions about the attitudes of employees toward and acceptance of responsibility. Managers who adhere to Theory Y solicit input from subordinates and delegate authority. Theory Y assumptions reflect positive views concerning enthusiasm of employees and their willingness to accept responsibility.

3. *Why do so few people attain Maslow's level of self-actualization?*

Maslow's hierarchy represents a logical progression in fulfillment of human needs. Self-actualization is the pinnacle of the hierarchy. Because of uncontrollable events that occur or personal limitations, relatively few people maximize their potential for growth and personal fulfillment. In reality, many persons simply do not take advantage of circumstances that might ultimately lead to greater self-actualization.

4. *How can managers motivate themselves?*

Maintaining a positive attitude is a key factor in motivation. By looking ahead and focusing on desired outcomes, managers can overcome many obstacles and inevitable disappointments. A willingness to learn from experiences and to be persistent contributes to achievement and satisfaction. The concept of a self contract is often useful as a tool for self motivation.

5. *What is the difference between Herzberg's motivator factors and hygiene factors?*

Motivator factors (advancement, more responsibility, achievement, nature of work, and recognition) contribute to job satisfaction and accordingly serve to motivate. Hygiene factors (relations with the boss, working conditions, company policies, salary, and quality of supervision) represent potential sources of job dissatisfaction.

6. *In equity theory, what is the importance of a comparison reference person?*

This person's situation (status, salary, benefits, working conditions) represents a standard for making equity comparisons. According to the theory, employees strive for equality and make subjective comparisons of their inputs and outcomes to comparison reference persons.

7.   *What are the important differences among the four types of reinforcement?*

It is important for managers to recognize the relationship between reinforcement and motivation. *Positive reinforcement* recognizes desired behaviors. *Negative reinforcement* focuses on behavior to avoid undesirable consequences. *Punishment* uses penalties to minimize undesirable behaviors; however, it sometimes causes those who are punished to become angry or resentful. When formerly rewarded behaviors are no longer recognized, *extinction* occurs; unwanted behaviors diminish.

8.   *Discuss the fundamental premise of expectancy theory.*

According to this theory, motivation is influenced by the relationship between the desire for preferred outcomes (value) and the likelihood of attaining them (expectancy). Expectancy theory recognizes the importance of individual differences in skills and abilities. It considers how role perceptions influence performance.

9.   *How does the concept of employee empowerment change the role of a manager?*

By empowering employees, managers delegate decision-making authority to them. Consequently, managers must be willing to concede some of their traditional power and authority and assume the role of adviser, coach, or facilitator. Managers who empower successfully establish boundaries (limits within which subordinates have discretion to make decisions) and clearly communicate expectations.

10.   *What can managers do to improve the organizational morale of their employees?*

A key factor is to treat employees as valued human assets and communicate effectively. To build morale, it is useful to solicit employee views and provide explanations of decisions. Managers can strive to practice fairness in dealings with subordinates and seek to create trusting relationships with them. Other relevant considerations are to assure a safe and healthy workplace, provide adequate equipment resources, and earn the respect of subordinates.

▦ Answers to CRITICAL THINKING INCIDENTS
■

Incident 10-1: THINGS CHANGE

1. **In terms of motivation, why do Carol and June react differently to the takeover by Travel and Cruises International?**

This incident illustrates the complexity of motivation and shows how the same situation can have different impact on productivity levels. While neither person likes the new compensation plan or Bryan's managerial style, Carol seems to experience greater personal frustration. Various explanations for Carol's behavior are possible. Carol values personal attention and support from her boss. She appears to have a close identification with her job; recognized job-related success is very meaningful to her. Conversely, June experiences internal satisfaction with her own job performance and does not appear to need as much recognition from management.

2. **How can Bryan become more knowledgeable about the basis of Carol's motivation.**

Bryan should try to better understand Carol's professional background and philosophy toward the workplace. He needs to focus on development of interpersonal skills and establish a more "open" communication environment. It is important to solicit Carol's views, especially those involving the management change. To become more knowledgeable, Bryan must demonstrate sincerity and evidence greater interest learning Carol's perspectives.

3. **Why should Bryan be perplexed about Carol's job performance?**

Bryan is not familiar with New World's corporate culture and has not spent much time in his new management position. He follows a manager who has taken much interest in Carol's job performance and career development. Bryan seems to have overlooked the nature of human behavior and assumes that employees will respond positively to directives simply because management desires them to do so.

4. **Specifically, how can Bryan motivate Carol?**

Carol values a manager who is concerned about how well she accomplishes job responsibilities and takes time to answer questions. Bryan should listen to Carol's views and encourage her participation in job-related decisions. In addition, he needs to evidence appreciation for her as a valued employee. Most likely, Carol will respond positively to personal recognition and praise, which should be earned through excellent performance of job duties.

Incident 10-2:   I'M STUCK HERE

1.   **How can Harriett gain control over the frustrations and avoid being so negative?**

Harriett must realize that negativism does not help establish a good work record at Westside Stores or with other employers. At some future date, she may need references from managers who are familiar with her job performance. It might be worthwhile for Harriett to share her frustrations with a friend, a trusted colleague, or even a professional job counselor. Actually, Harriett's job-related concerns are not as unique as she might think. A useful strategy is to develop a positive attitude toward job performance, while recognizing that her future career might not include employment at Westside Stores.

2.   **What can Wilma do to motivate Harriett?**

Although she may not exercise control over allocation of financial rewards, Wilma can emphasize the importance of doing good work and extend praise for demonstrated job-performance accomplishments. By recognizing good customer service, for example, Wilma reinforces repetition of desired behaviors. She should continue trying to develop an environment based on fundamentals of open communication by emphasizing a willingness to listen and discuss problems or concerns. Wilma might recommend participation in professional development activities and stress potential future benefits to be gained from them.

3.   **Do you agree with Tom's recommendation? Explain your response.**

Given her record of capable performance over a lengthy period of time, Tom's recommendation seems rather harsh. A blunt response might further irritate Harriett and lead to additional problems. It appears that Harriett needs opportunities to share her views with Tom and perhaps gain insights into rationales for management policies and actions. Tom needs to establish a more collegial work environment and use effective communication practices.

4.   **Is Harriett likely to regain her enthusiasm and be motivated if she changes jobs and works for another employer? Explain your response.**

This is a thought question that will evoke yes and no responses. A key point is for students to have a rationale for justifying their responses. From a perspective of career advancement and frustration with the recognition system, employment at another firm could certainly prove to improve Harriett's motivation and enthusiasm. Like many job-related decisions, however, the choice to leave may also involve moving to another location, learning a new organizational culture, and responding to another set of management expectations. Therefore, a job change is not without potential additional frustrations that could also negatively impact motivation. Should she seriously think about changing employment, Harriett should carefully consider employment factors that are important to her in selecting a new position.

Incident 10-3:   THE STAR PERFORMER

1.   **What factors motivated Sally to achieve her outstanding sales record?**

As a salesperson, Sally demonstrates self-confidence, job competence, and commitment to getting things done. She accepts challenges and is not hesitant to work hard or push for results. These factors contributed to her success. Probably, past successes further motivated Sally to strive for even greater accomplishments.

2.   **How can Sally be a star performer and be seemingly ineffective at motivating her employees?**

An outstanding salesperson is not necessarily an effective manager. Sally possesses the qualities necessary to motivate herself; however, motivation of employees is a separate challenge. People have different aspirations, abilities, and rationales for behaviors. She must avoid the tendency to base actions upon her own beliefs, values, and attitudes.

3.   **Does Sally have the potential to be a successful manager? Explain your response.**

Yes, Sally has an outstanding record of managing herself and appears to understand managerial functions. Assuming she is receptive to suggestions and willing to practice human relations skills, Sally has the potential to be a successful manager.

4.   **Sally's employees are using her as an excuse for their own ineffective job performances. What is your reaction to this statement?**

This question is not easily answered. It's convenient to rationalize many reasons for the existing difficulties and place some blame upon Sally who may be too impatient and demanding. Possibly, events beyond Sally's control (such as economic conditions, actions of competitors, or changes in consumer-usage patterns) have occurred. Most likely, a combination of factors is responsible for the decline in sales and increased turnover.

5.   **Would you like to have Sally as your manager? Why or why not?**

This question is intended to provoke discussion among students. While many students will respond negatively, Sally possesses considerable product knowledge and sales skills; seemingly, much can be learned from her. Perhaps, she can serve as a role model to employees who aspire to success. Also, her push for productivity might encourage some employees to recognize the need for exerting greater efforts, and as their personal sales increase, they may develop a more positive perspective toward Sally's philosophy.

Study Guide Assignments

In the individual case assignment, students serve as consultants to a manager who believes that he has no problems with motivation of employees. Students are given comments obtained from employees and asked to make an analysis of them. Finally, they are challenged to make recommendations to improve motivation based upon the perspectives of theories presented in the chapter.

The group case assignment involves development of a motivational approach for a manager and determination of the communication technique to use in explaining it to employees. This is an excellent exercise to gain greater insights into motivation, as it emphasizes the wide range of attitudes and opinions possessed by employees.

Video Case

Financial Service Corporation

Focus: **Motivation**

Summary:

The challenges to Financial Service Corporation (FSC) of Marietta, Georgia, were basic: survival and a return to profitability. Declining sales and high costs had yielded monthly operating losses. Independent representatives on whom FSC depended for sales were deserting it. Employees felt little loyalty and no motivation to perform well.

After finding some unique ways to motivate representatives and employees, FSC was in the black in less than three years, and income was rising. Sales were up, and costs were under control. The number of representatives had risen, and revenue per representative had doubled. Net worth went from zero to more than $2 million in less than two years.

The company credits this remarkable turnaround to the motivation of its people. The company heightened motivation primarily by getting employees involved in the organization, giving them a piece of the action, and developing a unique computer/automation system.

FSC's customers and sales representatives are scattered around the country. The company supplies information on insurance and investment opportunities – mutual funds, securities, limited partnerships – to hundreds of financial professionals who help consumers and small businesses with their insurance and investment needs. It also executes transactions, keeps records, and processes data.

Mutual Life Insurance Company of New York had bought the company from its management in 1986. Mutual Life sold it back, loss-ridden, in 1989. FSC Chairman E. James Wisner immediately met with employees and then field representatives. Ownership of the company, he promised, would be shared with the field representatives and the employees. In fact, that promise was kept in 1991 when stock was distributed – some shares were given, others sold – to field representatives, employees, and managers in varying rations. Wisner himself owns 26 percent of the company.

Employees were then given a choice of four compensation packages with fixed and variable components that, to different degrees, gave them the choice of guaranteed income or profit sharing if the company did well. The higher the fixed component, the lower the variable; the lower the fixed component, the higher the variable. Surprisingly, many employees at modest salary levels opted for the riskier – but potentially more rewarding – packages.

In addition to improving employee motivation, linking pay to profits strengthened FSC by making it easier to weather any future downturn without losing employees it wanted to keep. Normally, the fixed nature of salaries makes it difficult to cut payroll costs during business slowdowns except by firings.

Today's FSC is minus some people it didn't want to keep. The company has dropped representatives who were poor sales producers, replacing them with representatives who are more productive. It has also been able to cut the number of home-office employees, while improving quality of services, by investing $2 million in state-of-the-art computer software and taking other steps to improve efficiency.

FSC's progress is apparent not only in its better balance sheet, but in the number of the customer complaints it receives. They used to average 1,100 a month, the company says. Now they average ten.

Discussion Questions:

1.   Using Hertzberg's model of motivation, discuss the motivator and hygiene factors at FSC.

        Hertzberg's two-factor theory holds that pay and benefits are hygiene factors and factors such as recognition, achievement and advancement are motivators. One way to explain what happened at FSC using Hertzberg's model is that employees were dissatisfied with the old system, and dissatisfaction had to be eliminated before motivation could be addressed.

2.   If you were an advisor to Wisner, what other techniques to motivate employees would you suggest? Why?

        Students will have a variety of suggestions. One interesting aspect to bring up is the issue of personal control: individuals typically prefer self-control, and letting employees select their pay plan provided them with control. Other techniques to motivate people might work better if this element of control was included.

Chapter 11

Social Responsibilities and Ethics

▨ Chapter Overview

This chapter introduces the concepts of social responsibility and ethics. In the opening real world case, examples are cited that indicate a need for consideration of social responsibilities. This opening case indicates why more legislation is needed if society truly wants many firms to be more socially responsible. While many firms talk about this subject, fewer companies are actually taking initiatives on their own to be more socially responsible.

▨ Teaching Objectives

The teaching objectives of this chapter are to:

1. Define and understand what social responsibility means.

2. Discuss and appreciate the costs and benefits that a socially responsible business incurs in today's competitive environment.

3. Understand the different ways to measure social responsibility in the business world.

4. List and discuss some common ways to improve social responsibility.

5. Define and discuss the role of ethics in business today.

6.   Appreciate and explain some of the factors that affect ethics in business.

7.   Identify some ways to improve managerial ethics.

Chapter Outline of the Text

        I.   SOCIAL RESPONSIBILITY DEFINED
        II.   OPPOSING VIEWS ON SOCIAL RESPONSIBILITY
                A.   Economic Responsibility
                B.   Public Responsibility
                C.   Social Responsiveness
                D.   Social Issues in Management
        III.   BENEFITS AND COSTS OF BEING SOCIALLY RESPONSIBLE
        IV.   MEASURING SOCIAL RESPONSIBILITY
        V.   WAYS TO IMPROVE SOCIAL RESPONSIBILITY
                A.   Cause-Related Marketing
                B.   Advocacy
        VI.   MANAGERIAL ETHICS: PROBLEMS IN DEFINING ETHICAL
                BEHAVIOR
                A.   Level 1: The Law
                B.   Level 2: Policies, Procedures, Rules and Guidelines
                C.   Level 3: Moral Stance
        VII.   FACTORS THAT AFFECT MANAGERIAL ETHICS
        VIII.   WAYS TO IMPROVE MANAGERIAL ETHICS
        IX.   LOOKING BACK
        X.   KEY TERMS
        XI.   REVIEW AND DISCUSSION QUESTIONS
        XII.   CRITICAL THINKING INCIDENTS
        XIII.   SUGGESTED READINGS

Key Terms

        These terms are introduced in the chapter. Definitions are included in the glossary of the text.

Advocacy promotions   Environmental issues
Cause-related marketing   Equal employment opportunity
Code of business ethics   Ethics
Economic responsibility phase   Law
Energy concerns   Moral stance

Policies (procedures, rules, and guidelines)
Public responsibility
Quality of work environment
Social audit

Social investments
Social issues in management
Social responsibility
Social responsiveness
Stakeholders

Detailed Chapter Summary

I.   SOCIAL RESPONSIBILITY DEFINED

Teaching Objective 1:   Define and understand what social responsibility means in the business world.

A.   *Social Responsibility Defined*

While social responsibility is difficult to precisely define due to different perspectives, a good working definition is, "Actions and decisions which consider the legal, economic, and societal factors in both the short and the long run as well as the organizational interests." This definition does not ignore profits. It simply asks firms to also consider if their products meet society's expectations and are being produced in a safe and reasonable manner.

B.   *Social Responsibility and Ethics*

It is easy to condemn some of our early business leaders. However, we must keep in mind that what was considered ethical or legal in those days was different than today's expectations. Consumers and the government are forcing businesses of all types to become more socially responsible. Consumer groups have forced companies to produce safer and more environmentally safe products through protests and by pressuring government officials to pass new laws. The government itself has also initiated several pieces of legislation covering everything from reducing pollution to eliminating discriminatory hiring practices. While many business leaders are getting the message, recent surveys of retired business managers indicate that the great majority still see a definite need for more legislation if society wants the business world to raise its level of social responsibility.

II.   OPPOSING VIEWS ON SOCIAL RESPONSIBILITY

Social responsibility is a constantly-evolving process, and it will continue to change in the future. There are currently four distinct phases that a firm may pass through to become a truly socially-responsible firm.

A.   *Phase 1: Economic Responsibility*

In this phase, management's only concern is to make profits as large as possible for the stockholders. The stockholders are of primary concern. Businesspersons believe that by being economically profitable, the firm is also being socially responsible to its employees, as their jobs become more secure. Finally, by being profitable, companies are meeting consumer expectations in the products/services that are produced.

B.   *Phase 2: Public Responsibility Phase*

In Phase 2, the company still wants to be profitable, but it also recognizes the need to help society establish public policy on major social issues. Businesses feel indebted to society for profits; therefore, they believe they should help society. In this phase, businesses may help society set public policy on issues such as safety or AIDS in the workplace.

C.   *Phase 3: Social Responsiveness*

In Phase 3, businesses for the first time actually develop and implement social programs aimed at solving a problem. While this is obviously very good, usually businesses do not do this until they receive some form of public pressure to implement a program. Examples of programs that businesses have implemented include: (1) utilizing packaging materials that are recyclable; (2) eliminating product components that hurt the ozone layer; or (3) making products, such as cars, safer and more fuel efficient.

D.   *Phase 4: Social Issues in Management*

Here, firms voluntarily identify social issues or problems that they feel strongly enough about to want to make some changes. Some examples include: (1) helping to reduce unemployment in the intercity by building plants within those areas and (2) helping the field of education by providing resources of all types to help better educate the youth of America.

Teaching Hint: *There is considerable debate as to which phase most U.S. businesses would fall into. While most people answer phase 2 or 3, it may be interesting to ask your class this question.*

III.   BENEFITS AND COSTS OF BEING SOCIALLY RESPONSIBLE

Teaching Objective 2:   Discuss and appreciate the costs and benefits that a socially responsible business incurs in today's competitive environment.

When a business considers being more socially responsible, it normally does some type of cost/benefit analysis.

A.   *Benefits of Being Socially Responsible*

The benefits of being socially responsible appear to be the following:

1.   *Increased profits* -- Consumers are becoming aware of socially responsible firms and supporting them.
2.   *Improved image* -- Being socially responsible has a very positive image in the public's eye.
3.   *Helps avoid more restrictive legislation being passed in the future* -- Legislation is aimed at socially irresponsible firms. By being socially responsible, there is no need for more restrictive legislation.
4.   *The value of the firm's stock often rises* -- Socially responsible firms are often praised for their social programs, which makes them a more solid investment. There are non-profit groups that rate major companies on how they handle social issues and then publish the results for investors.
5.   *Solving some of society's problems helps create a better environment* -- Socially responsible firms make employees feel proud when they help the community solve problems.
6.   *Helps prevent problems from growing* -- Almost always, a problem is easiest to solve before it grows too large and becomes uncontrollable. Businesses can act far faster than the government in most cases.
7.   *Cooperation between business, government, and society helps everyone* -- The government cannot solve all of society's problems alone. If the business world helps out, everyone benefits.
8.   *Benefits outweigh the costs in most cases* -- While there are some costs, there are even greater benefits to the firm if the programs are done properly and the results communicated to the public.

B.   *The Costs Of Being Socially Responsible:*

1.   *Financial costs of running social programs may mean higher prices to consumers* -- Effective social programs whose results are communicated clearly to the public can have the same effect as good advertising. In fact, since the results are usually reported in the form of publicity, it usually is even more effective than advertising.

2.   *Social programs may not be cost effective* -- If the social issues that the firm is trying to solve are important to the public and not just the firm and the results are well published, then the program should be cost effective in the long run if not in the short run.

3.   *Businesses may be engaging in illegal social programs and not even be aware of it* -- A secondary effect could be harmful or even be illegal. This should not be a problem, however, if the program is well thought out and appropriate regulatory agencies are contacted first.

4.   *Social programs may cause a firm to stray from its main purpose of efficiency and profitability* -- Research has shown that social programs can be profitable if done properly. Thus, actions of a business do not have to deviate from its main purpose.

5.   *There is a general lack of public support for being socially active* -- The number of people who feel strongly about the business world and social issues is very significant and is growing larger every year. Even the business community recognizes this, according to a survey completed by INC magazine. In this survey, 76 percent of the businesses considered that being socially responsible was good for business, and 68 percent said they would continue doing social programs even it they were cutting into their profits.

Teaching Hint: Remind your students that most of the real gains from being socially responsible are long term in nature. Things like high customer retention are incredibly valuable to a firm.

IV.   MEASURING SOCIAL RESPONSIBILITY

Teaching Objective 3:   Understand the different ways to measure social responsibility in the business world.

A.   *Responsible To Whom?*

First remember that a firm is responsible to all of the members of its stakeholder group. These, of course, include anyone who is affected by the decisions or actions of the firm such as the stockholders, employees, managers, customers, and suppliers.

B.   *Measuring Responsibility*

Next, a firm must try to measure how it is responding to society as a whole on a number of various current social issues such as the following:

1.   *Environmental issues* -- Not polluting but actually trying to reverse pollution effects.

2.   *Energy concerns* -- Conservation and research on new forms of energy.

3.   *Quality of the work environment* -- How management treats employees, especially in terms of manager-worker relationships, wages and benefits, job security, promotional opportunities, recognition and financial incentives, concern for worker safety, participation in work-related matters, degree of communication throughout the firm, amount of autonomy, basic working conditions, and genuine concern for producing a high quality product or service.

4.   *Equal employment opportunities* -- Non-discriminatory practices in hiring, promoting, and dismissing employees. Also affirmative action programs to help increase the number of minorities, females, and disabled workers in management positions.

5.   *Community support* -- Helping the community through fund raising programs and actively encouraging managers and employees to volunteer their time and talents to community programs.

6.   *Social investments* -- Making a sizeable financial donation or even the outright purchase of something badly needed by the community. On-going donations, such as Ben and Jerrys' 7.5 percent of pre-tax earnings, are even more exemplary.

C.   *Continuum for Measuring Responsibility*

Trying to measure how socially responsible a firm has been is not easy, since it may rate high in some areas and poor in others. A continuum from -60 to +60 with points given in each area previously covered ranging from -10 to +10 helps to solve this problem.

Very Socially Irresponsible	-60 -50 -40 -30 -20 -10 0 +10 +20 +30 +40 +50 +60	Very Socially Responsible

Suggested Readings for this Section:
Davidson, Jacqueline. "Responsibility Reaps Rewards," Small Business Reports (February, 1993), pp. 56-64.

What can a small business do to make a meaningful social contribution? While their resources are small, small businesses can make a tremendous impact on a community if they will get involved in a personal and meaningful way, as the following four examples indicate.

Crib Diaper Service sells an environmentally safe cloth diaper service to over 5,000 residents, 40 day care centers, and one hospital. Their cause is the environment, and they take it seriously. The firm currently recycles over 90 percent of its solid waste including the lint from the diapers themselves. The lint is used to make paper. They are also planning on spending $80,000 on the latest water recycling equipment which will reduce the amount of water they use from 50 to 70 percent. This is a large investment for a firm of only 40 employees.

Stonyfield Farms decided to personally support the small local farmers who were in serious financial trouble. The firm now buys milk from over 40 local farmers at a premium price and makes yogurt out of it. It took eight years to get the consumers to buy into the concept and make the firm profitable, but now the firm has 85 employees and does $18 million in sales a year.

Nature's Recipe Pet Foods, a twelve year old 35 employee pet food firm, produces natural pet food which does not contain any chemical preservatives. The firm also is heavily involved in the drug prevention programs in the Los Angeles area in California. To date they have spent over $200,000 on "Just Say No To Drugs" campaigns which included printed cards, local school programs, press releases, and newspaper ads.

King's Collar Company, Inc. makes custom shirts in Philadelphia, Pennsylvania. The owner Nancy Gold also is incredibly active in helping the homeless people in that area. Nancy founded a non-profit organization called "I Do Care" which gives the homeless people vouchers that can be used at various kiosks and carts around the city. She also wants to open a training center so that these people can learn how to become fast-food employees. Nancy has chosen not to give the homeless money which they could use on other non-essential items. Instead, she has chosen to help them eat better, learn new job skills, and hopefully get off the streets.

Reynolds, Jerry. "A New Social Agenda For the New Age," Management Review *(January 1993), pp. 35-41.*

A new business trade group has recently been formed in Washington, D.C. called Business for Social Responsibility (BSR). This organization originally started with 55 charter members including some major manufacturers such as Stride Rite, Reebok, and Lotus Development. The majority of the members, however, are small to midsize firms such as Ben and Jerry's Ice Cream.

The organization hopes to concentrate initially on educating and training member companies on the benefits of expanding their community and workplace programs. BSR plans to show how environmental programs, healthy and fulfilling workplaces, and community activism are good for business. BSR hopes to get Congress to pass regulatory rules that will give firms a tax break if they become involved in social issues like helping to employ inner-city people. BSR members said they hope to present a new way of thinking and behavior for companies and public policy makers to consider before they act. BSR members also support the position that America's long-term competitive position in the global marketplace necessitates consideration of social and environmental costs of doing business. The organization even favors including these costs on corporate balance sheets and annual reports so that consumers can be better informed as to the real costs of the products they buy.

While BSR is still new, the group believes it will add 400 to 500 new members within a year or two and help develop a new "corporate soul" for its members and interested companies.

V. SOME WAYS TO IMPROVE SOCIAL RESPONSIBILITY

Teaching Objective 4: List and discuss some common ways to improve social responsibility.

If any firm is going to become more socially responsible, top management must set the tone. Top management needs to communicate this new stance to all managers and employees in both words and actions. Once employees and managers see how important this area is to top management, positive changes are more likely to occur. Providing financial incentives is also an important way to communicate this change.

A. *Cause-Related Marketing*

One method used by some firms to be more socially responsible is "cause-related marketing." Here, a firm ties the sales of products to a donation to a charitable or social cause. In most cases the firm's products have some kind of a natural "fit" with the cause. This approach to helping social causes has been both praised and criticized, as a firm's real intentions might not be evident.

B.   *Advocacy Promotions*

A second approach used by some firms to be more socially responsible is called, "Advocacy Promotions." In this situation, there is not any natural product tie-in to the cause. Instead, the promotions try to tell the public how businesses are helping to solve some critical social problem or how they are supportive of a popular social issue. Again, a company's true motives may not be obvious, and one will only know for sure in the long run.

C.   *Steps for Implementing a Social Program*

A good step-by-step procedure to assure success in implementing any social program is spelled out in the Remember to Communicate box in this chapter. The following steps must be carefully followed:

1.   Decide what social causes to support and how to support them.
2.   See if there are any common practices or precedents for this area.
3.   Social program coordinators must communicate with and involve both management and employees at every step of the program.
4.   The program goals must fit the corporate philosophy toward the social cause.
5.   Program coordinators need to communicate constantly with the community, so that the firm is perceived as being socially responsible.
6.   The coordinators must always communicate with all of the firm's stakeholder groups regarding its goals and intentions.
7.   The program coordinators need to audit and evaluate progress and results on a regular basis.

VI.   MANAGERIAL ETHICS: PROBLEMS IN DEFINING ETHICAL BEHAVIOR

Teaching Objective 5:   Define and discuss the role of ethics in business today.

Ethics involves many different aspects, but it is defined as "the roles of conduct and moral principles and values which define how individuals and businesses conduct business."

There are three basic levels of ethics:

A.   *The Law*

These, of course, try to prevent some of the worst forms of unethical behavior, such as falsifying records. The problem with the law is that it is always retroactive and subject to different interpretations.

B.   *Policies, Procedures, Rules, and Guidelines*

These help further define ethical behavior by giving people direction when confronted with difficult situations. However, they are generally not comprehensive and may not cover many situations that arise.

C.   *Moral Stance*

How persons respond to a situation not covered by the law or any type of guideline depends on their personal moral stance. This, in turn, is determined by a person's own personal values, beliefs, and (to some degree) the corporate culture within the firm itself. The most difficult problems fall into this category.

VII.   FACTORS AFFECTING MANAGERIAL ETHICS

Teaching Objective 6:   Appreciate and explain some of the factors that affect ethics in business.

Good ethics, like good social responsibility, starts at the top of the organization. Top management support efforts to exemplify good ethical behavior are key considerations.

A.   *Companies That Are Corrupt and Unethical*

A recent survey of retired executives cited poor ethics of top management, competition, and greed as the main reasons why some companies were so corrupt and unethical.

B.   *Poor Ethical Practices*

Poor ethical practices have been found to only give a firm a short-term advantage or gain. Poor ethical practices have also been found to give a firm disastrous results in the long run as the "word spreads" very quickly to a firm's customer base. Poor ethical behaviors have also been found to demoralize employees and local community citizens.

C.   *Fines and Penalties*

The fines and penalties for unethical behaviors can reach millions of dollars.

D.   *Good Ethical Behaviors are Profitable*

Research indicates that firms practicing good ethical behaviors are more profitable than those using unethical business practices.

Suggested Readings for this Section:
McGarvey, Robert. "Do Thee Right Thing," <u>Entrepreneur</u>, (April 1994), pp. 64-67.

Both large and small businesses suffer occasionally from the unethical acts of their managers and employees. While sometimes the ethical slip is not intentional, in many cases it is intentional.

How can businesses get everyone in the firm to act ethically? The following points may help any firm solve this problem. First, remember that ethical standards start at the top of an organization. The examples emphasize the importance of ethical behavior.   Next, develop a real code of ethics. It does not need to be very long or complex. Many firms print their codes on 3 x 5 cards and tape them on their telephones or dashboards. Third, give everyone training that really communicates what the code means. Also, be sure that the training is given by someone who is already known to trainees.   The training itself should emphasize many typical problem situations and how to handle them and can include some real-life stories told by the trainers themselves. Open the training to questions and invite employees to offer any situations they have faced. Finally, do periodic review sessions, especially if new employees are hired.

If a business is able to win employees over, in terms of practicing only ethical behaviors, top management will be able to observe results in the work environment and will likely receive positive comments from suppliers and customers.

Cox, Robert. "Good Ethics Mean Good Business," The Wichita Eagle, March 29, 1993, pp. D4-5.

The two main reasons that managers or employees act unethically are greed and fear. During good business times, it is greed, and during hard times, it is fear. What many businesses are finding is that unethical acts only have short-term gains at best.

To be competitive today, firms must have high quality products and services, and a firm must have employees and suppliers who have high ethical standards. "There are many studies that show that firms with strong ethics policies have twice as much net income as those who do not," according to Larry Axline, managing director of Management Action Planning, a management consultant service in Boulder, Colorado.

Another reason we are seeing new interest in ethics is because of the new federal sentencing guidelines, which significantly reduce penalties and fines for companies that have a strong ethics policy and active programs to train employees.

Boeing Aircraft is a good example of a firm that has increased emphasis on ethical behavior. Boeing increased ethical training, established protection for employees who report ethical violations by their superiors, established "hot lines" for employees to report violations, made addressing any potential violation a top priority at all times, and even required vendors and suppliers to comply with their rules. What all of these changes have done is to create a business environment that makes employees want to go the extra mile for customers, thereby, making Boeing even more competitive in the marketplace.

VIII.   SOME WAYS TO IMPROVE MANAGERIAL ETHICS

Teaching Objective 7: Identify some ways to improve managerial ethics.

    A.   *While the variety of ways to improve ethical behavior is almost endless, a sound, logical approach was developed by the Business Roundtable and others who surveyed over 100 companies. This approach utilizes the following steps:*

        1.   Top managers must be committed to ethical conduct and should provide leadership and incentives to encourage appropriate behavior. They also must communicate the message in words and actions.

        2.   The establishment of a written code of ethics. This code makes it clear that top management is serious about ethical behavior.

3.   Implementation of a good ethical program. This involves many things including communication, incentives, ethical audits, and enforcement.
4.   Involvement and commitment of all personnel at all levels. Everyone must be informed, involved, and committed, or it will not work.
5.   Measure results. Utilize surveys and audits to determine results. Consider utilizing outside firms for this function.

B.   *How should a person handle an ethical dilemma on an individual basis?*

If you have to deal with an ethical dillema and are not sure how management will respond, consider these useful steps:

1.   Determine if a real conflict does exist. Get the facts and see if the behavior is acceptable to the firm and the industry.
2.   Decide how much risk is acceptable.   Do a personal cost/benefit analysis.
3.   Initiate action. Inform management that improper behaviors are inappropriate and have an alternative technique for them to consider.
4.   If there is trouble, get help. Contact an influential person within the firm who will be a "receptive" listener.
5.   Consider a job change. If relief cannot be obtained and the clash in values is too high, it may be necessary to leave the position.

IX.   LOOKING BACK

This chapter introduces the reader to some issues and problems associated with ethics and social responsibility in today's business environment. Firms must recognize the importance of good ethical behaviors and being socially responsible or risk losing business to competitors.

Answers to CONSIDER THIS Questions   (Page 361)

1.   **Since more and more businesses are becoming socially responsible, why do we need more federal legislation in this area?**

Legislation is necessary for a number of reasons. First, research indicates that in many cases the business world, as a whole, will not take the lead in helping to solve social problems on their own. Second, legislation can actually help businesses that want to be socially responsible compete by forcing all firms to comply. Finally, because of the costs in some areas, such as pollution, legislation is the only way to get the business world to reach for truly high goals.

2. **Why is it wrong for businesses to only concentrate on making a profit when that is their main reason for going into business in the first place?**

    First, the business would not be profitable if the marketplace or society did not purchase a firm's product and provide employees and managers to run the company. Second, many firms have a strong influence in the community, and the community looks to them to provide leadership and support on social issues. The government is not able to handle all social problems on its own and needs the help of business.

3. **Can socially responsible firms really compete with firms that are not spending any money on social programs?**

    While there are definite costs in being socially responsible, research does indicate that firms that are socially responsible do as well or better, in terms of profits, than firms in general. The research also indicates a very negative public reaction to firms that are deemed socially irresponsible.

Answers to CONSIDER THIS Questions   (Page 368)

1. **Why is it so difficult to accurately measure the social responsibility of a particular firm?**

    Measuring social responsibility is difficult for a number of reasons. First, there is no agreed upon list of social issues on which all firms can be assessed. Second, what constitutes socially acceptable behavior in any given social area is not accurately defined. Finally, it is difficult to come up with an honest rating of a firm when it is socially responsible in some areas but socially irresponsible in other areas.

2. **What are some of the most important current social issues that should concern businesses?**

    While a current list of social issues is constantly changing, some major issues which will be with us for a long time are environmental concerns, energy concerns, quality of the work environment, equal employment opportunities, community support, and social investments in a number of different local and national areas.

3.   **Is cause-related marketing an acceptable way to be socially responsible? What about advocacy marketing?**

Cause-related marketing occurs when a firm ties the sale of products to a donation, charity, or social cause. The real question here is "Does the firm genuinely support this cause or is this just a marketing scheme to increase sales?" If the donation is a substantial amount, over a considerable period of time, and the firm stays with the cause even if the sales of related products do not substantially increase, then probably it is a socially responsible action on the part of the firm.

Advocacy marketing occurs when a firm does not have a natural product-cause tie in. Here, the promotion tries to elicit goodwill and a good public image by illustrating how some totally unrelated social problem or cause is being helped by the firm. Again, if the firm is strictly helping to promote the cause because of a sincere commitment, it probably is socially responsive. If, however, the firm is illustrating how a new "unrelated" product helps solve the problem, very possibly profit is the real motive.

Answers to CONSIDER THIS Questions   (Page 372)

1.   **What are the three levels of ethics?**

The first level is law. Federal, state, and local laws all apply. International laws and laws of foreign countries, if applicable, also apply. Second, are company policies, procedures, and rules. Third, is the moral stance a person takes when dealing with a situation that is not covered by the above factors.

2.   **Aren't individuals or firms being ethical as long as they are obeying all applicable laws?**

While the law does cover many of the major ethical problems such as falsifying documents or deceptive advertising, it does not cover every conceivable situation. There are also many different interpretations of the law, so it is sometimes difficult for a person or firm to know if they are breaking the law. Finally, the law may lag behind in terms of defining what is legal and what is not legal.

3. **What are the main reasons why businesses become unethical?**

While there are many reasons why a business starts acting unethical, the three most common appear to be greed, poor ethical standards on the part of management (especially top management), and finally, competitive pressures both from within the firm and in the marketplace.

Answers to REVIEW AND DISCUSSION Questions

1. *What are the four phases of social responsibility?*

   The four phases in order of acceptance by a firm are:
   a. *Economic responsibility* -- Firm is only profit oriented.
   b. *Public responsibility* -- Firm goes beyond a pure profit orientation and tries to help society establish public policy on major social issues.
   c. *Social responsiveness* -- Under some social pressure, the firm actually implements some type of program to help solve a social problem.
   d. *Social issues management* -- Here, the firm scans the internal and external environments to find issues or social problems that need addressing. Then, a program is implemented to help alleviate them.

2. *What are the main benefits of being socially responsible?*

   The primary benefits are:
   a. Increased profits
   b. Improved company image
   c. Avoidance of new legislation
   d. Stock prices usually rise to benefit both stockholders and the firm
   e. The environment is better off
   f. Help to prevent problems from growing is a logical approach
   g. Improved cooperation between business and society

3. *What are the real costs of being socially responsible?*

   a. Socially responsive programs do cost money and may force a firm to raise prices, which could hurt profits.
   b. Social programs may not be cost effective due to a firm's lack of expertise in running a program in a social area.
   c. Social programs may cause the firm to stray from its main objective of profits.

d.   Some of the social programs instituted may include illegal aspects, since the firm is not totally familiar with all considerations.

e.   The public may not strongly support socially responsible firms over non-responsible firms when buying products.

4.   *Why is it so important that social responsibility start with top management?*

Top management sets the tone and the direction of the firm. Everyone in the firm looks to top management for guidance on how to handle various situations. Top management determines what is rewarded and what actions are punished. A firm will only become socially responsible when top management decides to adopt socially responsible policies, procedures, and programs. These managers must also stress the importance of being socially responsible in both action and words.

5.   *What are some ways in which management communicates its social responsiveness stance?*

While there are many different ways to communicate a firm's social responsiveness stance, some of the more effective ones are the following:

a.   Involve both employees and managers in designing and implementing social programs.

b.   Have a reward system for those who accomplish social goals and objectives.

c.   Utilize constant on-going forms of communication, such as graphs or charts, which indicate progress toward a goal.

d.   Communicate with the public through the mass media what the firm is trying to accomplish.

e.   Periodically audit results and make changes accordingly. Input on how to improve results should be sought from everyone in the firm.

6.   *How does a firm benefit from advocacy promotions?*

Advocacy promotions do not have an obvious product/cause relationship like cause marketing programs do. They can still benefit a firm, however, by illustrating how it really feels about a specific social problem or issue. The main benefits are improved company image and goodwill, which may in turn lead to sales and better customer loyalty.

7. *What are some of the main factors that affect managerial ethics?*

Managerial ethics are influenced by a number of factors including the following:
a. The laws at all levels of government
b. The ethical stance of top management
c. Rules, policies, and procedures
d. The business culture, including types of actions that are encouraged or discouraged
e. The moral stance of an individual, which is also influenced by personal values, beliefs, and attitudes

8. *How can a firm improve its managerial ethics?*

The following steps will help any firm improve in this area:
a. Be sure top management is constantly communicating high ethical standards in both words and actions.
b. Establish a written code of ethics and communicate it to everyone.
c. Utilize a permanent ethics committee to clarify situations and actions.
d. Utilize an ombudsmen or someone from the outside who can give impartial insights about situations.
e. Establish "hot lines" to report unethical behaviors.
f. Do in-house seminars on ethics.
g. Establish training programs on ethics for all managers and employees.

9. *What are some of the factors that an individual should consider before challenging a questionable ethical problem?*

The following steps should be followed:
a. Be sure you have all of the facts and determine that a breach of ethics has occurred.
b. Decide how much you are willing to risk in reporting this situation.
c. Inform your boss of the situation and explain your feelings.
d. If the situation is still not resolved, go to a higher level, where you feel confident that that listener will be receptive to hearing your comments.
e. If you find that some of the firm's actions are strongly different from your values, consider changing jobs.

▒ Answers to CRITICAL THINKING INCIDENTS
■

Incident 11-1:   WHAT IS JOHN WATERMAN'S DILEMMA

1.   **Assuming that the developer's marketing plan is now in place, what ethical questions does it raise?**

This case presents the reader with both legal and ethical questions. While few reading the case probably have sufficient legal expertise to judge the total legality of the new marketing plan, lying about the true source of loanable funds is deceptive and probably fraudulent.

The marketing plan, as a whole, relies on deception. Raising the price from $85,000 to $119,000 for one week just so you can "lower" it to $89,900 is a deceptive act. As previously stated, lying about the source of funds so you can "justify" the incredibly low interest rate is probably illegal and certainly untruthful. Finally, utilizing a five year balloon mortgage means the entire balance of the mortgage becomes due at the end of the fifth year. Balloon mortgages are legal and used fairly often in real estate transactions. However, if purchasers are not clearly made aware of this situation, then they could be in serious trouble when the mortgage does come due. Finally, while "rebates" are commonly used in the automotive industry to increase sales, they too are seen by many people as deceptive, since some consumers are naive enough to think that someone is honestly "giving" them $1000 to purchase a product.

If the questions on the ethics guide of the Rotary Clubs given earlier in the text are applied to this situation, it is easy to see that it fails most, if not all, four of the test questions:
>   Is it truthful?
>   Is it fair to all concerned?
>   Will it build goodwill and better friendships?
>   Will it be beneficial to all concerned?

2.   **What possible problems could arise in this situation?**

Deceptive advertising falls under the jurisdiction of the Federal Trade Commission (FTC), and this marketing plan appears to be deceptive. The FTC can make the company stop running any advertisements and possibly even force them to run "corrective ads." The Real Estate Commission could very possibly be brought into this situation. If the commission feels that consumers have been hurt by this deceptive program, it can fine the development company or possibly take away their real estate license. Finally, consumers who were not "clearly" made aware of the balloon payment could sue the developers in court for damages and very possibly win.

3.   **Would you recommend that John take the position?**

The answer is a resounding, "NO."

Incident 11-2:   WAS AMERICAN PESTICIDE NEGLIGENT?

1.   **Do you feel that American Pesticide was acting in a socially responsible manner in this case?**

Very early in this chapter, social responsibility was defined as "actions and decisions which consider the legal, economic, and societal factors in both the short and long run as well as the organizational interests." Utilizing this definition, it is apparent that American Pesticide was not acting in a socially responsible manner. American Pesticide was operating a plant that produced a "lethal gas" that they knew could have devastating effects on the people in and around the plant. Yet, they failed to anticipate what might happen if a valve malfunctioned. The company also had not given any thought to the long run as indicated by the lack of a computerized safety system and siren warning system. Finally, the company was only thinking of the short run and of the organization when it cut back on training due to declining profits.

2.   **In what ways, if any, was American Pesticide negligent? Was anyone else to blame for the accident?**

American Pesticide was negligent in a number of ways.   First, the plant was not built to the same safety standards as the other plants. There was not any computerized safety system or siren warning system. The personnel in the plant were not properly trained on how to handle a leak such as this, as evidenced by two workers running away when they first saw the leak. There is no mention of the company doing safety training or having safety drills to simulate accidents of this type. Finally, the plant management was evidently relying totally on the Mexican government to do safety inspections.   No company safety inspection program is ever mentioned.

The second part of the question asks if anyone else is to blame here?

The Mexican government can certainly be held at least partially liable for not making sure that all safety systems were installed and operational before the plant opened. Also, it appears that the Mexican government may have been lax in doing regular safety inspections.

3.   **What options can American Pesticide exercise to solve this problem? Which option do you recommend and why?**

American Pesticide basically has the following options:
a.   Install the computerized safety and siren warning systems and do massive safety training before they reopen the plant and continue manufacturing the same products. This option is practical, as this is what the plant is currently set up to manufacture. This option may not be feasible, however, since people are going to be afraid to work there. Also, the Mexican government may force the firm to comply with some safety standards which are unrealistic, due to the obviously poor public relations that the firm now has with the community.
b.   Stop producing the current products and instead design the plant to make a product that does not produce any kind of lethal by-product. This option should help quell the fears of the local people and the government, but another "safer" product may not be available. This option could also be very expensive, depending upon how much new equipment is needed and how much training is necessary for the workers to produce the new product.
c.   Close the plant, sell it (if possible), or simply remove the equipment and walk away. While this is the simplest alternative, it is probably the most expensive. Selling the plant would be very difficult due to the circumstances. Walking away with just the equipment may mean leaving behind a very expensive facility and getting nothing.

The second part of question three asks for a recommendation and explanation. Option two, producing a new safe product, appears to be the best solution, as equipment and training costs are not prohibitive. The company has irrefutably damaged itself by producing its current product. With the number of people killed and hurt by the accident, it is unlikely that any public relations program could ever convince the people or the government that the plant is now safe. Walking away from the plant is definitely the worst possible scenario financially but may be the company's only alternative if a new safe product cannot be found.

Incident 11-3:   SO WHO REALLY WAS TO BLAME?

1.   **In what areas did Thiokol display poor, or at least questionable, ethics?**

The management at Morton Thiokol had known that there were problems with the "O" rings for almost nine years prior to the Challenger disaster. They had received reports of problems with the "O" rings on at least nine previous shuttle flights. Finally, even their own engineers noted damage to the seals and observed that low temperatures aggravated the problems. All of these reports were ignored since the "O" ring was so "cost effective." It seems that profit was more highly valued than safety. Morton Thiokol's management also suppressed any reports of problems to NASA out of fear that production would be hurt. They were also aware of the "cover ups" concerning any problems that did occur during production that could not be solved.

2. **Is it reasonable to state that the real cause of the Challenger disaster is the way in which contracts are awarded through the lowest bid process? Explain your answer.**

    The lowest bid process has been used for many years in a very successful manner. To be successful, however, specifications and standards must be very clearly and specifically spelled out. Any changes or deviations must be closely monitored to be sure nothing of significance is compromised. If Morton Thiokol had practiced openness with NASA about the problems, they probably could have resolved. The contract might have been reopened to reflect the increased costs necessary to design and produce any parts of the project which had safety problems.

3. **Is it reasonable to expect a company to absorb $500 million in cost overruns to correct a design problem that has seen a lot of success? Explain your answer.**

    It is unrealistic to expect any firm to absorb a $500 million dollar cost overrun all by itself. Virtually no business could survive a cost overrun of that magnitude. At the same time, however, NASA should have been made aware of the problems and degree of risk present in utilizing the present seal system. Since human lives were at stake here, continuing to use the same "O" ring system that had partially broken down on at least nine previous occasions does not make much sense. The logical answer in a situation like this is for NASA to reopen the contract so that Morton Thiokol could recoup these costs and raise the safety levels.

4. **How can NASA improve the way in which it awards contacts so disasters like this one can be avoided in the future?**

    One way is to stop using the lowest-bidder process and simply award contacts on the basis of reliability and quality of work. This, of course, will be more costly and, in some cases, difficult to judge as some products will be proto-types. Another method is to utilize open-ended contracts which allow for renegotiations when new problems are found that were not anticipated by either NASA or the manufacturer. If a company knows that cost overruns for designing and producing safer components is possible, it is far less likely to try and hide problems or cover them up.

5.   **What is your reaction to the fact that none of the managers at Thiokol were dismissed? Do you agree or disagree with this decision? Justify your answer.**

While it is easy to say that at least some of Thiokol's managers should have been dismissed, the real problem is determining which ones. If specific managers can be found that withheld, covered up, or failed to pass on vital information, all on their own, then they should be dismissed. If however, all of Thiokol's management was aware of what was going on, then it is a company-wide failure and not a specific manager's fault.

Study Guide Assignments

The individual case presents one person's very negative view of the business world. In particular, the case portrays business managers as people who only care about profits even at the expense of health and safety. Environmental problems, the exploitation of women and minorities, and even the exploitation of underdeveloped countries are all blamed on the business world. The case also states that it would be impossible for a business firm to be socially responsible today, as costs would be higher and reduce competitiveness. The case concludes by asking readers if they agree with the charges made, and it also asks them to review the phases of social responsibility.

The group case again continues with these same debatable social issues. It raises the question of how much government intervention may be necessary to keep businesses from harming employees, consumers, and the environment. The case concludes by asking the instructor to identify students who hold divergent views on business social responsibility and ask them to present their views to the class.

Video Case

U.S. Sprint

Focus: **Culture and Ethics**

Summary:

This training film for U.S. Sprint features Olympic track star Jim Ryun. A major part of the culture at U.S. Sprint is treating all people with dignity and respect. Ryun argues that ethical behavior creates a competitive edge and that integrity is vital to the success of the company. He states, "Success is measured in how you've treated people and how you feel about yourself."

Discussion Questions:

1.   This video advocates integrity and honesty. Are these universal virtues you would expect to see at all companies, or do some companies/industries place more emphasis on these virtues than other companies/industries?

     There are certain industries that seem to place a heavier emphasis on these virtues than others. Accounting firms, insurance companies, and banks usually have corporate creeds that specifically outline the importance of honesty.

2.   If you were an employee at U.S. Sprint, what would be your reaction to a training film like this one?

     While some students may view this film with some cynicism, it clearly indicates that senior management considers the topic important enough to spend money on the video. How much employees buy into the video's message depends in large part on whether senior managers exhibit the behavior advocated in the video.

Chapter 12

International Management

Chapter Overview

Global competition and global opportunities have never been clearer to today's business leaders. As trade barriers fall, the primary disadvantage that global competitors have will be transportation costs. With this in mind, it is imperative that domestic business leaders take steps to not only meet foreign price and quality standards but to exceed these standards if at all possible.

This chapter explains how the global business scene has evolved and changed over time. The chapter also discusses different ways a business firm can enter the international marketplace. Also, some of the environmental differences related to operating in a foreign market are presented. Finally, approaches to adapting management practices to international business are discussed.

Teaching Objectives

The teaching objectives of this chapter are to:

1. Understand how the field of business has evolved into a truly global scene.

2. Identify some of the major changes in the fluctuating international markets.

3.   Examine how multinational firms have evolved.

4.   Discuss global competition in the service industry.

5.   Differentiate between cultural and environmental trends and realize how they can impact the management of a foreign business.

6.   Find out how to apply American management principles to an international business world.

7.   Identify some definite problem areas that must be considered before a domestic firm becomes a multinational corporation.

Chapter Outline of the Text

I.   THE CHANGING GLOBAL BUSINESS SCENE
      A.   How Can U.S. Firms Become More Competitive Internationally?
      B.   Current Trends in the International Marketplace
          1.   General Agreement on Tariffs and Trade (GATT) which has recently been named *The New World Trade Organization*
          2.   The European Community (EC)
          3.   The U.S./Canadian Free Trade Agreement (FTA)
          4.   The North American Free Trade Agreement (NAFTA)
          5.   New Markets in Eastern Europe and Russia
II.   THE GROWTH AND DEVELOPMENT OF INTERNATIONAL MANAGEMENT
      A.   Different Forms of International Management
          1.   The Domestic-Market Approach to International Management
          2.   The Multinational Approach to International Management
          3.   The Global Approach to International Management
      B.   Global Competition in the Service Industry
III.   ASSESSING ENVIRONMENTAL DIFFERENCES
      A.   The Political and Legal Environment
      B.   The Cultural Environment
      C.   The Economic Environment
IV.   MANAGING IN THE INTERNATIONAL BUSINESS WORLD
      A.   Planning
      B.   Organizing
      C.   Staffing
      D.   Leading
      E.   Controlling
V.   SOME PROBLEM AREAS FACED BY A FIRM ENTERING THE INTERNATIONAL MARKETPLACE

Key Terms

These terms are introduced in the chapter. Definitions are included in the glossary of the text.

Customer focus

Domestic-market management approach

European Community (EC)

European Economic Community
    Agreement (EEC)

Foreign agent (broker)

General Agreement on Tariffs and Trade
    (GATT) or *The New World Trade*
    Organization

Global management approach

Global strategic partnership

International business firm

Joint venture (partnerships)

Licensure agreement

Manufacturing contract

Maquiladora program

Multinational firm

Multinational management approach

Nationalism

Protectionism

Quota

Regional trading area

Subsidy

Tariff

U.S./Canadian Free Trade Agreement
    (FTA)

Vertical integration

Wholly-owned subsidiaries (multinational
    and global)

Detailed Chapter Summary

I.   THE CHANGING GLOBAL BUSINESS SCENE

**Teaching Objective 1:   Understand how the field of business has evolved into a truly
                             global scene.**

The economies throughout Europe and Asia were badly damaged in World War II.
The U.S. economy, therefore, faced very little foreign competition until the European
and Asian countries rebuilt their economies with state-of-the art technology. Since the
early 1970s, the U.S. has seen a tremendous amount of competition in virtually every
product and service industry. The level of competition will only continue to grow as

Russia and Eastern European countries convert their socialist economies to capitalism, and trade barriers continue to fall.

A.   *How can U.S. Firms Become more Competitive Internationally?*

In order for U.S. firms to become more competitive, they must concentrate primarily on the following four areas:

1.   Customer Focus

This really means two things. First, U.S. businesses must establish an effective on-going communication system with their customers. Second, through this communication system, they must determine what customers really want in terms of innovative features and then provide them.

2.   Improved Quality and Productivity

To achieve higher levels of quality and productivity, managers of U.S. firms must be sure that the entire production process is properly synchronized and coordinated. Everything from product planning to actual production and customer satisfaction must be carefully orchestrated with communication again being the key element. Customers start the process by telling a firm what they want and finish the process by expressing their level of satisfaction with the firm's products or services. The firm must always be working on improving quality, efficiency, and customer satisfaction.

3.   The Development of Human Resources

The old saying that "nothing improves unless you work on it" is certainly true in this area. If firms do not educate and train their workers, chances are very slim that desired learning will occur. Management must also remember that an employee who does a specific job eight hours a day possesses very good knowledge about that job. Since this is the case, management needs to involve employees in problem solving and decision making situations. When developing human resources, management needs to assume a facilitator role.

4.   Continuous Improvement

Many foreign competitors and the Japanese, in particular, constantly work at improving every aspect of the firm.

Firms in the U.S. must also adapt this philosophy, even to the point of making it a part of their organizational culture. In today's business world, it is necessary to seek improvements, or the competition will gain a competitive edge.

B.   *Current Trends in the International Marketplace*

Teaching Objective 2:   Identify some of the major changes in international markets.

There have been three major changes that have tremendously impacted the entire international marketplace:

1.   Elimination of Trade Barriers Through the General Agreement on Tariffs and Trade/G.A.T.T.

Through G.A.T.T., now known as the World Trade Organization, trade barriers between 117 nations have been reduced. This agreement is revised every few years, and each time the number of trade barriers among member nations has declined. It is only logical to conclude that there will ultimately be worldwide free trade through this agreement. The regional trade agreements removed trade barriers among the participating nations, either immediately or over a stated period of time. The three largest regional trade agreements are the European Economic Community (EEC), The Free Trade Agreement (FTA), and the North American Free Trade Agreement (NAFTA).

a.   The European Community (EC)

The European Community (EC) began to operate on December 31, 1992. Originally, it consisted of the twelve common market nations, but several other European nations have applied for membership since then. This agreement eliminated all trade barriers, custom delays, and differences in national standards among the participating nations. It also has a provision for a common currency and a central bank by 1999. At least two nations, however, Denmark and Great Britain, have asked and been granted the right to use their own currency instead of the common currency.

b.   The Free Trade Agreement (FTA)

The Free Trade Agreement between the United States and Canada was established in 1988. Over the next ten years, all trade barriers between them will be abolished. This time frame was established to give selected industries that may be adversely affected time for adjusting to a duty free marketplace.

c.   The North American Free Trade Agreement (NAFTA)

The North American Free Trade Agreement took effect on January 1, 1994. This agreement is between the United States, Canada, and Mexico and will eliminate all trade barriers over a 15 year period. Again, this time frame is used to allow sensitive industries in all three countries to adjust to a duty free marketplace. NAFTA also has had some other countries in South America inquire about membership.

3.   New Markets in Eastern Europe and Russia

As the Eastern European and Russian economies convert to capitalism, there are some excellent opportunities for U.S. firms to establish themselves in these markets. This, of course, can be accomplished in a number of different ways ranging from strictly exporting to purchasing and operating existing firms within countries. While the opportunities are great, the risk and problems unfortunately may be equally great. Problems can range from a poor infrastructure to support the business to rules and regulations, which may make operating a business very difficult, imposed by a national government.

Teaching Hint: Students need to realize that the opening of the former communist countries to private investors is currently filled with difficulties and perils. However, it is a true "window of opportunity" which will not be open indefinitely.

II.   THE GROWTH AND DEVELOPMENT OF INTERNATIONAL MANAGEMENT

Teaching Objective 3:   Examine how multinational firms have evolved.

In the international marketplace, several factors are going to have an impact on the management of domestic firms. Some of the most important factors are the following:

1.   Many firms, especially ones in free-trade areas, are now looking at all global markets, since they have had to adopt products or services to fit

all of the people in the free-trade area. If this is the case, then it may make a lot of sense to take initial advantage of market opportunities.

2. As U.S. firms do grow internationally, domestic suppliers must either grow with them or lose them to foreign competitors. If the U.S. firm loses a supplier to a foreign competitor, it probably will not be long before the foreign competitor seeks to do business in the U.S. market as well.

3. In many high tech product areas, the cost of new product development has simply grown beyond the ability of one firm to handle it. It is going to be increasingly common for international competitors to form joint ventures so that they can share development costs and develop new products. The airline industry is a classic example.

4. Since many product and service markets in the U.S. are quite mature, new international markets are an excellent way to expand current product sales. Also, a product or service may have reached the end of its life cycle in the U.S. but still be accepted as a new product in a foreign market. This extension of a product's life cycle could be very profitable.

5. Entrance into new international markets grows increasingly difficult as time passes and other competitors enter them. Managers of U.S. firms must remember that they can enter some international markets on a relatively low-risk basis by exporting to firms. If that experience is successful, then they can consider getting involved on a larger scale.

A. *Different Forms of International Management*

Entering the international marketplace can be done by utilizing several different methods. In each case, the levels of risk and control move together. The three most common approaches are listed below:

1. Domestic Market Approach

    Their are three domestic market approaches to international management. Each approach has a different level of risk and control.

    a. First Domestic Market Approach - Exporting

        Exporting means to sell your firm's products to a foreign broker or agent. Here, the firm has virtually no control over how products are marketed once the foreign broker or agent purchases them. Once they have been paid for the products, the risk is quite low. The only real danger here is what the foreign agent may do with the products that could hurt the firm's or product's image.

b.   Second Domestic Market Approach - Licensure Agreement

This approach allows a foreign firm to either manufacture and/or sell products or the right to place a brand name or symbols on products. Disney World, for example, has licensure agreements with many foreign firms. This approach provides more control as, a firm can require that certain specifications be met, yet it is still not the manufacturer in the foreign market.

c.   Third Domestic Market Approach -- Manufacturing Contract

With this approach, a foreign manufacturer agrees to let the U.S. domestic firm actually supervise how its products are made. The two firms then share the profits. Control increases here but so does risk, as these contracts may be for substantial amounts of time.

2.   The Multinational Approach to International Management

With this approach, a U.S. firm is willing to make substantial commitment to a foreign market. Normally, products or services are modified to meet the foreign market and in many cases, substantial fixed investments are made in plants and equipment. The two most common ways to become a multinational firm are to form joint ventures or to establish wholly-owned subsidiaries.

a.   Joint Ventures

This involves a U.S. company forming a partnership with a foreign firm. Joint ventures may be formed to develop new products, to share technology, and/or to give each other access to local markets. Normally, the roles and responsibilities of each firm are clearly spelled out in the joint-venture agreement. This approach does increase both control and risk.

b.   Wholly-Owned Subsidiary

A U.S. firm purchases either controlling interest or all of a foreign firm. Often the subsidiary firm is given considerable freedom in terms of how to operate in the foreign market, and heavy use of foreign managers and employees is very common. The U.S. firm does have the most control, but it also has substantial investment risk.

3.   The Global Approach to International Management

The last and most extensive approach to the international marketplace is the global approach. There are two common forms in this approach.

a.   The Global Strategic Partnership

This approach is much larger than a simple joint venture. Two firms join together and make a long-term commitment in the form of time and investments to develop products or services that will dominate world markets. This approach does not modify products for a particular market but develops a single product market strategy which can be utilized in all markets. General Electric and France's state owned SNEEMA are good examples of this approach. They hope to dominate the worldwide jet engine market.

b.   Wholly-Owned Subsidiaries that are Vertically Integrated

A U.S. firm owns not only the manufacturer but also owns or controls distributors and retailers. Again, the main emphasis is on dominating a worldwide product or service area with a single product market strategy. True global products are very difficult to develop, and it is even more difficult to dominate all global markets.

Teaching Hint: Remind your students that a firm really does not have a choice as to whether it wants to compete internationally. Foreign competitors will come after U.S. markets, even if the U.S. firm decides only to do business domestically.

B.   *Global Competition in the Service Industry*

Teaching Objective 4:   Discuss global competition in the service industry.

While many U.S. companies have lost out to foreign competitors in various product areas, the service industry is still primarily dominated by U.S. firms. The areas of computer services and retailing are clearly dominated by U.S. firms, and they are making substantial gains in the fields of insurance, airlines, banking, and construction.

While U.S. firms are doing well in the service industry, they are vulnerable to competitors in this field as well as the product area. U.S. firms must be very careful to make sure that both quality and efficiency are constantly maintained and that they are striving for continuous improvement in both of these areas. There are five megatrends that will definitely keep the service industries growing:

1.   Technical Advancements

Rapid worldwide data transmissions of all types.

2.   The Globalization of Manufacturing

With more manufacturing plants being built throughout the world, the service industries that service them will also grow.

3.   Increased Income

Incomes are increasing, and this increases the demand for services.

4.   Deregulation of Government Barriers

Both the U.S. and many other countries have removed barriers of many types, such as extensive licensing requirements against foreign firms.

5.   Removal of Trade Barriers

The removal of trade barriers opens up markets, for example, to foreign firms.

Suggested Readings for this Section:
Cohen, Warren. "Exporting Know-How," U.S. News and World Report, August 20/ September 6, 1993, pp. 53-57.

While the U.S. is running large trade deficits with many foreign countries due to an excess of product imports over exports, the service sector shows a positive trade surplus. The U.S. has had a positive service trade surplus every year since 1970, and it was close to $68 billion in 1993. Even better news is that service exports have been growing at an average rate of 12.6 percent, which is almost double the growth rate for merchandise exports. The biggest single factor causing this large growth for service exports is the modernization of many countries around the world. In particular, Russia, and some eastern European countries are very interested in U.S. know-how.

Berry, Jon. "Don't Leave Home Without It, Wherever you Live," Business Week, February 21, 1994, pp. 76-66.

American Express spent over half of its $200 million advertising media budget in 1994 on international media. American Express is expanding its global business, which currently accounts for approximately 25 percent of revenues.. While this percentage is significant, it lags in comparison with VISA, which now does over 50 percent of its business internationally.

American Express Travel Related Services Unit launched a series of testimonial advertisements from some of the biggest fashion designers, hotel owners, and prominent merchants in Britain, Italy, Germany, and Japan. They also plan on serving Hong Kong, Singapore, Spain, and Brazil in an effort to reach nearly 30 countries. The ad campaign is aimed at the business traveler. In an effort to overcome VISA, they have reduced merchant fees, broadened their merchant base to include mass merchandisers, and offered frequent flier incentives to increase usage by current card holders. All of this is part of an American Express corporate restructuring, which is trying to change its image as a "yuppie" status symbol to that of a card used by businesspersons who travel a lot in their work.

Average spending per card in the international marketplace grew by 17.6 percent between 1991 and 1993. With growth like that, is it any wonder that American Express is big on global expansion?

III.   ASSESSING ENVIRONMENTAL DIFFERENCES

Teaching Objective 5:   Differentiate between cultural and environmental trends and realize how they can impact the management of a foreign business.

Managing a business in a foreign country requires managers to deal with a large variety of cultural and environmental differences. There are numerous examples of U.S. firms that tried to operate a new foreign subsidiary just like it was located in the U.S. The results have been disastrous. Cultural and environmental differences fall into three areas:

A.   *The Political and Legal Environment*

U.S. firms operating in a foreign country may not be treated the same as their domestic competitors. Tax laws and licensure requirements may be substantially different. Many times, foreign firms are viewed suspiciously by local governments. In particular, foreign governments can cause U.S. firms to encounter difficulties through these methods:

1.   Forms of Protectionism

Protectionism is intended to give domestic firms a competitive advantage. Typically it takes the form of tariffs (taxes on all incoming goods), quotas (limits on the number of goods that can be brought into the country), or subsidies (direct government payments to help domestic firms compete internationally). Nationalism, the last form of protectionism, occurs when local governments strongly encourage local people to purchase only their country's products.

2.   Bribes and Payoffs

While this is a common practice in many foreign countries, it is illegal for U.S. firms to use bribes and payoffs, even in a foreign country. The U.S. law has recently been amended to ease some of the restrictions, and the new law does clarify how to handle some of the more common problem areas. For example, U.S. firms can pay people to "facilitate" government action; they simply cannot pay someone to ignore the situation.

B.   *The Cultural Environment*

Cultural differences, which can be very subtle, are extremely important. Any firm that enters the international marketplace on virtually any level must make it a high priority to try to learn the cultural taboos and the proper cultural practices. If a U.S. business fails to understand the cultural methods of doing business, grave misunderstandings and a complete lack of trust may occur. Language differences are particularly important, and U.S. managers must remember that not all English terms translate into another language so that the exact same meaning is received. The Remember to Communicate box in this chapter is an excellent example of this fact.

C.   *The Economic Environment*

In assessing the economic environment, a business must look at four main areas:

1.   The Average Income Level of the Population

If the average income for the population is very low, then no matter how desperately they need your product or service, there simply is not much of a market for it.

2.   The Tax Structure

In some countries, foreign firms have much higher tax rates than domestic competitors. These tax differences may be very obvious or subtle, as in hidden registration fees.

3.   Inflation Rate

Inflation rates in the U.S. have been quite low and relatively stable for several years. In some foreign countries, however, inflation rates of 30, 40, or even 100 percent per year are not uncommon.

4.   Fluctuating Exchange Rates

The exchange rate, or the value of one country's currency in terms of another country's currency, is determined primarily by supply and demand for each other's goods and services. The government of a country can, however, cause this exchange rate to change dramatically by causing high inflation, by printing too much currency or by changing the value of the currency through devaluation. A foreign investor could sustain large losses if the value of the currency did drop substantially.

Suggested Readings for this Section:
Symonds, William, Malkin and Melcher. "Did Labatt Guzzle Too Much Too Fast?" <u>*Business Week*</u>*, May 29, 1995, pp. 55-56.*

Labatt, Canada's second largest brewer, was facing a flat Canadian beer market with little or no growth projected. To position for growth, Labatt purchased 22 percent of a Mexican brewer called Femsa Cerveza for $510 million in 1994. At that time, the deal looked favorable in terms of growth potential, but many analysts felt the price was a little too high. Barely six months later, the Mexican government devalued the Peso, making Labatt's share now worth approximately $175 million, or a $335 million loss according to Equity Research.

While no one could have predicted the Mexican devaluation, this loss is indicative of what can happen when a firm decides to enter the international marketplace.

Galuszka, Peter, and Sandra Dallas. "And You Think You've Got Tax Problems." <u>*Business Week*</u>*, May 29, 1995, p. 50.*

Investing in Russia has never looked better. At least that is what Coca-Cola Company thought when they decided to open a new bottling plant near Moscow. Coke had planned on investing up to $100 million in Russia in order to compete better with Pepsico, a company that has been in Russia for quite some time.

At the beginning of 1995, however, Coke got a very big surprise from the Russian government. Without any warning, it eliminated a tax exemption on imported construction materials and levied a $1.4 million tax against Coke's new plant. While Coke was still upset about this tax, the Russian government levied (in March 1995) an "excess wage" tax equal to 38 percent of the wages paid to their Russian employees. This second tax bill was almost identical in size to the first one.

Many foreign investors or potential investors in Russia state plainly that they can tolerate the political problems and even the fluctuating ruble, but they cannot handle the unanticipated tax increases that carry heavy retroactive penalties.

IV.   MANAGING IN THE INTERNATIONAL BUSINESS WORLD

Teaching Objective 6:   Find out how to apply American management principles to an international business world.

Global competition has forced U.S. business firms to change how they manage both at home and abroad. The increasing rate of change, technological advances, shorter product life cycles, and high speed communications are all factors that have created these changes. The new management approach focuses on establishing a new communication system that features high levels of employee involvement. Organizational structures must also be flexible enough to change with changing market conditions. On-going staff development programs and design-control procedures, which are understandable and acceptable, are outcomes from this new approach. Management values are changing, and managers must now have a vision and be able to communicate the vision to everyone in the firm.

Each of the five basic management functions also must change when operating in a foreign market:

A.   *Planning*

International firms must be sure that their plans fit the culture of the host country. Typically, U.S. firms feel that long-term plans should be three to five years in length, but in some cultures, this time period is too short. Through the regulations and bureaucracy, a foreign government may also influence how an international firm does its planning.

B.   *Organizing*

International businesses must be organized so they can adapt to cultural and environmental differences. No longer can U.S. firms just put a "carbon copy" or a clone of themselves in a foreign country. An international firm must organize so that it can be responsive to foreign customers, employees, and suppliers. An entire international firm may even be organized as one giant worldwide company that has several different divisions. Above all, the new organization design must establish a very open communication system so that problems, ideas, and grievances can quickly be heard and addressed at all levels of management. Without this, employees will not get involved, and their insights and ideas are crucial to the success of the business.

C.   *Staffing*

Since obtaining a good staff is so critical to the success of a business,
the hiring and development of employees must be done very carefully.
Management must be familiar with the country's national labor laws.
Next, it must decide how many managers and personnel to hire from the
local labor force or transfer from the U.S.   In most cases, U.S. firms
are better off hiring local talent and using only a few key expatriates.

D.   *Leading*

The style of leadership, which is acceptable to employees, varies from
nation to nation. In countries like France and Germany, informal
relations with employees are discouraged; leadership is quite rigid and
clearly spelled out. In Sweden and Japan, however, informal relations
with employees are strongly encouraged, and a very participative
leadership style is used. Incentive systems also vary tremendously. The
type of incentives used in the U.S. might not work very well in Europe
or Japan, where stable employment and benefits are more important than
bonuses.

E.   *Controlling*

In order to be as flexible and adaptive as needed in today's international
markets, a form of self control by each individual employee must be
established. This calls for a large amount of commitment to the firm by
employees and, in turn, will only come from effective leadership on the
part of the managers at all levels. Some critical areas, such as the
financial area, will still be rather tightly controlled; however, many
other areas may be turned over to employees who have knowledge and
experience. This will give employees a real feeling of involvement and
help them see how they can impact the success of the company.

*Teaching Hint: Remind your students that managing a business in a foreign country is quite
different and at times very difficult. Most, if not all, problems can be overcome if the firm
studies the culture of a country before entering it and hires local managers for key positions.*

V.   SOME PROBLEM AREAS FACED BY A FIRM ENTERING THE
      INTERNATIONAL MARKETPLACE.

**Teaching Objective 7:   Identify some definite problem areas that must be considered
                           before a domestic firm becomes a multinational corporation.**

There are four basic potential problem areas that a U.S. firm may face when
entering the international marketplace.

A.   *Selecting the Right Market*

      The firm's products or services must be acceptable to the new market.
      Without acceptance, the U.S. firm will fail. The U.S. firm must also try
      to select markets abroad that are relatively stable in terms of the
      government and the local economy, or a bright future could disappear
      very fast.

B.   *New Competitors*

      New competitors can originate from countries most Americans may not
      have heard of, and they may be very competitive. Before making a
      major foreign commitment, U.S. firms must try to learn of any possible
      new competitors.

C.   *Economic Reforms in Foreign Countries*

      In foreign countries economic reforms are usually slow and may not be
      as successful as anticipated. Infrastructures, such as roads, airports,
      water and sewer systems, and even telephone systems, may be very
      poor for a long period of time.

D.   *Getting Into the Marketplace Too Late*

      Many times, it is prudent to "wait until things level out." However, this
      may cause a firm to be late in entering the market. U.S. firms are not
      the only ones looking at foreign markets, and the first companies into a
      market get first chance at the most desirable locations, distributors, and
      suppliers. Also they may establish large market shares that can be
      difficult to compete against.

VI.   LOOKING BACK

This chapter looks at how the field of management is changing due to international competition and international opportunities. The world is becoming a global business arena.   Firms in the U.S. must realize that they may not have any real choice as to whether or not to compete with foreign competitors. Although the international competition can be very challenging, U.S. firms must also realize that there are some competitive strategies that do not require huge international investments.

Answers to CONSIDER THIS Questions   (Page 395)

1.   **What is NAFTA and what impact will it have on U.S. business?**

NAFTA or the North American Free Trade Agreement went into effect on January 1, 1994. This agreement between the U.S., Canada, and Mexico created the largest single trading partnership in the world. Under NAFTA, all trade restrictions of any type will be eliminated; however, some specific products will be "phased in" over a fifteen-year period. NAFTAs impact on U.S. business is both positive and negative. For those U.S. businesses that are strong competitors, these new trade-free markets provide opportunities. On the other hand, for those U.S. industries that have very labor intensive products, such as clothing, the lower cost of wages in Mexico could be disastrous.

2.   **How will the European Community (EC) affect foreign competitors?**

The EC created the second largest trading partnership, and it also eliminated all trade barriers of any type between the member nations.

The EC will allow member countries that are very competitive to produce products in larger quantities, which will lower costs and make them even tougher worldwide competitors. As the EC adds new countries and grows even larger, the markets for a given firm's product will also expand. While non-member foreign producers will not be kept out of the European markets, they may encounter some trade restrictions, which may put them at a significant disadvantage.

3.   **What does the transformation of Russia and eastern European countries to capitalism mean to U.S. businesses?**

For the first time, U.S. businesses will be able to enter these markets and receive currency that is fully convertible to U.S. dollars. They will also be able to purchase existing companies or set up new ones and actually own them outright. The markets themselves are very large, and while there are significant problems to overcome, the rewards may be very beneficial.

Answers to CONSIDER THIS Questions (Page 407)

1. **What communication problems does a firm commonly encounter when doing business in a foreign market?**

   The most obvious communication problems occur if the business firm does not have anyone who fluently speaks the foreign language. Words do not always translate as literally as desired. The second problem deals with different views of nonverbal gestures. Behaviors that are not offensive to Americans may be very insulting to a foreign person. To establish a good relationship with foreign businesspersons, knowledge of their language can be quite advantageous.

2. **What is meant by nationalism? How does it affect foreign competitors?**

   Nationalism refers to businesses or customers who feel very strongly about only purchasing products or services produced in their home country. If nationalism is practiced by a large percentage of the population, it will eliminate foreign competitors. The problem here is that so many products today consist of parts from all over the world and may even be assembled outside of the country. Thus, it is very difficult to determine which products originate in a particular country.

3. **Why is the foreign exchange rate so important to the operation of a foreign business?**

   The foreign exchange rate is the value of one country's in terms of another country's currency and is determined by the supply and demand for each others goods and services. This rate can change on a daily basis. If a firm in the U.S. enters a foreign country with a substantial investment and then that country's government decides to "devalue" its currency, the U.S. firm could sustain huge losses. To counter this, many firms constantly "hedge" their investment. The foreign exchange rate can also hurt a firm if the price of the foreign country's currency rises very sharply, and the firm is trying to sell internationally from that country. A high-valued currency will make the goods coming out of that country very expensive, and this will hurt sales.

▓ Answers to REVIEW AND DISCUSSION Questions
■

1.   *What factors led to the U.S. decline in so many different product areas during the 1970s and 1980s?*

The main factor that lead to the decline of many U.S. products was the fact that prior to the 1970s the U.S. had little or no foreign competition, since Europe and Asia were still rebuilding from World War II. This caused many U.S. producers to become careless, and in many cases, they failed to build high quality products in an efficient manner. When the countries of Europe and Asia finished rebuilding, they had "state-of-the-art" technology, which provided both high quality and cost efficiency. In many cases, the foreign competitors were also much more customer oriented than their American competitors.

2.   *What are the four key elements that U.S. companies must address if they are going to become more competitive internationally?*

These four main areas are the following:
1.   Strong customer focus
2.   High quality and increased productivity
3.   Development of their human resources
4.   Continuous improvement in all areas of the firm

3.   *Why will most firms probably be involved in international markets, at least to some degree?*

There are many good reasons for entering international markets including the following:
1.   As foreign competition attacks U.S. firms, they are going to be forced to counter this threat and will then be in an advantageous position.
2.   Suppliers of all types are going to be forced to follow major customers abroad or possibly lose them to foreign suppliers.
3.   In some areas new product development costs have risen so steeply that it becomes tenable to form a joint venture with foreign manufacturers to help split the costs.
4.   As American markets mature, international markets offer tremendous growth opportunities.
5.   Some new market opportunities, such as Russia and eastern Europe, may be too good to pass up.

4.   *What are the different forms of international management?*

The Domestic approach consists of:
1.   Exporting to a foreign agent or broker.
2.   Establishing a licensure agreement with a foreign firm.
3.   Signing a manufacturing contract with a foreign manufacturer.

The Multinational approach consists of:
1.   Joint ventures or partnerships.
2.   Establishing wholly-owned subsidiaries.

The Global approach consists of:
1.   Establishing global strategic partnerships.
2.   Setting up vertically integrated wholly-owned subsidiaries.

5.   *How important is the service industry to international markets?*

The service industry is tremendously important in the U.S., as it is the area where the U.S. still has world dominance. As new technology allows U.S. firms to sell services worldwide, it will become even more important in the future. Finally, the service sector is the sector that in the future will provide the most new jobs.

6.   *What are the three main areas of environmental differences that a firm must consider before doing business in a foreign country?*

The three main environmental areas are the following:
1.   Political-legal environment
2.   Cultural environment
3.   Economic environment

7.   *What impact has the international scene had on the way in which U.S. businesses manage their foreign firms?*

The main factors forcing U.S. businesses to change how they manage are the following:
1.   The ever-increasing amount of new technology
2.   Product life cycles are growing shorter and shorter
3.   New high speed communications technology and its impact on the service industry
4.   The ever-increasing rate of change in so many different areas
5.   The ever-increasing amount of foreign competition from all over the world

8.   *Briefly, what kind of changes are managers going to have to make, in each of the five management functional areas, when they start operating in a foreign country?*

In the planning area, firms must be sure their plans fit the culture of the people in another country. They must also learn to plan on a longer-term basis, as a whole, and to take into consideration the impact of the foreign government. In the organizing area, the firm must be sure that it is organized so it takes advantage of all of its worldwide talents. It also needs to be very flexible and able to change quickly. Open communication systems will be critical.

In the staffing area, the firm needs to do absolutely the best job possible in finding, hiring, and developing new employees. The use of local talent must be emphasized to keep costs down and gain local knowledge.

In the leading area, the firm must be sure the style of leadership chosen fits the culture. Incentive systems must be appropriate for the culture, and the amount of employee participation will also have to be determined.

Finally, in the control area, a firm must be sure that the control system is understood and acceptable to the employees. Eventually control always comes down to self control, and this must be established in any country.

9.   *What are some of the general guidelines which most businesses will follow upon entering the international scene?*

The most common guideline that will apply to virtually all businesses is the need to establish a very open communication system between the firm and all of its stakeholder groups. In most cases, the firm is also going to do the following:
1.   Increase levels of employee participation in virtually every aspect of the firm.
2.   Develop organizational structures so that they are very flexible and adaptive to market changes.
3.   Provide inspiring leadership at all levels of management.
4.   Develop the staff on a constant on-going basis.
5.   Design control procedures that are understandable and acceptable to personnel.

10.   *What are some of the real dangers that a business must be aware of before becoming an international firm?*

There are four basic potentially dangerous problem areas:
1.   Be sure the firm selects the right market to enter.

2. Be aware that new competitors can come from anywhere in the world.
3. Be aware that new economic reforms may take a very long time.
4. Be sure the company is not getting into a market area too late.

▦ Answers to CRITICAL THINKING INCIDENTS
■

Incident 12-1: SOUTHERN FRUIT DRINK COMPANY

1. **What are some specific factors that Terry should know before he agrees to Erin's proposal to enter international markets?**

   As pointed out in the text under dangers or problem areas to consider before going into an international market, a firm must look at several key factors:
   1. Will this local market accept a fruit juice drink?
   2. If the market is acceptable to a fruit juice drink, what kind or flavor is preferred, what size containers, etc.?
   3. Will this market accept a carbonated fruit drink? Do potential customers have the income to handle the premium price?
   4. What kind and amount of competition is there?
   5. What kind of a distribution system is available?
   6. How should this product be priced and promoted?
   7. What kind of legal problems might exist?
   8. How far toward capitalism has this country advanced? Is there an adequate infrastructure to produce this product locally?
   9. Is Southern already too late in getting into this market?
   10. What are some of the cultural aspects to consider?

2. **What are some reasons for and against marketing Southern in eastern Europe versus the western part of the United States?**

   The favorable points for going to eastern Europe appear to be as follows:
   1. If there is a local market that is receptive to a fruit drink, there is a good chance that competition will be small, and a very large market share could be captured.
   2. If competition is weak, a premium price can be charged to give the firm larger profit margins.
   3. By getting into the eastern European market first, the company can capture the best distributors, retailers, etc.
   4. Competition on the West Coast will probably be much greater than in eastern Europe.

The favorable points for going to the western part of the United States are as follows:

1. Southern remains in its own country and understands the culture and political systems.
2. Distribution and infrastructure are readily available and adequate.
3. The firm has test marketed current products in this country, and there is no reason to believe that potential customers will not accept them.
4. The West Coast has the income to handle the new premium-priced product, Sparkle.
5. Going to the West Coast is the easiest and most natural progression for this firm at this time.

3.   **Which market do you think Southern should attempt to enter? Why?**

The company really cannot answer this question until it answers all of the questions stated under question number one of this case. But even assuming that the answers to these questions do look favorable, the West Coast of the United States is still preferable because it is so much less risky. There is a large market on the West Coast so growth potential is there. The international market may be something to enter after Southern has reached maximum market saturation in the U.S. but not at this time.

Incident 12-2:   TRAIL RITE MANUFACTURING MOVES SOUTH

1.   **What basic cultural, political, and economic factors did Trail Rite fail to see?**

Culturally, Trail Rite should have been aware of the makeup and nature of the work force. They should have known the skill levels of the work force, and they should have been aware that effectively managing these people would take a different style than the one they used in Los Angeles. Politically, Trail Rite should have been aware that the Mexican government has had a history of treating foreign firms differently than domestic firms. They also should have been aware of the possibility that the minimum wage could be substantially raised due to their current economic situation. Economically, Trail Rite should have foreseen the possibility of a raise in taxes, since the government was so heavily indebted. Also, the devaluing of the peso was something the government had done before to curb inflation, and it was only logical that it would possibly be done again.

2.   What options does Trail Rite have at this point in time?

1.   Trail Rite can try to sell the plant at the best price possible and leave while there is still a company to salvage.
2.   If they cannot sell the plant, they can just strip it clean, and walk away from it.
3.   The firm can stay and try to get some concessions from the government in the future. Also, Trail Rite can change its management style to gain the support of the workers and lower costs.

3.   What is your recommendation to the management of Trail Rite?

At this point, Trail Rite probably cannot find a buyer for the plant at anywhere near the price needed to breakeven. Walking away from the plant with only the movable asset is definitely the worst case scenario, but it may be the one the company is forced to take in the future. The firm needs to stay and try to win some concessions from the government. Management should lobby hard and often and emphasize the situation. Also management needs to turn its management/employee relationship around. Trail Rite needs to develop incentives that the workers will accept for increased productivity and lower costs. Some type of profit sharing program may be the answer, along with a much more participative management style.

Incident 12-3:   FIRST QUALITY TOOLS GOES GLOBAL

1.   **What are the pros and cons of establishing factories in foreign countries?**

On the "pro" side are the following points:
1.   Market acceptance of the products is higher, since the products are made locally by local people.
2.   Costs may be lower due to lower shipping costs, no tariffs to pay, and even labor rates may be lower.
3.   By having the plant located in the country, you can hire local nationals who understand the cultural climate, the political process, and the market.

On the "con" side are the following points:
1.   By building a plant in a foreign country, the firm is subject to the political problems of that country. These can range from high taxes to outright confiscation of the plant.
2.   The labor force in a foreign country may not be as well trained, and they may have to be managed very differently than domestic workers.
3.   When building plants in a foreign country, American jobs are exported.

2.   **At what point do you think a firm should definitely consider putting a factory in a foreign country?**

While this question is certainly open to debate, the following points seem to indicate the time to establish a factory in a foreign country:
1.   When international sales reach a point where it is difficult to meet demand from domestic factories and still serve the domestic market.
2.   If the foreign government is making it very difficult to be competitive because of high tariffs or possibly even quotas.
3.   If shipping costs are fairly substantial and competitors are making it difficult to pass these costs on to consumers.
4.   If the size of the market potential is great, the acceptance of products is good, and the political, cultural, and economic factors all look favorable.

3.   **What is your opinion of First Quality's compromise between the two types of saws preferred by French and English customers?**

First, the company needs to determine how strongly each market feels about the items (handles and saw teeth) in question. If either market is very strongly opposed to any other type of handle or saw teeth, other than the one they desire, then the firm must either accept the cultural desires or get out of the market. Many times, a compromise such as the one First Quality made turns out not to please either market, and the firm ends up at a competitive disadvantage in both markets. However, if customers are not strongly opposed to a different type of handle or saw teeth, then the compromise may work.

Study Guide Assignments

The individual case for this chapter takes the student through several different ways that a firm could enter the international marketplace. In this case, a firm tries exporting, licensing to manufacturer, and operating a wholly-owned subsidiary, all of which fail. The case then asks the student what might have been done differently. It is a good case to use to show your students that challenges can be encountered whenever companies enter the international marketplace.

The group case illustrates an American company that is losing market share to foreign competitors due to their lower costs of production. Five possible solutions are given, and the instructor is asked to form groups of five people and have each person set forth reasons as to why his or her recommended course of action is best for the company. It is a good case to use to illustrate that there are always alternative options to consider when confronted by a competitor. The case also asks for a group consensus on a course of action, and new alternative solutions for this problem should also be encouraged.

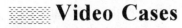

Video Cases

3 Cases From the Blue Chip Enterprise Initiative"

Chipco International

Focus: **International Business**

Summary:

In buying the 90-year old Burt Company of Portland, Maine, in 1985, John Kendall knew he was taking a big gamble.

The manufacturing business, owned for three generations by a family named Burt, had only one product then, a poker chip. Hand-built of compression-molded clay, the chip was a Burt invention, and the company had long enjoyed a worldwide monopoly.

Now an identical chip was being made in low-wage Mexico and sold to casinos by a full-service supplier of gaming accessories–tables, dice, etc. The Burt Company, which couldn't compete on price, was losing $30,000 a month. Unless Kendall could turn the firm around, the odds favored its demise.

Kendall who had been a turnaround specialist for a major venture-capital firm, thought of switching to another type of product but decided to bet on inventing a new, better chip. He went to Las Vegas, Atlantic City, and Europe to see the company's distributors and casino executives. If they could have everything they wanted in a new chip, what would that be?

From what he learned, he listed requirements, including: prices no higher than existing chip prices; clay or ceramic material, not slippery like plastic; 10-gram weight; washable; unbreakable; customized designs; prompt deliveries; suitable for automated handling; and security against counterfeiting.

Contacting people he knew from his venture-capitalist experiences, Kendall investigated various technology and manufacturing options and used dwindling resources for investment. He also was able to attract new money. "I was a part-time mad scientist and part-time financial juggler," he says.

And he gave the customers what they wanted. In subsequent months, research conquered manufacturing challenges at a company that Kendall renamed CHIPCO International. Employees were retrained.

Ceramic chip blanks were injection-molded in large quantities, keeping cost low and production capacity high. An injection-moldable resin kept chip weight at 10 grams. A new decoration-coloration process permitted customization of chips without retooling expense or long delivery delays. A system was developed to implant invisible bar codes on chips, making them counterfeit-proof and permitting automated handling.

CHIPCO's first delivery of its Pro-Tech chips was to a casino in Puerto Rico in November 1988. Deliveries of the old chips had been good for years; after all, the chips were virtually indestructible. These were too, but decorations made them "designer" chips, and many patrons took one home as a souvenir. The casino reordered in a month and six months later.

A new casino profit center had been born. If a casino ordered "designer" chips instead of plain, at 65 cents a pop, and the customer bought chips for $1 or $5, everytime a customer took a chip as a souvenir, the difference went to the casino's bottom line.

Kendall's sales rose, and his bottom line improved, too, but his first profitable year didn't come until 1991, after six years of losses. Sales then were $1.2 million; last year they were $2.8 million. The company's 31 employees are fewer than its 56 when Kendall bought it, but there would be none if it hadn't been turned around.

CHIPCO, which supplies machines to sort, count, validate, and pay for cashed-in chips, has expanded into slot machine tokens. Its anticounterfeiting technology is applicable to many industries, Kendall says, thinking of gambles to come.

Discussion Questions:

1.   Why was CHIPCO able to be competitive and experience success against its international competition?

Innovativeness, foresight, and a willingness to listen are relevant factors. CHIPCO used available information to differentiate its product and respond to requirements of customers. Introduction of "designer" chips enabled customers to add more money to profits.

2.   Is it likely that CHIPCO will continue to be competitive in the international
        marketplace?

        In responding to market conditions, the firm not only met pressing challenges but
        developed technologies that should be valuable in the future. For example, the
        anticounterfeiting technology can increase sales. Continued emphasis upon innovative
        product adaptations and expansion into slot-machine tokens represent opportunities
        with considerable potential.

Orion Network Systems

Focus: **International Business**

Summary:

        In the 1980s, Orion Network Systems was a tiny enterprise with big ideas. Today,
        larger but still small, it has acquired big partners and is about to take off.

        Orion is scheduled to launch a space satellite, and it has plans for more. Not bad for a
        company, founded in 1982, that had no more than five people on its staff in its early
        years and only a dozen as recently as 1990. It has 70 now.

        Headquartered in Rockville, Md., just outside the nation's capital, Orion was the first
        private firm to seek a Federal Communications Commission license to own and run an
        international satellite system.

        At the time INTELSAT, the International Telecommunications Satellite Organization,
        had a 20-year-old monopoly on communications by satellite, and the FCC had been
        granting access to such operations only through COMSAT, the Communications
        Satellite Corp. COMSAT, a part-owner of INTELSAT, was the U.S. signatory to the
        treaty that created it.

        But federal policy makers and congressional leaders during the 1980s encouraged
        development of private satellite systems in competition with INTELSAT. Orion seized
        the opportunity.

        It adopted a strategy that focused on a niche market that was relatively insignificant to
        INTELSAT in terms of size and revenue. INTELSAT was concerned with the mass
        telephone and television markets. Orion was after the private communications
        market—business teleconferences, for example, or intrabusiness data transmission.

        The strategy worked. Orion got its licensing.

Then there was financing. Where would a company with shallow pockets find funds on which to function during further years of incubation, let alone funds for a satellite?

John Puente, an investor in Orion from the beginning, became its chairman, in 1987, bringing with him a wealth of experience in communications business start-ups. Puente persuaded friends to join him as investors.

For the big money, he went to big business at home and abroad. A Partnership was formed between Orion and seven companies, including General Dynamics, British Aerospace, and Japan's Nissho-Iwai, and Orion's partners put up $90 million. that opened the way to a $400 million bank credit line.

Orion and its partners are employing technology that provides direct access to customer locations, bypassing other communications firms by using small, inexpensive, roof satellite terminals. Also, the satellite that is due to be launched includes transmission improvements vis-a-vis existing satellites that make for cost-effective customer services.

The satellite will be launched over the Atlantic. John Puente and Orion's president and CEO, W. Neil Bauer, don't intend to stop there. They want to launch over the Pacific, too, and build a private satellite system that is global.

Discussion Questions:

1.   How important was selection of a market niche to the success of Orion?

      This was a major strategy, as it enabled Orion to serve customers without experiencing major competitors that would have been encountered in the mass markets, which were of primary concern to INTELSAT. Without such a strategy, the company might not have been so successful in obtaining necessary licensing and financing.

2.   What is the benefit of having partners such as General Dynamics, British Aerospace, and Japan's Nissho-Iwai?

      In addition to the critical need for funds, this arrangement may assist Orion's expansion into international markets. These companies represent sources for additional loans and possess expertise that will be valuable in identifying and serving specific market segments.

Emma Ayala Enterprises

Focus: **International Business**

Summary:

Emma Ayala de Rodriguez learned a lesson in trying to sell a new teaching system to beauty schools in Puerto Rico. Talking about the system's theoretical merits was not nearly as persuasive as showing actual results.

Ayala and her husband, owners of a well-regarded beauty salon, began representing a Chicago-based company called Pivot Point International in 1967. They got nowhere when they went around the island commonwealth, trying to get beauty-school owners to sign up for Pivot Point's system of training hairdressers. None of the school owners wanted to risk introducing a new methodology to their instructors.

How to convince school owners and teachers that the system was reliable and that using it would make students more successful hairdressers?

"We decided to open a beauty school and train our teachers with the system," Ayala says. That way, other school owners could "see the difference between our teachers and students and theirs."

The first step was to apply for and get a U.S. Small Business Administration loan. The next: Sell the beauty salon and open a school. Emma Ayala Enterprises, Inc., of Mayagnez, P.R., was born.

Once the school was established, Ayala set out to show off her teachers and students at beauty fairs held around the island. The fairs have hair-dressing competitions for beauty-school students. Ayala would register students as competitors, and they began winning. Registering herself, she became a winner, too. Two schools signed up.

Today there are many more. Ayala and her husband, Radamen Rodriguez, opened a second school themselves in Ponce, P.R., and over the years they have persuaded another nine Puerto Rican schools to adopt the Pivot Point system, bringing its adherents on the island to 13.

Rodriguez has extended their sales area to other Caribbean islands, Central and South America, and Miami's Latin community, signing up 12 other clients. Ayala has been doing a lot of traveling, too. She has taught the Pivot Point system in Europe and Asia, as well as closer to home.

In addition to educational programs, Emma Ayala Enterprises sells tools to be used by teachers, students, and professional hairdressers. Sales last year topped $750,000. The payroll—once just Ayala and her husband—totals 21.

"It has not been easy," Ayala says. "We put in a lot of effort." But it was worth it.

Discussion Questions:

1.   Why has Emma Ayala Enterprises evolved into a successful firm?

Development of a reputation for excellence is a key ingredient to organizational success. This firm illustrates the importance of strategy selection and implementation (selling the salon and opening the school). Also, it demonstrates how sales of complementary products (tools used by teachers, students, and professional hairdressers) can enhance revenue income.

2.   How might Emma Ayala's role change as the firm continues to experience growth.

With continued growth, Ayala and her husband will likely be less involved in day-to-day operations and become increasingly dependent upon obtaining the services of capable managerial talent. Expansion will necessitate even more travel with greater amounts of time spent on exploring opportunities for opening additional schools.

Source: Excerpted from Real-World Lessons for America's Small Businesses 1994, *pp. 85-86, 160-161, and pp. 188-189, Connecticut Mutual Life Insurance Company.*

Chapter 13

Productions/Operations Management

Chapter Overview

Since every business produces some type of product or service, it is imperative to do so efficiently and with the highest quality level possible. This chapter presents some of the main decision areas that every business must consider, regardless of whether it produces a tangible product or an intangible service.

In this chapter, the main decision points are classified by the level of management that normally must handle them. Therefore, top management must deal with the long-term strategic decisions; middle management must handle the tactical-level decisions and operations; and the supervisory level must deal with the operational-level decisions. When all three areas are combined, the firm has its master operational plan.

Finally, the role of quality is highlighted, and several important quality issues are discussed.

Teaching Objectives

The teaching objectives for this chapter are to:

1.   Define the role and importance of operations management.

2.   Examine pros and cons of applying production/operations management principles to the service industry.

3.   Describe how strategic decisions in operations management have changed due to increased competition.

4.   Outline the basic steps involved in establishing a new product or service facility.

5.   Describe how to control production/productivity, quality, and inventories.

6.   Explain how scheduling, purchasing, and cost management are accomplished.

Chapter Outline of the Text

   I.   DEFINING PRODUCTION/OPERATIONS MANAGEMENT
            A.   The Role and Importance of Operations Management
            B.   Operations Management in the Service Industry
   II.   STRATEGIC DECISIONS IN OPERATIONS MANAGEMENT
            A.   New Product and Service Development
            B.   Determining Where to Locate a New Facility
            C.   Determining the Size or Capacity of the New Facility
            D.   Determining How to Produce a Product or Service
            E.   Determining the Layout for the New Facility
   III.   TACTICAL DECISIONS IN OPERATIONS MANAGEMENT
            A.   Quality Control
            B.   Productivity Control
            C.   Inventory Control
   IV.   OPERATIONAL-LEVEL DECISIONS IN OPERATIONS MANAGEMENT
            A.   Scheduling
            B.   Purchasing
            C.   Cost Control
   V.   LOOKING BACK
   VI.   KEY TERMS
   VII.   REVIEW AND DISCUSSION QUESTIONS
   VIII.   CRITICAL THINKING INCIDENTS
   IX.   SUGGESTED READINGS

Key Terms

These terms are introduced in the chapter. Definitions are included in the glossary of the text.

ABC inventory classification system	Operations management
Benchmarking	Program evaluation and review
Cellular (group-technology) layout	technique (PERT)
Computer-aided design (CAD)	Process layout
Computer-aided manufacturing (CAM)	Process planning
Computer-integrated manufacturing (CIM)	Product layout
Critical path method (CPM)	Production layout
Deming circle	Production management
Deming's chain reaction	Productivity
80/20 rule	Qualitative method
Fixed-interval inventory system	Quality circle
Fixed-point inventory system	Quantitative method
Fixed-position layout	Reengineering
Flexible manufacturing system (FMS)	Robotics
ISO 9000	Safety stock
Just-in-time (JIT) inventory system	Statistical process control
Master production schedule	Stockout
Materials requirement planning (MRP)	Total quality management (TQM)
Materials requirement planning II (MRPII)	

Detailed Chapter Summary

I. DEFINING PRODUCTION/OPERATIONS MANAGEMENT

The term production management only applies to firms that make tangible products. Since service firms make intangible products, a new term, operations management, has evolved. Operations management includes all of the management operations involved in producing either a product and/or a service.

A. *The Role and Importance of Operations Management*

Teaching Objective 1: Define the role and importance of operations management.

U.S. firms are facing more competition, especially foreign competition, every day. Many of these foreign competitors have developed techniques that allow them to produce extremely high quality products and services at amazingly low costs. In many industries, U.S. firms have lost substantial market share to foreign competitors. In operations management, planning involves various key decisions, which ultimately lead to development of a master plan for a firm. The planning process must be carefully developed and executed.

1.   Long-term strategic operations decisions involve determining what new products or services to offer, where to locate a new facility, how much capacity should be available for a new facility, which production processes to use, and how to arrange the layout for a new facility.

2.   Tactical operations decisions are concerned with quality, productivity, and inventory control.

3.   At the operations level, decisions focus on scheduling, purchasing, and cost control.

B.   *Operations Management in the Service Industry*

Teaching Objective 2:   Examine the pros and cons of applying production/operations management principles to a service industry.

The service industry produces intangible products that cannot be inventoried but must be created on demand when requested by a customer. Consequently, there is always going to be a larger variation in quality of services than for products.

1.   The operations management model utilized in many service organizations today is basically the same model that is used in producing products. There is a lot of emphasis on technology, job specialization, and cost cutting. Unfortunately, there is very little emphasis on the people who produce the service.

Teaching Hint: While cost controls and technology are important in the production of services, they are not the key or critical areas affecting the quality of services provided and ultimately customer satisfaction. The employees who provide the services are the key factors that must be carefully managed.

2.   To have an efficient service operation, a firm must emphasize customer satisfaction; this can only come from placing the emphasis on the employees who are actually giving the customer the services requested.

3. In order to improve a service operation, a firm must carefully define an acceptable range of quality that will be accepted by customers. Then it must work with the employees to give customers services at this level.

Suggested Readings for this Section:
Armstrong, Larry and William C. Symonds, "Beyond 'May I Help You?'," Business Week (Special Quality Issue, 1991), pp. 100-103.

While manufacturing firms have had quality improvement programs for many years, the service industry is just getting serious about them. The most difficult quality problems with the service industry are the short time that the service exists and the need to create service on the spot to serve customers. To measure the quality of a firm's services, customer satisfaction and customer retention must be measured. From the perspective of quality, these are the two factors that really tell a service firm how it is doing. To get high marks in both of these areas, firms must start by having employees who are well trained and really like their jobs.

Some other factors that have been found to be important to achieving high quality services are careful hiring of new employees and empowerment training for all employees.

Oneal, Michael, "Straighten Up and Fly Right," Business Week (Special Quality Issue, 1991), pp. 116-117.

The airline industry is sometimes cited for providing less than optimal customer service. While most passengers realize that there are going to be weather delays and an occasional mechanical problem, rude treatment and customer insensitivity irritates customers.

Until recently, most airlines could generally count on keeping their customers. However, with many U.S. airlines entering the global arena and with foreign airlines coming into the U.S., the level of competition and quality of service is about to change. Both Singapore Airlines and British Airways are known to give very high quality personal service to passengers. Even in the U.S. at least two airlines (Delta and Southwest) have earned high marks for customer service. It is beginning to look like the industry standard is changing, and those airlines that do not change will be quickly left behind.

How can airlines improve the quality of their services? The answer to this question is through employee training and empowering employees to help customers solve problems. Northwest Airlines is placing a coordinator at each airport who will be responsible for keeping passengers informed on delays and helping them get a hotel room or an alternate flight. Airlines could also do a better job of tracking customers and their baggage.

II.   STRATEGIC DECISIONS IN OPERATIONS MANAGEMENT

Teaching Objective 3:   Describe how strategic decisions in operations management have changed due to increased competition.

To compete in a global economy, it is necessary to develop and market innovative products or services. New product and service-development times continue to grow shorter. Technology has become increasingly important; utilization of advanced technology is a key to survival and growth.

What new products and services will be in demand in the future? The answer to this question is difficult to obtain and crucial for the survival of the firm.

1.   Communication System

A firm must have a communication system that includes its customers, managers, employees, suppliers, and even its competitors. All of these groups must be monitored on a continuous basis for changes and new ideas that could possibly lead to a new product or service idea.

Teaching Hint: You may want to mention to your students that a firm can take three basic approaches to new product development. (1) It can develop new innovative products. (2) It can take new, successful products produced by competitors and develop similar ones. (3) It can do new product innovations and copy successful competitive products.

2.   Design and Production Process

Whatever new products or services a firm does decide to produce, it must be sure that every department is actually integrated into the design and production process. This is necessary so that many potential problems can be identified before the actual production process begins.

Teaching Objective 4:   Outline the basic steps involved in establishing a new product or service facility.

A.   *Determining Where to Locate a New Facility*

To determine where to locate a new facility, a firm will make up a list of factors in order of priority and then look for the location which most closely fits its needs. Some of the main factors to consider in this decision are the following:

1. Location of firm in terms of market consideration.

   Normally service firms must locate quite close to their markets and be very convenient for customers. Some manufacturers of component parts have found that a major customer may want close proximity, especially if the customer is utilizing a Just-In-Time (JIT) inventory control system.

2. Cost of Utilities

   If large amounts of electricity are used, the cost of utilities may be a major factor in selecting the new location. This is why many large manufacturers located near the Tennessee Valley Authority facility in Tennessee.

3. Cost or Availability of Labor

   If a firm is very labor intensive, it may consider locating in a foreign country where labor rates are low.

4. Building or Operating Costs

   Many communities offer tax incentives and very low-priced land.

5. Climate and General Living Conditions

   A nice climate and an attractive area to live in is helpful in attracting good personnel.

B. *Determining the Size or Capacity of the New Facility*

   It can be a challenge to determine the size or capacity of a new factory, retail store, or restaurant. It requires determining potential demand for the product or service.

   1. Quantifiable Data

      Numerical data, such as industry and company sales, and economic data are gathered to determine trends.

   2. Qualitative Data

      These data rely on the judgements of people, such as potential and current customers, executives, salespersons, and suppliers.

C.   *Determining How to Produce a Product or Service*

It is necessary to determine how to produce the new product or service. This decision is frequently referred to as "process planning." All of the following key factors must be considered in determining the production process.

1.   How should the product or service "flow" through the facility?

2.   What type and how much equipment will be needed?

3.   What type of workers and how many of them will be needed?

4.   What type of production system should be used? (for example, a mass assembly line or small work groups, self-service or professional sales personnel)

5.   How much, if any, will the facility utilize computer-integrated manufacturing (CIM) techniques such as computer-aided design (CAD), computer-aided manufacturing (CAM), and flexible manufacturing system (FMS)?

6.   Will the firm utilize robotics extensively or at all?

D.   *Determining the Layout for the New Facility*

Determining the actual physical layout of the facility is also of utmost importance. Here, a firm must determine where machines will actually be placed, where offices will be located, where cashier stands will be, and where storage areas will be located. There are four basic layout designs and an unlimited number of variations of them.

1.   The Product Layout

This is illustrated by the mass assembly line. It works well for standardized products or services, such as registering for college or mass producing automobiles.

2.   The Process Layout

Here, specialized departments are formed. This layout allows a firm to customize the products or services.   An auto service center is a good example.

3.　　　The Fixed-Position Layout

People, equipment, and materials are brought to the product being manufactured or serviced because it is too large or cumbersome to move. Repair of large appliances or lawn maintenance are examples from the service sector.

4.　　　The Cellular or Group-Technology Layout

Small groups or clusters are formed to produce a product or service. This "team" approach is being used more often today and will probably be used to a greater extent in the future. Some computers are currently manufactured this way.

Teaching Hint: Remind your students that it is important for correct decisions to be made at every management level. If strategic decisions are not made correctly, there probably is not any way for the firm to be successful, regardless of how efficiently the decisions are made at the lower levels of management.

III.　　TACTICAL DECISIONS IN OPERATIONS MANAGEMENT

Teaching Objective 5:　Describe how to control production/productivity, quality, and inventories.

Tactical decisions are usually made on a one year time-frame basis. The three main tactical decisions concern: quality, productivity, and cost control.

A.　　*Quality Control*

Quality control is extremely important in the production of all goods and services. Consumers have come to expect high quality standards. Any firm that is not producing high quality goods or services will suffer in the marketplace.

1.　　　Total Quality Management (TQM)

Total quality management is a term used to describe the quality control process used in a typical firm. There are almost an infinite number of variations of TQM, but most of them contain the following eight points:
a.　They are customer driven.
b.　They focus on continuously improving quality.

    c. They concentrate on improving quality by improving the work processes.

    d. They try to eliminate reworking products.

    e. Everyone is involved, and all vital information is shared.

    f. There is an emphasis on teamwork, and workers are empowered.

    g. Everyone is trained and recognized for achievements.

    h. There are inspired leaders who have a vision and communicate it through their actions as well as their words.

2.   Deming's Statistical Control Procedure

W. Edwards Deming's statistical control procedure is a form of TQM that embraces all eight of the above points and has worked well for many firms in both Japan and the United States. Deming's 14 points, illustrated in Figure 13-4, summarize his basic philosophy and have been applied by Ford, General Motors, and Xerox.

3.   Instituting Total Quality Management (TQM)

To be effective, TQM programs must be instituted properly or problematic results may occur. The proper way to institute TQM considers the following points:

    a. There must be total commitment of everyone in the firm, starting with top management.

    b. The firm must not try to do too much too fast. As one level of quality is attained, it can then reach for a higher level. Training of all workers is essential.

    c. The return on quality (ROQ) improvements must make financial sense.

    d. The use of benchmarking or comparison to the industry leader is a good technique. However, a firm must be careful not to try to leap ahead too rapidly.

    e. Reengineering, rethinking the total work flow process that a product or service goes through, can be a very effective way to increase quality and productivity. This rethinking process is then repeated over and over continuously. This is called the "Deming circle."

    f. Everyone must be thoroughly trained to work in teams, and incentives must be in place to encourage this constant improvement in quality.

    g. A communication system must be established that starts with customer needs, flows through the entire firm and its suppliers, and ends with customer satisfaction. This continuous communication system is the key to high quality and high customer satisfaction.

Suggested Readings for this Section:
Radding, Alan, "Quality is Job #1," Datamation (October 1, 1992), pp. 98-101.

If Total Quality Management (TQM) is going to be effective, the information systems within the firm must play a number of key roles. The information system department may act as merely a tool provider in the TQM program. Tools such as statistical programs and E-mail are very common. Another role is a support role. By providing information on quality improvement or inventory levels, a firm's information system department supports the TQM program. Another role is that of process analysis. Here, the information systems department examines, documents, and benchmarks production processes or even design changes. Finally, the information system department can play the role of leader of the total quality effort. This role is filled by getting actively involved in the quality efforts of the business units. Since improving quality is really about providing ways to link the company with customers and suppliers, this role is a natural fit for the information systems department.

Henricks, Mark, "Reality Checks," Profit (September/October 1994), pp. 40-42.

While lowering costs, programs such as Total Quality Management, reengineering, team building, and empowerment all promise to increase quality and productivity. However, many small firms do not have the time or the money to properly learn and implement these programs.

Many of the popular management concepts are primarily aimed at large bureaucratic companies that need to get "lean." Small firms are already lean and need more help with areas such as competitive advantages than with cost reduction.

Many small firms have found that they can get good results by asking employees to watch videos on team building and then discuss how the team concept can be implemented.

One firm, Paranetics, a small manufacturer of parachutes, found that it improved quality by (1) developing a small library on quality, (2) purchasing and showing a six week video course, and (3) photocopying a brochure on quality that the president thought was very enlightening. While this sounds like a very simplistic quality program, it did fit the company's resources and it worked.

B.   *Productivity Control*

Productivity, or the amount of goods or services received from a given amount
of resources (usually measured in terms of labor hours), is also a crucial
tactical decision area. If a firm has a higher productivity rate than its
competitors, it likely has lower costs. Firms must be certain that they can at
least match the industry average. Quality improvements and productivity
improvements do go hand in hand, which is just another reason why a firm's
management needs to concentrate on quality. To improve productivity, the
following methods have been found to be effective:

1.   Participative Management Style

      A more participative management style between management and the
      employees encourages productivity.   Good communication practices
      have been found to be effective.

2.   Autonomous Work Teams

      With this approach, management establishes employee work teams and
      gives them considerable authority and freedom to act on their own.
      Management then acts primarily as a facilitator. Good communication
      is the key to the success of autonomous work teams.

3.   Profit Sharing

      Profit sharing, particularly cash payment plans as opposed to deferred
      payment plans, have worked very well in improving productivity.

4.   Technological Improvements

      Technological improvements, such as flexible manufacturing systems,
      can be very effective.

5.   Improving the Work Environment

      Negative environmental effects, such as poor lighting, noise, stale air,
      and extreme temperatures can decrease productivity.

C.   *Inventory Control*

Inventory control is a major financial component and must be balanced against the production rate and level of customer service desired.

1.   Inventory Costs

Inventory costs consist of handling or order processing costs; storage costs; losses due to damage, theft, or obsolescence; and the cost of capital tied up in inventory.

2.   Types of Inventories

There are three types of goods that may be inventoried: raw materials, work in progress, and finished goods.

3.   Controlling Inventories

The following are the most common methods of controlling inventories:

a.   Fixed-Point and the Fixed-Interval Inventory Controls.

The fixed-point method adds a specified amount of inventory when the present inventory level reaches a specific point or number. The fixed-interval method adds a predetermined amount at predetermined times, regardless of the current level of inventory.

b.   The ABC Classification System.

Utilizing the marketing 80/20 rule, all inventory items are classified as an A, B, or C item. "A" items are those 20 percent of the products or services that account for 80 percent of your sales. The firm usually carries sufficient safety stock of "A" items so that stockouts never occur. Therefore, approximately 75 percent of the inventory dollars go into "A" items. "B" items are the next most important products and services, and 15 to 20 percent of the firm's inventory dollars are given to them. Some stockouts will occur with "B" items. Finally, "C" items are given the last 5 to 10 percent of the inventory dollars, and stockouts may be fairly common with these items.

      c.   Materials Requirement Planning (MRP) and Materials Requirement Planning II (MRPII).

             Both MRP and MRPII utilize a computer program to make sure that sufficient inventory levels of raw materials and component parts will be on hand to accommodate the production schedule. Purchasing, lead times, and current inventory levels are then coordinated with the production schedule. MRPII goes a step further and coordinates every major area of the firm with the production process.

      d.   Just-In-Time (JIT)

             This inventory control system keeps very minimal levels of inventory. To work effectively, a manufacturer must work very closely with suppliers. Quality of materials and parts must be very high. Long-term contracts are usually utilized with suppliers for this reason. Since inventories are so low, there is a significant cost savings. To work well, however, there must be a very good communication system so that potential problems or bottlenecks can be quickly resolved. JIT has also been found to work best with firms that have a relatively constant demand for products and do production runs on a constant basis.

Teaching Hint: Remind your students that while JIT looks very good, it definitely is not a good inventory control system for every firm. Also, it can be time consuming to implement a JIT program and work out all of the problems that can occur.

IV.   OPERATIONAL-LEVEL DECISIONS

Teaching Objective 6: Explain how scheduling, purchasing, and cost management are accomplished.

             Normally, operational-level decisions are made by first level or supervisory management. These decisions are typically made on a daily, weekly, or monthly basis. The three main decision areas involve scheduling, purchasing, and cost control.

A.   *Scheduling*

Scheduling of materials, parts, equipment, and personnel is very critical to the efficiency of any organization. Scheduling usually starts by examining the master production schedule which gives all the current and projected production runs. There are two scheduling techniques that are used a great deal with the construction of large projects.

1.   Program Evaluation and Review Technique (PERT)

PERT is a system that starts by breaking a project down into every activity that must be completed from start to finish. The steps or activities are then laid out in sequence, and any activities that can be done at the same time are overlapped on the PERT chart. Finally, three time estimates are made for each activity: the most optimistic, the most probable, and the most pessimistic.

2.   Critical Path Method (CPM)

A variation of PERT is Critical Path Method. CPM is done exactly like PERT but only one time estimate is made: the most probable. CPM is utilized for projects that are familiar to the firm, which explains why only one time estimate is needed. Both PERT and CPM illustrate the longest path, which then becomes the critical path because any delays along it will move the whole project back from a time perspective.

B.   *Purchasing*

Purchasing costs are classified as either ordering costs or holding costs.

1.   Order Costs

Order costs are the costs that are derived from placing the order, follow-up on deliveries, and inspection of the order upon arrival.

2.   Holding Costs

Holding costs include monies tied up in inventory; the storage costs of warehousing the inventory; and the costs incurred due to loss from theft, deterioration, or obsolescence.

3.   Economic Order Quantity (EOQ)

One way to minimize these two types of purchasing costs is to utilize a technique called the economic order quantity. The EOQ point balances ordering and carrying or holding costs and can be found by utilizing the following formula:

$$EOQ = \sqrt{\frac{2 \times \text{Order costs} \times \text{Annual demand in units}}{\text{Cost of item} \times \text{Carrying Cost percentage}}}$$

4.   Purchasing

Purchasing is now done much more frequently with a few well established suppliers who will work with a firm in providing the quality levels and quantities desired. This normally translates into long-term contracts which, in essence, makes them a partner of the firm.

C.   *Cost Control*

Cost control is obviously crucial for every firm. To practice effective cost control, a firm needs to:

Have very accurate cost figures on all direct costs, such as labor and materials.

Determine as closely as possible all indirect costs or overhead costs, such as design costs, office expenses, public relations, maintenance fees, and even rework and downtime costs.

Consider using activity based cost management (ABC). This computerized form of cost control adds all costs at each step of the production process. This technique also helps management identify areas where costs are abnormally high so that corrections can be made.

V.   LOOKING BACK

This chapter examines the planning process in operations management. Decision areas at the strategic, tactical, and operations level are analyzed. If any firm is going to be competitive today, it must very carefully and efficiently handle each and every one of these decision areas.

Answers to CONSIDER THIS Questions   (Page 430)

1.   **How is production management similar to operations management? Different from operations management?**

The term "production management" applies only to firms that produce tangible products. "Operations management" is a term that applies to all firms, whether they are producing tangible products or intangible services. Both terms are identical in the sense that they utilize the basic management functions to produce their goods or services. They are also alike in the way they develop a master operations plan.

2.   **What special problem does the service industry have that product industries do not have?**

The service industry produces intangible services, on demand, which cannot be inventoried or mass produced to very specific quality tolerances. Because of this, the quality of services is always going to vary more than that of tangible products. What this really means to a service firm is that it must try to limit the range of quality variation as much as possible and constantly check with customers to maintain an acceptable quality level. For example, there is not much planned variation in quality of service from one McDonald's restaurant to another or from one Holiday Inn to another.

3.   **Describe the best way to conduct new product planning. Who should be involved in this process?**

The best way to design any new product or service is to get all of the departments in the firm working together on the project. This way marketing can provide information on what the customer is looking for and what the competition looks like; production can point out problems in producing the new product or service; human resources can be instrumental in providing staffing needs; and finance can recognize possible financial limitations.

In addition, a firm also needs to be sure that it has a considerable amount of customer input. Finally, it needs to bring in primary suppliers to see if they have any problems with the new product or service being considered.

Answers to CONSIDER THIS Questions (Page 451)

1.   **What are the four main questions that management must answer before a new facility can be built?**

The four main questions are:
a.   Where to locate the facility?
b.   What size or capacity will the facility be?
c.   What type of production process will be utilized?
d.   What will be the physical layout of the facility?

2.   **Explain the essence of Deming's statistical process control approach to quality control.**

While Dr. Deming's total quality management (TQM) approach utilizes statistical process control as a central procedure, the real "heart" of his approach is that total quality management must become a *management philosophy* that is accepted by everyone within the firm. Every employee, manager, and even supplier must be totally committed to providing the highest quality product or service available. Finally, there must be constant customer contact to make sure that they are satisfied with the level of quality being produced.

3.   **How can a typical firm improve productivity?**

There are four main areas that have proven to increase productivity in almost all firms. These areas are:

a.   A more participative management style. This approach can utilize autonomous work teams.

b.   Profit sharing. As a method to increase productivity, it encourages greater worker involvement. Giving employees cash payments instead of deferred payments and giving them a percentage of the profits rather than a percentage of their pay have also been found to work very well.

c.   Technological improvements. At the forefront are flexible manufacturing systems, which can turn out a wide range of products very quickly on the same production line.

d.   Improving the working environment. This emphasizes reducing noise, improving lighting, and eliminating stale air.

Answers to REVIEW AND DISCUSSION Questions

1. *Why is so much emphasis placed on constantly increasing quality and lowering costs in both product- and service-oriented firms?*

    While there has always been a lot of competition, the United States is now experiencing more foreign competition than ever before. Many of these foreign firms have increased quality and lowered costs to the point where they have captured large market shares and in some cases the entire market. If U.S. firms do not at least match these quality and cost levels, they will not be able to compete effectively in the global marketplace.

2. *Why is it so important to develop new products or services fast and get them to the marketplace first?*

    As global competition increases, every industry is going to see its markets divided up into smaller and smaller segments as competitors develop new products or services. In order to stay competitive, every firm in the industry must be constantly communicating with its customers in order to ascertain what new products or services they desire. Being first in the marketplace also allows a firm the opportunity to charge a premium price if desired, as it will not experience direct competition for a while at least. Finally, by being first in the marketplace, a firm may be able to capture market share if its new product or service is significantly better than current ones.

3. *What are the four basic layout designs for a new facility? Briefly what type of product or service appears to fit each design the best?*

    The four basic layout designs are:
    a. Product layout -- Good for smaller mass produced products, such as cars and TVs that can be produced on an assembly line.
    b. The Process layout -- Customization is very common, and specialization is always utilized. A large medical clinic is a good example of this type of layout.
    c. Fixed-position layout -- This is used when the product is so large that it is easier to move people and equipment to the product. It is also used if the service must be done at the customer's location, such as custom-built homes or a roof repair service call.
    d. Cellular layout -- This grouping of machines and people allows for both specialization and "mass customization." Products that have a large number of options and variations can be produced best by utilizing this method. Products, such as computers, are now being produced this way by some manufacturers.

4.   *How has the role of robotics in the service industry changed over time?*

Robotics, or the use of robots, were once required solely as a production tool
for manufacturers. With improved technology, robotics now are also being
used in the service industry as they receive better vision, sensors, and even
artificial intelligence. In the service industry, robots are currently used
primarily to do hazardous tasks like inspecting nuclear plants or cleaning up
chemical spills. In the future, however, robots will be doing a lot of the
mundane tasks like cleaning floors, cutting grass, and taking your order in a
fast-food restaurant.

5.   *Define ISO 9000 quality controls and their impact on U.S. firms.*

ISO 9000 is a series of comprehensive international quality standards that apply
to both products and services. They are designed to ensure constant quality
levels both now and in the future. Designed by the European Community,
many EC firms are already making it mandatory that all firms doing business
with them be certified. Since almost one-third of the U.S. exports go to
Europe, this new certification will affect a lot of U.S. firms.

6.   *Briefly describe some of the benefits of utilizing quality circles?*

Firms use quality circles for a number of reasons. Quality circles are a form of
participative management to get employees involved in solving job-related
problems. They also encourage upward communication and generally improve
management/employee relations. While quality circles may not always be cost
effective, in the great majority of cases they have saved money, and in some
cases, the savings have been very substantial.

7.   *How can a firm lower costs and improve product or service quality at the same
time?*

Many times, quality improvements also lower the cost of producing the product
or service.   First, one of the most common ways to improve quality is to
improve the process used to produce the product or service. A more efficient
process also lowers costs. Second, higher quality means less rework, lower
waste costs, and less downtime in a manufacturing or service setting. This
lowers the costs of production.

8.   *Why isn't a Just-In-Time (JIT) inventory control system suitable for use in all
firms?*

Just-in-time inventory control system is not a good system for firms that
produce products with highly-fluctuating demands. JIT also requires extensive

training of all personnel and may require the firm to buy new and expensive capital equipment to simplify production as much as possible. Finally, JIT forces a firm to make long-term contracts with suppliers who must be located close to them. Suppliers must be treated almost as partners and brought in often for discussions.

9. *In which areas do firms tend to have the most cost-control problems? What, if anything, can be done about them.*

   The real problem area in cost control is usually not with direct costs (such as materials and labor) but with indirect overhead costs (such as design costs, maintenance costs, public relations costs). These indirect costs are rapidly rising as a percentage of a product's total costs. At the same time, direct costs are falling due to automation and increased production efficiency. In terms of a solution utilizing computerized cost-control programs, such as "activity based cost management" (ABC), should help considerably. This program measures all costs at each stage of a products development and assesses these costs accordingly.

10. *What does the new service model for the service industry stress?*

    The new service model stresses the following five points:
    a. Investing substantial amounts of money in employee training.
    b. Doing a much better job of recruiting and selecting employees.
    c. Using technology to assist front-line employees, not to replace them.
    d. Compensation is linked to performance.
    e. A new role for supervisors: one that stresses communication, coaching, and developing employees rather than just monitoring them.

Answers to CRITICAL THINKING INCIDENTS

Incident 13-1:   JOHN CASEY'S DILEMMA

1. **What does Dr. Deming mean when he states that pay for individual performance is bad because of "differences in the system?" Give an example.**

A typical manufacturing firm, has all the different departments commonly found in most companies. Some of these departments make up "support systems" in the firm, such as accounting and human resources. Other departments (like production and marketing) are direct customer-oriented systems. If a firm is successful in selling its products, the amount of bonus available to each department and each individual within the department based on his or her role in the success of the sales performance may be impossible to ascertain. Therefore, Dr. Deming preferred incentives like company-wide profit sharing on an equal basis.

2. **Why doesn't Deming like Management by Objectives (M.B.O.)?**

M.B.O. goals for each individual are quite narrow and concentrate on specific tasks. If these are the only areas in which a person is evaluated, an employee or manager may stress them too much and at the expense of other areas which also need attention. For example, suppose a sales representative has an annual sales goal of $1 million, and this person gets a bonus if he/she reaches that figure. If the year is almost over and the goal has not been reached, the person may do some rather inappropriate things in order to reach this goal, even if it will hurt the company later on. In other words, the individual's goals may supersede the company's goals.

3. **Do you agree with Dr. Deming that pay is not a primary motivator? Why or Why not?**

Dr. Deming notes, as many psychologists do, that pay is only a motivator for most people in the short run. Dr. Deming stresses the fact that employees become truly motivated when they feel pride and an integral part of the firm. If pay is a real motivator, people would not focus their efforts toward success of the entire company. Finally, as people reach a certain level of income, it becomes less important; and other areas, like the need to grow and be recognized, are emphasized to a greater extent.

4. **Why does Dr. Deming state that mass final inspections are no longer needed? Do you agree or disagree? Why?**

Dr. Deming's statistical control process stresses checking products at key points in the production process. He also stressed learning to anticipate when mechanical problems will happen and intervening before they do occur. With emphasis on quality, it is not necessary to do a final mass inspection, since high quality is likely to be assured.

Incident 13-2:   CON-TECH ENCOUNTERS FOREIGN COMPETITION

1. **List the advantages and disadvantages of Con-Tech entering this new market. Based on your analysis, what do you recommend?**

The advantages of entering this new market are:
a.   The market is close to 70 million units and growing.
b.   The U.S. market, while only at 10 million units, is also growing.
c.   If the company ignores this new market in the U.S., they are inviting foreign competitors to come into the U.S. and take market share from them.

The disadvantages of entering this new market are:

a.   Substantial costs will be incurred to design and tool up for this new product.

b.   With only 10 million units sold in the U.S. today, the market may be too small to go after right now.

c.   By entering this new market, the company may hurt their present markets, as resources will be spread too thin.

While a good case could probably be made for either decision, the best choice is probably to enter the market and at least try to protect the U.S. market share.

Competitors like these do not normally go away. In fact, they usually get stronger. Therefore, the best time to initiate acting is while a firm still dominates a market.

2.   **Assuming that Con-Tech does decide to enter this market, do you recommend responding solely to the U.S. market demand for these products or adopting a global approach? Justify your decision.**

This is a new product for Con-Tech, which initially may have some problems that have not been foreseen. Con-Tech should start by serving only the U.S. market. After development of a product that is superior in some way to the competition, the company could justify investing in larger facilities. In other words, a company needs to "learn how to walk before it starts running."

3.   **Which of the three production alternatives do you think Con-Tech should select? Again, justify your answer.**

In entering any new market, it is always best to minimize risk and potential losses as much as possible. Since Con-Tech does have the capacity within the plant to serve its share of the U.S. market, this option seems the safest, and it gives the most control. It also may be the least expensive initially when storage and distribution costs are carefully analyzed (such as in a country like Mexico). Finally, quality control is especially crucial when a firm starts producing a totally new product, and its current plant would definitely assure the highest quality.

Incident 13-1:   SHOULD WATERWORKS "HIRE" THE ROBOT WELDER?

1.   **Describe the types of applications that robots can perform better than people.**

Robots are very good at performing relatively simple routine tasks that are repeated over and over again. Robots also are useful in doing relatively dangerous or dirty tasks such as painting or welding. Since programs can be pre-set, robots also are much more consistent in terms of the quality of work completed.

2.   **What kinds of applications can people perform better than robots?**

Anytime the task involves analysis and decision making on an on-going basis, people tend to outperform robots. Some robots do have sensors and computer brains that are capable of making some decisions. This form of artificial intelligence, for the most part, is rather primitive. As newer technology is developed, however, this could change.

3.   **Determine the pros and cons of purchasing the robot welder in this case. Based on your analysis, should Waterworks purchase the robot welder?**

The pros of purchasing the robot welder appear to be:
a.   Lower costs of producing the water tower.
b.   Higher quality welds.
c.   Faster completion time.
d.   It may give Waterworks a true competitive edge.

The cons of purchasing the robot welder are:
a.   High initial cost and high debt service payments increase Waterworks' fixed costs. This could hurt them very badly if the economy turns downward and business slackens considerably.
b.   Without any experience with robot welders, the firm could have a lot of problems learning how to operate them properly.
c.   The robot welder may have some technical problems that have not been totally worked out.
d.   Purchasing the welder requires the firm to layoff almost 70 percent of its labor force.

Based on the information available, a sound decision cannot be made at this time. Waterworks needs to know the answer to the following questions:
a.   Are their competitors using this type of equipment?
b.   What does it cost their competitors to produce a water tower?
c.   Are there some other ways to lower costs at Waterworks?
d.   How much training and support will the manufacturer of the robot welder provide?
e.   How large will the debt service payment actually be?
f.   Have the technical problems really been corrected?
g.   If the robot welder is purchased, will Waterworks be able to somehow assist the workers who must be laid off?

Study Guide Assignments

The individual case for this chapter is interesting, as it asks the student to give advice on how to set up a hypothetical tee shirt printing business. The case asks the student to consider many of the strategic and tactical decisions that would have to be made in order to establish this business. Strategic questions include what products to produce, location of the facility, and size of the facility. Tactical questions include quality, productivity, and inventory control.

The group case continues with the same problem explained in the individual case. Some new potential problems are emphasized by asking what impact an economic downturn, as well as new competition from major discounters might have on the business. The group case also discusses the problems of foreign competitors who utilize very low cost labor. Finally, the idea of utilizing technology to combat the cheaper foreign labor is discussed. The group case concludes by asking each person to take one of the strategic and tactical decisions and develop a recommendation.

Video Case

Oregon Cutting Systems

Focus: **Control, Total Quality Management, and Just-In-Time Approach**

Summary:

Cutting technology is the science of designing and manufacturing cutting tools for various applications. This is the business of Oregon Cutting Systems (OCS). Each day OCS converts cold rolled steel into over 20 miles of cutting chain. Output varies from one-quarter-inch pinch chain for consumer markets to three-quarter-inch pinch chain used in mechanized forestry harvesters. OCS also manufactures related products, such as chain bars. It is the industry leader with more than one-half the world's chain saw market. OCS is also an original equipment manufacturer, supplying the world's best-known brands of chain saws through its own network of distributors and dealers.

In the early 1980s, it became apparent that business as usual was no longer going to be good enough for OCS. According to Noel Hingley, division vice president for manufacturing, "the initial impetus for changing things came from a discomfort with quality problems that were too large and problem solving that took too long and resulted in problems that weren't permanently solved." Self-inspection revealed an operation that was ripe with opportunities for improvement. Jim Osterman, president of OCS, notes that "when somebody came in with a problem or a complaint we were certain that it had to be their problem and not our product problem. As a consequence, we earned a reputation in the field of not covering our products." According to Charlie Nicholson, division vice president for quality, "We felt we knew so much about the market and the needs of our customers (our end users) that we could pretty well design for them, and we made a lot of assumptions regarding their needs and expectations. We did develop chains without direct data from them for awhile, and we did design chains for large market segments. We've learned since that there are a lot of different market segments out there that demand different types of products."

OCS began its improvement program by implementing a just-in-time (JIT) approach to inventory management. This was not without problems, though. OCS found that it could go only so far with JIT before it encountered obstacles in the form of machinery that wasn't reliable enough to maintain consistent production and interruptions in production because of quality defects. OCS found that it couldn't maintain as low an inventory as it wanted or make further gains. The company shifted its focus to quality and continuous improvement. A strong emphasis on statistical process control was adopted. Production workers were trained in its procedures and were given the authority to make decisions and solve problems. At that point, operations improved dramatically. Work in process was reduced to 30 percent of pre-change levels, and new goals for an additional 50 percent cut in inventory and a 20 percent reduction in costs were set. A major element in OCS's success is its effort to translate customer requirements into product characteristics. In a process it calls Strategic Product Development, OCS starts with customer inputs and designs products to meet those customer needs. As a result of these changes, OCS now delivers value that is far above what it previously delivered. Customer problems that were chronic in the past are now nonexistent. At the same time, OCS production workers have become happier and more fulfilled on the job and are proud of their accomplishments.

In retrospect, President Osterman says, "I think what I would have done differently is understood the ramifications of total quality commitment a little better and started on the quality side before starting on the just-in-time side."

Discussion Questions:

1.   What kinds of ways can a company like Oregon Cutting Systems use to stay close to customers and learn what they want from products?

       While useful information can be gained from distributors, the best information comes from the ultimate consumer. Customer satisfaction cards, surveys and focus groups are two ways such information can be gathered as part of the control process.

2.   Discuss what you feel are the reasons that OCS met with limited success with JIT
      before it addressed the quality issue, and why such dramatic improvements were
      possible after the focus on quality and continuous improvement.

      Because materials arrive on the factory floor within a short time of when they are
      used, JIT requires extraordinarily high quality standards. A problem with JIT that
      many American companies have experienced is that, unlike many Japanese companies,
      American companies have typically purchased supplies from the lowest bidder. Many
      Japanese companies prefer to develop close working relationships with their suppliers,
      which helps ensure high quality supplies.

Note to Instructors:

The following chapters are not included in the basic textbook. However, they are available in modules which you may or may not wish to use. If you choose to cover Chapters 14 through 20, or any combination of these chapters, you may use the following materials in this instructor's resource manual. If you cover only the thirteen chapters of the basic text, you may stop here.

Chapter 14

Working With Groups

Chapter Overview

Groups in organizations have the potential in many cases to accomplish more than individual employees working alone. However, the extent to which managers are familiar with and able to utilize the strength of groups can determine the effectiveness of groups in organizations.

In examining how groups in organizations function, this chapter emphasizes that managers are responsible for creating an environment that is conductive to group success in a company. A distinction is made between formal and informal groups. Other topics discussed include stages of group development, communication patterns in groups, and important aspects of work groups. Attention is also given to groupthink and the importance of group goals.

Teaching Objectives

The teaching objectives of this chapter are to:

1. Define the four types of formal groups traditionally found in organizations.

2. Describe two common types of informal groups found in many organizations.

3. Trace the common stages of group development.

4.   Explain the difference between explicit and implicit group norms.

5.   Identify factors that influence group cohesiveness.

6.   Distinguish between achievement goals and maintenance goals.

Chapter Outline of the Text

I.   THE IMPORTANCE OF WORK GROUPS
       A.   Definition of a Group
II.   TYPES OF GROUPS
       A.   Formal Groups
              1.   Long-standing Work Groups
              2.   Project Groups
              3.   Prefabricated Groups
              4.   Quality Circles
       B.   Informal Groups
III.   COMMON STAGES OF GROUP DEVELOPMENT
       A.   Forming
       B.   Storming
       C.   Norming
       D.   Performing
       E.   Adjourning
IV.   COMMUNICATION PATTERNS
V.   IMPORTANT ASPECTS OF WORK GROUPS
       A.   Group Size
       B.   Member Roles
VI.   GROUP NORMS
       A.   How Group Norms Develop
VII.   GROUP COHESIVENESS
       A.   Factors That Influence Group Cohesiveness
       B.   Guiding Group Cohesiveness
       C.   Risky-Shift Phenomenon
       D.   Groupthink
VIII. GROUP GOALS
       A.   Two Types of Group Goals
       B.   Behaviors That Help a Group Accomplish Its Goals
       C.   The Importance of Clear Goals
IX.   USING TEAMS WISELY
       A.   Carefully Analyze Team Tasks
       B.   Consider Using Integration Teams

Key Terms

These terms are introduced in the chapter.

Achievement goal	Nonoperational goal
Adjourning stage	Norm
Explicit norm	Norming stage
Formal group	Operational goal
Forming stage	Performing stage
Friendship group	Prefabricated group
Group	Process-focused team
Group cohesiveness	Process measure
Groupthink	Project group
Implicit norm	Quality circle
Informal group	Risky-shift phenomenon
Interest group	Role
Long-standing work group	Self-centered role
Maintenance goals	Storming stage
Maintenance role	Task role

Detailed Chapter Summary

I.   THE IMPORTANCE OF WORK GROUPS

Predictions of future trends in management indicate that organizations will make increased use of self-managing or self-governing work groups.

A.   *Definition of a Group*

A group can be defined as two or more people working together and satisfying needs through interaction.

Teaching Hint: Emphasize that although people often prefer to work on a solution to solving a problem alone rather than in a group, it is common for groups to be more creative and productive than individuals working alone.

II.   TYPES OF GROUPS

People in organizations may belong to more than one group, and each group can have a different purpose. As a result, several types of groups frequently exist in organizations. These groups can be classified as formal or informal.

A.   *Formal Groups*

Learning Objective 1:   Define the four types of formal groups traditionally found in organizations.

The common types of formal work groups found in organizations are long-standing work groups, project groups, prefabricated groups, and quality circles. Long-standing work groups serve a permanent function for an organization and have well-defined responsibilities. Project groups assemble highly-trained members for the purpose of completing a specific project in a specified period of time. Prefabricated groups have a meticulously defined goal and a rigid structure that allows any collection of members to produce at a specified level of performance. Quality circles are groups of employees that meet on a regular basis to identify and solve departmental quality problems.

B.   *Informal Groups*

Learning Objective 2:   Describe two common types of informal groups found in many organizations.

The two groups are interest groups and friendship groups. Members of an interest group share a common cause or interest. On the other hand, individuals who assemble together as a result of friendship and the pleasure of association form a friendship group.

Suggested Readings for this Section:

Scott, K. Dow and Anthony Townsend. "Teams: Why Some Succeed and Others Fail." HR Magazine *39, August 1994, pp. 62-67.*

This article investigates why some teams perform better than others. To examine team performance, the authors studied team productivity in an apparel manufacturing company. The company had 122 teams containing more than 1,200 employees. The team approach is an important part of the company's strategy for success. The Team Productivity Study conducted in this company occurred in three phases over one year. The findings of the study indicate that team performance is determined in large part by attractiveness of performance, agreement with team goals, team goal level, willingness to use cross-training, perceived participation, team efficacy and team commitment.

Hopkins, Edward J. "Effective Teams: Camels of a Different Color?" Training & Development Journal *48, December 1994, pp. 35-37.*

The author of this article indicates that in the past, when a committee was instructed to create a horse, it built a camel of a different color. Today, teams are supposed to operate in a more effective and productive manner than has been the case with many committees. Eight guidelines for effective teams are identified and discussed in the article.

III.   COMMON STAGES OF GROUP DEVELOPMENT

Learning Objective 3:   Trace the common stages of group development.

Research indicates that group development occurs in five specific stages: forming, storming, norming, performing, and adjourning.

IV.   COMMUNICATION PATTERNS

Research has shown that patterns of communication can influence productivity and morale in groups. Two general patterns through which messages flow in groups are the circle and the star. The circle structure is considered to be democratic in nature. The star structure is autocratic in nature. The process of disseminating information for the purpose of solving problems occurs much faster in a star structure than in a circle structure. However, the open nature of communication in the circle structure encourages members to share their views and therefore promotes high-quality decisions.

V.   IMPORTANT ASPECTS OF WORK GROUPS

Interrelated aspects of work groups influence the effectiveness of groups in organizations. Four especially important aspects are group size, member roles, group norms, and group cohesiveness.

A.   *Group Size*

As group size increases, there is more ability, knowledge, and skill available to the group, but the potential for conflict in the group increases. Many group members tend to participate less in group discussions as group size increases. Also as size increases, more pressure is placed on members to conform. Generally, group members seem to be more satisfied in small groups than in large groups.

B.   *Member Roles*

In groups, roles are the behaviors expected of members based on the requirements of the position each holds or occupies. Three important classifications of group roles include task roles, maintenance roles, and self-centered roles.

VI.   GROUP NORMS

Group norms are the standards of conduct that group members accept as their behavioral guidelines regardless of their positions within the group.

Learning Objective 4:   Explain the difference between explicit and implicit group norms.

Explicit norms are explicitly identified rules of appropriate behavior. Implicit norms are rules of behavior that most group members generally understand are in place without being formally stated.

A. *How Group Norms Develop*

Some norms develop as a result of explicit statements made by managers or coworkers. Critical events that occur over time as the group acquires a history can set norms. The behaviors of group members at their initial meeting can establish norms for the group. In addition, transfer behaviors from past situations can establish norms for the group.

VII. GROUP COHESIVENESS

Group cohesiveness refers to the liking group members have for each other, to their attraction to the group, and to their motivation to remain in the group.

A. *Factors that Influence Group Cohesiveness*

Learning Objective 5: Identify factors that influence group cohesiveness.

Several factors appear to have a positive influence on group cohesiveness. Frequent interaction by members of a small group usually produces high group cohesiveness. Also, members tend to be attracted to and feel comfortable with people who they perceive to be similar to themselves. Furthermore, an increase in competition and success will enhance group cohesiveness.

B. *Building Group Cohesiveness*

To build group cohesiveness, managers should select individuals for a task force who are compatible and who will work well together. Managers should also help the group to experience success, encourage cooperation, and promote acceptance among group members.

C. *Risky-Shift Phenomenon*

Groups, especially those with high levels of cohesiveness, are vulnerable to the risky-shift phenomenon, which refers to the fact that individuals are more likely to advocate risky strategies when they are in a group than when they are acting alone.

D. *Groupthink*

When group cohesiveness is high, the desire to be a good group member and to be accepted by other members may encourage conformity. This tendency, called groupthink, occurs when members of a group avoid critically testing, analyzing, and evaluating each other's ideas in order to minimize conflict and reach a consensus.

VIII.   GROUP GOALS

Goals provide group members with a sense of direction to follow in planning and coordinating their activities.

Teaching Hint: Groups work best when they have an important goal that is meaningful to the members of the groups. It is hard to motivate group members to work on tasks that they consider to be unnecessary or irrelevant.

   A.   *Two Types of Group Goals*

   There are two broad types of group goals: achievement goals and maintenance goals.

Learning Objective 6:   Distinguish between achievement goals and maintenance goals.

   An achievement goal represents the outcome or product that the group wishes to produce. A maintenance goal focuses on maintaining and strengthening the group itself.

   B.   *Behaviors that Help a Group Accomplish Its Goals*

   A manager should make an effort to define the group's goal clearly. Doing so will help group members stay focused and get back on track if a discussion begins to stray. In group discussions, it helps if the manager periodically summarizes what has been accomplished in the discussion, what points are unclear, and what still needs to be accomplished. The group will also benefit when the manager shares his or her personal expertise and provides the group with pertinent information.

   C.   *The Importance of Clear Goals*

   Employees look to their manager for guidance in understanding specific group goals. Clear goals help employees to be productive. Techniques to clarify goals include making them more specific, operational, workable, measurable, and observable.

IX.   USING TEAMS WISELY

Employees working in teams can often accomplish much more than working alone. However, to be most productive, teams need to maximize their group resources.

A.   *Carefully Analyze Team Tasks*

Make sure that the task assigned to a team requires a team effort instead of delegating it to one particular individual.

B.   *Consider Using Integration Teams*

Integration teams help other teams to work together in companies. They can coordinate input from different groups and improve horizontal communication to help solve problems associated with different tasks being performed by a company.

C.   *Keep Team Morale High*

Much can be accomplished by teams when they have high morale. Establishment of a high level of trust between managers and employees is very helpful in developing high team morale.

Suggested Readings for this Section:
Pacanowsky, Michael. "Team Tools for Wicked Problems." Organizational Dynamics 23, Winter 1995, pp. 36-51.

When groups attempt to analyze and solve some especially difficult problems in companies, they may end up going in circles after hours of discussion. Problems with group problem-solving discussions at W. L. Gore & Associates, makers of Gore-Tex, are examined in this article. Techniques for groups to use in attempting to solve complex company problems are identified and discussed.

Coradetti, William R.. "Teamwork Takes Time and a Lot of Energy." HR Magazine 39, June 1994, pp. 74-77.

This article describes what Perdue Farms Inc. experienced when the company decided to create self-managed work teams. The author of this article indicates that it is important to be patient when developing self-managed teams. Such teams can not be created overnight and expected to function smoothly at first. The team members at Perdue were accustomed to being led. As a result, participation in group discussions was low for the self-managed teams. The department manager dealt with this reluctance to participate initially, by requiring that individual members lead different group discussions. This experience helped them become comfortable in participating. It was also necessary to help the team members feel like a group, instead of individual workers who are assembled together. Now, when problems on the job develop, the "team" takes care of them, instead of waiting for one employee to assume the responsibility.

X.   PROCESS MEASURES FOR TEAMS

To be more efficient and to improve quality, many firms are developing a process-focused approach to producing products and services. In doing so, process measures are needed to monitor the work and interactions throughout a company that produce a needed product or service.

XI.   TEAMWORK AND TQM

For total quality management (TQM) to achieve its potential, the top managers of a company must make a commitment to pursue continuous improvement. Managers need the help of other employees, working in groups, to implement this commitment. Teamwork in companies is most effective at improving product or service quality when groups work toward continuous improvement, when different groups engage in collaboration while working on related problems, and when they use a process-oriented approach. Maintaining a customer orientation is also necessary for improving product or service quality.

XII.   LOOKING BACK

This chapter examines the importance of work groups in organizations, and it covers key concepts associated with the way in which groups function.

▦ **Answers to CONSIDER THIS Questions**
■

1. **Each group has its own "personality." How much does a group's personality influence its ability to be productive?**

    A group's personality can have a significant influence on its ability to be productive. Some groups have a very positive personality and are motivated to accomplish much. Many of the members of these groups assume needed group task roles and group maintenance roles. They are willing and able to accept responsibility. As a result, these groups often compile many achievements. In leading such groups, however, it is important not to burn them out by overloading them with things to accomplish. There are also groups, unfortunately, that generally lack motivation and the ability to accomplish much. In some cases, these groups have a long history of accomplishing little. It almost becomes a self-fulfilling prophecy in that they don't expect to get much done, so they don't try to achieve much. These groups often have members who assume self-centered roles that are unproductive. Such behaviors must be changed before the group can be productive.

2. **Although groups can be very creative, prefab groups often do not adapt well to new situations that may develop. Why?**

    A prefabricated group has a meticulously defined goal and a rigid structure that allows any collection of members to produce at a specified level of performance. Fast-food restaurant chains have embraced the concept of prefab groups. As a result, even with high turnover, each restaurant still is able to produce the same items, with similar levels of quality, in about the same amount of time. The training prefab groups receive allows them to perform tasks in a reliable manner. However, they do not adapt well to new situations that may develop, because they are typically trained to perform in a standard way. They are not expected to be creative. Instead, they are expected to be consistent.

3. **Have you ever belonged to a group whose members have lost their enthusiasm and ability to be effective? What factors were responsible for the decline of this group?**

    Students frequently indicate that when top management loses interest in a group's work or fails to accept group recommendations, the group will usually lose its enthusiasm and ability to be effective. Another common cause is when a group is no longer challenged by a task or problem. Also, when a group lacks the resources to perform a task well, the members of the group will often lose their enthusiasm and ability to be effective.

Answers to CONSIDER THIS Questions

1.   **Which self-centered role do you believe is the most disruptive and damaging to groups? Why?**

Students often indicate that they think the "aggressor" is the most disruptive and damaging self-centered role that can be played by group members. Students with this view frequently explain that for a group to be creative and effective, the members must feel comfortable in expressing their ideas and opinions. However, an open communicative climate is less likely to exist when an "aggressor" is present in a group. An "aggressor" often expresses disapproval of others' ideas, bruises the egos of others, and generally has a negative attitude.

2.   **If you were placed in charge of a group that had low cohesiveness, what would you do to increase its cohesiveness?**

Students frequently explain that they would first try to learn why the group had low cohesiveness. If it was due to incompatible members of the group, then many students indicate that they would replace some of the members of the group. If members of the group could work well together, students often suggest working with the group to help it better utilize its human resources so that some early successes could be achieved by the group, which would help cohesiveness. Making sure that members of the group agree with and support the goals of the group is important. In addition, you should get as many members involved in group discussions as possible. Also, you should create a work climate in which employees feel valued. Such a climate encourages group members to demonstrate trust and respect for each other. Group members who show tolerance and encourage each other to excel tend to develop high levels of cohesiveness.

3.   **Why is it important for group leaders or managers to make sure that group maintenance goals are given careful attention?**

A group maintenance goal focuses on maintaining and strengthening the group itself. An example of a maintenance goal is to make sure there are satisfactory interpersonal relations among the members of the group. When, for example, dissension and strife in a group is high, little if anything productive can be expected to be accomplished by the group. Therefore group maintenance goals are important to the success of a group.

Answers to REVIEW AND DISCUSSION Questions

1.   *What is the distinction between long-standing work groups and project groups?*

A longstanding work group serves a permanent function for an organization and has well-defined responsibilities. A specific department or work unit in a company can be considered a longstanding group. Examples include an accounting department, a marketing department, or a human resources department. On the other hand, project groups assemble highly-trained members for the purpose of completing a specific project in a specified period of time. When special project groups are created, they cannot rely on the goals and modes of operation employed by the longstanding groups from which the members were borrowed. Instead, the newly-formed group must accept new goals and learn to work together.

2.   *What typically occurs during the storming stage of group development?*

After group members get acquainted and have a chance to assess the characteristics of the group, they often begin to unveil more about their personalities, in what is called the storming stage. Differences in personalities become more apparent at this time, and these differences often foster some conflict in the group. As various members of the group begin to assert themselves, disagreements over group goals or strategies for accomplishing the goals frequently develop. Factions within the group may begin to form with different factions vying for power to control the group agenda. As a result, there is generally a lack of cohesiveness. This is a critical time for the group. If the group members see the value and benefits to be gained from working together, the group will likely have a productive future. On the other hand, if the group drifts toward polarization, it may not progress beyond the storming stage.

3.   *How is the norming stage of group development different from the performing stage?*

Norming, the third stage in group development, is characterized by a resolution of conflict and differences of opinion in the group. Divisiveness in the group diminishes due to some dissatisfied members leaving the group or the understanding that more will be accomplished by putting differences aside and working together. In either case, unity begins to develop and group roles emerge. The group leader needs to take advantage of this lull to push for the establishment of group standards and specific goals. As a result, group members begin to accept individual responsibilities for the purpose of helping the group achieve its objectives.

On the other hand, in the performing stage, group energy is focused or channeled into accomplishing the group task. Issues that earlier held the group back get resolved, and the members are committed to the group task. As a result, they coordinate their efforts and accommodate the special needs of each other. Personality differences among the group members are accepted and tolerated because they need to work together and pool their strengths to accomplish group goals.

4.   *As a manager, why is it important for you to discourage group-member behaviors that are associated with self-centered roles?*

The sole function of self-centered roles is self gratification of individual group members, even at the expense of the group. An example of a self-centered role is the "Aggressor." Such a person in a group often expresses disapproval of others' ideas, bruises the egos of others, and generally has a negative attitude. When one or more members of a group engage in behaviors associated with self-centered roles, the group's overall performance will be harmed. Therefore, managers need to discourage behaviors associated with self-centered roles.

5.   *What are the four ways in which group norms develop?*

Certain norms exist when a group is formed, while other norms appear over the history of the group. For the most part, however, norms develop in the following four ways. First, some norms develop as a result of explicit statements by managers or coworkers. Second, critical events in the groups' history can set norms. Third, initial behaviors by group members can establish norms for the group. Fourth, transfer behaviors from past situations can establish norms for the group.

6.   *Why does the presence of new or increased competition tend to promote cohesiveness in a group?*

Typically, when a group is confronted with new or increased competition, the group members seek the support of each other in meeting the challenge. Differences in opinion between the members are set aside so they can focus on working together to beat the competition.

7.   *What can managers do to promote and build group cohesiveness?*

High-cohesiveness can have a positive effect on the satisfaction of group members and the productivity of the group. Four strategies can be especially helpful to managers in building group cohesiveness. First, managers should encourage compatible membership in groups. When a group is composed of members who work well together, cohesiveness often occurs. Second, help the group succeed. Group success at a task can frequently produce increased cohesiveness. Third, encourage cooperation. When group members cooperate rather than compete with each other, cohesiveness develops. Fourth, promote acceptance among group members. That is, create a work environment in which employees feel valued.

8.   *What can managers do to help work groups avoid groupthink?*

Certain strategies used by managers can help groups avoid groupthink. For example, tell group members that you expect them to be critical evaluators. When you instruct your group members to analyze a company problem, do not provide hints on the solution you think would be best. To really get impartial decisions, consider having two different groups analyze the same problem. You may seek the opinions of people outside the group to expose the group members to ideas uninfluenced by any group pressure. Even consider having an outside person who is knowledgeable about the discussion topic attend your group discussions.

Answers to CRITICAL THINKING INCIDENTS

Incident 14-1:   NEW COMPETITION

1.   **The employees in groups 1, 2, and 3 view final assembly as their only customer. What problem does this view create for Saniv.**

Although final assembly is an internal customer, it is not the only customer of groups one, two, and three. Individuals who purchase the company's finished product are also customers of the sections produced by groups one, two, and three. The three groups need to realize that it is not important enough to please only final assembly. These three groups also have external customers who must be pleased. In this case, the standards set by external customers appear to be higher than those of final assembly. Until the three groups improve their performance to meet the expectations of external customers, the company will continue to have serious problems.

2. **What problems exist in the way in which Saniv uses groups in its manufacturing process?**

    The activities of the three groups are not coordinated very well by the company. Final assembly frequently does not detect problems in the work performed by groups one, two and three until it is too late and bottlenecks have developed in the final assembly process. With the three groups operating rather independently of each other, the groups focus more on their needs and goals rather than the needs and goals of the company itself.

3. **What changes should Saniv make? Why?**

    Saniv should make sure that groups one, two, and three realize that they have external customers and that the needs of those customers must be met. The three groups should meet with some of these external customers periodically or get feedback from these customers on how the customers perceive the quality of their work. A process approach that better coordinates the activities of the three groups should be adopted by Saniv. In doing so, company goals need to be emphasized and assigned greater priority over individual group goals. Quality should be emphasized at each stage of the manufacturing process instead of at the end of the process.

Incident 14-2:   A GROUP CAUSE

1. **What type of formal group did Ted Becker form? How did you determine that it was that type of group?**

    The formal group formed by Ted Becker is considered to be a project group for several reasons. First, the members of the group have special talents and backgrounds that are needed by the group. That is, two employees are experienced in the company's mining business, and two employees are familiar with logging procedures. The fifth member is an environmental sciences specialist. Second, they have a specific threefold mission or purpose. Last, they have a time limit of six months to complete their review.

2. **Through what stages in group development have the members of the group progressed? What group developments did you observe in determining the group's progress?**

    The members of the group have progressed through the "forming" and "storming" stages of group development. Initially, none of the group members are familiar with each other. The "forming" stage of group development occurs with group members getting acquainted. Therefore, when the group members spent a lot of time getting to know one another in their first group meeting, they were engaged in the "forming" stage of group development. Once group members have assessed the characteristics of the group, they become willing to unveil more significant aspects of their personalities, in what is called the "storming" stage of group development. After the members of the group created by Ted Becker become acquainted with each other, they begin to learn more about the different personalities represented in the group. Some of the differences in personalities are threatening to produce conflict in the group. As a result, it is appropriate to conclude that the group has also progressed into the "storming" stage of group development.

3. **Which one of the three group roles is Alfonso performing? What did you observe about Alfonso's behavior that led you to this conclusion?**

Alfonso is performing a maintenance role. A maintenance role is performed for the purpose of supporting and nurturing other group members. For example Alfonso attempts to mediate differences that exist between the two different factions within the group. He also works to reconcile any disagreements that surface between individual members. Alfonso uses jesting in an effort to relieve group conflicts.

Incident 14-3:   A FALSE SENSE OF SECURITY

1. **The small group assembled by Rachel can best be classified as what type of formal group due to what characteristics of the group?**

The small group assembled by Rachel can best be viewed as a project group. The group has a specific goal, that is, to help Rachel select one of the three advertising approaches created by the advertising agency. A decision is expected to be made during the time allotted for the meeting. These conditions typically apply to project groups.

2. **What problems did the group experience in its effort to select the best advertising campaign for the company?**

The group members Rachel selected tend to view things the same way, which makes it difficult for the group to be exposed to different ways of evaluating the three advertising campaigns. Opening remarks by Rachel to the group included the statement "I think we should use the humorous approach, but I want to know your views." This statement can influence or bias the thinking of some group members in that they feel pressure to agree with their boss. The high cohesiveness of the group also increases the likelihood that they will experience groupthink. The desire to conform and to be in agreement probably led some of the group members to dismiss Larisa's concerns about Rachel's recommendation.

3.   **As manager, what should Rachel have done to help the group overcome the problems it experienced?**

Rachel should select people to be on the group based primarily on their qualifications and the skills they can offer the group, not primarily employees she works well with and likes. People with a wide range of experiences relevant to the group task can be especially valuable group members. To avoid unduly influencing or biasing the group discussion, Rachel should not initially signal which solution she thinks is best. Instead, Rachel should ask the group for their views on the different marketing programs she is considering for adoption. Rachel should also be aware of the dangers associated with groupthink. For example, Rachel should make sure that Larisa's concerns are fully examined and that Larisa is made to feel comfortable in expressing relevant concerns.

Study Guide Assignments

A matching exercise at the beginning of the study guide helps students to check their familiarity of key terms used in the chapter. A useful concept application exercise follows which contains six scenarios that deal with important group concepts.

An individual case assessment is provided that focuses on frustrations three individuals experience with groups in their companies. The group case assessment enables students to benefit from sharing ideas about how teleconferencing can help companies make better use of groups.

Video Case

Motorola

Focus: **Work Teams**

Summary:

This video profiles Motorola's cellular telephone plant. Motorola faced a problem with their cellular telephones because Japanese companies were selling phones at below market value. Motorola's management recognized that slow progress was no longer acceptable.

Cellular phones were designed and built in traditional ways. A design team developed plans for the product, the purchasing department ordered raw materials, and the operations group manufactured the product. As a result of this organization, the people from various departments did not talk with one another or work on problems together.

Motorola brought these people together into project teams. By bringing them together, Motorola was able to decrease costs and increase the quality of their products. In order to accomplish this change, Motorola worked to educate employees about the change, moved the technical employees' offices to the manufacturing floor, and started working with suppliers as partners. This Motorola plant went from seven layers of management to three layers. Their new phone is 1/3 the size, 1/3 the weight, and uses 1/3 the number of parts of the old phone, and it is three times as reliable.

As a result of the product changes, Motorola's cellular phones are now a hot export item to the Far East.

Discussion Questions:

1. What was the method of technological interdependence at Motorola before the change?

   Before the change, Motorola used pooled interdependence: the output of one department became the input for the next department. The design team's work became input for purchasing; purchasing's work became input for operations.

2. In an autonomous work group, what kind of coordination mechanisms would be most important?

   In work groups, communication is the key coordination mechanism.

Chapter **15**

Managing Change and Conflict

▒ Chapter Overview

Managers must be prepared to deal with change and conflict in organizations. Success in implementing change can depend on whether a manager has anticipated likely resistance to the change. Therefore, some of the common sources of resistance to change and techniques for dealing with resistance are identified and discussed. The influence of corporate culture on change is also examined.

A change process is presented and its application to organizations is examined. Levels of change and the difficulty associated with achieving the different levels in companies are identified and analyzed. The participative change cycle is presented. Two common techniques utilized as part of organizational development efforts to make large scale or organization-wide changes are covered.

Common causes of conflict in organizations are discussed, along with the influence of corporate culture on conflict. Different strategies for dealing with conflict are described. Communication skills that help reduce defensive feelings that can produce conflict are presented. In addition, two key issues associated with negotiating agreements are discussed.

▒ Teaching Objectives

The teaching objectives of this chapter are to:

1.   Identify the common sources of resistance to change in organizations.

323

2.   Explain how to apply force-field analysis for making change.

3.   Indicate the steps involved in Kurt Lewin's three-phase model of change.

4.   Explain how to implement a participative change cycle.

5.   Identify some of the common causes of conflict in organizations.

6.   Discuss the different conflict management strategies available to managers.

Chapter Outline of the Text

    I.   CHANGE
          A.   Why Change Is Often Resisted
          B.   Dealing with Resistance to Change
          C.   Consider Competing Forces
          D.   Corporate Culture Influences Change
          E.   Considerations When Attempting Change
    II.   THE CHANGE PROCESS: KURT LEWIN'S THREE-PHASE MODEL
    III. LEVELS OF CHANGE
          A.   The Participative Change Cycle
    IV.   ORGANIZATIONAL DEVELOPMENT
          A.   Survey Feedback
          B.   Team Building
    V.   CONFLICT IN ORGANIZATIONS
          A.   Constructive Conflict
          B.   Destructive Conflicts
    VI.   COMMON CAUSES OF CONFLICT
          A.   Competition for Scarce Resources
          B.   Ambiguous Job Responsibilities
          C.   Task Interdependence
          D.   Personality Differences
          E.   Authority Differences
          F.   Miscommunication
    VII. THE QUESTION-AND-ANSWER COMMUNICATION PROGRAM
    VIII. INFLUENCE OF CORPORATE CULTURE ON CONFLICT
    IX.   CONFLICT MANAGEMENT STRATEGIES
          A.   Avoidance Strategy
          B.   Accommodation Strategy
          C.   Competition Strategy
          D.   Compromise Strategy

Key Terms

These terms are introduced in the chapter.

Accommodation strategy

Avoidance strategy

Bridge the gap

Changing stage

Collaboration strategy

Competition (forcing) strategy

Compromise strategy

Conflict

Conflict management

Corporate culture

Force-field analysis

Fundamental attribution error

Gap

Lose-lose solution

Objective criteria

Organizational development (OD)

Participative change

Participative change cycle

Proactive change

Question-and-answer communication
    program

Reactive change

Reciprocal interdependence

Refreezing stage

Self-serving attributional bias

Sequential interdependence

Survey feedback

Team building

Unfreezing stage

Win-lose solution

Win-win solution

Detailed Chapter Summary

I.   CHANGE

Today, with an emphasis on continuous quality improvement, change occurs on a
fairly regular basis. As a matter of fact, managers must be prepared to anticipate and
plan in advance for change.

A.   *Why Change Is Often Resisted*

Learning Objective 1:   Identify the common sources of resistance to change in organizations.

Employees may fear that they will fail and lose their jobs if significant changes are made in their work environment. In addition, they may fear the loss of a comfortable routine. There is also fear of the unknown or a disruption in career plans. Furthermore, employees often fear that change will disturb established work relationships with others.

B.   *Dealing with Resistance to Change*

Much of the anxiety associated with change can be eased by educating employees about the change beforehand. Employees also tend to resist change less if they have a chance to participate and be involved in necessary change. In addition, managers who offer to facilitate employees as they make needed changes and support them in doing so help reduce resistance to change.

C.   *Consider Competing Forces*

Learning Objective 2:   Explain how to apply force-field analysis for making change.

Managers should identify and analyze the key driving and restraining forces that affect any situation they wish to change in an organization. A two-step strategy for making the desired change should then be developed by the manager. First, identify ways to reduce or eliminate all or some of the restraining forces. Second, identify ways to improve or strengthen as many of the driving forces that affect the situation as possible.

D.   *Corporate Culture Influences Change*

The tenets of a corporate culture can be very strong, and they can influence the behavior patterns within an organization. If top management wishes to introduce change that is not compatible with the firm's culture, there will be much resistance to it, and the change will be difficult to implement.

E.   *Considerations When Attempting Change*

Managers should consider the scope of change, that is, should a particular change be implemented throughout the organization or just in one department initially? It may be appropriate to start with a trial run in one area so that unanticipated problems can be corrected before the change is more widely implemented. The timing of change should also be considered, as well as how the change will be coordinated, and the impact of the change.

Suggested Readings for this Section:

Harari, Oren. "Why Don't Things Change?" Management Review 84, February 1995, pp. 30-32.

According to the author of this article, many managers feel overwhelmed, and they believe their companies must change in order to survive. However, much of the needed change does not occur. Why doesn't the necessary change occur? The author claims there are two fundamental impediments to appropriate change. First, too often managers tolerate a culture of mediocrity, which acts as a barrier to change. That is, in a culture of mediocrity, blaming substitutes for accountability. Furthermore, mediocrity becomes addictive, causing inefficient work routines to be retained. Research, for example, indicates that many of the in-house activities of companies add little value to the products or services acquired by their customers. The second impediment is the quest for a quick fix. Undoubtedly, the desire for solutions that can be implemented risk-free, quickly, and cheaply are in great demand. Such solutions, however, usually produce little change.

Fisher, Anne B. "Making Change Stick." Fortune, April 17, 1995, pp. 121-131.

To be successful in implementing change in organizations, managers must often respond to fear and anger expressed by employees. Key ingredients to making change work is to empower employees, listen to their suggestions, and communicate frequently with employees in order to clarify the company's goals and strategy for achieving them. The approach used to make needed changes at the Jaguar car maker is discussed.

II. THE CHANGE PROCESS: KURT LEWIN'S THREE-PHASE MODEL

Learning Objective 3: Indicate the steps involved in Kurt Lewin's three-phase model of change.

The first stage, unfreezing, makes the individual, group, or organization aware that change is required. In the second stage, changing, some type of change is made to improve whatever needs to be corrected. Refreezing, the final stage, occurs once the change or new behavior becomes a current way of thinking and/or acting.

III.   LEVELS OF CHANGE

Four general levels of change apply to organizations. Specifically, they are changes in knowledge, attitudes, individual behavior, and group behavior.

Teaching Hint: An unpopular change that is forced by managers will often require close supervision by them to maintain. Emphasize that the extra time needed to involve employees in understanding the need for change and in developing a strategy for implementing the change increases the likelihood that the change will be long-lasting without time-consuming, close supervision.

A.   *The Participative Change Cycle*

Learning Objective 4:   Explain how to implement a participative change cycle.

The participative change cycle is most appropriately applied to situations in which employees are motivated and ambitious, actively seek responsibility, and have the knowledge and/or experience to implement a particular change. First, employees are provided with new knowledge about a problem. Second, they are involved in developing a strategy to solve the problem. Third, their commitment is converted to actual behavior.

IV.   ORGANIZATIONAL DEVELOPMENT

Organizational development focuses on large-scale or organization-wide changes and can be defined as the use of applied behavioral science principles to make major improvements in the capability and effectiveness of an organization.

A.   *Survey Feedback*

In organizations, survey feedback is a technique that assesses the attitudes of employees, disseminates the results of these assessments for review, and facilitates company-wide discussion which leads to change.

B.   *Team Building*

Team building is a technique designed to help work groups function in an effective and productive manner. Team building may deal with such issues as determining how groups accomplish various tasks and the quality of interpersonal relations in groups.

V. CONFLICT IN ORGANIZATIONS

Conflict is a condition that exists whenever the goals, methods, or objectives of two or more parties are in opposition and therefore hinder the parties from pursuing their interests. The possibilities for conflict in organizations are numerous.

A.   *Constructive Conflict*

Probably the most beneficial aspect of conflict is that it can force individuals who are frustrated with each other to discuss their concerns together. Through open communication, situations are clarified, and the individuals involved are better able to understand each other's predicament. They may even be able to determine how to help each other.

B.   *Destructive Conflicts*

A conflict becomes destructive when the parties involved are dissatisfied with the outcome and believe they are worse off as a result of the conflict. The frustrations associated with conflict can distract employees from the organization's important goals and hurt company morale.

Suggested Readings for this Section:
Pascale, Richard T. "Intentional Breakdowns and Conflict By Design." <u>Planning Review</u> 22, May/June 1994, pp. 12-19.

Breakthroughs, according to this article, seldom occur without breakdowns, and the author indicates that companies must encourage conflict internally to jump-start the creative process. Japanese managers, for example, can disagree with each other without being disagreeable. This approach allows them to harness conflict to their advantage. To the Japanese, tension is good if it promotes frequent dialogue and communication, and a breakdown in a process is not automatically bad. As a matter of fact, the Japanese permit an entire manufacturing assembly line to be stopped when a worker spots any defect. The logic is that dramatizing a breakdown is the best way to permanently eliminate the underlying cause.

Kaye, Kenneth. "The Art of Listening." <u>HR Focus</u> 71, October 1994, p. 24.

Companies should have a conflict-resolving system as part of their corporate culture. If employees treated fellow employees as their most valued clients, more time would be spent in listening to the needs and concerns of others, which reduces the likelihood of conflict. Listening techniques that can promote productive working relationships and can be beneficial for resolving conflicts are discussed.

VI.   COMMON CAUSES OF CONFLICT

Learning Objective 5:   Identify some of the common causes of conflict in organizations.

Conflict can occur in organizations as a result of competition for scarce resources, ambiguous job responsibilities, and task interdependence. Differences in personality and authority can also result in conflict. In addition, miscommunication can create conflict in organizations.

VII.   THE QUESTION-AND-ANSWER COMMUNICATION PROGRAM

The question-and-answer communication program is designed to reduce misunderstandings associated with downward communication in organizations. In this program, after supervisors provide downward communication to their employees, the employees have a chance to ask questions. If the supervisors do not know the answers to certain questions, they get answers for the employees from top management.

VIII.   INFLUENCE OF CORPORATE CULTURE ON CONFLICT

Top management's job is to blend a corporate culture in a way that defuses subcultural conflicts and turns them into complementary forces that mutually reinforce the best aspects of the subcultures.

IX.   CONFLICT MANAGEMENT STRATEGIES

Learning Objective 6:   Discuss the different conflict management strategies available to managers.

Several conflict management strategies are used by managers. For instance, a manager who employs an avoidance strategy basically does nothing and avoids a conflict. When an accommodation strategy is in force, a manager works hard to get along with others at all costs and hopes that conflict will be eliminated. Managers employ a competition or forcing strategy whenever they use their position power and authority to force others to accept a particular solution. On the other hand, a compromise strategy is an attempt to reach a solution that meets some of the needs of the individual parties in a conflict. When a collaboration strategy is implemented, both parties in a conflict focus on each other's concerns in an effort to reach a mutually beneficial agreement.

X.   DEFENSIVE AND SUPPORTIVE COMMUNICATION BEHAVIORS

Language that appears to the listener to be negative in its evaluation tends to increase defensive behavior, but descriptive statements reduce defensiveness. Statements that are designed to control promote defensive behavior, but problem orientation statements produce the opposite result. Strategy statements with a hidden agenda increase defensiveness, but spontaneity statements have the opposite effect. Neutrality, "just-the-facts" statements appear detached and insensitive. As a result, they increase defensiveness, but empathy statements reduce defensiveness. Superiority statements and certainty statements increase defensiveness, but equality and provisionalism statements tend to reduce defensiveness.

XI.   HOW TO NEGOTIATE

Managers must be prepared to negotiate agreements on the job. Good negotiators realize that the needs of both parties in a negotiation must be considered in order to develop long-lasting agreements.

Teaching Hint: Negotiators sometimes refer to the other person in the negotiation as the adversary. Emphasize that it is easier to negotiate with a friend than an enemy. When negotiating, show an interest in understanding the other person's needs. This behavior will be viewed positively by the other person and will help create an environment in which you are negotiating with a friend, not an opponent.

A.   *Negotiate From Objective Criteria*

Objective criteria are independent, established standards against which any possible solution can be measured. If a proposed solution in a negotiation does not meet the objective criteria established, it will likely produce problems if accepted.

B.   *Bridge the Gap*

The gap in a negotiation is the distance between differing positions taken by two people on an issue. Sometimes, the gap that exists appears to represent an impasse. One way to deal with this situation is to bridge the gap by introducing new issues. These new issues can create the foundation for a workable and acceptable agreement.

XII.   LOOKING BACK

This chapter examines key issues managers should be aware of concerning change in organizations and how to deal with conflict.

Answers to CONSIDER THIS Questions

1.   **Consider a change you would like to make. What driving and restraining forces affect that change? How could you alter some of these forces to make the desired change easier?**

Students typically can think of a lot of changes they would like to make, but they have not generally considered driving and restraining forces connected with them. Instead, students usually conclude that they have not made certain changes because they don't have time to do so, or something else must be done first. However, when they do attempt future changes, they will find that awareness of driving and restraining forces can help them better understand what must be done to succeed in making changes. Now is a good time for students to begin considering what driving and restraining forces might exist for changes they will attempt to make in the future.

2.   **What difficulty will you probably experience as a manager if you do not consider the causes of resistance to a change before you attempt to implement it?**

Resistance to change in organizations is common and should be expected. You may fail in your effort to implement a change if you are not prepared for certain forms of resistance that are likely to occur. For example, educating employees on how the benefits of a change outweigh the weaknesses can be critical to gaining acceptance of the change. In addition, understanding that employees accept change more readily if they participate in its development will allow you to get the employees involved early in discussions concerning changes that are needed. These forms of preparation and others can reduce or eliminate some forms of resistance to change that could otherwise be significant.

3. **Is it better to implement change in an organization quickly or slowly? Why?**

    Some students will claim that it is best to act quickly in making changes so that there is little time for resistance to gain momentum. Other students will argue that it is wise to go slowly when implementing change so people have time to adjust to the change and unexpected problems can be dealt with in an orderly fashion. An important factor for students to consider is the expected impact of an anticipated change. If a particular change will have a wide impact on a company, it may be appropriate to implement the change slowly. Otherwise, the change may not succeed. On the other hand, a change that affects few areas and has limited impact on a company can often be implemented quickly with little risk.

Answers to CONSIDER THIS Questions

1. **In what ways does a manager's personality influence how well he or she will be able to deal with conflict?**

    Personality can make a big difference. Some managers, for example, take disagreements very personal. For these managers, you are viewed as rejecting them if you reject their ideas. As a result, it is difficult for them to deal with conflict. Their uncomfortableness with disagreements often limits them to two options concerning conflict. First, they may do everything possible to avoid conflict. That is, the absence of conflict means ideas don't get rejected. Second, as soon as disagreement occurs, the manager may become very aggressive in an effort to overwhelm and end the confrontation quickly to eliminate any continuation of conflict. Managers with personalities that enable them to accept disagreement without feeling rejected personally, are able to manage conflict situations better.

2. **How open-minded do you think you are in considering opposing viewpoints?**

    Most students believe they are open minded. For these students, being open minded indicates that they are willing to listen to new ideas. For managers, being open minded should indicate that in addition to listening, they are also willing to accept and implement new ideas. Beyond having managers listen to their ideas, employees want to see action taken. If employees do not see action taken on their upward communication, they will likely conclude that their managers are not open minded even if they are good listeners.

3.   **What types of conflict do you think are the most difficult to deal with for most managers? How would you deal with these types of conflicts?**

Conflicts that do not appear to have acceptable solutions are often perceived as the most difficult to deal with by managers. Frequently, a narrow, traditional view of a problem is responsible for the inability of managers to find a solution. Creativity is needed to deal with these situations. When the specifications for an acceptable solution are very restrictive, options are limited. To increase the acceptable options available, managers must be willing to consider nontraditional ways of viewing the situation. In doing so, relevant goals and objectives should be reviewed to see if changes in these areas are appropriate.

Answers to REVIEW AND DISCUSSION Questions

1.   *How should managers attempt to overcome resistance to change in organizations?*

Much of the anxiety associated with change can be eased by educating employees about the change beforehand. Through communicating with employees, managers can explain the need for and the logic of the change. Giving employees a chance to participate and be involved in making needed changes can help reduce resistance to change. Offering assistance to employees who will be affected by change helps to reduce concerns about the change. That is, such facilitation and support often helps to smooth the way for change to occur. Understanding and working with competing forces that affect change can also reduce resistance to change.

2.   *What are the typical characteristics of top executives who are successful in implementing major changes in corporate culture?*

Research indicates that top executives who are successful in implementing major changes in corporate culture typically are effective leaders, have an outsider's perspective, and maintain an insider background.

3.   *What issues should a manager take into consideration before actually implementing change in an organization?*

Attention by managers to certain considerations often smooths the path for change. For example, managers should give attention to the scope of change. That is, should a particular change be implemented throughout the organization or just in one department initially? Starting with a trial run in one area makes it easier to correct unanticipated problems that develop as a result of the change. The timing of the change should also be considered. Instituting change during an especially busy period for a company, for instance, may not be wise. Windows of opportunity for the successful implementation of change can become more open or closed at different times in companies. Last, managers should consider how a change will be coordinated.

4. *Why is it easier to implement change in a company when employees perceive themselves as agents of change instead of as targets of change?*

People generally resist change that is forced on them more so than if they helped to design and implement it. When, for example, employees are given an opportunity to investigate a problem facing a company and suggest needed change, they are likely to support the change. Participation generally leads to commitment due to the fact that the participants better understand and appreciate the proposed change. After all, it is the participants' change because they helped develop it, and they can be utilized to help sell the needed change to others in the organization.

5. *How can conflict actually be beneficial to a company?*

Conflict can force individuals who are frustrated with each other to discuss their concerns together. Through open communication, situations are clarified and the individuals involved are able to understand each other's predicament better. Conflict that allows differing views to be discussed and examined can also reduce tension that might otherwise build. In these discussions, creativity may be stimulated. Conflict between groups of employees can actually increase both the cohesiveness and performance of work groups when the members band together to meet the challenge.

6. *Why is conflict between line and staff individuals predictable in organizations?*

Staff departments often enjoy high placement in the organizational structure of a company. Therefore, they typically have the attention of top management. As a result, they enjoy informal command authority, which may concern line managers who fear that their control is being undermined by the staff departments. Differences in personality that can characterize employees in line departments compared to those in staff departments may also contribute to line-staff conflict.

7.   *Under what conditions would it be appropriate to use avoidance as a conflict management strategy?*

It may be appropriate to use avoidance as a conflict management strategy if the pressures that are causing the conflict will soon subside. As a result, intervention is not necessary because the problem will correct itself over time. Also, managers with poor conflict management skills may do more harm than good if they attempt to resolve a conflict. For these managers, avoidance is the least-risky approach.

8.   *What problems are associated with using compromise as a strategy for resolving conflicts?*

Just because some of the needs of both parties in a conflict are met in a compromise solution does not mean that they will like or be committed to it. As a result, the compromise solution may not be fully honored by one or both of the parties. Also, managers who compromise on key issues affecting their departments may be taking unwise risks.

9.   *How does the "bridge the gap" strategy work during a negotiation?*

The "bridge the gap" strategy is used to deal with an impasse in a negotiation. A negotiator using this strategy introduces new ideas into the negotiation. The person introducing the new issues offers something of value to the other person. In exchange, the other person is motivated to make some further concessions that will allow the gap or impasse in the negotiation to be closed. As a result, an agreement is finally reached.

Answers to CRITICAL THINKING INCIDENTS

Incident 15-1: MISGUIDED STRATEGIES

1.   **What approach is top management at Marianne's company taking to implement change? How appropriate is this change strategy?**

Change in Marianne's company is being forced. As explained in the chapter, there are four general levels of change that apply to organizations. Specifically, they are changes in knowledge, attitudes, individual behavior, and group behavior. Executives at Marianne's company simply announce new policies that change the way the company operates. Since these new policies affect all employees, group behavior is forced to change. Each individual in the group, of course, is affected. Therefore, individual behavior also is forced to change. The executive's logic is that once the employees see the wisdom of the new policies (a change in knowledge), the employees will like the new policies (a change in attitude). Forced change in an organization, (except in crisis situations) is inappropriate when the employees are highly motivated, very skilled, like being challenged, are well educated, and have the willingness and ability to accept responsibility on the job.

2. **What approach is top management at Jim's company taking to implement change? How appropriate is this change strategy?**

Jim's company is using a participative change approach. In using this approach, employees are provided with new knowledge concerning a problem that needs to be corrected. The employees are then directly involved in developing a strategy to achieve a desired goal. Last, they are encouraged to engage in behaviors that will enable the strategy to be implemented. The participative change approach is most appropriate for change situations in which employees are motivated and ambitious, actively seek responsibility, and have the knowledge and/or experience to implement a particular change. The employees in Jim's company do not have a lot of formal education. Their jobs are fairly routine in nature and do not require a lot of skill. These employees are more concerned about how much they earn per hour than what they actually do on their jobs. In addition, they do not expect or want to make many decisions on the job. As a result, it is probably not appropriate to ask these employees to take a lot of time away from their jobs to analyze changes top management is considering. The employees are not especially interested in attending decision-making meetings, and they probably lack the training necessary to fully participate in discussions of problems management is analyzing.

3. **What change strategies should be used by each of the two companies? Why?**

Due to the fact that employees at Marianne's company are motivated, skilled, well-educated, like being challenged, and have the willingness and ability to accept responsibility on the job, the company should probably make heavy use of the participative change strategy. There is less need for management at Jim's company to pull employees away from their work to attend meetings in which options for change are discussed.

Incident 15-2:   IT'S ALL AROUND YOU

1.   **What common cause of conflict was responsible for the argument that developed between the manager and the employee?**

The manager instructed the employee to "stack the sheets of drywall against the north wall." However, the meaning the employee gave to this statement was different than the meaning intended by the manager. As a result, conflict occurred between the manager and the employee. This conflict, therefore, was due to miscommunication.

2.   **How should the manager and employee have dealt with this situation?**

The manager should not have assumed that the new employee would automatically know the proper way to stack sheets of drywall. Instead, the manager should have been more specific in explaining what needed to be done. For example, the manager should have said, "Please stack the sheets of drywall against the north wall by placing each sheet on its long, narrow edge and lean one against the other." The employee should have clarified what the manager wanted by asking, "In what way do you want the sheets of drywall stacked?"

3.   **Why did the disagreement between Manuel and Sharon develop?**

The disagreement between Manuel and Sharon developed due to miscommunication. In this situation, Sharon thinks that Manuel wants each training session to be longer in duration. Manuel doesn't want the sessions themselves to be longer. Instead, he wants more sessions over a longer period of time. Sharon would not have objected to Manuel's suggestion if she had realized that he was not advocating that the length of each training session be increased.

Incident 15-3:   GOING NOWHERE

1.   **Which of Grabriella's statements can be classified as communication behavior that demonstrates superiority, according to the discussion of defensive and supportive communication in this chapter? What are the negative consequences of communication behavior that indicates superiority?**

Gabriella's first two statements can be classified as "superiority" communication behavior. As individuals interact, superiority communication behavior will increase defensive feelings on the part of the recipient of such behavior.

2.   **Which one of Gabriella's statements is an example of communication behavior that demonstrates certainty? How should this statement be rephrased?**

Gabriella's last statement represents an example of a "certainty" type of communication behavior. This statement should be phrased provisionally, such as, "Could it be that growth in the furniture business is only available in the low-priced market?"

3.   **Which one of Gabriella's statements is an example of communication behavior that indicates control? How should this statement be rephrased?**

Gabriella demonstrates a "control" type of communication behavior when she says, "It doesn't matter. I've analyzed the situation, and for us to increase sales, we must produce low-priced furniture." This statement should be phrased using a problem orientation, such as, "The furniture industry remains in a recession, and I am wondering what we should consider doing to correct this problem." This rephrased statement represents a problem orientation communication approach and signals a desire to collaborate in understanding and solving a mutual problem.

Study Guide Assignments

For this chapter in the study guide, students can use the helpful matching exercise to identify correct definitions for key terms. Six scenarios for students to analyze in relation to key organizing concepts are provided. An individual case assessment has also been prepared that gives students an opportunity to think about the difficulty employees face when they know changes are needed in their company, but they realize the changes will have a negative impact on them.

The group case assessment provided gives students an opportunity to share their views on how some of the forms of resistance to change that exist in the case should be dealt with by the CEO of the company. A helpful self assessment questionnaire is also available to help students better understand how receptive they are to change.

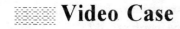 **Video Case**

Marion Carpets

Focus: **Adaptive Organizations**

Summary:

Marion Skoro founded Marion's Carpets in 1965. He started as an upholstery shop but soon changed to selling carpet to commercial accounts. As more of his children became involved in the business, he decided to expand.

Skoros decided to enter the retail carpet business in Portland. Because carpet is normally ordered only when the customer places an order, the major costs in this move were space costs. To lower these costs, Skoros formed alliances with complementary businesses, sharing space and costs with a chain of paint, wallpaper, and miniblind stores. In addition to saving space, these alliances created total design stores, increasing sales for both businesses.

Commissioned sales people were reluctant to work at Marion's Carpets without major expenditures on advertising. In addition to radio and television ads, Skoros took the unusual step of guaranteeing customer satisfaction with their carpet purchase. If the customer was dissatisfied after installation, Marion's Carpets provided no-cost replacement.

Sales at Marion's Carpets topped $9 million in 1993, and the firm is Portland's largest carpet chain.

Discussion Questions:

1.   How would you describe the organizational design at Marion's Carpets?

       Based on the video, the design at Marion's Carpets appears to be relatively flexible. In addition to Skoros, key family members have assumed key leadership positions. In family businesses, cooperation and communication appear to be keys to successful design.

2.   As Marion Carpets continues to grow, how might its design change?

       How the organizational design at Marion Carpets changes depends to a large extent on what direction the growth takes. For example, if Marion Carpets expands into new geographic areas, it may need to structure the organization based on geographic regions.

Chapter **16**

Employee-Management Relations

▚▚▚ Chapter Overview

This chapter provides students with an overview of formal appraisal programs used by managers to appraise the performance of employees. The need for managers to promote self-discipline among employees is emphasized. In the event that self-discipline is not practiced, procedures available to managers for disciplining employees who fail to follow company rules, standards, or policies are also discussed.

Key aspects of compensation programs in organizations that managers should be aware of are examined. Unique issues associated with managing employees who are represented by a labor union are presented. In addition, techniques for promoting good labor relations and efficiency in nonunionized companies are discussed.

▚▚▚ Teaching Objectives

The teaching objectives of this chapter are to:

1.   Identify three important considerations that managers should make when selecting performance-appraisal standards.

2.   Explain how behaviorally anchored rating scales can be used in performance appraisals.

3.   Identify the four key principles of the "hot-stove rule" for administering discipline.

4.   Explain why managers should focus on employees' strengths, rather than on their weaknesses, when preparing performance appraisals.

5.   Describe the five-step procedure for establishing pay rates for jobs.

6.   Indicate what factors typically encourage employees to seek representation by a labor union.

▓ **Chapter Outline of the Text**

I.   APPRAISING PERFORMANCE
        A.   Selecting Performance Standards
                1.   Relevance
                2.   Distinguishability/Measurability
                3.   Reliability
II.   PERFORMANCE-APPRAISAL METHODS
        A.   Graphic Rating Scales
        B.   Behaviorally Anchored Rating Scales (BARS)
        C.   Management by Objectives (MBO)
        D.   Essay Method
        E.   Customer Feedback
        F.   Peer Evaluation
III.   ADMINISTERING DISCIPLINE
        A.   Self-Discipline
        B.   The Responsibility to Discipline
        C.   Progressive Discipline
        D.   Discipline Without Punishment
IV.   COMPENSATION
        A.   Legislation Affecting Compensation
        B.   Determining Pay Rates
        C.   Pay-for-Performance Programs
        D.   Pay-at-Risk Programs
V.   EMPLOYEE BENEFITS REQUIRED BY LAW
        A.   Costs of Providing Benefits
VI.   LABOR UNIONS
        A.   Good-Faith Bargaining

Key Terms

These terms are introduced in the chapter.

Behaviorally anchored rating scale (BARS)
Benefits
Collective bargaining
Compensation
Discipline
Distinguishability
Employee-management committee
Empowerment
Essay method
Featherbedding
Graphic rating scale
Halo error

Hot-stove rule
Labor union
Management by objectives (MBO)
Measurability
Open meeting communication program
Pay-for-performance system
Pay-at-risk program
Progressive discipline
Relevance
Reliability
Self-discipline

Detailed Chapter Summary

I.   APPRAISING PERFORMANCE

Managers are expected to provide employees with periodic appraisals of their performance. When conducted properly, employee-appraisal programs benefit employees and managers by providing employees with feedback that will help them to grow professionally and by helping companies to fully utilize the potential of their human resources.

A.   *Selecting Performance Standards*

Learning Objective 1:   Identify three important considerations that managers should make when selecting performance-appraisal standards.

The three considerations of relevance, distinguishability/measurability, and reliability should be given attention when selecting performance standards.

II.   PERFORMANCE-APPRAISAL METHODS

Several performance-appraisal methods are available to managers. Depending on the employees and the work they perform, some appraisal methods are more appropriate and effective than others for evaluating the performance of employees.

A.   *Graphic Rating Scales*

Graphic rating scales compare employees' performance to an absolute standard. A graphic rating scale may contain several dimensions, such as quality of work, quantity of output, punctuality, and congeniality by which to evaluate employees.

B.   *Behaviorally Anchored Rating Scales (BARS)*

Learning Objective 2:   Explain how behaviorally anchored rating scales can be used in performance appraisals.

Behaviorally anchored rating scales (BARS) use observable job behaviors, rather than traits, knowledge, or skills, as evaluative dimensions. A detailed description of an actual on-the-job behavior is provided as a standard against which a manager can compare the performance of employees. The descriptions range from those indicative of success on the job to those indicative of failure. These descriptions become aligned with appropriate positions on a scale.

C.   *Management by Objectives (MBO)*

The strategy of Management by Objectives is to evaluate the performance of employees based on how well they achieve objectives that they and their manager have established together.

D.   *Essay Method*

When employing the essay method, a manager writes a brief narrative that describes the general performance of an employee. The narrative usually addresses preset areas of performance. As part of the essay, the manager identifies both the strengths and weaknesses of the employee's performance. The essay method offers managers an opportunity to elaborate on certain behaviors and clarify why they are valued or need attention.

E.   *Customer Feedback*

To learn how well their products and services are received, companies often survey the opinions of their customers. These surveys can be structured to help companies gain customer feedback on the performance of their employees.

F.   *Peer Evaluation*

On the job, peers often have unique opportunities to observe each other's performance in ways that may not always be available to managers. Especially given the increased use of self-managing work teams in companies today, peer evaluation is becoming more appropriate. Employees are apt to assign a great deal of credibility to the observations and suggestions that their peers make about them.

Teaching Hint: When employee performance is viewed as unsatisfactory, it may be due to poor communication rather than inability or lack of motivation. Failure on the part of managers to clearly indicate expectations, standards, and priorities can confuse employees in ways that result in them receiving poor performance evaluations. You can ask for examples of how the students or others have had incorrect interpretations of what was expected on the job.

III.   ADMINISTERING DISCIPLINE

In organizations, discipline is any action directed toward an employee for failing to follow company rules, standards, or policies. Traditional disciplinary procedures are established to promote compliance with rules and to deal with any infractions.

A.   *Self-Discipline*

Employees demonstrate self-discipline whenever they voluntarily follow established company policies and rules.

B.   *The Responsibility to Discipline*

Managers who are responsible for the performance of employees are also expected to deal with infractions of rules and policies. Any approach a manager takes toward employees who disregard company rules and policies should incorporate basic principles of the "hot-stove rule."

Learning Objective 3:   Identify the four key principles of the "hot-stove rule" for administering discipline.

The "hot-stove rule" emphasizes the four key elements of advanced warning, immediacy, consistency, and impersonality in administering discipline.

    C.   *Progressive Discipline*

In organizations, progressive discipline is a procedure that sets increasingly stiffer penalties for repeated or serious misconduct. Its purpose is to apply corrective measures in increasing degrees to get an employee to voluntarily correct inappropriate behavior. A guiding principle of progressive discipline is the belief that when misconduct occurs, the seriousness of the infraction should determine the severity of the corrective measure. Most progressive discipline programs in companies have six steps. In order, they are informal talk, oral warning, written warning, suspension, demotion, and discharge.

    D.   *Discipline without Punishment*

The discipline without punishment approach is based on the belief that the employees themselves must be the real source of discipline. As a result, employees who behave in a manner that requires disciplinary action get an oral reminder. The manager meets with the offending employee to discuss the problem and to get a commitment from the employee to resolve the problem. If the problem continues, the next step is for the manager to issue a written reminder. Once again, the manager discusses the problem with the employee. Together they agree on how the employee is going to eliminate the gap between actual and desired behavior or performance. Should the disciplinary discussions fail to produce the desired changes, the employee is instructed to take a day off from work with full pay. The employee is told to return on the day following the leave and to have made a decision to change and stay or to quit. If the offender does not improve after agreeing to do so, he or she is discharged.

Learning Objective 4:   Explain why managers should focus on employees' strengths, rather than on their weaknesses, when conducting performance appraisals.

A manager who focuses on weaknesses when appraising employees will probably encounter defensive behavior that will only complicate efforts to correct an employee's inappropriate conduct. A more beneficial approach is to view a weakness simply as the absence of a strength. Focusing on an employee's strengths gives a manager a better chance of gaining that employee's cooperation when exploring ways to build on his or her strengths to improve performance.

Teaching Hint: Emphasize that careful attention given during interviews to make sure that only employees who are well suited for employment in the organization are hired will minimize discipline problems.

IV. COMPENSATION

Employee compensation represents the pay or rewards that individuals receive for their employment. There are three broad classifications of employee compensation: 1) direct financial payment 2) indirect payments 3) nonfinancial rewards.

A. *Legislation Affecting Compensation*

Managers are subject to laws governing the compensation of employees. Specifically, the following legislation has had a significant influence on how employers administer compensation: The Davis-Bacon Act of 1931, Walsh-Healey Public Contract Act of 1936, Fair Labor Standards Act of 1938, Equal Pay Act of 1963, Civil Rights Act of 1964, and Americans with Disabilities Act of 1990.

B. *Determining Pay Rates*

Learning Objective 5: Describe the five-step procedure for establishing pay rates for jobs.

The first step in this procedure is to conduct a salary survey. A job evaluation is performed as the second step. Third, group comparable jobs into pay grades. Develop a wage curve as the fourth step. The fifth and last step is to develop rate ranges.

Suggested Readings for this Section:

Ghorpade, Jai and Milton M. Chen. "Creating Quality-Driven Performance Appraisal Systems." Academy of Management Executive 9, February 1995, pp. 32-39.

It is important for managers to select performance appraisal methods that are congruent with the culture of their organizations. Seven suggestions or prescriptions are offered for improving quality-driven performance appraisal methods. Each of these suggestions is discussed and its implications for improving quality efforts in organizations are analyzed.

Hawk, Elizabeth J. "Culture and Rewards." Personnel Journal 74, April 1995, pp. 30-37.

A company's corporate culture and its system for rewarding employees go hand in hand according to the author of this article. Attempts to change cultures without re-examining reward systems can send mixed signals which may hurt the productivity of employees. Likewise, changing the reward system in hopes that certain changes in the company's culture will automatically occur is very risky. Experiences of two companies that changed only one key aspect of the organization are examined.

C.   *Pay-for-Performance Programs*

A pay-for-performance system links the pay given to employees with their productivity levels.

D.   *Pay-at-Risk Programs*

A pay-at-risk program attempts to provide an incentive by holding back a certain amount of pay that can only be received if an employee achieves an established performance target.

V.   EMPLOYEE BENEFITS REQUIRED BY LAW

Benefits are a form of rewards or compensation provided as part of employment but not paid directly to employees in the form of wages or salary. Employee benefits that are required by law include social security, unemployment compensation, and workers' compensation.

A.   *Costs of Providing Benefits*

Employees often underestimate the actual costs to their employers of the benefits they receive. Also, employees are often confused about the various provisions of their benefits. Managers, therefore, need to help employees better understand the benefits available to them and the true costs of these programs.

VI.   LABOR UNIONS

A labor union is a formal association of workers that represents its members for the purpose of promoting their welfare. Through collective bargaining, representatives of the union and management negotiate an employment contract for workers in an organization. Organized labor unions embrace the following four goals and target strategies to achieve them: First, organized labor unions seek to improve their members' economic status and security. To do so, unions engage in collective bargaining. Second, unions try to shield their members from difficulties that result from market and technological changes or management decisions. In order to accomplish this objective, unions work to have rules established that will protect members' job rights, and they seek a system of due process. Third, unions attempt to influence political decision making in ways that will benefit them. In this endeavor, unions lobby for favorable legislation. Fourth, unions seek to improve the welfare of workers in general, regardless of union membership. To achieve this goal, unions back political policies that will create a stable economy and fair treatment for workers.

Learning Objective 6:   Indicate what factors typically encourage employees to seek representation by a labor union.

Many factors can prompt employees to seek representation by a union. For example, failure of management to show concern or respect for employees, poor lines of vertical communication, and unfair and inconsistent discipline practices are factors. Also, failure of management to provide employees with a reasonable mechanism for voicing complaints and receiving a response and allowing unsafe or unhealthy working conditions to exist creates dissatisfaction. Furthermore, refusing to provide adequate training, an unwillingness to resolve legitimate problems raised by employees, and offering below standard wages will heighten employees' interest in a union.

A.   *Good-Faith Bargaining*

If employees in a company are represented by a labor union, top management must agree to bargain in good faith with the union's representative to reach a labor agreement. The union usually presents its demands first. Management then responds. It is illegal for an employer to refuse to bargain collectively with chosen representatives of employees.

B.   *Unfair Labor Practices*

Unions are prohibited from pressuring employers to discriminate against specific employees who have been denied membership in the union or expelled from it. Labor unions must also agree to bargain in good faith with employers. Furthermore, labor unions are prohibited from engaging in featherbedding, which requires a company to pay for work or services that have not been performed.

C.   *Trends in Union Membership*

In 1994, nearly 16.7 million U.S. wage and salary employees were members of a labor union; about 15.5 percent of total employment. After a 14 year decline, union membership rose in 1993 and again in 1994. Union membership in the public sector has been increasing steadily since 1984.

Suggested Readings for this Section:
Gibson, Virginia M. *"The New Employee Reward System."* <u>Management Review</u> 84, *February 1995, pp. 13-18.*

Use of a one-size-fits-all approach to compensation and benefits can be unwise for companies. It may be better, instead, for companies to give business units the flexibility to develop compensation programs in ways that address specific goals. New trends in developing compensation programs are discussed in this article. A case study that explains how one company compensates employees who work as part of a team is also contained in the article.

Sunoo, Brenda Paik. *"Managing Strikes, Minimizing Loss."* <u>Personnel Journal</u> 74, *January 1995, pp. 50-60.*

Human resources managers for companies that operate in a union environment act wisely if they assume and plan for the possibility of a strike. This article contains interviews with three human resources executives who experienced strikes in the transportation, trucking freight, and baseball industries. The ways in which these executives managed the activities of their companies during the strikes are discussed.

VII.   CHALLENGES RAISED BY UNIONIZATION

Some of the special challenges facing managers in a unionized organization are reduced decision-making flexibility, bilateral review of labor policies, and diminished managerial authority.

VIII.   THE NONUNION APPROACH

Common characteristics of successful nonunion companies include: 1) a commitment to provide employees with job security and necessary training for promotion, 2) selection of company locations that are near quality schools and have a strong work ethic, 3) strong market leadership and steady growth, 4) maintenance of steady levels of employment, 5) opportunities for promotion, 6) outstanding human resources departments, 7) good-paying jobs with benefits, 8) encouragement of upward communication, 9) selection of managers who promote good employee relations.

IX.   THE EMPLOYEE-MANAGEMENT COMMITTEE

The primary objective of an employee-management committee is to establish and promote effective, open communication between employees and management. This committee does not act as a bargaining agent for employees. However, it does provide management with input from employees before major decisions, programs, or policies concerning them are implemented. The joint committee also considers job-related concerns and complaints raised by employees.

X.   THE OPEN MEETING COMMUNICATION PROGRAM

This program is designed to tap the important company resource of upward communication. To do so, small groups of employees, assisted by a facilitator, provide managers with information on what company procedures are working well and how the company can improve operations and the jobs and working environment of employees.

XI.   LOOKING BACK

This chapter examines key issues associated with conducting performance appraisals, administering employee discipline, establishing pay rates for jobs, and managing a unionized workforce.

▦ Answers to CONSIDER THIS Questions

1. **As a manager, what aspects of conducting a performance appraisal would make you feel uncomfortable? What would you do to overcome this uneasiness?**

    Many students say that they would feel most uncomfortable discussing weaknesses of employees. The possible conflict and confrontation that may develop in discussing weaknesses is often identified by students as something they would like to avoid. To overcome this uneasiness, it is wise to view a weakness as the absence of a strength. Consider the employee's strengths and look for ways to build on the strengths to eliminate the weakness. That is, managers should look at the things they do well and determine what strengths were displayed that could be applied in a way to reduce or eliminate weaknesses.

2. **Think about improperly conducted performance appraisals that you or others have experienced. What mistakes do you believe were made in those reviews?**

    In identifying performance appraisals that were improperly performed, students usually recall situations in which their boss led them to believe that they were doing everything right. Later, however, when they were fired or failed to receive a promotion, they learned that the boss had not been completely pleased with their performance when the appraisal was conducted. The obvious mistake made was that the boss had not been open and honest with them. The second most common example that many students give of an improperly performed performance interview is one in which they had little involvement. That is, final decisions about how well they were performing were made without any input from them. The mistake in this approach is that the employee does not have a chance to correct any incorrect information or assumptions used in the appraisal.

3. **How has your working relationship with a supervisor in either a full- or part-time job affected the appraisal of your performance?**

    Naturally, some students who remember receiving poor evaluations of their performance believe it was due to the fact that they had a negative working relationship with their boss. Interestingly, after careful consideration, other students indicate that they believe a very good working relationship with their boss has hindered them at times from receiving a thorough performance evaluation. As a result, many students say they are likely to be especially trusting of a performance evaluation from a manager with whom they have neither an especially good or bad working relationship. In considering this issue, students also often conclude that they should evaluate their own performance and that they need to be candid and honest with themselves in doing so.

Answers to CONSIDER THIS Questions

1. **How compatible are the goals of labor unions and the goals of top management in most companies?**

    It is not uncommon for lively debate to occur among students in response to the above question. Generally, the debate really springs from strong beliefs by some students that labor unions are either good or bad for the United States. If the discussion is then changed to address the modified question, "How compatible can the goals of labor unions and the goals of top management be?," students have an opportunity to examine how responsible managers and union representatives can work together for their mutual benefit and the success of their company.

2. **Are you more interested in working for a company that is unionized or nonunionized? Why?**

    Predictably, different views are typically expressed by students in regard to the above question. Some of the views, of course, are based on whether the students believe that labor unions are good and beneficial. In some cases, for example, students will be strongly opposed to paying union dues. Views on working for a unionized or nonunionized company will also vary depending on whether the students believe they will be better off working for a unionized company. The discussion should soon be directed to what type of company the students would most like to work for as employees. Are there examples of companies with characteristics desired by the students that are unionized or nonunionized? As managers, how can they make their companies like the ones they have indicated they would like to work for as employees?

3. **What do you believe labor unions need to do to improve their membership in the private sector?**

    Many students can be expected to indicate that in order for labor unions to increase their membership, they will need to offer employees more than the right to strike. Students also often explain that to be more successful in increasing membership, unions need to be less confrontational and to find better ways to work together with management. If employees believe they are being treated fairly by top management, they often will not see a need to join a labor union.

Answers to REVIEW AND DISCUSSION Questions

1. *What is the difference between distinguishability/measurability and reliability as considerations for selecting performance appraisal standards?*

    The performance standards used in conducting performance appraisals should be capable of distinguishing between effective and ineffective performers. A standard that has this capability is said to meet the necessary consideration of "distinguishability/measurability." On the other hand, "reliability" refers to consistency of judgment. That is, if capable evaluators can all reach the same conclusion using a common, specific standard, that standard is considered "reliable."

2. *How should a manager determine which dimensions to include in a graphic rating scale?*

    The manager should review the individual employee's job description and select specific employee behaviors that are critical to the performance of that job. The manager then selects a scale to use in evaluating all of the dimensions selected.

3. *What is the halo error?*

    A halo error occurs when the evaluation of one dimension of performance influences the evaluator's perception of the person being evaluated on all of the different areas of performance. A negative perception of an employee in one regard, for example, may bias the evaluator's perception of the employee in other areas of performance. The reverse can be true if an employee is evaluated highly in one certain area of performance. As a result, the manager may tend to give the employee the same evaluation in other areas of performance.

4. *What disadvantages are associated with using behaviorally anchored rating scales?*

A significant disadvantage of using behaviorally anchored rating scales (BARS) is that they are time consuming to develop. In addition, a BARS scale constructed for one job will not apply to other jobs that require different behaviors for successful performance. The large amounts of time required to develop BARS scales for many jobs can make them an expensive assessment instrument.

5.   *What are the characteristics of a good goal?*

Specifically, a goal should be *both* realistic and challenging. For example, a goal may be very realistic but too easy, or exceptionally challenging but unlikely to be achieved.

6.   *In progressive discipline, why is it important to suspend before discharging an employee?*

Suspending before discharging gives a manager a chance to review all relevant evidence. A careful review gives the manager an opportunity to make sure that a decision to discharge is correct and not being made in haste. A suspension also gives the manager a chance to document the reasons for discharging.

7   *What are the key provisions of the Americans With Disabilities Act of 1990?*

The Americans With Disabilities Act outlaws discrimination against individuals with physical or mental impairments that substantially limit major life activities. It is now unlawful to ask job applicants "Do you have any disabilities that would preclude you from doing this job?" Questions that might intrude into a person's ability to perform physical or mental tasks must be specific and relevant to the job. For example, an employer may ask an applicant "Can you lift a 40-pound sack from a wheelbarrow six times a day?" Beyond prohibiting discrimination, the Americans With Disability Act requires employers to make whatever reasonable accommodations are necessary for a disabled employee who can otherwise handle the essential functions of the job.

8.   *What are the goals of labor unions?*

Organized labor unions embrace four major goals with targeted strategies for achieving them. First, organized labor unions seek to improve their members' economic status and security. To do so, unions engage in collective bargaining. Second, unions try to shield their members from difficulties that might result due to market and technological changes or management decisions. In order to accomplish this objective, unions work to have rules established that will protect members' job rights, and they seek a system of due process. Third, unions attempt to influence political decision making in ways that will benefit them. In this endeavor, unions lobby for favorable legislation. Fourth, unions seek improvements in the welfare of workers in general, regardless of union membership. To achieve this goal, unions back political policies that they believe will create a stable economy and fair treatment for workers. These goals are more attainable with a large union membership. Therefore, unions attempt to recruit new members in areas where they think their recruiting efforts will succeed.

9. *What behaviors or actions on the part of management contribute to workers seeking representation by a union?*

The following eight behaviors or actions on the part of management can contribute to workers seeking representation by a labor union.
1) Failure by management to show concern or respect for employees.
2) Tolerating poor lines of communication, both upward and downward.
3) Administering discipline in an unfair and inconsistent manner. Also, capricious firing of employees for no apparent justification.
4) Failing to provide employees with a reasonable mechanism for voicing complaints and receiving a response.
5) Allowing unsafe or unhealthy working conditions to exist.
6) Refusing to provide employees with adequate training to perform their job duties effectively.
7) Unwillingness to resolve legitimate job-related problems called to the attention of management by dissatisfied employees.
8) Offering below standard wages and benefits.

Answers to CRITICAL THINKING INCIDENTS

Incident 16-1: MISAPPRAISALS

1. **What mistakes does Rita make in developing a graphic rating scale?**

The best approach in developing a graphic rating scale is to review the individual employee's job description and to select specific employee behaviors that are critical to the performance of that job. If the behaviors selected for evaluation are not critical or commonly performed by the employee, the value of the graphic rating scale selected is in question. A mistake Rita is making is that not all of the performance dimensions she has selected for evaluating Bill are necessarily critical to his job or commonly performed by him. For example, "typing speed" is seldom critical to the performance of a mechanic. Rita's decision to complete the graphic rating scale without involving Bill is also unwise. The time it takes to include Bill and to give him a chance to provide input in his evaluation is time well spent. The approach Rita is using will likely produce a performance appraisal that is invalid and harms her working relationship with Bill.

2. **What mistakes does Barry make in attempting to use the management by objectives method?**

Barry is focusing on weaknesses, a common approach used by managers when conducting performance appraisals. Weaknesses should not be ignored by managers when evaluating employees, but it is predictable that an employee will become defensive if a manager begins a performance appraisal by focusing on the employee's weaknesses. It is best to view a weakness as the absence of a strength. In doing so, Barry should first focus on Kevin's strengths and then discuss with Kevin ways Kevin can build on his strengths to reduce or eliminate his weaknesses. For example, what are Kevin's communication skills? How could those skills be built upon, utilized, or applied to situations Barry believes Kevin is not handling well due to inappropriate methods of communicating with others?

3. **What difficulty is Myrasol going to experience in attempting to use the behaviorally anchored rating scale she developed?**

The difficulty Myrasol is going to experience is that a behaviorally anchored rating scale (BARS) constructed for one job will not apply to other jobs that require different behaviors for successful performance. A little bit of knowledge can sometimes be a dangerous thing. Myrasol is correct in her understanding that she needs to select behaviors ranging from those that represent success on the job to those that indicate failure. However, those behaviors must be selected from one job description, not different job descriptions. Also, a BARS scale constructed for one job will not apply to other jobs that require different behaviors for successful performance, as Myrasol plans to do.

Incident 16-2:   BAD BLOOD

1. **How is the union engaging in unfair labor practices?**

Apparently, the union representing employees at the Consolidated Ore Mining Company tries to get the company to discriminate against any employee who won't support the union's positions. However, the Taft-Hartley Act prohibits unions from pressuring employers to discriminate against specific employees. In addition, the union pressures the company to pay loyal union employees extra for work they do not perform. This practice is called featherbedding, and it is considered to be an unfair labor practice.

2.   **What actions did management take that indicate it is not bargaining in good faith with the union?**

If employees in a company are represented by a labor union, top management must agree to bargain in good faith with the union's representative to reach a labor agreement. The union usually presents its demands first. Management then responds. The Wagner Act makes it illegal for an employer to refuse to bargain collectively with chosen representatives of employees. The practice by management at Consolidated Ore Mining Company of simply presenting the labor union with a new labor contract and saying, "take it or leave it," is not considered to be an example of good-faith bargaining. Also, once a labor agreement is reached, management's attempt to change the agreement without discussing it with representatives of the labor union is improper.

3.   **Does the company benefit from this type of behavior by its management and the union? Explain.**

No. Positive labor-management relations in companies enhances efficiency and productivity. The types of behavior engaged in by the labor union and management at Consolidated Ore Mining Company can harm labor-management relations. The relationship between the union and management at the company is described as confrontational. The improper behaviors of the union and management described in the case will not improve relations between them. Instead, these behaviors will distract all involved from focusing on ways to accomplish organizational goals and to help the company prosper.

Incident 16-3:   ALL IN A DAY'S JOB

1.   **What mistakes is Rex making in the way he deals with Beth?**

Both Jim and Beth are equally qualified in terms of experience and ability. Although Jim and Beth both perform well, Beth learns that she is paid less than Jim. According to the Equal Pay Act, employees of one sex may not be paid more than employees of the opposite sex for doing basically the same work equally well. Differences in pay based on superior performance or longer service are lawful, but those distinctions do not apply to Beth and Jim. Therefore, it is improper for Rex to pay Beth less than Jim. The justification Rex gives to Beth for why Jim is paid more is inappropriate.

2. **How is Rex violating provisions of the Americans With Disabilities Act of 1990?**

One salesperson, Joel, uses a wheelchair. Joel's wheelchair makes it difficult for him to use the desk and telephone in the office assigned to him. Although Joel is performing well, Rex ignores his requests for a different desk and style of telephone that would enable him to perform his job without so much fatigue. Rex's failure to make reasonable accommodations necessary for Joel is a violation of the Americans With Disabilities Act, as is his practice of asking job applicants, "Do you have any disabilities that would create problems for you in this job?" Questions that might intrude into a person's ability to perform physical or mental tasks must be specific and relevant to the job.

3. **How appropriate is it for Rex to discipline Joel?**

When Rex noticed what appeared to be improper behavior by Joel, he should have dealt with the problem quickly. It was improper for Rex to wait three weeks before deciding to discipline Joel. Also, it is not entirely clear that Joel is actually guilty of stealing company property. If Rex was concerned that Joel violated company policy or engaged in some form of misconduct, he should have discussed the behavior with Joel. Instead, Rex only informed Joel that he was issuing Joel a written warning for stealing company property. This behavior by Rex was inappropriate.

Study Guide Assignments

A matching exercise at the beginning of the study guide helps students to check their familiarity of key terms used in the chapter. A useful concept application exercise follows which contains six scenarios that deal with important issued related to employee-management relations.

An individual case assessment is provided that gives students an opportunity to consider how the manager in the case could have avoided the problems he experienced in conducting performance appraisals of employees. A group case assessment also contained in the study guide offers students the chance to discuss and evaluate how well the manager in the case deals with an employee who misses an important meeting.

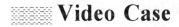 **Video Case**

Northwestern Mutual Life Insurance

Focus: **MBO and Peer Review**

Summary:

This training video highlights the performance review program at Northwestern Mutual
Life Insurance company. The program, called Peer Review and Feedback, combines
elements of management by objectives with peer review. All associates are reviewed
by their peers. The review covers customer management, managing work objectives,
self-management styles, technical skills, and interpersonal effectiveness. In each of
these areas, associates are rated as below, met, or exceeded expectation.

Like most performance reviews, the reviews at Northwestern Mutual are used for
making decisions about pay increases, bonuses, and promotions. The company
emphasizes that the program is used as a process for discussing an employee's
strengths and development needs, and the people performing the review are those who
know the employee best: his or her fellow workers.

Discussion Questions:

1.   What aspects of the Northwestern Mutual Peer Review and Feedback program contain
      elements of Management by Objectives?

      The areas to be covered in the review are set by senior management, as well as the
      standards that will be used. These elements are related to the company's overall goals
      and objectives.

2.   How comfortable would you be with a review program like this?

      One way to spark discussion on the pros and cons of this program is to ask how peer
      review could be used in class to assign grades. Some of the difficulties with this type
      program are: (1) letting personal biases enter into the review and (2) determining the
      specific standards that will be used.

Chapter 17

Promoting Job Satisfaction and Productivity

Chapter Overview

In this chapter, the importance of job satisfaction in organizations is discussed, and common methods for measuring levels of job satisfaction are described. Key factors that have an important influence on job satisfaction are analyzed.

Chapter 17 also indicates that for employees to perform well and to be productive, management must create a work environment that encourages collaboration, commitment, and creativity. The influence of job satisfaction on the overall performance of companies is examined. The relationship between communication satisfaction and organizational productivity is also discussed.

The chapter concludes with a discussion of the value of creative work schedules for many companies. Four examples of alternative work schedules are identified and described.

Teaching Objectives

The teaching objectives of this chapter are to:

1.   Indicate the important aspects of work life that can be influenced by job satisfaction.

2.   Examine common methods for measuring levels of job satisfaction.

3.   Identify factors that contribute to job satisfaction.

4.   Describe the stages associated with job satisfaction that employees go through as they experience irritants on the job.

5.   Explain the influence of job satisfaction on productivity.

6.   Discuss four popular examples of alternative work schedules.

Chapter Outline of the Text

I.   JOB SATISFACTION
     A.   Absenteeism and Turnover
     B.   Mental Health
     C.   Safety
II.   ASSESSING JOB SATISFACTION
     A.   Questionnaires
     B.   Critical Incidents
     C.   Interviews
III.   THE OPEN-LINE COMMUNICATION PROGRAM
IV.   FACTORS THAT CONTRIBUTE TO JOB SATISFACTION
     A.   Mentally Challenging Work
     B.   Personal Interest in the Job Duties
     C.   Work That Is Not Physically Exhausting
     D.   Just Rewards for Performance
     E.   Comfortable Working Conditions
     F.   High Self-Esteem
     G.   Assistance from Others in the Workplace
V.   LITTLE THINGS INFLUENCE JOB SATISFACTION
VI.   PRODUCTIVITY
     A.   Influence of Job Satisfaction on Productivity
     B.   Communication Satisfaction and Productivity
VII.   ALTERNATIVE WORK SCHEDULES
     A.   Flextime
     B.   Telecommuting
     C.   Compressed Workweeks
     D.   Part-Time Employment
VIII.   LOOKING BACK
IX.   KEY TERMS
X.   REVIEW AND DISCUSSION QUESTIONS
XI.   CRITICAL THINKING INCIDENTS
XII.   SUGGESTED READINGS

Key Terms

These terms are introduced in the chapter.

Acceptance stage
Communication satisfaction questionnaire
   (CSQ)
Compressed workweek
Critical incident procedure
Flextime
Interview

Job description index
Open-line communication program
Part-time employment
Questionnaire
Rejection stage
Telecommuting
Tolerance stage

Detailed Chapter Summary

I.   JOB SATISFACTION

Job satisfaction refers to the amount of enjoyment or contentment individual employees experience on the job.

Learning Objective 1:   Indicate the important aspects of work life that can be influenced by job satisfaction.

In organizations, job satisfaction can affect employee absenteeism and turnover. The mental health of an employee can also be affected by the level of job satisfaction. In addition, high job satisfaction can act to enhance safety on the job.

II.   ASSESSING JOB SATISFACTION

Learning Objective 2:   Examine common methods for measuring levels of job satisfaction.

Some of the most common methods for measuring levels of job satisfaction include questionnaires, critical incidents, and interviews. The critical incident procedure asks employees to identify and describe incidents that have influenced their level of job satisfaction.

III.   THE OPEN-LINE COMMUNICATION PROGRAM

The open-line communication program is a mechanism that permits upward communication to be expressed in a confidential manner. Specifically, employees can write out their ideas, comments, or concerns on a form and mail it to the Special Coordinator (SC) for the program. The SC retypes the comments on any open-line form received, deletes the employee's name, and assigns the same code number to the original and retyped form. The SC then sends the retyped message to the appropriate person in the organization for a response. It is a requirement that a response must be provided within a set period of time. The SC reviews the response to make sure it is complete. Once an acceptable response is prepared, the SC matches the code number of the comment or question with the original open-line form containing the writer's identify and address. The reply is then mailed to that person by the SC. In addition, the SC makes the inquiry and response public within the organization, often through a bulletin board or newsletter, so that others can also benefit from the response.

Teaching Hint: It is important to emphasize that upward communication often does not occur on its own. Instead, it must be encouraged, and programs need to be established to get valuable upward communication flowing from employees.

IV.   FACTORS THAT CONTRIBUTE TO JOB SATISFACTION

Learning Objective 3:   Identify factors that contribute to job satisfaction.

Research indicates that seven key factors have an important influence on job satisfaction. Mentally challenging work, personal interest in job duties, work that is not physically exhausting, and just rewards for performance can influence an employee's level of job satisfaction. Other factors that influence job satisfaction include comfortable working conditions, high self-esteem, and assistance from others on the job.

V.   LITTLE THINGS INFLUENCE JOB SATISFACTION

Managers should realize that an accumulation of little problems occurring on a job can have a strong negative influence on job satisfaction. Specifically, as the number and severity of job irritants grow, job satisfaction declines.

Learning Objective 4:   Describe the stages associated with job satisfaction that employees go through as they experience irritants on the job.

Initially, during the acceptance stage, employees decide that no job is perfect and conclude that it is only normal to experience a few irritants or nuisances on the job. When the number of irritants and their severity increase, job satisfaction declines and employees enter the tolerance stage. At this point, they begin to doubt whether management has the competence, sincerity, and willingness to tackle existing problems. If the situation worsens and the number and severity of irritants continues to increase, employees often move into the rejection stage. In this stage, employees have lost interest in their work, and some will quit, while others will put forth only the minimal effort required to keep from getting fired. As a result, the organization has lost the opportunity to maximize its human resources.

VI.   PRODUCTIVITY

Research indicates that for employees to perform well and to be productive, management must create a work environment that encourages collaboration, commitment, and creativity.

A.   *Influence of Job Satisfaction on Productivity*

Learning Objective 5:   Explain the influence of job satisfaction on productivity.

The influence of job satisfaction on productivity is mixed. If productivity is measured only in terms of quantity of output or quality of performance, then a direct relationship does not always exist between productivity and job satisfaction. However, employees can and do make many important contributions on the job that indirectly influence organizational efficiency and productivity. Employees who experience high levels of job satisfaction engage in more of these behaviors than employees who experience low levels of job satisfaction do. Thus, the benefits of creating a work environment that provides employees with high levels of job satisfaction are wide-ranging for organizations.

Teaching Hint: Although it may not always be possible to show an increase in commonly measured forms of productivity when job satisfaction of employees increases, the consequences of ignoring job satisfaction can be great. For employees to perform well and to be productive, management must create a work environment that encourages collaboration, commitment, and creativity. Creating such an environment when low job satisfaction exists is next to impossible.

B.   *Communication Satisfaction and Productivity*

Research indicates that feedback from managers helps employees feel good about themselves and their work. As a matter of fact, it is common for employees to indicate that they are motivated to work harder by personal feedback they receive from their manager.

Suggested Readings for this Section:

Dumaine, Brian. "Why Do We Work?" Fortune, December 26, 1994, pp. 196-204.

Research indicates that most employees work not only to earn money, but to satisfy important psychological needs. The type of work that employees perform has a significant impact on their self-esteem. This article profiles three individuals and describes their efforts to make the work that they perform more fulfilling.

Firestien, Roger L. and Kenneth F. Kumiega. "Using a Formula for Creativity to Yield Organizational Quality Improvement." National Productivity Review 13, Fall 1994, pp. 569-585.

A company's ability to survive and thrive is dependent in part on how well it utilizes the creativity of its workforce. This article identifies a model for implementing creativity in organizations. The specific formula is: Creativity Skills + Environment + Application = Creative Output. Each of the factors in the above formula are discussed. The benefits of using creative problem solving in companies are examined.

VII.   ALTERNATIVE WORK SCHEDULES

Various experiments and settings indicate that creative work schedules are associated with improvements in job satisfaction, morale, and performance. Four examples of alternative work schedules are flextime, telecommuting, compressed workweeks, and part-time employment.

Learning Objective 6:   Discuss four popular examples of alternative work schedules.

One alternative work schedule, flextime, offers employees the flexibility of choosing when they will begin and end their workday. However, all of the employees must work at certain set times and for an established number of hours per day. Telecommuting gives employees a different type of flexibility by allowing them to work at home instead of traveling to the office. In another alternative work schedule, compressed workweek, an employee's job duties are compressed into four 10-hour days each week. The company or department is then usually closed on Monday or Friday of each week. The fourth alternative work schedule, part-time employment, occurs when an employee works less than a full-time work schedule.

Suggested Readings for this Section:

Barnes, Kathleen. "Tips for Managing Telecommuters." HR Focus *71, November 1994, pp. 9-10.*

It is estimated that by the year 2000, at least 25 million employees will telecommute. However, before allowing employees to engage in telecommuting, managers should develop telecommuting policies. This article identifies issues managers need to address to ensure that telecommuting is productive for their companies.

Bencivenga, Dominic. "Compressed Weeks Fill an HR Niche." HR Magazine *40, June 1995, pp. 71-74.*

A 1993 survey of 55 companies with 1.5 million employees indicated that 40 percent of the companies utilized compressed work weeks. Most of these companies have implemented their compressed work week programs since 1990. The possible effects of a compressed work week schedule on the economic efficiency and productivity of companies are discussed. Important issues that should be considered by managers before implementing a compressed work week schedule are also examined.

VIII. LOOKING BACK

This chapter examines key issues associated with job satisfaction and productivity and with the increased use of alternative work schedules.

Answers to CONSIDER THIS Questions

1. **Why do you think so many executives claim that having regular meetings with employees is the best thing they can do to improve productivity?**

Executives do not generally have a detailed understanding of all the jobs performed by employees in their companies. Even if they did have a comprehensive understanding of the different jobs performed, they cannot be expected to have the unique perspective and ability each employee has for identifying changes that could improve productivity. For these reasons, meetings with employees give managers an opportunity to receive valuable upward communication that they might not get otherwise.

2.   **To what extent do you think job satisfaction can influence creativity?**

Mentally challenging work can help produce high job satisfaction. Furthermore, mentally challenging work is usually stimulating to employees and promotes creativity. If employees take a personal interest in the work they perform, they will likely find the work satisfying. In turn, employees who are interested in their work generally enjoy analyzing their jobs in ways that promote creativity. As a result, factors that contribute to job satisfaction can also often be expected to help increase creativity.

3.   **Why is hiring the right person for a job so important to promoting job satisfaction?**

Several individuals may be able to perform a job in a satisfactory manner, but they may not all enjoy the job. As a manager, you should attempt to hire people who can perform a job well and who enjoy performing the job. Low job satisfaction, even for capable employees, will often lead to high employee turnover. In addition, low job satisfaction can lead to increased frustration and defensiveness among employees. This type of negative work environment hinders productivity and makes it difficult to get employees who would be right for the job to accept a job offer.

Answers to CONSIDER THIS Questions

1.   **Think of a job that you have had that you enjoyed. In what ways did you exert extra effort because you liked the job?**

In comparing different jobs and bosses they have had in full-time or part-time jobs, students can quickly think of a job they liked the best. Also, as they think of their favorite job, they can usually identify different ways in which they exerted more effort than required. Some students, for example, indicate that they make a stronger effort to offer suggestions concerning how the company can save money when they like their jobs. They also acknowledge that they will work harder to meet company goals if they enjoy their work. Many students also explain that if they like their jobs, they feel more loyalty to the company.

2. **In your opinion, what are the long-run prospects for a company if its employees consistently experience low levels of job satisfaction?**

Employees are the most important resource of a company, especially in the long run. Whenever a company allows its most important resource to be put at risk, the long-run consequences are likely to be negative. For example, absenteeism and turnover are often higher among employees with low job satisfaction. These employees may also have more accidents and experience more health problems, compared with employees who experience high job satisfaction.

3. **To what extent does the size of an organization influence how well flextime will work?**

Generally, it is easier for a large organization to accommodate flextime than it is for a small organization. It is not uncommon, for example, for employees in small companies to wear several different hats. Due to the fact that these employees take care of different jobs as needed, their absence is noticed quickly. In large companies, more employees are available to cover critical job duties when a flextime schedule is in operation.

Answers to REVIEW AND DISCUSSION Questions

1. *To what extent does job satisfaction affect employee absenteeism and turnover?*

Research indicates that job satisfaction is closely associated with levels of absenteeism and turnover for many jobs. That is, the more satisfied employees are with their jobs, the less likely they will be absent from work. In addition, research indicates that when employees' job satisfaction is high, they are less likely to resign.

2. *How is the critical incident procedure used to assess job satisfaction?*

The critical incident procedure asks employees to identify and describe incidents they have experienced on the job that influenced their level of job satisfaction. For example, an employee may recall a supervisor providing confusing directions. Due to the confusion, the employee performed an assignment incorrectly and had to redo much of the work. The employee's level of job satisfaction declined as a result of the frustration associated with this problem. If several employees recall having experienced miscommunication with the same supervisor, communication skills training will likely be appropriate for the supervisor. Employees also identify incidents that have had a positive outcome for them and increased their level of job satisfaction.

3. *What are three important elements of the open line communication program?*

The first key element is that the program is confidential. Second, it guarantees that comments, concerns, complaints, or suggestions voiced through the program will receive a written response. Third, it enhances employee-management relations by meeting the needs of employees to communicate upward and by providing management with information on how to improve the effectiveness of the organization.

4. *What strategy is being used by organizations to retain talented employees when there are few opportunities for promotion?*

Organizations are experimenting with shifting employees sideways instead of up when few opportunities for promotion exist. Moving employees sideways gets them out of the bottlenecks that have been created when upward movement is blocked. Companies hope that lateral moves requiring new skills will provide the challenge and interest necessary to retain talented employees.

5. *If employees who are exposed to irritants on the job have reached the rejection stage, how should their manager deal with the situation?*

Once employees have reached the rejection stage, it is likely that they have lost confidence and trust in management. As a manager in this situation, you will need to demonstrate through deeds, not simply words, that you are going to turn things around. One way to demonstrate action is to hold a meeting with employees. At this meeting, compile a list of irritants the employees experience and indicate a strategy for dealing with them. For some problems, it would be a good idea to ask a group of employees to investigate and recommend solutions. Indicating that you want to work with the employees to solve the problems is an important prerequisite for increasing their level of job satisfaction.

6. *What three conditions in the work environment must management create if employees are to perform well and be productive?*

Research indicates that for employees to perform well and be productive, management must create a work environment that encourages collaboration, commitment, and creativity.

7.   *To what extent can it be claimed that job satisfaction influences productivity?*

It is not necessarily accurate to say that happy workers are automatically productive or that unhappy workers are always slow and unproductive. For example, some employees find it very satisfying to have a job that puts them under little pressure to produce. On the other hand, employees who hate their jobs may work hard so their productivity will be rewarded with a promotion that gets them out of the jobs they dislike. In general, however, employees who experience high job satisfaction engage in behaviors that can contribute greatly to the overall performance of a company. For example, they are more likely to help coworkers, to accept orders without a fuss, or to tolerate temporary impositions without a complaint. They also generally make an effort to conserve organizational resources. These and other behaviors that result from high job satisfaction can directly and indirectly improve productivity in a company.

8.   *How does a flextime work schedule operate?*

As a nontraditional work schedule, flextime offers employees the flexibility of choosing when they will begin and end their workday, as long as they work at certain set times and for an established number of hours per day. During certain parts of the work day, called core times, all employees must be present. However, under flextime, employees have the opportunity to take a half-hour or one-hour lunch break, as long as it occurs sometime between 11:30 a.m. and 1:30 p.m. Once they have worked the minimum number of hours required for the day, employees may leave their job anytime between 3:30 and 6:30 p.m.

9.   *What key difficulties are associated with compressed workweek schedules?*

Some companies do not have the flexibility to close one day during the workweek. Also, a 10-hour workday can be very fatiguing for employees.

Answers to CRITICAL THINKING INCIDENTS

Incident 17-1:   THREE PROBLEM COMPANIES

1.   **How do the situations at Southwest Design Associates and Byrne Manufacturing differ?**

Sometimes, it is the little things that count. Certainly, an accumulation of little problems that occur on a job can have a strong influence on job satisfaction. The accumulative effects of little, work-related frustrations on job satisfaction are such that employees experiencing these frustrations progress through three separate stages: the acceptance stage, the tolerance stage, and the rejection stage. The situations at Southwest Design Associates and Byrne Manufacturing differ in that the employees at Southwest Design Associates are in the acceptance stage as they experience irritants on the job. The employees at Byrne Manufacturing, however, are in the tolerance stage as they experience irritants on the job.

2.   **What should Nadia recommend be done by Matt Jenkins?**

Right now, Matt does not have a lot to worry about with employee job satisfaction. The good news is that the employees view him as being on their side and as willing to correct whatever problems do exist. Matt should make the best of this situation by talking to the employees directly to find out what things irritate them on the job. He then needs to determine which of the problems appear to be the most severe. Next, Matt should start making changes and keep the employees informed of the progress he is making on these problems.

3.   **What management training does Greg Clark need to succeed as a store manager?**

Greg certainly needs to be trained on how to better utilize human resources. Greg also needs to understand that the employees at Star Business Products are the most valuable resource the company has. This important resource is at risk due to low job satisfaction of employees at the company. Through training, Greg needs to realize that job satisfaction of employees can have both a direct and indirect influence on company productivity. He also should receive training on some common methods for measuring levels of job satisfaction. In addition, Greg should be aware of key factors that contribute to job satisfaction. Greg should be trained on how to keep employees from progressing to the rejection stage as they experience job irritants, which is where his employees are now.

Incident 17-2:   A DIFFERENCE OF OPINION

1.   **How is the company likely to benefit from the changes Tran has made?**

Tran began considering ways to make some of the routine and repetitive jobs more challenging. In cases where routine jobs could not be changed much, he allowed employees to rotate among these jobs so they got a break from doing the same old thing. Routine and repetitive jobs are generally very boring because they offer little challenge. Doing the "same old thing" day after day can cause employees to lose interest in their work. Employees not only prefer work that is challenging, but they also want jobs in which they have some control over the way tasks are completed and the pace of the work. As a result, the more opportunities employees have to be creative and make decisions on the job, the greater the likelihood that they will experience high job satisfaction. Under these conditions, the employees will also probably feel a sense of commitment to the job. It should also be noted that physically exhausting jobs will usually produce low job satisfaction for employees who perform these tasks. Some of Tran's employees are experiencing job fatigue. As a result, Tran hired a consultant to study the situation and make recommendations for modifying jobs to reduce fatigue. These changes should help improve job satisfaction. Tran also set up a system to encourage suggestions from employees on how their jobs could be improved. This effort should improve job satisfaction and help the company to operate more effectively. In addition, the special effort made by Tran to recruit employees who are well suited to specific jobs will promote high job satisfaction and high productivity. Tran's efforts to offer competitive pay and to praise employees for their accomplishments should also promote high job satisfaction and increased productivity.

2. **Why are the hiring practices of the company critical to improving job satisfaction?**

Tran is making a special effort to make sure that new employees hired are well suited to their jobs. If employees enjoy the work they perform and are well qualified, they will likely experience high job satisfaction.

3. **Why might Jack Stoll be incorrect in concluding that improved job satisfaction has not helped the company.**

There are many ways in which employees can make important contributions on the job. For example, when employees experience high job satisfaction, they often engage in behaviors that can indirectly improve productivity in a company. Such behaviors include: helping coworkers with their job-related problems; accepting orders without a fuss; tolerating temporary impositions without a complaint; helping to maintain a clean and uncluttered work area; making timely and constructive statements about the work unit or its head to outsiders; promoting a work environment that is tolerable and minimizes the distractions created by interpersonal conflict; and protecting and conserving organizational resources. These behaviors can result from increased job satisfaction and can benefit the company. Therefore, it may be incorrect for Jack Stoll to conclude that improving job satisfaction has not helped the company.

Incident 17-3:   WEAK LINKS IN A CHAIN

1.   **Based on the material covered in this chapter, what is a likely reason for the poor performance of some of the restaurants in this chain?**

Employees in the poor-performing restaurants are experiencing a lot of stress. Their levels of absenteeism and turnover are high, they make little effort to help each other with job-related problems, and they will not accept any change in duties without a fuss. Due to the bad reputation of these restaurants, it is difficult for them to hire good people. In essence, the poor-performing restaurants have working environments that make it difficult for employees to experience high job satisfaction. As a result, the employees do not exert the effort needed to help the restaurants succeed. In addition, these restaurants are probably not hiring employees who are a good fit for the jobs, which increases the likelihood that they will perform poorly and experience low job satisfaction.

2.   **What should the company do to help reduce the level of stress experienced by employees in the restaurants that are failing?**

First, the company should determine what is causing the employees to experience a lot of stress. In performing this analysis, the company should determine the extent to which the high stress experienced is due to hiring employees who are not a good fit for the jobs. The levels of stress experienced by employees at the company's profitable restaurants should also be examined. If these levels of stress are lower than the stress experienced by employees in the poor-performing restaurants, an analysis should be performed to determine why. Once the causes of high stress are identified, strategies for dealing with these causes can be developed. Attempts to improve the job satisfaction of employees at the poor-performing restaurants will probably help to reduce the stress these employees experience.

3.   **What should the poor-performing restaurants do to improve the job satisfaction of their employees?**

There are several problem areas that need to be addressed in order to improve the job satisfaction of employees at the restaurants. The employees are experiencing a lot of stress. An effort should be made to identify the causes of stress and to reduce as much as possible the forms of stress the employees experience on the job. The causes of absenteeism and turnover by the employees should also be investigated. The employees in the poorly performing restaurants make little effort to help each other with job-related problems. Addressing and correcting this problem in a way that emphasizes the need for cooperation on the job to benefit all employees will almost certainly help to improve job satisfaction. It is also important to deal with the resistance to change that exists among the employees. In addition, hiring practices should be re-examined to make sure that employees who are hired are a good fit for the job. Efforts to improve the reputations of the restaurants will also make it easier for the employees to feel good about themselves and their jobs.

Study Guide Assignments

For this chapter of the study guide, students will find six scenarios to analyze. The scenarios deal with important concepts related to job satisfaction and productivity. Many thought-provoking issues are raised in the scenarios to help students apply key concepts in the chapter and appreciate the interrelated aspects of job satisfaction and productivity for organizations. An individual case assessment has been prepared that gives students an opportunity to analyze changes in job satisfaction and productivity that exist in a company acquired in a hostile takeover by an overseas company.

The group case assessment that exists in the study guide provides students with an opportunity to examine and discuss a report prepared by a management consultant. Material contained in the chapter can be used by the students to critique the report. A helpful self assessment questionnaire is also available to increase students' awareness of how their approaches to managing others are likely to affect the job satisfaction of employees.

Video Case

Studio 904

Focus: **Employee and Customer Satisfaction**

Summary:

Although Studio 904 had a strong customer base of about 1,800 regular customers, the company faced some serious issues concerning its future growth. The Seattle-based hairdressing company utilized commissioned sales, leased chairs, and tipping systems in its operating procedures. While these practices were standard for the industry, Studio 904's management believed the company's long-term growth goals could not be achieved unless drastic changes were made.

The most significant change at Studio 904 shifted the company emphasis from profits to customer service. Instead of focusing on the acquisition of new customers, the company began to focus on increasing the satisfaction of its current customers by establishing long-term relationships. Although attracting new customers remained an essential component of the company's future growth, Studio 904 planned to generate greater loyalty among its current customers in order to increase repeat business. To support its new emphasis on customer service, Studio 904 developed a quality assurance program that included weekly training sessions for all employees. An environmental awareness program was also established to emphasize the company's use of environmentally safe products and its sensitivity to environmental issues. To further support Studio 904's emphasis on customer service, the method of employee compensation was changed from a tip-based system to hourly or, in most cases, salary-based compensation. Studio 904 also provided its employees with medical and dental benefits, sick pay, and vacation pay.

Studio 904 has received many benefits from its new emphasis on customer service and satisfaction. In particular, its customer base has risen from 1,800 to more than 5,000 customers. As a result of its rapid growth, Studio 904 has opened a second location in Seattle. The greater number of satisfied, repeat customers and improved compensation benefits have led directly to increased employee satisfaction, which in turn has resulted in a reduction in the level of employee turnover. Finally, because of its environmental awareness program, Studio 904 has been recognized by the city of Seattle for its leadership and responsibility within the community. With these factors in place, Studio 904 has positioned itself to attain greater profitability and to achieve its future goals.

Discussion Questions:

1.   How did the management at Studio 904 alter its human resource management practices to improve the overall performance of the company?

The major changes at Studio 904 involved: (1) the method of employee compensation was changed from a tip-based system to hourly or, in most cases, salary-based compensation. (2) Studio 904 provided its employees with medical and dental benefits, sick pay, and vacation pay. These changes reduced turnover at Studio 904, which in turn allowed the company to emphasize customer loyalty.

2.   What other human resource management changes might Studio 904 make to further improve employee relations, quality, and financial performance?

Some of the HRM changes other companies have made include ownership in the company through employee stock ownership plans and in-house day care for working parents.

Chapter **18**

Human Resource Issues

▓▓ Chapter Overview

This chapter discusses several relevant human relations issues. These are managerial concerns because human resources represent an organization's most important asset. It is important to create and maintain a workplace environment to maximize the productive contributins and job satisfaction of personnel.

Topics discussed are safety and health, substance abuse, tobacco consumption, AIDS, and sexual harassment. A safe and healthy workplace reduces the likelihood of accidents and illnesses. Alleviation of alcohol and drug abuse relieves many personal and professional problems. Elimination of tobacco consumption leads to improved health. Managers need to understand causes of AIDS and know the rights of employees who have the disease. Finally, the chapter concludes with coverage of concerns related to prevention of job-related sexual harassment.

▓▓ Teaching Objectives

The teaching objectives of this chapter are to:

1.   Emphasize the importance of promoting safety in the workplace.

2.   Understand the negative consequences of alcohol and drug abuse.

3.   Recognize potential health complications caused by smoking.

4.   Stress the need for managers to develop an understanding of AIDS.

5.   Explain the importance of eliminating sexual harassment from the workplace.

Chapter Outline of the Text

▨ Key Terms

These terms are introduced in the chapter.

Acquired immune deficiency syndrome
   (AIDS)
Drug abuse
Drug testing
Employee assistance program
Human immunodeficiency virus (HIV)

Occupational Safety and Health Act
Passive smoking
Safety
Safety audit
Sexual harassment

▨ Detailed Chapter Summary

I.   SAFETY: A CONCERN FOR HUMAN RESOURCES

Teaching Objective 1: Emphasize the importance of promoting safety in the workplace.

Safety involves protecting people from accidents and injuries. Safety problems arise in all areas of the workplace. One source estimates that unsafe work behaviors are the reason for between 70 and 95 percent of on-the-job accidents involving injuries.

    A.   *Accident Prevention*

    Prevention of accidents is the key to a safe workplace, and education plays an important role. The safety audit is a process for examining the extent to which safe work practices are followed. The safety audit includes four steps: decide, observe, act, and record.

    Congress passed the Occupational Safety and Health Act (OSHA) to assure a safe and healthy workplace. Figure 18-2 summarizes the purpose of OSHA legislation. Even though OSHA has its critics, it has been responsible for getting employers to pay more attention to safety and health issues. Characteristically, Third World nations have not enacted strict regulations to assure a safe and health workplace.

    B.   *Management's Role in Promoting Safety*

    Management is responsible for creating and maintaining a safe workplace. A positive attitude toward safety consciousness is instrumental in promoting job safety. Concern for the health and safety of people is a priority managerial concern.

Teaching Hint: Point out the need for managers to (consistently) stress accident prevention. There are no opportunities to replace eyes, hands, fingers, arms, or legs.

II.   ALCOHOL AND DRUGS IN THE WORKPLACE

Teaching Objective 2:   Understand the negative consequences of alcohol and drug abuse.

In the U.S., the annual cost of alcohol and drug abuse exceeds $140 billion. Alcoholism is an illness and involves consuming alcohol to such an extent that an afflicted person cannot function normally in everyday life. Drug abuse involves improper use of various substances, including stimulants, depressants, or even alcohol. Alcohol or drug addition is defined as a disease.

A.   *Recognizing Substance-Abuse Problems*

Figure 18-3 lists symptoms of alcohol and drug problems. Drug addition can evolve rapidly or emerge gradually over an extended period of time. Dependency on alcohol emerges more slowly and progresses through several stages. Figure 18-4 presents a brief summary of the effects and dangers of drug usage.

B.   *Drug Testing*

Drug testing is a controversial issue. Some people consider it to be an invasion of privacy; others emphasize the need to maintain safe and healthy working conditions. Drug testing programs include pre-employment and random testing as well as testing in cases of suspected drug use. The scope of programs should be clearly communicated to employees and prospective employees. Unless legally authorized, random testing of all employees without reasonable suspicion is not a recommended course of action.

C.   *Employee Assistance Programs*

These programs provide professional counseling to rehabilitate troubled workers and enable them to be healthy and productive employees. Deterioration of work performance is a key indicator of a possible need for referral. Workers who cooperate and volunteer to seek diagnosis and treatment are able to retain employment. Participation in an EAP is kept confidential.

D. *Eliminating Alcohol and Drug Abuse*

Strong management commitment is an essential step toward elimination of alcohol and drug problems. Managers can enforce compliance with safety standards and consistently stress the need to maintain a substance-free workplace. Communication is another primary consideration. Managers need to emphasize the rationale for having policies and programs to alleviate substance abuse.

III. SMOKING: A HAZARD TO HEALTH

Teaching Objective 3:   Recognize potential health complications caused by smoking.

Although the number of smokers is declining, Americans smoke over 500 billion cigarettes each year. Nicotine is addictive; it affects neuro-transmitters and sedates as well as stimulates.

A. *Smoking and the Workplace*

Controversy over rights of smokers and nonsmokers has led to adoption of policies to govern smoking in the workplace. Communication is a key factor in development of policies to regulate smoking. Passive smoking, inhalation of secondhand tobacco smoke, is believed to be a source of deaths and respiratory illnesses. Smokeless tobacco products contain poisons and carcinogens and are not healthful alternatives to smoking.

B. *Alleviating Addiction to Tobacco*

Alternatives available to those who desire to quit smoking include smoking cessation programs, nicotine gum, nicotine patches, and personal decisions to cease using tobacco. By giving encouragement and extending congratulations to subordinates who quit smoking, managers can encourage workers to have the self-confidence needed to become nonsmokers.

Suggested Reading for this Section:
Brownlee, Shannon, Steven V. Roberts, and others. "Should Cigarettes be Outlawed?"
U.S. News and World Report 116, April 18, 1994, pp. 32-38.

This article discusses health concerns, political issues, and economic factors related to
smoking. Comparisons are presented (1965 and 1994) for the numbers of smokers and
tobacco-related deaths. While the total number of smokers has declined, more females are
smoking. Benefits and costs associated with a nationwide ban on producing,
manufacturing, consuming, and exporting tobacco products are identified. Benefits include
longer lives and fewer illnesses; costs involve job losses in the tobacco industry and
reduced government revenues.

IV.   AIDS: A DEADLY DISEASE

**Teaching Objective 4:   Stress the need for managers to develop an understanding of
                            AIDS.**

AIDS is an incurable disease that impairs functioning of the body's immune system. It
is caused by a virus called HIV, which weakens the body's ability to fight infection.

A.   *Understanding AIDS*

High-risk persons who are more likely to acquire AIDS include those who
engage in sexual activities with already-infected partners, intravenous drug
users who share contaminated needles, children who acquire the virus from an
infected mother, and people receiving blood transfusions before the introduction
of blood-screening techniques. AIDS progresses through three stages:
infection, AIDS-related complex, and the disease itself. Figure 18-7 lists
possible symptoms of AIDS.

B.   *AIDS and the World of Work*

Existence of AIDS cannot be used as a reason not to hire or to terminate a
person having the disease. Managers cannot base employment or termination
decisions on the opposition of colleagues working with AIDS victims, and the
confidentiality of persons with AIDS must be protected. Although the AIDS
issue is not specifically addressed in many company policies, a special policy
on AIDS can improve communication. Education can be provided through
seminars, newsletters, brochures, and videotapes.

V. SEXUAL HARASSMENT: AN IMPORTANT ISSUE

Teaching Objective 5: Explain the importance of eliminating sexual harassment from the workplace.

Sexual harassment is unwelcomed, verbal or physical, sexually-oriented behavior. The Equal Employment Opportunity Commission sets forth two forms of harassment: Quid pro quo and hostile environment. The issue of sexual harassment is not new to the workplace; however, events, such as the allegations by Anita Hill during the confirmation proceedings for Supreme Court Justice Clarence Thomas have focused media attention on the topic.

A. *An Overview of Sexual Harassment*

It is impossible to know the extent of sexual harassment in the workplace. In 1986, the first sexual-harassment case (*Meritor v. Vinsen*) was decided by the U.S. Supreme Court. A Circuit Court of Appeals decision (*Ellison v. Brady*) established the "reasonable woman" standard to determine if a hostile environment exists. Sexual harassment is not exclusively a problem existing only in the United States.

B. *Preventing Sexual Harassment*

A supportive management attitude and educating of workers are important factors in prevention of sexual harassment. Development of a sexual-harassment policy communicates management's determination not to condone sexual harassment. Assuming a complaint has merit, several alternatives are available to prevent undesired behaviors. A letter may be sent specifying the behaviors and asking that they cease. Sometimes, a verbal warning is sufficient to stop the harassment. In other circumstances, it may be necessary to initiate disciplinary action.

Teaching Hint: Emphasize that seriousness of the managerial stance against sexual harassment must prevail. For example, telling and/or listening to sexually-oriented jokes does not communicate an appropriate message to employees.

Suggested Readings for this Section:
*Baridon, Andrea P., and David R. Eyler. "Workplace Etiquette for Men and Women."
Training 31, December 1994, pp. 31-37.*

More communication is a key factor to elimination of sexual harassment in the workplace.
Practical business etiquette is recommended as a guideline to govern behaviors between
men and women. Suggestions are given on ways of responding to invitations and
propositions, the "boys will be boys" syndrome, stereotyped behavior, and the competition
mentality that sometimes exists between males and females. In addition, appropriate
responses of managers to these circumstances are noted.

*Fisher, Anne B. "Sexual Harassment: What to Do." Fortune 128, August 23, 1993, pp.
84-88.*

Some companies are actively trying to eliminate sexual harassment, which is a major
concern in the workplace. According to a survey by Freada Klein Associates, 90 percent
of Fortune 500 firms have experienced complaints involving sexual harassment.
Consultants and managers who have taken workshops believe that the best training gives
participants opportunities to talk with one another about the appropriateness of various
behaviors in the workplace. Having a sexual-harassment policy is not enough, firms need
to make sure that employees clearly understand its provisions.

VI.   LOOKING BACK

This chapter covers several important human relations issues: safety, substance abuse,
smoking, AIDS, and sexual harassment. Managers need to recognize the importance
of providing a workplace environment that encourages the most effective usage of its
human assets.

Answers to CONSIDER THIS Questions

1.   **Is it fair for OSHA to hold employers responsible for the safety of
employees?**

Even though managers sometimes consider OSHA standards to be vague,
unreasonable, or costly, it is generally considered appropriate to hold employers
responsible. Accountableness helps to assure that the intent of OSHA
legislation is fulfilled and keeps attention focused on safety and health issues.

Also, firms have an incentive to provide the education and training needed to reduce or eliminate accidents and promote health consciousness.

2. **What is the most important action managers can take to reduce workplace accidents?**

Prevention of accidents is the key to safety. The most important action is to educate workers about their jobs and the work environment. Training, safety meetings, and safety audits are key considerations. Managers must demonstrate a commitment to health and safety. Continual emphasis on safe work practices is necessary to promote acceptance for the principle of "think safety."

3. **Why is legislation necessary to help ensure a safe and healthy workplace?**

Through legislation, society sets rules and regulations to govern behaviors and specifies penalties for infractions. In practice, actual behaviors do not necessarily coincide with desired behaviors. In terms of compliance, voluntary compliance is too often more of an ideal than a reality. Since safety and health issues are of major importance, legislation assures the best interests of all personnel are considered.

Answers to CONSIDER THIS Questions

1. **Considering the potentially harmful consequences of alcohol, drugs, and smoking, why do people continue to use these substances?**

Chemical dependency is thought to be caused by one or a combination of psychological, emotional, or social factors. Too frequently, use of these substances becomes habit forming. Depending on the type of substance, the amount of time for addiction to occur varies from several weeks to a number of years. Once a habit becomes well established, it can be extremely difficult to break without professional intervention and much personal effort on the part of the afflicted individual.

2. **As a condition of employment, who should be subjected to drug testing?**

Student answers to this question depend on their perspectives. Some persons consider drug testing to be an invasion of privacy. Others believe pre-employment testing is essential, especially for occupations (such as train engineers or airplane pilots) involving public safety. Among the public, there is likely much support for pre-employment testing of all job applicants. Without doubt, this view is favored by employers because of the desire to have a drug-free workplace.

3.   **How can managers use communication as a "tool" to reduce substance abuse?**

Communication techniques can be used to emphasize reasons for implementing and supporting policies and programs that alleviate substance abuse. Managers can provide explanations and ask questions to inform employees about the firm's position on substance-abuse issues. At meetings, a few minutes might occasionally be taken to address the importance of a substance-free workplace. Posters, brochures, and informative handouts are other items to keep the topic at the forefront of attention.

Answers to REVIEW AND DISCUSSION Questions

1.   *Why did Congress pass the Occupational Safety and Health Act?*

Congress passed this act to assure a safe and healthy workplace. Review Figure 18-2, which cites a number of specific reasons for creating this legislation. These include encouraging employers and employees to reduce workplace hazards and to implement new or improve existing safety/health programs.

2.   *What is OSHA's most noteworthy accomplishment?*

OSHA has been responsible for reducing the number of job-related injuries and encouraging research into harmful toxic materials. However, its greatest contribution is getting employers to pay more attention to safety and health issues.

3.   *How can managers promote safety awareness in the workplace?*

A positive attitude toward safety consciousness is instrumental in promoting job safety. Immediate attention needs to be given to repair of unsafe equipment and elimination of unsafe work behaviors. The importance of accident prevention merits continual emphasis, and employees should be trained to operate equipment properly. Managers can emphasize understanding the costly nature of accidents, and employees should be encouraged to suggest ways to improve safety.

4.   *Why should managers be knowledgeable about the issue of alcohol/drug addiction?*

Substance abuse is a major workplace problem. It takes a tremendous toll on the physical health and welfare of many workers and their families. In addition, alcohol and drugs are responsible for a tremendous amount of lost productivity. Knowledge helps managers better understand issues related to substance abuse and initiate preventive actions in their companies.

5.   *What are the symptoms of possible alcohol or drug abuse?*

Figure 18-3 lists symptoms of possible drug and alcohol abuse. The presence of one or more symptoms does not necessarily confirm abuse but does serve as a signal to be alert.

6.   *Why has drug testing emerged as a controversial topic?*

Some people consider drug testing to be an invasion of privacy. Many persons who share this view tend to distinguish between on- and off-the-job workplace behaviors and consider that employers should not exert influence on private lives of workers. Others emphasize the need to maintain safe and healthy working conditions. These people support the view that actions taken to assure such a workplace environment are justified.

7.   *Discuss the importance of the Supreme Court's decision in Meritor v. Vinson?*

This was the first sexual-harassment case to be decided by the Supreme Court. The decision concluded that a key factor involved the "unwelcomed" nature of sexual harassment and supported the premise that loss of economic benefits is not necessary to establish a valid complaint. Also, the court set aside a ruling that an employer is always liable for sexual harassment of workers by supervisors. The decision served to focus public attention on the issue of sexual harassment and likely served as an impetus for victims of sexual harassment to file cases with the court system.

8.   *How is the virus that causes AIDS transmitted?*

The AIDS virus can be transmitted from engaging in sexual activities with infected persons, sharing contaminated hypodermic needles, or (less frequently) receiving blood transfusions. Also, children can contact the virus from an infected mother prior to or during the birth process. Evidence does not indicate that the virus is transmitted through casual contacts with others.

9. *Whatelements should a corporate sexual-harassment policy contain?*

Essentially, the policy states the corporate position on sexual harassment, specifies inappropriate behaviors, and explains the procedure for reporting complaints. Development of a policy is important because it signals management's position not to condone sexual harassment.

10. *What can managers do to educate workers about the issue of sexual harassment?*

Periodically, managers can remind workers of the company's sexual-harassment policy, or if none exists, they can support development of a formal policy. Brochures or other literature, which include relevant information, are a relevant education resource. The topic can be covered at training sessions. Communication is relevant because employees need opportunities to ask questions and clarify misunderstandings.

Answers to CRITICAL THINKING INCIDENTS

Incident 18-1:   OBEY THE RULES

1. **Based on her skills, excellent job performance, and accident-free record, should Ginny be exempted from compliance with the safety rules? Explain your response.**

Ginny can be proud of her safety record, especially since it was achieved while doing a difficult job. Even though she is a skilled, experienced operator, Ginny must adhere to established safety rules. Granting an exemption to Ginny sets a precedent and is an invitation for others to avoid compliance with the rules. Karen simply cannot let such a situation occur.

2. **If Karen forces Ginny to choose between following the safety rules or resigning, how do you think the operator will react?**

Ginny might react negatively and become defensive. However, if she wants to keep her job, there is no alternative but to obey. Ginny will most likely elect to comply and remain with McClennen Industries. Karen must clearly communicate these key points. Subordinates are expected to follow company rules and, unlike Joe Johnson, she will not overlook violations of safety rules.

3.   **How can Karen persuade Ginny to comply with the safety rules?**

An appeal can be based on logical reasoning; rules are essential for a safe, accident-free workplace. Karen can praise Ginny's job accomplishments and emphasize that it is not characteristic of work done by most personnel. It is important for Karen to justify the rationale for having safety rules and stress the difficulty of enforcement in circumstances where its optional whether personnel obey them.

4.   **How might Ginny's reluctance to abide by the safety rules be viewed by her co-workers?**

The colleagues might agree with her views because required safety apparel is uncomfortable and sometimes makes it more difficult to operate equipment. If feasible alternatives exist, however, workers should recommend them to management. Perhaps, different types of protective devices might be adopted. The vast majority of workers understands that safety rules exist for their own protection. Some people think that accidents happen only to others and consequently do not recognize safety as a foremost consideration. This is unfortunate because accidents can happen suddenly and without warning.

Incident 18-2:   A CHANGE IN BEHAVIOR

1.   **Identify symptoms indicating that Deborah may have a substance abuse problem.**

Several behavioral changes reveal the possibility of substance abuse. Deborah has a valued reputation for excellent job performance. Recently, however, she missed deadlines and submitted inaccurate reports. A disoriented appearance and resumption of smoking are indicators of potential problems. Students need to remember that symptoms, by themselves, do not conclusively evidence substance abuse. It is important for managers to observe a pattern of changes, which represent a departure from normal behaviors.

2.   **When recognizing Deborah's disoriented behavior, should Nola have inquired about alcohol or drug consumption? Explain your response.**

In the absence of recurrent symptoms or prior problems, Nola should not make a direct inquiry. Such directness might be taken negatively and put Deborah on the defensive, especially if the behavior resulted from taking medication prescribed by her physician. Nola might ask an indirect questions such as, "You appear to not be feeling well. Are you ok? Might I be of assistance?" In any event, Deborah should not continue to work if her condition might impair her own health and safety or the health and safety of others.

Chapter 18: Human Resource Issues

3.   **As a manager, how should Nola respond if Deborah's declining job performance becomes clearly evident?**

Managers have an obligation to be concerned about an employee's job performance and must take the initiative to assure that performance expectations of human resources are met. Therefore, Nola should arrange to visit with Deborah and address the difficulty. She should focus her comments on job-related factors and not let the conversation digress to a discussion of personality issues or issues unrelated to job performance. If a problem exists, Deborah should be informed about availability of the substance abuse program. Like most managerial challenges, such a situation necessitates the practice of excellent communication skills to attain desired results that benefit both the employee and employer.

4.   **If referral to the employee assistance program becomes necessary, why should Nola think carefully before discussing the topic with Deborah.**

Personal criticism and placement of blame are not productive solutions for remedying the problem. It is advantageous for Nola to demonstrate a supportive attitude and encourage Deborah to make the commitment needed to alleviate her substance abuse. In any case, Nola should try to avoid causing detrimental emotional outbursts, which might possibly occur during a discussion. She needs to avoid negatively influencing the future superior-subordinate relationship with Deborah and focus efforts on getting her to have a cooperative attitude toward participation in the program.

Incident 18-3:   SHE'S QUITE A PACKAGE

1.   **Is Darla victim of sexual harassment?   Explain your response.**

Darla is a victim of sexual harassment. The sexually-oriented jokes and sexual advances interfere with performance of her job responsibilities and create an offensive work atmosphere.

2.   **How should Darla handle her predicament?**

Every effort should be make to document the offensive behaviors. These data will enable Darla to substantiate her allegation of sexual harassment and provide evidence in case she is threatened with dismissal. In private and separate discussions with each executive, Darla could express her willingness to be a capable, productive employee and ask for the sexually-oriented behaviors to cease. Another strategy is to send a letter to each offender specifying the undesired behaviors, requesting they not continue, and indicating actions to be taken in event they do not stop. As a final resort, Darla has the option to initiate action through appeal to higher management and filing of a formal grievance.

3.   **Assuming she personally confronts each executive, how should Darla prepare herself?**

A personal confrontation creates anxiety, but in Darla's case, it is a strategy to alleviate an uncomfortable job-related situation. Darla should make an outline of anticipated remarks and mentally rehearse how she will deliver them. It's necessary to review her notes for accuracy and avoid arguments. When visiting with each executive, Darla must be firm, tactful, and attempt to be understood clearly.

4.   **Should Darla give up her Job? Explain your response.**

Apparently, Darla is a capable employee who likes her job and the salary she earns. As a victim of sexual harassment, Darla's legal rights to employment are protected. After Bob and Gene become aware of her views, it's possible that the work atmosphere could become strained. From the perspective of personal satisfaction, Darla might retain the position until other employment, which is personally and professionally attractive, can be secured.

Study Guide Assignments

The individual case assignment deviates from stereotyped tradition and involves a female sexual harasser. It introduces students to the difficulties encountered by the possibility of unwelcomed sexual conduct in the workplace. Also, the case illustrates how the reaction of a colleague to an incident involving the possibility for inappropriate sexual behavior can be embarrassing to a potential victim.

The group case assignment reflects what is likely an unfortunately too common reaction among managers to allegations of sexual harassment. Students are challenged to determine how an employer can avoid trouble. The discussion should involve a lively exchange of views among groups as they strive to resolve complications related to an allegation of sexual harassment.

 **Video Case**

Age Discrimination

Focus: **Age Discrimination (a Human Resource Issue)**

Summary:

Herman, the manager at Rally Motors, is interviewing candidates for a mechanic's position. Jake applies for the job. If anything, Jake is overqualified for the position, but Herman is concerned about Jake's age. Rather than tell Jake his concerns, Herman tells Jake that the job has already been filled. Jake asks Herman if he thinks he is too old for the job.

Discussion Questions:

1.   What are the legal requirements on age discrimination?

       The Age Discrimination in Employment Act of 1967 (as amended) prohibits discrimination against persons age 40 or older. Generally, unless age is a condition of legal employment (for example, in most states you must be 21 to serve alcoholic beverages), age may not be a factor in employment.

2.   Why should Herman tell Jake his concerns about Jake's age?

       At a minimum, if Herman openly tells Jake his concerns, Jake can address them. In lying to Jake, Herman forces Jake to be confrontational.

Chapter **19**

Current Trends in Management

▒▒▒ Chapter Overview

      Chapter 2 (Philosophies of Management) presented an overview of how the field of management evolved from the early classical managers to the most recent innovative managers. This chapter examines some of the main trends that are continuing to influence how managers must manage an organization in today's business world if they want to remain competitive and profitable. There are three major trends that every organization must learn how to adapt to if they are going to survive and prosper. These trends are: the increasing amount of new technology being developed, the globalization of the business world, and the ever increasing rate of change. These trends definitely affect how managers handle the basic management functions, and the success of the organization will depend on their ability to adapt successfully.

▒▒▒ Teaching Objectives

The teaching objectives of this chapter are to:

1.   Identify the major trends that will impact future management.

2.   Discuss the main changes in the business environment that will affect future business managers.

3.   Explain the future relationship between government and business.

4.   Examine the changes and trends that will affect how managers handle the basic management functions.

5.   Identify the changes in the make-up of the future labor force.

6.   Examine management training techniques that will be utilized in the future.

Chapter Outline of the Text

I.   CHANGES THAT WILL AFFECT MANAGERS
    A.   Technology
    B.   Globalization
    C.   Increasing Rate of Change

II.   CHANGES IN THE BUSINESS ENVIRONMENT
    A.   Downsizing
    B.   Information-Based Organizations
    C.   The Role of the Government in the Business World in the Future

III. SOME TRENDS IN APPLYING THE BASIC MANAGEMENT FUNCTIONS
    A.   Planning
    B.   Organizing
    C.   Staffing
    D.   Leading
    E.   Controlling

IV.   STRATEGIES FOR THE CHANGING WORK FORCE
    A.   The Aging of the Work Force
        1.   Automation
        2.   Recruiting
        3.   Women
        4.   Minorities
        5.   Older Workers
        6.   Immigrants
        7.   Disabled

    B.   The Multicultural Work force
        1.   Communication
        2.   Language
    C.   Both Parents in a Household Working

Key Terms

These terms are introduced in the chapter.

Controlled chaos   Planning
Controlling   Rate of Change
Downsizing   Scenario planning
Globalization   Self-managed work teams
Information Based Organization   Synchronized work teams
Leading   Span of control
Mentors   Staffing
Networking   Technology
Organizing   Vision

Detailed Chapter Summary

I. CHANGES THAT WILL AFFECT MANAGERS

Teaching Objective 1: Identify the major trends that will impact future management.

While there are many changes that have occurred in the business world, three have had a tremendous impact on how managers must manage a business organization. While managers may very well not like these changes, they must recognize them and adjust to them as best they can.

A.   *Technology*

All of the new technology available today is truly amazing. What may be more amazing, however, is the rate at which new technology is advancing. Computers have changed how businesses operate. Desktop computers have literally eliminated entire levels of middle managers whose main duties were to relay communications and assist lower-level managers in problem solving. The development of computers seems to have no end, and the usefulness of computers is constantly improving. Computers are invaluable to any business organization and serve to assist management in doing everything from data storage to problem solving, product design, and manufacturing.

Another major area of technology that is impacting business organizations is the use of robotics. As discussed in the chapter on production/operations management, applications of robotic technology are continuously increasing. Robots will very possibly take over the great majority of the dangerous, monotonous, and distasteful jobs in this country.

B.   *Globalization*

As trade barriers disappear, worldwide competition will increase in virtually every product and service industry. Already, we see major regional free-trade zones being established. Without trade barriers, a foreign competitor's only disadvantage in competing with local businesses is shipping costs, which may or may not be significant. Globalization of markets will definitely increase quality standards and force businesses to reduce costs through efficiency.

While global markets may possibly threaten some businesses in the U.S., they also open up many new opportunities. Most foreign markets are not nearly as saturated as those in the United States, and many businesses in this country are well equipped to enter foreign markets. To be successful, however, U.S. firms must carefully segment foreign markets; adopt the most efficient management procedures; and establish on-going communication between the firm and its customers, suppliers, managers, and workers.

C.   *The Increasing Rate of Change*

Change is not only inevitable, it is increasing and is impacting many significant areas of business. For example, as Tom Peters quotes, "There are no mature products anymore. Everything can be reinvented, usually with the help of technology." Technology, products, services, competition, government, free trade, and the labor force are among the areas experiencing changes. Managers must anticipate these changes and try to take advantage of them.

This proactive way of managing relies heavily on communication, and its key role in business today cannot be overemphasized.

II.   CHANGES IN THE BUSINESS ENVIRONMENT

Teaching Objective 2:   Discuss the main changes in the business environment that will affect future business managers.

A.   *Downsizing*

Reducing costs by eliminating personnel is hardly a new idea in the business world. What is new, however, is the frequency and magnitude that it is being done today. Many major U.S. corporations have downsized or permanently eliminated close to 50 percent of their personnel. The real concern is the need to assure efficient and effective operations.   Along with efficiency, quality, and morale, competitiveness must be considered. The literature is full of examples where firms downsized to improve profits only to experience negative long-term results.   To accomplish downsizing properly, a firm must systematically analyze every task in the organization and determine how crucial it is to operations. It is necessary to determine who else could do each task and even consider whether tasks should be centralized or possibly contracted to an outside organization. This procedure is called "rightsizing." It considers both the short- and long-term impacts of decisions on the personnel who are retained.   The success of rightsizing depends on maintaining open channels of communication with everyone in the firm.

Suggested Readings for this Section:

Greengard, Samuel. "Don't Rush Downsizing: Plan, Plan, Plan." <u>Personnel Journal</u>, November 1993, pp. 64-76.

Reasons for downsizing a firm are many and varied but some of the most common reasons involve global competition, a slow economy, new technology, mergers and consolidations, and organizations that have become too bureaucratic.

The consequences of downsizing, however, can be disastrous if not handled properly. An American Management Association survey found that less than one-half of the companies that downsized reported a profit in the long run. The Conference Board also found that 64 percent of the firms with 10,000 or more employees that downsized had lower morale, 30 percent had to increase overtime costs, and 22 percent eliminated the wrong people.

The best way to deal with this issue is to have a strategic plan in place from the beginning. By having this plan, adjustments are constantly being made as things change, and a firm can hopefully avoid the typical "slash and burn" response that some firms experience when poor profit figures are released.

The techniques typically used to decide who stays and who goes have not worked well. Traditionally seniority is used as a basis; senior employees may be the most willing to leave, and they are the most expensive to keep.

Performance evaluations are another method that has experienced problems. Houston Lighting and Power laid off almost 1,000 people in February 1992. More than 900 of these employees filed a class action lawsuit claiming their supervisors used an "inaccurate" point grading system which was "prejudicial" on their performance evaluations.

One system that does seem to work is the one used by Sea-Land, a cargo shipping firm. The firm uses a zero based staffing system that literally places every employee and manager at risk. New job descriptions were developed for the organizational structure, and skills and abilities were matched to the new job descriptions. Every employee in the redundant category who lived over 50 miles away or who would have to drop over two levels in the company was offered a severance package. They all had the right to ask for new jobs in the firm; approximately a third of these persons took new positions, and others went into outplacement. Sea-Land eliminated over 800 employees and five layers of management without experiencing major problems.

Byrne, John A. "There is an Upside to Downsizing." <u>Business Week</u>, May 9, 1994, p. 64.

While there have been many documented cases of the horrors of downsizing, not all of them are completely accurate, and there have been many well documented success stories after downsizing. In a 1993 study, researchers found that financial performance worsens two years after a company downsizes. In other words, there are only short term gains to this procedure. In reality, however, the study only analyzed the financial records of 17 companies who announced layoffs in 1989. Review of financial data did not fully account for the recession of 1990-91. While financial performance deteriorated in 1991, a good case could be made that it would have been even worse if people had not been laid off in 1989 because of the recession.

Another study conducted by the Wyatt Company found that fewer than one-half of the companies that downsized met subsequent financial goals or operational goals. The study also cited that morale was hurt in 56 percent of the firms surveyed. The researchers also concluded that downsizing led to improved productivity, higher quality, better customer service, and a greater willingness of the survivors to take risks.

Many firms have experienced sizable increases in revenues and profits after downsizing, including Boeing, Chrysler, Hewlett-Packard, Motorola, and Texas Instruments. Possibly the best results, however, have been reported by the General Electric Company. In 1981, GE had 420,000 employees, and by mid 1995 they had approximately 220,000. The company had tripled its net profits and more than doubled its revenues during this same time period.

While massive layoffs should be avoided when possible and downsizing should not be considered a "quick fix," there are some very possible real gains if it is done properly.

B.   *Information-Based Organizations*

The most competitive businesses in the future may very well be the ones with the best information gathering systems. Information based organizations constantly communicate with customers, suppliers, employees, and those who can make an impact on operations. These types of organizations typically utilize specialists, autonomous workteams, and try to "mass customize" products or services for customers. Information technology allows a firm to gather, store, and retrieve huge amounts of data that can provide a competitive edge. Teams of workers representing all of the major areas of a firm jointly design new products and services in an incredibly short period of time. Finally, levels of customer service are brought to new heights as businesses begin to realize the importance of this data base in attracting and retaining customers.

C.   *The Role of the Government and Business in the Future*

Teaching Objective 3:   Explain the future relationship between government and business.

The relationship between the U.S. government and the business world has not always been cooperative and cordial. At times both sides have viewed the other somewhat negatively.   Businesses and government are starting to view each other more positively. This point is very important, since governmental actions influence the business world. In countries like Japan, the relationship between the government and the business community is one of cooperation and even assistance. This relationship reduces costs and increases competitiveness. The U.S. government can assist its national companies by maintaining fair competition, assuring adequate infrastructure and an educated work force, trying to keep the playing field level in terms of trade, reducing unnecessary paperwork and regulations, and helping to maintain strong economic growth. The business sector needs to assist the government by being socially responsible and understanding that some government intervention is necessary, since not all businesses play fair.

Teaching Hint: Students need to realize that the business environment is always changing, and the really good managers look constantly for new factors that will impact them and then try to make the proper changes before they are negatively impacted. The whole key to this situation is an effective communication and information gathering system.

III.   SOME TRENDS IN APPLYING THE BASIC MANAGEMENT FUNCTIONS

Teaching Objective 4:   Examine some of the changes and trends that will affect how managers handle the basic management functions.

There have been a number of changes that have impacted how a manager needs to manage a business. These changes have initiated some new trends related to basic management functions.

A.   *Planning*

The factor that has impacted planning the most has been the rapid increase in the rate of change. Long-term strategic planning is tremendously influenced by this factor. In response to change, the following trends are evident.

1.   Develop several different plans based on various possible outcomes. This is called "scenario planning" and has been very effective for many firms.

2.   Keep plans flexible so that many different scenarios can be dealt with quickly. Focus on "core competencies" or the things that the firm does exceptionally well and which generate profits.

3.   Finally, realize that new products are being developed at incredible speed. Therefore, every firm needs to stay very close to its customers by communicating with them and determining their new-product preferences.

B.   *Organizing*

The main changes in the organizing area center around the following trends:

1.   Companies are implementing flatter, more decentralized organizational structures. Today's organizations are pushing decision making and responsibility downward.

2.   Large firms are breaking up into smaller companies that are closer to the customer. Johnson & Johnson's 166 separately-charted companies are a prime example.

3.   Self-managed work teams, which are empowered to make many decisions, are used to a greater extent. Many of these teams are cross-functional as they cut horizontally across the organization for their members.

4.   Outside firms are accustomed to performing tasks that are not part of a company's "core area." This is called *networking*, and these outside firms then become a very integral part of the organization itself.

C.   *Staffing*

Staffing trends are also changing. First, there is a growing shortage of entry-level/low-skill level employees. The baby bust group, which follows the baby boomers, is much smaller, and the number of 18 year olds recorded in 1989 will not reach this level again until the year 2003. This means that businesses needing entry-level employees will have to compete for them. Secondly, new sources of highly-skilled and managerial workers will also have to be utilized. In the future, women, minorities, immigrants, disabled persons, and older

workers will be key sources of skilled workers. Businesses will also lease
more employees on a temporary basis to fill certain needs. Finally, there is a
definite trend toward giving employees more training on an on-going basis. As
new technology emerges, the need for training is obvious. Employees also will
need more training in communicating, problem solving, working on teams, time
management, and working with a diverse and multicultural work force.

D.   *Leading*

In the future, the best leaders will be ones that can effectively communicate a
vision to everyone in the organization. To achieve this, leaders must utilize a
large variety of ways to communicate with their employees and other
stakeholder groups.   The new leaders must set the direction of the firm and
give people in the firm more freedom, authority, and autonomy. Good leaders
know that they can only succeed if they get everyone in the firm to understand
and "buy into" the vision of the firm. They know that their actions speak
louder than their words, so they make sure that everything they say is backed
up with appropriate actions. Good leaders encourage a free exchange of ideas,
and they encourage appropriate employees to make direct contact with suppliers
and customers on a regular basis. Finally, good leaders understand that
everyone in the firm must reap the rewards for achieving the vision.

E.   *Controlling*

The use of autonomous work teams and empowered employees means that
different types of control systems are necessary. In many organizations, the
primary mechanism of control will be self control. Since employees will have
a lot of autonomy or freedom, they must control themselves. This type of
control will only work if the employees definitely buy into the vision and
direction of the firm's top management.

Suggested Readings for this Section:
Hendricks, Mark. "Who's the Boss?" Entrepreneur, January 1995, pp. 54-55.

Stewardship is an idea popularized by author Peter Block in his text entitled *Stewardship*. It is also an idea that is catching on in many firms across the country. Stewardship is very similar to empowerment and participative management. Stewardship goes a little further than empowerment a practice in which employees are given the authority to make individual decisions. Under stewardship, an employee must utilize this authority for the good of the entire company as well as for the good of the individual or work group.

Basically, stewardship has two elements: (1) to make employees accountable for the well being of the company and (2) to give order to the distribution of power among the employees. Under stewardship, employees organize their own work including scheduling materials, tools, and people. Employees vote on capital expenditures and even have access to financial information; they are also more accountable under stewardship.

Stewardship does have its limitations, however. If a business owner wants tight control over every major decision, especially in crisis situations, then it will not work. To be effective, stewardship really means letting go of self interest and acting for the greater good of the firm.

Stewardship does not cost a lot in terms of capital outlays, but there are some definite training costs, especially in the beginning. It does take some courage to institute this program, but the results for many small- and medium-sized firms have been tremendous. BriskHeat, a Columbus, Ohio manufacturer of flexible electric heating elements, saw its sales rise from $6.1 million in 1993 to almost $10 million in 1994.

Burns, Greg. "The Trouble with Empowerment." Quality Digest, February 1994, pp. 47-49.

Empowerment is a term that brings on a negative reaction in a lot of firms because employees have learned that it is just a buzzword with no real meaning.

The biggest problems with empowering employees come in two forms: (1) If you really think about it, only the employees can truly empower themselves, and (2) to really work, there must be some very real and even sometimes radical changes in the work environment.

Many managers simply want to tell employees that they are empowered and then go on with business as usual. When employees start making decisions of any magnitude, management grabs the power back. This is analogous to putting a 100-yard leash on a dog to get up a good speed before snapping back.

If management really wants to empower employees, it must create an environment that genuinely encourages personnel to empower themselves. For example, in some firms, the idea of pushing decisions downward can be viewed by the employees as either being "dumped on" with additional work or as a chance to develop more skills and really take charge of the work they are doing. The difference between these two viewpoints is usually determined by how management presents the decision-making opportunity to the workers and how much *real* authority they have in making and implementing decisions. If management honestly shows workers that it is more concerned with developing human resources, than "supervising" them, a positive attitude is normally the outcome of the process.

Empowerment can achieve dramatic results for almost any firm but only if the proper organizational climate is established.

IV.   STRATEGIES FOR THE CHANGING WORK FORCE

Teaching Objective 5:   Identify the changes in the make-up of the future labor force.

Change in the work force throughout the 1990s is going to impact how managers recruit, train, and retain personnel.

A.   *The Increasing Age of the Labor Force*

The baby-boomer generation will start to retire in the year 2010. This, of course, means that the average age of the work force is now over forty. The baby-bust generation which follows is significantly smaller, and this fact, which has been previously mentioned, is going to cause a real shortage of highly-skilled and entry-level workers. Some alternative strategies for handling this problem include:

1. Utilize automation, whenever it is feasible and practical. The field of robotics has advanced to the point where many jobs can be automated if a firm can afford it financially.

2. Start a serious recruiting program to attract as many of the baby bust employees as possible. Establishing school/work programs and internships have worked well.

3. Actively recruit more female employees. Firms may develop more flexible job schedules and possibly offer some type of child care arrangements.

4. Attract more minorities. Firms need to establish programs that will attract more minorities, such as mentor programs and scholarship/internship programs.

5. Recruit more older workers. Many entry-level jobs are filled by retired workers who just want to work on a part-time basis. Fast-food restaurants and grocery stores, in particular, have actively recruited this group of workers.

6. Seek qualified immigrants who represent yet another source of employees. Our entire work force is definitely becoming more multi-cultured so it is a logical extension to recruit even more immigrants. While there may be communication problems initially because of differences in language and perceptions, these can be overcome; diversity of this type has been found to be a real asset for a number of firms.

7. Hire more disabled workers who are a source of new employees. With the American Disabilities Act (ADA) making it unlawful to discriminate against disabled people in hiring, all businesses need to look seriously at this group of workers. A recent study showed that the disabled population has also been found to be very hardworking, reliable, and productive. According to the EEOC (Equal Employment Opportunity Commission) accommodations for workers with disabilities averages only $260.00.

B.   *Both Parents Working in the Household*

Today, over 70 percent of all women who have children between the ages of 6 and 17 are working. This means that there are some very real family issues that firms must address. The main family issues appear to be child care and care of the elderly.

1.   *Child Care* — Child care is a major issue for all families where both parents work and for single parent families. Since these two groups make up the vast majority of workers today, it must be dealt with. Some possible alternatives are:
   a. On site child care
   b. Subsidized child-care benefits
   c. Assistance in locating affordable child care.
   d. Money, space, or land to assist a non-profit company to build a child care facility close by.
   e. Work with local schools or other agencies on after-school programs.
2.   *Care of the Elderly* — Currently 30 percent of all workers are responsible for caring for an elderly parent or relative, and this figure will definitely grow as the baby-boomer generation ages. Elder-care facilities, similar to child care facilities may be the logical answer.

C.   *Single Parent Families*

Single parent families now make up one-eighth of the working population, and over 90 percent of them are female. Child care is a critical issue here, but these persons often need more flexible work schedules. These parents must handle the various tasks and duties that two parent families normally split. Two other alternatives for both single-parent families and families in which both parents work include:
1.   Alternative career paths, which allow for pregnancy leaves for both men and women.
2.   Alternative work locations, such as working at home when it is a feasible option.

Teaching Hint: Remember to remind your students that equally important with attracting good workers is retaining them. Firm that deal with the issues discussed in this section should have a real advantage over those that do not.

V.   MANAGEMENT TRAINING IN THE FUTURE

Teaching Objective 6:   Examine management training techniques that will be utilized in the future.

Since the world of business is constantly changing, it is only logical that managers need on-going training to handle these new changes.

A. *Managerial Skills*

Skills that managers will need both now and in the future are
1. Good communication skills
2. Good interpersonal relationship skills
3. The ability to work in teams
4. The ability to handle a multicultural work force
5. Understanding the true role of an effective leader

B. *Training Methods*

Training methods vary from standard classroom training to programs that build a team orientation by having small groups scale cliffs or paddle down rapids. Some basic recommendations that seem to be both essential and effective are:
1. Top management must both actively sponsor training and become actively involved with it.
2. There should be identified career transition levels with different types of training to take managers to the next level.
3. Both current and future organizational needs must be addressed. Real problems and strategies should be discussed.
4. Appropriate methods should be utilized. The use of real problems in a simulated setting is worthwhile.
5. Support individual improvement with diagnostic tools. Managers need to be assessed through some form of instrument that can really show them their strengths and weaknesses. Standardized instruments such as the Leadership Practices Inventory or the Mahler Coaching Practice Survey are useful..
6. Ensure practical and relevant content. Using real problems in simulated situations is recommended.
7. Emphasize interpersonal relations and teamwork. Here is where a lot of the outdoor team-building activities are appropriate.
8. Conclude with individual action plans. A personal growth plan, which is reviewed periodically, is worthwhile.

VI. LOOKING BACK

This chapter presents the major changes and trends in the field of management. Management is a dynamic field, not a static one, and new changes and trends will continue to occur. Managers must learn to look ahead and try to anticipate new changes and figure out the best way to deal with them. Those business organizations that have this kind of foresight will be successful in the future, as businesses around the world will be adjusting to these changes.

Answers to CONSIDER THIS Questions

1. **Name some current advances in technology that will affect how you will manage in the future?**

    New advances in computers and computer software are by far the largest change for both managers and employees. The computer in the business world acts as a data storage and retrieval system, a communication device, and assists in problem solving. Another area of technology that will have a large impact is the whole field of robotics. As robots become increasingly sophisticated and less expensive, they will play a larger and larger role in all businesses. Finally, new information technology literally "puts the world at your finger tips." More companies are becoming information-based organizations. This technology will help firms interact with customers and suppliers and will change how firms do business.

2. **Explain the main difference between downsizing and rightsizing?**

    Downsizing refers to reducing costs by eliminating personnel. In most cases downsizing simply continues to lay off personnel until the cost-reduction goal is reached. The tasks of the people that are laid off are simply redistributed to the workers who survive the layoff. Typically, the results of downsizing show short-term gains at best and long-term problems of an even greater magnitude. Rightsizing asks a firm's management to do some real planning before the layoff of personnel. In rightsizing, management must think about what tasks each individual in the company does, how valuable these tasks are to the company, who will assume these tasks if this person is laid off, and how this change will impact quality and the employees that remain. In short, rightsizing attempts to keep the most valuable personnel and make sure that efficiency and quality stay high while costs are reduced. Rightsizing, if done properly, can give a firm both short- and long-term gains.

3. **Define an information-based organization.**

Information-based organizations are companies that have established high-tech data gathering, analyzing, storage, and retrieval systems that are available to all personnel. In an information-based company, everything of importance is monitored and tracked on a continuous basis. Customer satisfaction and desires are major considerations. Line employees are able to utilize the system to make decisions related to production or ordering products. In an information-based company, there are several specialists who are working on autonomous work teams that have substantial authority to perform assigned tasks. Possibly, this is because the necessary information is available for making the kind of decisions that are needed.

Answers to CONSIDER THIS Questions

1. **Why do some companies now use "scenario planning" for their long-term strategic planning?**

With the worldwide competitive environment changing at a faster rate, there is a definite need to be prepared for both potential disasters and potential opportunities. Scenario planning allows a firm to do this by laying out plans for different possible situations. If one of the situations does occur, the firm is in much better shape to act on it quickly and decisively. Scenario planning gives a firm the most flexibility and realistic long-term planning options, especially in a volatile industry.

2. **All organizations cannot make good use of autonomous or self-managed work teams. Why?**

Self-managed work teams have been found to work best in firms that have jobs that are fairly complex and require the interaction of people to accomplish their tasks. Also, it is important to ask these questions:
a. Do the employees want to work in teams?
b. Do employees have the skills needed to work in teams, and/or is the company willing to train them?
c. Would a team format require the hiring of several duplicate specialists for each team?
d. How will the team members be compensated?

If a firm does not have the right kind of jobs or personnel, the team approach might be problematic.

3.   **How does a leader really instill a "vision" in an organization's people?**

Employees and lower level managers in an organization will normally start accepting a "vision" when they see top management basing actions on this vision, not just talking about it. Also, top management has to clearly communicate how this vision will help employees as well as the company. In any organization people need to be reminded about the vision and its importance to them and the company. This can be communicated in a number of different ways, but getting them personally involved is definitely the best way. When people become involved and participate in planning how to achieve a vision, then it becomes a personal as well a corporate vision.

Answers to REVIEW AND DISCUSSION Questions

1.   *Name the three biggest changes in the work world that will affect the way we manage in the future.*

While there are certainly many areas that will affect the way managers must manage in the future, the three biggest ones are:
a.   The constantly increasing amount of new or improved technology that is being developed, which includes everything from more advanced computers and computer software to robotics and fully automated assembly lines.
b.   The globalization of world markets is growing every day. Large regional trade blocks, such as NAFTA, will very possibly eventually lead to total worldwide trade.   Increased trade will be accompanied by new competition as well as additional market opportunities.
c.   Changes in technology, products and services, competition, and the composition of the labor force are all occurring at faster and faster rates of speed.

2.   *Explain what autonomous work teams consist of in the business world today.*

Autonomous work teams are permanent groups or clusters of workers, typically from various departments within the firm. They are "self-managed" and "empowered," or given considerable authority and freedom in accomplishing their tasks. Autonomous work teams work best in industries and firms that have fairly complex tasks to accomplish, and the tasks require the interaction of people to accomplish them.

3. *Explain what Tom Peters means by "mass customization."*

Tom Peters was referring to the fact that if firms are going to be really effective in meeting needs of customers, they must individually customize products for each customer as much as possible. While individually customizing products, however, they are also going to learn how to mass produce them so that the costs remains low. The Hewlett-Packard computer is a good example.

4. *Why might a company "network" many of its functional areas out to outside firms?*

Networking refers to contracting with an outside firm to do all of the tasks in a functional area. A firm may decide to "network" some or all of its "non-core" areas because of lower costs or higher quality of service. Possibly, firms simply do not want to be involved with anything except core functional areas. For example, a small bicycle manufacturer could retain all of the production and marketing functions but network out accounting, human resources, and clerical functional areas to outside firms.

5. *Explain how a firm can emphasize both flexibility and focus in doing its strategic planning?*

Firms are "focusing" when they are concentrating on their core competencies or the areas or skills that they do best. These core areas make a firm distinctive from competitors. A firm must be sure all long-term plans stress these core areas. At the same time, every firm must be prepared for opportunities and threats. A firm can stay "flexible" by doing scenario planning. In scenario planning, a firm makes more than one set of plans (all of which are focused) for different possible situations, which they honestly feel could occur in the future. By having these plans, the most appropriate plan can readily be adopted.

6. *How is our labor force changing?*

There are three main ways in which our labor force is changing that will impact on managers. First, our current labor force, which is primarily made up of workers from the baby-boomer generation, is getting older in terms of their average age. With an average age over forty now, most firms need to start thinking about where they are going to find replacements for all of these people in a few years. Second, the newcomers represent a smaller group than the present labor force. Our present labor force is the baby-boomer generation, and the baby-bust generation also consists of fewer people. Finally, to make up for this difference in size, businesses are going to have to recruit a much more culturally diverse labor force, which includes more women, older workers, minorities, immigrants, and disabled workers.

7.   *How can a manager honestly improve communication at a company?*

While there are many different ways to improve communications, some of the best ways are:
a.   Use a more participative management style that encourages upward as well as downward communication.
b.   Utilize "groups" to encourage more communications. For example, quality circles, task forces, work teams, and committees.
c.   Use a variety of communication methods such as memos, flyers, tapes, live television, conference calls, coffee hours, roundtable discussions, and newsletters.
d.   Make sure management at all levels maintains contact with customers, suppliers, and employees so they know what is going on in all areas of the business. This can be accomplished by surveys, phone calls, and personal contacts.

8.   *Define the term "controlled chaos."*

Today, firms are encouraging everyone in the business to act creatively and intuitively in solving problems and generating new ideas and ways to get work accomplished. In order to get this kind of creativity, managers must give the employees a lot of freedom and authority. They must also instill a vision that provides direction self control. When employees believe in this vision and also see personal benefits, they will focus on development of self control.   Finally, management must constantly stress the importance of the vision through actions and by walking around, talking, and listening to employees.

9.   *What skills will be important for future managers?*

In the future the most competitive firms will be those that are the most creative in problem solving, introducing new products and services, and developing a true "team" orientation. In order to be successful, managers must be good communicators, have excellent interpersonal skills, utilize the "team" approach, deal with a culturally-diverse work force, and understand the role that a leader plays in an organization.

10. *Name some strategies for dealing with changes in the labor force.*

With the labor force getting older and the new labor force being smaller, businesses must derive strategies to deal with this circumstance. Some possible strategies are:

a. Automate as much as possible.

b. Utilize temporary workers.

c. Heavily recruit women, minorities, and older workers.

d. Establish school based programs with high schools, vocational schools, and colleges.

e. Implement the necessary changes to attract disabled workers.

f. Utilize immigrant workers.

g. Respond to the problems of child care and elder care that employees have by utilizing a variety of methods including flextime, child care centers, and alternative work locations.

h. Train personnel and establish pay and benefit packages that will retain your workers.

Answers to CRITICAL THINKING INCIDENTS

Incident 19-1: DATA MATE COMPUTERS

1. **What factors did David Wilson fail to consider when he announced his across-the-board 20 percent staff reduction?**

In the text this is referred to as the "lumber-mill approach" to downsizing. This approach assumes that all departments, and in this case all subsidiaries, are of equal value. Therefore, cutting them all equally will not hurt the firm to any greater extent than an unequal loss of personnel. This assumption is usually wrong both in terms of departments and subsidiaries. Mr. Wilson also failed to consider what might happen to the profitable subsidiaries that may lose 20 percent of their personnel. Mr. Wilson never involved any of the subsidiary people in this decision, so it will probably be met with a lot of anger and lack of real understanding. Finally, no thought was given to which tasks or jobs can be cut, who is going to assume these tasks, or what might be the reaction of the "survivors."

2.   **What are some of the arguments for and against Mr. John Ackerman accepting or fighting this decision?**

Arguments for accepting this decision are:
a.   Since Mr. Wilson is a *new* CEO, he may become very defensive and negative toward anyone who "fights" him on this decision.
b.   The corporation is obviously in trouble financially, and this is top management's decision in terms of solving this problem.
c.   Data Mate's director of finance admits that there is some excess personnel on the staff
d.   It is the easiest choice to follow.

Arguments against accepting this decision are:
a.   It is definitely wrong to treat every subsidiary and every department equally in this decision. Some are more important than others and should be treated accordingly.
b.   This reduction in personnel needs to be very carefully planned. At all levels, personnel need to be involved to open acceptance of the decision. Otherwise, the firm could experience some negative outcomes.
c.   Alternative forms of cost reduction need to be developed. A loss of 20 percent of the entire staff all at once is a huge reduction and may make it impossible to stay efficient and maintain quality.
d.   The great majority of personnel will expect resistance to the decision.

3.   **How should Mr. Ackerman proceed? Please be specific in your answer.**

Mr. Ackerman needs to request a meeting with Mr. Wilson to discuss this decision. He should stress that he would like to clarify some points and discuss some ideas. This meeting is *not* a confrontation but a negotiation. When Mr. Ackerman goes to the meeting, he should have all of his information and ideas in hand. He needs to get his managers involved in helping him generate these facts and ideas. He needs to find out what would be the maximum number of people that the firm could possibly lose without losing effectiveness. They must also determine what departments can absorb the most personnel reductions and which specific positions can be eliminated.

Various cost-cutting measures, such as cutting the new equipment, might be an acceptable alternative to reduction of personnel. Approaches to reducing personnel include early retirement, job sharing, and reduced work weeks. The object in the meeting with Mr. Wilson is not to "fight" him; it is to *justify* reasoning for not cutting 20 percent of the staff and give him some alternative answers. If this is done properly, Mr. Ackerman has at least a chance of solving what appears to be a problematic decision.

Incident 19-2:   RILEY AND SONS CORPORATION

1.   **As a management consultant, develop potential alternative solutions and a recommendation for solving this problem.**

Mr Riley should avoid staffing solely on the basis of gender or unsubstantiated gender-based observations. Persons who are selected for management positions need to meet job qualifications as specified in job descriptions and job specifications. Various alternative solutions are possible, and students will likely suggest a wide range of possibilities. An incentive program, which includes length of service as one of the variables, might be considered. With a focus on reducing time needed to become a manager, additional managerial training might be introduced. Provision of child-care facilities and alternative working arrangements, such as flextime or job sharing, could accommodate the needs of some persons.

Recommendation: Management positions should be held by qualified and capable personnel with rewards based on job performance. Provision of job-specific training is a worthwhile consideration. Training serves to prepare persons for promotion to management and provide both managers as well as aspiring managers with additional insights into managerial roles and responsibilities. A survey might be used to determine preferences toward various types of accommodations (such as child care or work scheduling arrangements). Whenever feasible, efforts to accommodate employee needs should be considered. These considerations can improve job satisfaction and promote the concept of an "employee-friendly" workplace.

Incident 19-3:   PLAYSTAR CORPORATION

1.   **Name some possible ways to improve new product developments.**

Playstar utilizes a new product development department which is totally responsible for new product developments. In order to get more new ideas, the company needs to collect information from customers. Then, management could set up new product development task force groups consisting of people from all of the major functional departments in the company. Management could also solicit ideas for new products from all of their employees and offer a cash incentive if one of the ideas becomes a new product for the company. Finally, management could utilize a computer assisted design (CAD) program that enables the firm to design three dimensional products on the computer screen, thereby holding costs down.

2.   **What are some techniques to cut costs and improve quality?**

Reducing costs and increasing quality go hand in hand. If Playstar can increase
quality, the company will cut costs at the same time because of less rework and waste.
To increase quality, the firm needs to institute a quality control program that offers
incentives for the employees. Employee suggestions on how to cut costs and/or
increase quality should be considered for financial rewards. For example, offer
employees 10 percent of one year's savings that can be verified. If the actual amount
of savings cannot be exactly determined, a joint management labor committee could
determine a fair amount. If management wants to increase quality and cut costs, it
must get the employees to buy into the program or it will never happen.

3.   **How could Playstar reduce employee turnover?**

Since Playstar utilizes an assembly-line production layout, the work is likely to be
boring. First, ask the employees for suggestions and check with competitors and non-
competitors for ideas. In order to help alleviate this boredom, there are a number of
different techniques to try:
a.   Utilize job rotation so the workers can at least learn a new tasks..
b.   Consider setting up work teams to take a new product from design to
        completion.
c.   Utilize quality circles, task force groups, and other forms of employee
        involvement in the company's decision-making process.
d.   Utilize flextime work schedules or compressed workweeks. These alternative
        work schedules are very appealing to many workers.

Study Guide Assignments

The individual assignment illustrates the attitudes and beliefs of many students today:
things are changing so fast that it is impossible to effectively prepare for a career in
today's business world. While it is difficult, the fact is that if persons do not prepare
for careers by doing some planning, they are at even more risk.

The group case assignment presents five major trends in a negative light. It asks
group members to see if they can come up with some creative ways to change these
negative views into positive opportunities (making lemonade out of lemons). This is a
good assignment to utilize in class as many, if not most, people fear these changes and
tend to think of them in a negative rather than a positive sense. Everyone needs to see
that there are some very real opportunities for people working and managing
businesses.

▨ Video Case
■

First Bank Systems of Minneapolis

Focus: **Usage of Information**

Summary:

As recently as 1990, First Bank Systems (FBS) of Minneapolis was a constant topic of conversation in the banking community. Many executives had left the bank, and newspaper stories frequently questioned the bank's ability to survive, while speculating that it might be bought out. One of FBS's biggest problems was its antiquated information system which had been developed in a piecemeal fashion in the early 1970s. The code and the file structures in some of the data bases were home-grown and did not conform to the industry standard. The systems for check processing were very old, and customer records were barely capable of identifying what products FBS had. As an illustration of how antiquated the system was, at one point in time customers actually had to go to the bank where they were signed up if they wanted to make a deposit. Customer service agents had a particularly difficult time responding to customer inquiries. For example, if a customer called with a question about her credit card account, the customer service agent had to access the credit card system. This system was developed with its own unique mode of entry, its own format for the layout of data, and its own idiosyncrasies. If that same customer were to inquire about her checking account, then another system would have to be accessed, and it too had its own mode of entry and unique screens. If there was a savings account inquiry, yet another system would be accessed.

FBS established a mission that in part could be achieved via a goal of growth through acquisition. This seemed reasonable because the market was right for the purchase and sale of banks at that time. In order to acquire these banks and the new customers that would come with them, FBS's challenge was to put an information system in place that would be able to handle the additional volume. Any newly acquired banks would then be converted over to this new information system. FBS's new information system was to be a totally integrated system, having centralized customer records with considerable information about customers, their households, and the amount of business conducted with FBS. Six major systems would be replaced by this system. This posed a considerable challenge because there are accounts of banks that planned to replace only their checking accounts and ended up spending up to three years and $40 million on the project. FBS decided that the information system changeover should be accomplished by buying and implementing packaged software because vendor support of the software after installation would be assured.

FBS was quite efficient in the information system changeover; it replaced the six major systems in eighteen months. In addition to the customer service advantages that accrue from its centralized information system, FBS streamlined the bank acquisition process. It can convert a major bank in 21 weeks and often needs only 13 weeks to convert smaller banks. The FBS "cookbook" process for acquisitions greatly facilitates the growth objective of its mission.

Discussion Questions:

1.   Discuss what you feel were the levels of quality, timeliness, and completeness for the information that FBS's old information system provided.

       Quality information is accurate and clear. Timely information means the information is current, frequent, and provided when needed. Complete information is of sufficient scope for the user, with appropriate summaries and adequate detail. FBS's old system failed on all three qualities.

2.   List and describe as many areas you can think of where you would like the new information system to provide you, an FBS customer, with information on your accounts, transactions, or interactions with the bank.

       At a minimum, bank customers want current account information in the teller line, at the ATM, and by phone.

3.   Do you feel it was a good or bad idea for FBS to restrict itself to buying packaged software? Why?

       The key reason for FBS's decision to use packaged software was time; the old system needed to be replaced as quickly as possible in order for the bank to accomplish a turnaround. From that perspective, packaged software made sense.

Chapter 20

Preparing for Management Careers

In order to be successful in any career, a person must develop a personal career plan and then carefully execute that plan. This chapter tries to help the student to implement a sound strategy for obtaining employment and advancing professionally in the field of management, which has changed and will continue to change in the future. It is very evident that each person must take charge of planning his or her own career. No longer can employees expect their present employers to lay out a nice step-by-step career plan for them. Businesses must be very flexible and change with the trends, and individuals must do exactly the same thing.

This chapter examines which fields look promising in the future, what skills a person needs to possess, how to do an effective job search, even how to survive during these rapidly changing times.

Throughout this chapter, the need to communicate with various people on an on-going basis is stressed as a key element in making sure that a career plan is on track.

░░░ **Teaching Objectives**

The teaching objectives of this chapter are to:

1.   Identify the fields that hold the most potential for a management career.

421

2.   Analyze the main factors to consider in managing both a career and a personal life.

3.   Identify the skills necessary for a successful management career.

4.   Identify the specific steps to follow in the job-search process.

5.   Determine some basic guidelines for advancing in a career.

6.   Analyze future management career opportunities for women and minorities.

7.   Identify some considerations for career survival.

Chapter Outline of the Text

I.   THE FUTURE OUTLOOK FOR MANAGEMENT CAREERS
        A.   Major Trends Affecting the World of Work and Your Career
                1.   Technology
                2.   Global Competition
                3.   The Aging Population
                4.   Growth in Small Businesses
                5.   Skill's Gap
                6.   Trends inIndustry, occupation, and location
II.   MANAGING YOUR CAREER YOUR PERSONAL LIFE
        A.   What Is Your Career Goal?
        B.   What Skills and Abilities Do You Need to Reach This Goal?
        C.   Where Do You Have to Go to Obtain These Skills and Experiences?
        D.   Personal Points on Managing Your Career
III.   BASIC SKILLS IN POTENTIAL MANAGERS
        A.   Versatility
        B.   Creative Abilities
        C.   Ability to Work in Teams
        D.   Ability to Communicate Effectively
IV.   STEPS IN THE JOB SEARCH PROCESS
        A.   Identify Sources of Possible Career Opportunities
        B.   Contact Potential Employers and Obtain a Job Interview
        C.   Submit a Job Application
        D.   Evaluate Job Offers
V.   SOME GUIDELINES FOR GETTING AHEAD IN YOUR CAREER
        A.   Start a Career Development Program
        B.   Modify Your Present Position
        C.   Move to Another Company

Key Terms

These terms are introduced in the chapter.

Career
Career development program
Career path
Career plan
Career plateau
Career survival plan
Career stages
Glass ceiling

Headhunter
Information interview
Mentor
Moonlighting
Networking
Primary job information source
Secondary job information source

▨ Detailed Chapter Summary

I.   THE FUTURE OUTLOOK FOR MANAGEMENT CAREERS

It has been stated that the world of work will change more in the decade of the 1990s than it did in the previous 100 years. If this is true, then preparing properly for a career has never been more important for virtually everyone.

A.   *Major Trends Affecting the World of Work and Your Career*

Currently there are five major trends that will affect the world of work and careers.

1.   Technology

New technology means learning new job skills. Computers, in particular, will impact virtually everyone's job. Everyone needs to accept new technology and not "fight it," as accelerated development will continue in the future.

2.   Global Competition

As U.S. businesses expand globally, many new career opportunities will present themselves for those people who are ready. Being bilingual and familiar with the customs and culture of a foreign country are extremely valuable skills.

3.   The Aging Population

As the baby-boomer generation hits retirement in 2010 and beyond, there will be shortages of workers and managers in certain occupations. A large elderly group will create many new opportunities in fields such as health care and hospitality fields.

4.   Growth in Small Businesses

It is estimated that during the 1990s up to one-half of all new jobs will be in new small businesses. The number of new small business start ups is also expected to grow, especially among females who are projected to start up over half of them.

5.   Skills Gap

Businesses want employees and managers to possess a variety of skills. Everyone needs to have a basic understanding of the business world and must continually train and educate themselves.

6.   Trends in Industry, Occupation, and Location

Teaching Objective 1:   Identify the fields that hold the most future potential for a management career.

The total number of new jobs between 1990 and 2005 is expected to be 24 million, according to the Bureau of Labor Statistics.

1.   The three fastest growing occupational areas are executive, administrative, and managerial. These three areas are expected to grow by 27 percent.

2.   The service industry is expected to be by far the strongest sector accounting for 19.2 million of the 24 million new jobs.

3.   The strongest fields for management positions appear to be in the hospitality field, marketing, advertising, and public relations.

4.   The fields that are losing the most jobs are manufacturing and farming. Any industry that can be automated with new technology will experience considerable decline in the future.

The fastest growing areas normally mean the areas which will offer the most job opportunities in most occupational fields. The South and West continue to be the fastest growing areas in the U.S.

Teaching Hint: Stress to your students that even though the strongest occupational fields and industries will change over time, these changes will, for the most part, be gradual. Therefore, selecting a career in a growth industry today does make a great deal of sense even if it will be a few years before entering it.

II.   MANAGING YOUR CAREER AND YOUR PERSONAL LIFE

Teaching Objective 2:   Analyze the main factors to consider in managing a career and a personal life.

First and foremost, realize that each person today is "personally" responsible for his or her own career. Companies are changing too fast to be able to lay out career paths for employees. The days of working for one firm for 30 years and progressing up the corporate ladder are virtually gone. Managing a career is not easy. Career paths vary for the same career goal, as changes along the way force adjustments. The sequence of jobs and occupations may zig-zag considerably before reaching a career goal, but this just further evidences a need to plan to reach a career goal.

A.   *What Is Your Career Goal?*

This first question may be the most difficult to answer, but it must be very carefully researched, since this goal is the focal point of an entire career plan. In order to determine a career goal, you need to examine yourself and future job opportunities.

1.   What skills, abilities, interests, aptitudes, and personality traits do you currently possess? You can find out by undergoing a series of tests and assessments at a number of different places including college career centers, state employment or job services offices, private career consulting firms, or even by doing your own computer analysis. You want to try to find a match between yourself and occupations that seem to "fit" you. Once you have narrowed your choices down to a few possibilities, contact people who are currently working in the field and get more information. Possibly, the best way to get insights is to gain actual experience by working part-time or doing an internship. Finally, you always want to consider at least one other career possibility in event that employment circumstances change dramatically.

Teaching Hint: Stress the fact that no matter how much research on an occupation persons do, they will never know if they are really going to like a job until they do it themselves. Therefore, internships and work experience are crucial in making a career decision.

B.   *What Skills and Abilities Do You Need to Reach This Goal?*

A person should identify the "core" or main skills needed for a career choice and try to be highly skilled at performing them. Also, determine what some of the secondary skills are and what unique or special abilities are highly desired. By talking to workers doing jobs, observing them, and gaining actual work experiences, people can determine skills needed.

C.   *Where Do You Have to Go to Obtain These Skills and Experiences?*

Once necessary skills are known, it is necessary to plan a way to obtain skills not currently possessed. Several options are possible:

1.   Get more education. This can take the form of something as simple as attending seminars and trade shows or attending college to earn a degree.

2.   Change jobs or positions at a current employer. By assuming a new position, which is not necessarily a promotion, a person may be able to learn valuable skills.

3.   Start a part-time "sideline" career. This is a good way to learn new job skills.

D.   *Personal Points on Managing Your Career*

In order to really be happy in a career, a person should consider these questions:

1.   What is your real definition of success?

It does not always have to mean moving "up" in an organization. It can mean performing a variety of tasks and experiencing success by excelling at a currently-held position.

2.   How important are some of the main quality of life issues?

Issues such as working hours, stress, travel, job security, working conditions, and night work need to be examined carefully.

3.   Is it worthwhile to assume the responsibility and stress that goes along with being in top management?

The old cliche` "Closer to the Top - Closer to the Door" does accurately describe the level of job security in positions.

Suggested Readings for this Section:
Special Report. "The New World of Work."   <u>Business Week</u>, *October 17, 1994, pp. 26-28.*

At many firms, the "typical job" is anything but typical. Working at home or in the field utilizing computers and modems, spending four out of five days a week out of the office on the road, meeting in teams, having the authority to set prices and solve problems and stopping by the office once a week to see associates and pick up E- mail are some of the "typical" changes.

Today, firms no longer promise lifetime employment. The days of working for one firm for 35 years and retiring are all but over.   Employers will help employees improve job skills, but each person is responsible for his or her own career.   Almost every employment situation is contingent upon the employer being able to stay in the same business without major changes in products and technology. If these factors do dramatically change, so will the number and types of people who will be employed.

What job skills will be demanded in the future? A good clue is the occupational forecast for the year 2005, which is developed by the Bureau of Labor Statistics. The winners on this list are the high-skilled jobs in the professional, managerial, and technical areas. The losers are the low skilled crafts, operators, and laborers.

Farnham, Alan. "Out of College, What's Next?" <u>Fortune</u>, *July 12, 1995, pp. 58-64.*

The world of work is changing dramatically.   Today, companies are restructuring. Technology is another major factor in reducing the number of entry-level jobs. For example, computerized CAD/CAM programs have reduced the need for new engineers.

Another rather common trend is to hire interns based upon their success in co-op work programs or summer internships. At General Mills, up to one-third of all offers to new graduates are based upon these experiences.

Some other good rules to follow in searching for a job are: 1. Start developing a career plan in the freshman year of college. This not only shows planning ability but evidences a desire for an occupational field. 2. Get experience. Experience can be an important factor in obtaining employment Again, internships are particularly good. 3. Seek out employers. Many medium and small firms do not recruit at colleges. 4. Do the homework. Learn as much as possible about the firm and know what skills are marketable. For example, global management personnel is in demand; therefore, fluency in a foreign language can be a big asset. 5. Have grit. Job searching is a full-time job that can take five to six months or sometimes more. 6. Make connections. It is important to develop networks. 7. Do not avoid extracurricular leadership positions. Build a record of job accomplishments. 8. Finally, pull out every last stop. Dress properly, even if that means buying new clothes. One recent graduate hired a search firm to help him find the right employer.

III.   BASIC SKILLS THAT EMPLOYERS ARE LOOKING FOR IN POTENTIAL MANAGERS

Teaching Objective 3:   Identify the skills necessary for a successful management career.

While the actual number of skills sought by employers varies tremendously, research does indicate that in addition to good technical skills, most employers value the following skills in hiring or promoting people into management positions:

A.   *Versatility*

Most employers define versatility as the ability to deal effectively with change. The versatile person can also do a wide variety of tasks, work with a culturally diverse work force, and be competent in working with other managers in the different functional areas of the firm.

B.   *Creative Abilities*

Everyone likes a person who can come up with creative new ways to solve problems or go after opportunities that really work.

C.   *The Ability to Work in Teams*

The utilization of teams in business has never been higher, and it is continuing to grow. Being able to work on a team means having the ability to be either a team leader or an effective member. It also means being willing to set aside some personal goals to help the team achieve its goals. Working in teams sounds easy, but in reality, it can be very difficult and demands good interpersonal relationship skills.

D.   *Ability to Communicate Effectively*

All managers spend the vast majority of their time communicating; therefore, it is obviously a very important skill to have. Communicating, both orally and in various written forms, is crucial. Miscommunicating is one of the most common reasons for problems. Good communication skills are essential to effective management.

Teaching Hint: Ask your class what other basic skills they see employers desiring in today's business world.

IV.   STEPS IN THE JOB SEARCH PROCESS

Teaching Objective 4:   Identify the specific steps in the job-search process.

Searching for the right job and company that fits a career goal is not an easy task. According to a recent worldwide survey of outplacement consultants, the average time in the 1990s is 5.2 months. Obviously, it can take even longer if the search is not well planned and carefully executed. The steps in a job search do vary, but the following steps are commonly followed in most job searches:

A.   *Step 1: Identify Sources of Information About Possible Career Opportunities in Your Chosen Career Field.*

It is important to utilize every possible source that may help to get a lead on a job opportunity. There are two primary types of information:

1.   Secondary Sources

These include trade magazines, trade journals, and some more general career-oriented magazines and newspapers such as *Careers and Majors,* and the *National Business Employment Weekly.* There are also some computerized job search programs such as Job Hunt, which is illustrated in Figure 20-10.

2. *Primary Information Sources*

Primary information sources are usually even better sources than secondary ones. These include contacting college placement departments, public and private employment agencies, professional and trade organizations, and personal contacts. The Department of Labor states that 80 percent of all jobs come from personal contacts.

B. *Step 2: Contact Potential Employers and Obtain a Job Interview*

It is often best to contact employers by telephone first to find out the names of people who do the actual hiring. The main goal, at this point in time, is for a person to secure an interview and be in a position to "sell" him- or herself and secure information about the firm.

Responding to an employer's request for a resume is another way to make contact. The resume should be well prepared and "slanted" toward that particular job and company. There are several books and firms that can help in resume development.

Finally, consider making some "cold calls" on perspective employers. While some employers like this approach, others do not.

C. Step 3: *Submit a Job Application*

The job application process varies considerably from firm to firm, but most firms utilize the following steps:

1. The Job Application Blank

The job application blank is used to obtain background data and may be a "test" of an applicant's ability to be neat, accurate, and to follow directions.

2. Job-Related Testing

Tests on job-related knowledge, personality factors, communication skills, problem-solving skills, decision making, and the ability to handle stress are all very common.

3.   Job Interviews

Job interviews enable employers to collect a considerable amount of information. Persons can *prepare* for an interview by gathering information on the firm and the position that is available. In addition to technical expertise, the interview is a test of a person's ability to handle stress, interact with new people, and communicate orally. It is important to be aware of body language and remain calm. Also, questions can be asked about the firm and the job. After an interview, it is appropriate to send a note of thanks to the interviewer.

4.   Reference Checks

The employer does this step, but the applicant should submit all of the appropriate information about references: name, title, address, phone number, and capacity in which the applicant knows them. Applicants should obtain permission before using a person's name as a reference.

5.   Other Job Requirements

Physical exams, drug testing, and driver's license checks may or may not be done as a last step.

D.   Step 4: *Evaluate Job Offers*

It is important to have the "right" job with the "right" firm! Job offers should be compared to career plans, quality of life issues, and future possibilities. Taking a job and leaving a few months later can be frustrating to employees as well as employers.

Teaching Hint: Students need to realize that doing a job search can consume considerable time. If a job search is poorly planned and half-heartedly executed, poor results are the norm.

Suggested Readings for this Section:
Moreau, Dan. "How I Got my Job." Kiplinger's Personal Finance Magazine, January 1993, pp 67-70.

Many times, the standard methods of doing a job search do not work as well as might be anticipated. If you find yourself in that situation, try some of the following ideas which have worked for many people in the past.

1. Be creative in your approach. For example, Guy de Brantes was being considered for an executive position at a premium pet food company. To really impress the firm that he knew its customer--dogs, he took his spaniel to the job interview with him. The dog behaved perfectly, and he got the job.

2. Propose what you will do for the firm. This can be difficult, but if you understand the industry and the firm, some honest ideas and proposals may be advantageous. Thomas McCormally, a man who desperately wanted an editor's position with a magazine publisher, gave the firm 100 ideas for cover stories in the interview.

3. Scope out the job. Do some research that shows you understand the company and the job. Steve Grupe wanted a job with IBM working on a project to revamp the nation's air traffic control system. He studied all he could find on the topic and was very impressive in the interview.

4. Become a solution. Determine the basic problems faced by a prospective employer and develop a solution for one of them. Rob Sikorsky states there are usually only four or five basic problems in any field and finding a potential solution to one of them shows your problem solving abilities.

5. Tell everyone you know you are looking for a job. Network everywhere you go, whether it is through your church, friends, or clubs. Finding ways to meet employers in a social setting is a particularly good strategy.

6. Stay flexible. Consider doing consultant work or even starting your own business.

7. Get organized. Use computer spreadsheet programs to classify possible leads and word processors for letters of introduction, resumes and follow-up letters.

*Sacino, Sherry. "What Employers Want." National Business Employment Weekly -
Managing Your Career. (Special Edition) Fall 1994, pp. 19-20.*

Getting a job means convincing an employer that you have the right abilities and that you
will fit well with the company's employees. This is especially true if you are just
graduating from college, and your work experience is limited. The following ten abilities
are skills that almost everyone is looking for:

1.   Enthusiasm - Everyone needs to show a spark of energy to a prospective employer.
2.   Fresh ideas - New perspectives are always welcome.
3.   Initiative - Mention how you are willing to go the extra mile for an employer.
4.   Mobility - Employers like people who are geographically flexible.
5.   Hard working - No one wants a "clock watcher."
6.   Technical skills - While these vary, almost all employers expect you to be computer
     literate.
7.   Knowledge of the industry jargon - Learn the terminology of the trade as fast as
     possible.
8.   Empathy - When employers make decisions you may not particularly agree with,
     practice empathy.
9.   Organizational skills - Sloppy workers very seldom impress employers.
10. Be a team player - Realize that business owners see themselves as leaders of a band
     with employees as musicians.

If you are wondering about technical skills obtained through your education and work
experience, they may be considered after candidates have been examined for the ten traits
listed above.

V.   SOME GUIDELINES FOR GETTING AHEAD IN YOUR CAREER

Teaching Objective 5:   Determine some basic guidelines for getting ahead in a career.

    A.   *Start a Career Development Program*

          Formulating a career development plan is essential to get ahead. This plan is
          aimed at an eventual career goal and includes lateral as well as vertical moves.
          In every situation, start by looking ahead one or two positions and try to

determine that most logical moves to make in order to get to the next position. Each move should add skills which are necessary for your ultimate career goal. These points are worthwhile considerations:

1.   Job Performance

     Job performance is almost always the main criteria for promotion. Make the extra effort to produce the desired results on time and within budget.

2.   Creative Approaches

     Try some new creative approaches. Think them out carefully and seek managerial approval. Keep in mind, not all creative approaches will be successful.

3.   New Job Responsibilities

     Assume new job responsibilities and tasks that increase job skills. While this can create anxieties, it is also a good way to grow.

4.   Develop Interpersonal Relationships

     Seek out a mentor or advisor and ask for advice. These relationships represent opportunities to gain many valuable career insights.

5.   Avoid Negative People

     When possible, avoid association with negative employees or managers. Being associated with this type of person is generally not worthwhile.

6.   Communicate Your Progress

     Communicate regularly with superiors so that they are aware of job-performance accomplishments. Keeping them informed is a good strategy to consider.

B.   *Modify Current Position*

Career growth is enhanced by volunteering to assist with various types of assignments as well as modifying job duties to learn new skills.

C.   *Move to Another Company*

Changing jobs is an alternative for persons experiencing career plateaus. It is worthwhile to consider both large and small firms and recognize various advantages and disadvantages.

D.   *Start Your Own Business*

Consider starting a business. This is a challenging opportunity that requires considerable personal enthusiasm and hard work to attain desired success.

VI.   FUTURE MANAGEMENT OPPORTUNITIES FOR WOMEN AND MINORITIES

Teaching Objective 6:   Analyze future management and career opportunities for women and minorities.

Opportunities for women and minorities in management are quite promising. There still are some potential problems that must be considered at some firms.

A.   *Opportunities for Women*

The "glass ceiling" is an invisible barrier beyond which women and minorities have not been able to advance in some firms. One of the major reasons that has created the "glass ceiling" for women is maternity. Maternity can often interrupt the career of a woman. While this has happened in many cases, more companies are recognizing that this interruption does not have to terminate careers. Many women continue their careers after maternity leave, especially if child care is available and some flexible scheduling is possible. The traditional "role" of women is to care for the family and not be a primary breadwinner. Again, businesses all over the world are realizing that this "role" has definitely changed in many marriages. Finding the employers who have a contemporary view of the workplace can provide additional job satisfaction.

B.   *Opportunities for Minorities*

Some minorities have failed to "network" or develop contacts with role models or others who can positively influence their careers. In particular, development of mentor relationships has been a challenge. These problems are diminishing as businesses realize the need to assist personnel to develop their career skills. Many businesses are establishing "success plans" for minorities that help to establish mentor relationships.

VII.   REALISTIC POINTS TO CONSIDER IN CAREER SURVIVAL

Teaching Objective 7:   Identify some considerations for career survival.

With the changing business environment, businesses must change in order to adapt. This may mean restructuring, merging, or even eliminating entire divisions. As a manager or as an employee, persons need to be aware of trends. Look for the warning signs and ask this key question: How strong is my industry, company, and division position and my own skill level?

A.   *Career Survival Plan*s

These considerations are relevant:

1.   Employment opportunities are strengthened by having a large variety of skills to offer employers. Versatile people are valuable people.

2.   Prior experience in core (or main functional) areas of business is valuable.

3.   Stay visible and act, think, and talk positive. Personal promotion for assignment to high visibility projects can be beneficial strategy.

4.   The need to "network" should not be overlooked.

5.   Maintain contacts with private employment agencies.

6.   Offering skills or abilities directly to other firms on a part-time basis can generate new contacts and possibly evolve into full-time employment.

B.   *Long-Term Unemployment*

For unemployed persons, a key to survival is preparation and foresight. While no career survival plan is perfect, those who do not have one are really the most vulnerable during tough times. These are some strategies to cope with extended unemployment:

1.   Try doing consultant work for small firms or even individuals.

2.   Utilize the services of temporary employment agencies. Some of these temporary jobs turn into permanent jobs.

3.   Look for job openings in different parts of the country or even different parts of the world.

4.   Review basic skills and see if other industries need them. It may be as simple as going from manufacturer to sales representative for the same product.

5.   Start a business. This has already been discussed but is always an option.

VIII.   LOOKING BACK

This chapter attempts to examine some of the factors that have influenced how to prepare for a career and career advancement. Changes in the business environment have forced business firms to alter the way they deal with employees and managers. Each person must take charge of his or her own career. Everyone must practice effective career-planning strategies.

Answers to CONSIDER THIS Questions

1.   **Why do businesses no longer provide a high level of assurance for continued employment to loyal, faithful, hard-working employees?**

Two factors that have had a major impact on how business organizations treat their employees are the ever-increasing rate of change and the increasing amount of global competition. Both of these factors force organizations to continually analyze their competitive standing and make necessary adjustments. Unfortunately, these adjustments may include major restructuring of the firm or even merging with another firm.

2. **In terms of job skills, how can a person be both a generalist and a specialist?**

    Every business organization has a group of "core" job skills that all personnel should possess. These generalist skills typically include computer, communication, and math skills, as well as at least a general understanding of each of the basic functional areas of the firm. Businesses also seek employees with at least one functional area of specialization.

3. **What are some alternative ways of acquiring necessary job skills?**

    There are three basic ways to acquire new job skills. First, try to get a new job assignment with a current employer. This new job assignment must be very carefully chosen to give appropriate experience. If that is not possible, consider changing employers. A key is for the new employer to give the desired type of job assignment. If neither of these options is available, starting a part-time career is a possibility. Another option is to seek additional education, which can take many forms from full- or part-time college degree programs to attending professional seminars, trade shows, and even reading books and periodicals. Whatever option or combination of options is chosen, there is always a way to learn new skills.

Answers to REVIEW AND DISCUSSION Questions

1. *Identify several major trends that will influence career options.*

    The major trends are: (1) new technology; (2) increasing global competition; (3) new career opportunities due to the large number of baby boomers who will be retiring in the near future; (4) career opportunities due to the increasing number of new small businesses; and (5) the widening skills gap between what the labor market wants and what the typical new worker possesses. Everyone is going to be impacted, to some degree, by virtually all five of these trends; and, in some cases, one or more of the trends will have a major impact on career choice.

2. *What occupational fields are growing the fastest? Which fields are declining? What areas of the country appear to hold the best prospects for future employment?*

The three fastest growing occupations listed in Figure 20-1 are home health aid, paralegals, and computer system analysts. The three fastest declining occupations are telephone installers and repairers, communications equipment mechanics, and precision assemblers. The fastest growing areas of the country, in terms of job opportunities, are Florida, Nevada, Texas, Arizona, California, North Carolina, and Utah.

3.   *What main job skills do employers look for when hiring or promoting people?*

There are four basic skill areas that virtually all employers are looking for: versatility, creative abilities, ability to work in teams, and the ability to communicate effectively. One other basic skill desired by almost all employers is the ability to operate computers.

4.   *What is the single most important source of job leads in the business world today?*

Personal contacts are the single most important source of job leads. The Department of Labor estimates that 80 percent of all job leads come from personal contacts.

5.   *How does a person prepare for a job search?*

First, a person must identify a career goal. Next, it is necessary to understand that the search process may be time consuming (5.2 months was the average in the early 1990s). Third, find the right company that offers growth opportunities as well as a career choice. Finally, be familiar with the four steps in the job search process: identify sources of possible career opportunities, contact potential employers and secure a job interview, go through the job application process very carefully, and evaluate job offers in terms of career goals.

6.   *Name the five most common errors made in managing a career.*
The five most common errors in managing a career are somewhat debatable; however, some of the most common ones are (1) not developing a well thought out career plan; (2) not carefully selecting a career goal; (3) not developing or obtaining the necessary skills needed to achieve a career goal; (4) not doing the job search process very carefully; and (5) not managing both career survival and growth properly.

7. *Why is good job performance not enough to advance in a career?*

    While good job performance is a major criteria for advancing, a person also has to look ahead at the skills needed to handle the job at the next level. Skills such as having good problem solving abilities, being able to develop creative strategies, being a real team player, and being an effective communicator are always in demand. When top managers look at a potential candidate for a higher-level position, they ask, "Does this person have the ability to handle this position?"

8. *Name some advantages and disadvantages of moving from a large firm to a small firm.*

    The advantages of going to a small firm are: (1) positions in a small firm typically handle a wide variety of duties and tasks in the business; (2) decisions are usually made faster; and (3) chances of being involved in top management decisions are much greater. Some of the disadvantages are: (1) lower salaries; (2) fewer well-defined career paths, and (3)necessity of doing tasks that may be perceived to be of lesser importance.

9. *What basic questions should a person ask to determine if job loss is likely to occur?*

    As indicated in Figure 20-15, five basic questions should indicate whether or not a job is in jeopardy?:
    a.   How strong is your industry?
    b.   How strong is your company?
    c.   How strong is your division?
    d.   How strong is your job?
    e.   How strong are you?

10. *What specific tactics can a person use to prepare for a possible layoff?*

    First, have marketable job skills. Second, try to hold a job position that involves the company's main core functions. Third, be visible and positive in both speech and actions. Fourth, always be actively networking. Fifth, keep a resume on active file with employment agencies. Finally, do some moonlighting or selling of skills directly to customers on a part-time basis.

11.   *What strategies are available if you become unemployed?*

First, consider doing consultant work. Next, try utilizing the services of temporary employment agencies. Third, look for jobs in different parts of the country. Fourth, look at basic skills and see if other industries need them. Finally, consider starting a business.

Answers to CRITICAL THINKING INCIDENTS

Incident 20-1:   LOOK OUT AHEAD

1.   Briefly describe Jonas's current situation.

Currently, Jonas Miller experiences a career plateau in a noncore area of a firm. Jonas needs to verify the accuracy of rumors involving potential staff reductions and recognize possible implications for him. Finally, he needs to determine relative strength of the bicycle industry and the Hudson Corporation. Jonas needs to note possible changes affecting the human resources division and the future of his position as a personnel specialist. Finally, Jonas should examine his own personal skills and abilities.

2.   Describe a career development program that you feel Jonas should begin immediately.

Jonas needs to:
1.   Verify his career goal of being a director of human resources.
2.   If this is his goal, ascertain the customary career path to attain the director's position.
3.   Determine the skills needed for each of these positions.
4.   Start working to obtain new skills that are needed immediately.
5.   Determine the best approach for getting the next position.
6.   If a job search is in order, implement a plan.

Incident 20-2:   WHAT TO DO?

1.   **What major errors did Mike make prior to losing his job?**

Mike's biggest error was not anticipating the demise of the bank and not preparing for it. Most businesses do not experience immediate bankruptcy, and the signs are often obvious for several months. Mike should have been actively networking, including contacting employment agencies that specialize in the banking industry, so that he had some good information on the availability of banking jobs. Since the banking opportunities locally were limited, he should have been working on alternative job possibilities.

2.   **What strengths does Mike have?**

Fortunately, Mike does appear to have some good skills. As the top loan officer for eight years, he obviously has good people skills and good financial skills. He has completed a financial management program and continued studying to become a financial planner. Finally, his computer skills look very impressive, and since this is a rapidly growing field, there may be options available to him in this area.

3.   **Develop a plan for Mike that includes various available options.**

First, Mike needs to decide what new career goal he really wants to go after and what new skills he is going to need to achieve it. Next, he needs to determine the best way to obtain these skills. Finally, he needs to do a thorough job search to achieve the first position toward his career goal. He has three options: banking, financial management, and the computer industry. To stay in banking, it may very well mean moving to another part of the country. To enter financial management, he could set up his own business or explore opportunities with an established firm. To enter the computer industry, Mike has the most options including hardware development, programming in both the banking and personal finance areas, and working for firms in other industries.

Incident 20-3:   WHEN A CAREER GOES WRONG

1.   **What went wrong with Betty's original career plan?**

Betty's original career plan was to be a Russian interpreter at the U.N. What Betty failed to fully comprehend was the small number of job openings for this type of career and the difficulty of getting the skills necessary for the position. When the job of acquiring these skills became very difficult, she decided to quit. Betty also never had any alternative careers in mind, should her first choice not materialize. Betty's career plan was too narrow and not well developed.   Once her career goal changed, she had no plan at all in mind to replace it, outside of just getting a job.

2.   **What can she do now to help develop her career?**

Betty needs to start a new career plan from scratch. First, she needs to determine a new career goal, possibly in banking.   Next, she needs to recognize skills needed for this career goal and determine the best way to achieve them. Finally, she needs to develop a job-search program to attain an initial position that will lead to her job goal.

Study Guide Assignments

The individual case assignment illustrates a very negative young man who firmly believes that planning for the future is a complete waste of time. Many of his arguments have some validity, but he fails to see that planning, while not perfect, is at least an attempt to proceed in the right direction. It may be interesting to see how many of your students agree with the points this young man makes.

The group case assignment asks the class to divide up into three groups to discuss the pros and the cons of each of Frank's three main points. While a clear definitive answer to these points may not be possible, be sure the class at least realizes how proper analysis can help prepare a person for a worst possible case scenario.

Video Case

Beyond the Glass Ceiling

Focus: **Women in Management Careers**

Summary:

In 1970, two percent of U.S. executives were women; by 1990, the percentage of female executives was less than six percent. While increasing numbers of women are in the work force, women are still blocked from top positions by the glass ceiling. They can see the top, but an invisible barrier prevents them from rising to the executives rank. Even women who do advance are paid less than their male counterparts; female executives earn 1/3 less than male executives in the same jobs.

This video, part of CNN's Special Reports series, profiles the problems faced by women managers and what some companies are trying to do to help women advance. Companies are attempting to improve this area not so much from a sense of fairness but because women constitute half of the labor force. It is a waste of human resources to overlook half the labor force.

Discussion Questions:

1. What kinds of industries do you think would be most receptive to women executives? Least receptive?

   Studies on this indicate that industries that are relatively new and/or are faced with major change in their environment are most receptive to women executives, such as the computer industry, publishing, and high-tech companies. Traditional manufacturing companies are among the least receptive.

2. Women cost companies more than men because women take time off to have children. Should this be a factor in how companies compensate women?

   This argument does not meet the test for employee fairness in compensation. Differences in pay among employees in the same job are acceptable only if the differences are attributable to differences in performance or seniority.